AIRBNB AND REAL ESTATE INVESTING MASTERY

4 BOOKS IN 1

LEARN HOW TO RUN A SUCCESSFUL AIRBNB, INCREASE BOOKINGS & INCOME, AND BUILD WEALTH WITH RENTAL PROPERTIES, HOUSE FLIPPING AND THE BRRRR STRATEGY

FRANK EBERSTADT

TABLE OF CONTENTS

HOW TO SET UP AND RUN A
SUCCESSFUL AIRBNB BUSINESS

HOW TO UNLEASH YOUR AIRBNB'S FULL POTENTIAL

THE ULTIMATE REAL ESTATE INVESTING BEGINNER'S BOOK

Part One

BUILD A BASE

THE ULTIMATE HOUSE FLIPPING AND BRRRR REAL ESTATE INVESTING BEGINNER'S BOOK

Part One
LEARN THE STRATEGIES

Part Two
TAKE ACTION AND MAKE SMART MOVES

Part Three
BUILD SMART AND GROW BIG

HOW TO SET UP AND RUN A SUCCESSFUL AIRBNB BUSINESS

OUTEARN YOUR COMPETITION WITH SKYROCKETING
RENTAL INCOME AND LEAVE YOUR 9 TO 5 JOB
EVEN IF YOU ARE AN ABSOLUTE BEGINNER

INTRODUCTION

The longer you're not taking action the more money you're losing.

— CARRIE WILKERSON

Imagine a life in which you get to visit the most beautiful and interesting places in the world. Imagine meeting new people, visiting historic sites, hiking beautiful trails, and finding local treasures. People want to have these kinds of experiences. Back in my single days, I lived that life and saw parts of the world that others could only dream of visiting. Then, after marrying my amazing wife and starting a family, I got to share my travels with my wife and kids. You might be wondering how this was possible. The truth is, if it weren't for Airbnb, I wouldn't have had these experiences and been able to see the world in so many unique ways.

As a solo backpacker, you don't have much money for travel—the main goal is to see the world's amazing sights. You also want to meet people and experience culture by immersing yourself in it—you want to stay where all the action is. Then, when you trade this life in for growing a family, you have to be more conscious of the little ones. Vacations become more about spending time with your family and enjoying the immediate surroundings. While you might still have a few adventures here and there, the main goal is to connect with your family in a special place. Being an avid traveler in both stages of my life allowed me to stay in a variety of Airbnbs—I know what works and what doesn't.

If all the traveling adventures weren't enough, we decided to make a huge move that came with many challenges and so many beautiful memories. We picked up our lives and emigrated to the Land Down Under.

Shortly after arriving in Australia, I knew I wanted to be in the accommodation business—I started working for an investment group that operated hotels and motels. Alongside this, I established my own property business. You could say that I have a passion for property and travel. What better way to combine these two than with Airbnb?

If you are someone with the same interests, then Airbnb is definitely for you. It provides a unique opportunity to deliver a fantastic travel experience to other people. If you have traveled before, you will know what a huge difference accommodation can make. I know that, out of all my travels, the accommodations were the travel experiences that I enjoyed the most.

If there was anything I wanted to make money from, it would be through properties. I loved the industry, and I knew that so many other people did as well. Everybody wants a fantastic vacation. There are so many complexities when starting a business and building an additional income that you want to enjoy the process—this is why Airbnb is such a great opportunity. Hosting people is an absolute pleasure if you know how to do it right. Not only that but investing in property means you have future security. Not only will you make an income, but you will always have your property to fall back on if you ever need additional income or a place to stay—a terrific method for maximizing control over your finances and avoiding economic unpredictability.

Currently, I have six properties and still work for the investment group I mentioned earlier. I'm quite experienced in the real estate industry, and more importantly, I have an Airbnb business. Throughout my time in this industry, I've learned quite a few lessons, and I've had to do them independently. That is the more challenging option, but you don't have to take that route. The knowledge that has taken me twelve years to accumulate, I want to pass on to you so that you can build up your Airbnb business and have it run smoothly without going through all my ups and downs.

When you start an Airbnb business, you will be able to become financially stable and simultaneously enjoy the process. When you become an Airbnb host, you open your doors to the rest of the world. The types of people you meet, the experiences you will have, and the stories you will get to tell all add to the wealth-building you will be participating in. Developing an Airbnb business is an investment in a better future for you and your family. By now, you are probably itching to find out how you can step into this journey so let's dive straight into Chapter 1.

AIRBNB BASICS

Over 150 million users worldwide have booked over 1 billion stays using Airbnb[1]. That is a lot of people who are looking for a unique and convenient place to stay when they go away. The traveling market has opened up, and people are looking for more affordable places to stay when they are traveling. It is essential to understand the basics of Airbnb before you can move on and create a strategy that will help you tap into all the benefits that come with it.

WHAT IS AIRBNB?

In the simplest of terms, Airbnb is an alternative to hotels. It allows individual property owners to list and rent their properties or rooms via the platform. The average property owner has access to a whole list of new clients they would not have otherwise. It also allows guests to find new, interesting, and often, inexpensive options for their vacation, business, or other travel needs. Before, you would need to be a hotel or a large rental chain to get enough business. Now, any person who has an available property can rent it out and make additional income.

The origin story of Airbnb is quite interesting. To say that it was something intentional wouldn't be true. It all started in 2007 when Brian Chesky and Joe Gebbia were completely broke and looking to make some extra money.[2] They lived in an apartment in San Francisco and needed a way to help pay their rent. They discovered a conference happening in their area and decided to rent out an empty room with an air mattress in their apartment for some extra cash. They called the service "AirBed & Breakfast." As you can see, this is where the name originated. Over a few years, this small idea grew, with the help of Nathan Blecharczyk, into the Airbnb platform we know today.

It is easy to look at the company and think it was an easy ride. Everybody loves to travel, and doing it uniquely and cheaply makes sense, right? However, the conception of this idea was purely accidental. When they were trying to build up the company, people genuinely thought they were crazy. Very few people thought this would be a good idea that would be profitable in the future. If you look at it in the context of 2007 or 2008, who wants to pay money to stay on an air mattress? They struggled to get investors to buy into their idea.

While you can see things from the investors' point of view, the people booking with them were telling a different story. People were even sharing their resumes and LinkedIn profiles to show that they were responsible and not security risks. They wanted a unique spot to stay, and this was when the founders believed they were onto something. After a while, they were accepted into a start-up accelerator program in San Francisco called Y Combinator, one of the points where the company pivoted. The idea suddenly started to catch fire and gain traction.

Airbnb has opened up real estate investing to the general public. You can make some money even if you are a recent graduate with only a small property. You don't even have to own the property yourself. Many renters are able to utilize Airbnb to make some extra money. It has opened up a whole new world for travel and for making extra money for yourself.

HOW IT WORKS

Airbnb is an interesting concept. One important thing that people often misunderstand is that the Airbnb platform does not own any of the properties that are advertised on the website. Most of the control is left up to the host. The host will decide if they are comfortable with the offer, the price, and many other aspects of their rental property. The Airbnb platform is simply the intermediary between the guest and the host. Some rules and regulations need to be followed to ensure that the guests have the best experience possible and the hosts are protected.

Guests

If you have stayed in an Airbnb before, you will probably understand how it works for a guest. It's a pretty straightforward process, and it's user-friendly. To utilize the platform as a guest, you just set up an account on the platform.

Once your profile is complete, you can scroll through the listings until you find a property you like and want to stay in. Since there are millions of listings on the platform, you can utilize the filters to help narrow it down, so you're not scrolling for hours. Guests can view pictures, amenities, features, and descriptions of the various listings to better understand what they are getting into. There are also reviews left by previous guests. This helps each guest get a better idea of what the service is like and what other people's experiences have been. The higher the rating, the better the experience is likely to be.

Once the guest finds a listing that they like, they can go ahead and book it. There are additional prompts that they are taken through to pay and confirm the booking. In most cases, the booking request goes to the host to be confirmed, and then the payment process will continue. The exception to this is if the listing has an instant booking option. This allows them to skip the host verification step and book immediately.

Hosts

The process for a host is a bit more detailed because you have to create your listing and ensure everything is in order. There are plenty of options for Airbnb hosts, so regardless of the type of property you have, you will likely find an option that will suit you. You can rent out an entire property, just a room, a shared room, or a specific portion of the property. There is even an option to list events on the platform.

You will need to create an account with Airbnb. This account is completely free, but in some areas it may vary, so it is a good idea to look at the fees and restrictions that will affect you. Certain areas might also have restrictions on Airbnb or rental properties in general. It is wise to research if any of these apply to you and your property. To complete your account, you will follow the prompts and upload the necessary documents and files. You will also need to ensure that your listing looks attractive so people will want to book with you. This means you need to write a description, upload pictures, and create a title for your listing. You will also be able to set a price. The price is completely up to you, but it is a good idea to set a competitive price, as setting it too high won't get you that many bookings.

You will also be directed to a calendar function where you can indicate when your property will be available to rent out. Some people only rent out their property during certain months; others do it throughout the year. It is completely up to you, so you can decide what will work best for your schedule. Once you have completed your information and followed all the prompts, you can publish your listing. Then, all you have to do is wait for people to start booking with you. This is just the basic overview of how Airbnb works for a host, but we will dive into more in-depth steps throughout the book.

IS AIRBNB SAFE?

One of the biggest concerns that people have is whether Airbnbs are safe or not. The platform creators have developed many systems and tools to ensure the safety of both guests and hosts. Identity verification, reviewing procedures, and private internal messaging make it much safer for both parties. Since payment is made through the platform, money can be held until check-in. This provides security to the guest, as they know they will not lose their money. Many people are scared of being scammed, so the fact that the host is not paid until after check-in reassures the guests.

Multiple verification methods are put in place for both hosts and guests. Both will have to enter personal details that must be confirmed. As a host, you can see how much information somebody has uploaded. The more information somebody provides, the more trustworthy they are likely to be. The same goes for guests who are looking for trustworthy hosts. The review system is an incredibly valuable part of the platform. Both guests and hosts review each other. This means you will be able to see any negative reviews about a potential guest, and they would be able to see the same about you. This helps you to make better choices when you are accepting a booking request.

With all of this being said, there have been some Airbnb horror stories. Before this puts you off, consider the fact that Airbnb is a massive company. There are likely to be a few bad experiences with the millions of properties worldwide that advertise with Airbnb. Airbnb does its best to help mitigate the situation and ensure that any guest or host that does not meet the standards is permanently removed. Since Airbnb cannot be in direct contact with every guest and every host, it is best to ensure that you take precautions to ensure your safety. We will be diving more into the nitty-gritty of this in later chapters.

DIFFERENT TYPES OF AIRBNB ACCOMMODATIONS

One of the biggest draws of Airbnb is the fact that there are many different types of accommodations for a guest to choose from and that a host can list. This gives incredible flexibility to all parties. Understanding the types of accommodation you can list on the platform will allow you to make better investment decisions, especially if you are looking to purchase a new property to list on Airbnb.

FOUR MAIN TYPES OF PLACES OFFERED VIA AIRBNB

Airbnb offers extreme flexibility for a host. You can rent out any type of space as long as customers are looking for that particular type of rental. There are four main types of places that Airbnb offers. We're going to dive into these now.

- **Entire Place**: The traveler will book the whole property for themselves and will not have to share the space with anybody else. An entire property could include a garden, a pool, and other amenities.
- **Private Rooms**: This is a larger property divided into common areas for the guests. A guest will have their own bedroom and possibly bathroom, but share the other amenities with other guests.
- **Hotel Rooms**: These are simply hotel rooms that are rented out on Airbnb.
- **Shared Rooms**: This is similar to hostel-style living. It is targeted more toward younger travelers because it will be a room with multiple beds where the amenities are shared by everyone.

SPECIALIZED ACCOMMODATIONS

In addition to the four main types offered on Airbnb, there are many specialized accommodation types that you can list. This provides even more flexibility to both the host and the guests.

Airbnb for Work

This is a spinoff from Airbnb, which allows corporations to use the platform to make bookings for business trips. It allows a business to plan trips for their employees and to keep track of the bookings that have been made. The more 5-star reviews that your property gets from business travelers, the more likely it will show up on Airbnb's work trip feed. There are also a few other criteria that need to be met in order to show up on this filter. For example, you would need to have high-speed Wi-Fi, well-equipped workstations, after-hour access, be close to transportation and cities, and possibly offer on-site laundry facilities. All of this provides for the needs of a business person who is traveling into town for a meeting or other business purpose.

Airbnb Plus

Airbnb Plus is reserved for the finest quality homes with great reviews. In order to become an Airbnb Plus host, you will need to be verified by Airbnb. There will also be an in-person inspection to make sure that you fit the criteria. You will definitely need to put in some extra effort in order to gain this status. It comes with additional maintenance requirements as you will need to provide above and beyond what other Airbnb hosts generally offer. This might mean that you need to ensure that your kitchen is stocked with amenities like cooking oil, basic cooking supplies, dishes, and cutlery. You might also need to stock your bathrooms with hair care products, bubble bath, high-quality bathing products, and other amenities. Your property also needs to have something different about it. Exceptional design is part of the qualifications that are required.

Airbnb Luxe

This option allows travelers to access amazing properties as well as trip designers to help them plan their experience. These homes are hand-picked from around the world and pass a very strict verification process. Standards need to be met in both design and function, as well as 300 different criteria. This is not just about offering guests great accommodation, but ensuring their trip is transformational and unforgettable. It is essentially about creating an experience.

Unique Stays

Many travelers out there are looking for unique experiences and uncommon spaces to rent out. These are non-traditional properties or spaces that can be rented out on the platform. There are so many types of unique stays that are available, so if you have a property that fits the bill, you will be able to utilize it for Airbnb. Perhaps you have a houseboat, a yurt, or a treehouse. There are even igloos are available on the platform.

Properties Run by Superhosts

In order to achieve Superhost status, you need to complete 100 nights of hosting over three completed stays or have ten completed stays over a period of a year, maintain a 90 percent response rate, have less than a 1 percent cancellation rate, and maintain a rating of 4.8. There are many guests out there who adjust the filters to look for Superhosts. Since a Superhost needs to meet these additional criteria, the guests can be sure that they are in for a good experience. It is definitely worth your while to try and earn this status.

It does take a bit of work to get there, but if you can maintain quality standards you will be able to become a Superhost. There are many incentives that are offered when you are a Superhost. You will be able to charge a bit more in your pricing since you have been verified and meet the higher standards. You will also get dedicated Airbnb support, improvement in listing visibility, and a badge signifying your Superhost status.

The fact that there are so many options available on Airbnb means that you will likely find one that's going to work for you. You can offer specialized accommodation or simply fit into one of the four primary categories. Either way, you will be able to make some good money through Airbnb if you utilize the right strategies. In the next chapter, we are going to be looking at being an Airbnb host and what it is really like.

THE TRUTH ABOUT AIRBNB HOSTING—MYTH VS. REALITY

Many people are put off from using Airbnb because of the many myths that surround it. It is really helpful to be able to see what is true and what is a lie. This way, you will be able to move into your Airbnb journey with confidence.

MYTH 1: THE VACATION RENTAL INDUSTRY IS SKETCHY

There are so many people out there who think the vacation rental industry is sketchy. The truth is that vacation rentals have been organized by individual property owners for many, many years. The only difference between Airbnb and other privately owned vacation rentals is that the platform makes it a lot easier for people to connect with each other. Airbnb is simply a place for property owners and travelers to meet. Previously, it was a lot more difficult to find a private property owner who offered a unique place to stay. Now, it is just more convenient.

MYTH 2: BEING A HOST MEANS YOU CAN'T GO ANYWHERE ELSE

A common myth is that you will never be able to leave your property. If you are somebody who loves to travel and spend time away from your home, this belief may keep you from pursuing an Airbnb business opportunity. However, there are plenty of options available to you if you want to leave your property and travel. In most cases, you are not going to be expected to stay on-site while you have guests. Unless you are providing a service to them each day, you really don't need to be there to babysit. This is especially true if you have private property or private rooms that are being rented out. Most of the time, people want to be left alone, so if you have ensured that everything is up to date and maintained on your property, then you are not likely to need to be there at all.

With this being said, it is always a good idea to have somebody available who will be able to assist your guests if necessary. You could hire a property manager to handle all the affairs of your property while you travel and do the things you enjoy. Another option would be to have a friend or someone else that you know take care of the property while you go on holiday.

MYTH 3: AIRBNB IS ONLY PROFITABLE IN THE WEST

If you do not live in the west, a common myth is that your Airbnb is not going to be successful. This is definitely not true. Although Airbnb was started in San Francisco and founded by Americans, it has expanded to the rest of the world. There are over 7 million active listings across the world. These listings span 100,000 cities in 220 countries and territories.[1] There are millions of hosts worldwide, and they are making good money out of it. People want to be able to travel all over the world, not just in the west. Airbnb has a global approach to ensure that it thrives all over the world. You will be able to receive payment in your local currency and the platform allows you to process those payments easily.

MYTH 4: AIRBNB GUESTS ARE MOSTLY PARTY PEOPLE WHO CAUSE TROUBLE AND DESTROY FURNITURE

This myth is fueled by a few horror stories that have come to light. The truth is, there have been some bad experiences for hosts who have had to deal with crazy partygoers who have ruined their property. With 103.7 million stays in the second quarter of 2022 alone, if there are one or two bad experiences that come out of it, it really is not that much.[2] Not only that, but Airbnb does take these things very seriously and will ban guests from using the platform if there is a reason to do so.

Even if you do have a bad experience with a guest at your Airbnb, the chances that it will be a massive blow to your income and your property are quite small. When dealing with people, there's always going to be the possibility of having a bad guest experience. These things are quite easy to handle and typically blow over. If you take the time to screen your guests before you confirm the bookings, you shouldn't really have an issue finding decent houseguests. Communication is always important so that you can set the standard for what you expect from your guests. This will prevent potential miscommunications down the line.

MYTH 5: BECOMING AN AIRBNB HOST IS ONLY ABOUT BUSINESS

Some people truly want to run Airbnb as a business, and that is completely valid. However, there are other people who do not want to do that. Either way, how you want to run your Airbnb is going to be completely up to you. Becoming an Airbnb host is not solely about business. When it first started, it was about offering experiences and making connections. If this is your main motivation, then this is what you can offer to your guests. Of course, making a profit is a big part of running an Airbnb, but your true motivation could lie in the hospitality side of it.

Airbnb is different from traditional hotels and formal vacation rentals. You are allowed to make it feel as homey as you would like. It is an expression of your creativity and hospitality. People know that when they book with Airbnb, they are not going to get a crisp, clean, and formal experience. They'd rather get something that feels a bit more personal. If you are passionate about hospitality and want to open your doors to strangers so that you can form new connections and relationships, then let this be your motivation and run with it. That extra-special personal touch is what has gotten many people 5-star reviews.

MYTH 6: AIRBNB RENTALS ARE BAD FOR MY NEIGHBORHOOD

People love comfort and things that stay exactly the same. The problem with this is that comfort does not often lead to growth or improvement. If you look at anything good that has happened over the past few years, you will see that it came about due to some sort of change. Many people are quite afraid of inviting Airbnb rentals into their area because they think it's going to lead to neighborhood deterioration. This is definitely a myth, and the opposite is actually true. When you invite more tourists into your area, you are spurring on the economy. You're leading to more economic growth for small businesses and for the people who live in the neighborhood.

Adding new people to the area also introduces diversity and allows for new thoughts and ideas. You will find that neighborhoods that open themselves up to new cultures and experiences are ones that tend to grow. If a neighborhood has growth potential, then more money would be invested in it, and the quality of life would increase for those who live there.

Of course, this can be a scary process if you are somebody who is not used to change, but it is absolutely worth it because the positives definitely outweigh any potential negatives. Airbnb is simply an advancement of an already established industry. It is something that has always existed but has now been improved upon. In the next chapter, we will look at helping you decide whether starting your own Airbnb business is the right decision for you.

9 SIGNS STARTING AN AIRBNB BUSINESS IS RIGHT FOR YOU

To date, Airbnb hosts have earned more than $150 billion. With 14,000 new hosts joining every single month, that number is only going to increase.[1] While this is enticing, it is important to understand whether Airbnb is right for you. Here are a few things you should consider and ask yourself before moving forward.

SIGN #1: YOU HAVE A KNACK FOR HOSPITALITY

Hospitality is definitely a talent, and there are many people who have it. If you are somebody who genuinely enjoys hosting people and doesn't mind playing hotel manager, then this could be the perfect fit for you. You will be able to invite many different people from all over the world into your home. You can cater to them and ensure that they are having a good time while they staying with you.

SIGN #2: THE MARKET CONDITIONS ARE THERE

Above all, Airbnb is designed to help you make some money. If you're unable to make a profit, it is definitely not going to be worth your time and effort. This is why it is so important to understand the market conditions where you are. There should be enough demand in your area or in the area you are looking to purchase a new property. This demand should be sufficient to facilitate your business and make financial sense.

You should have a look at whether your property is somewhere that people want to stay. This is why it is so important to do research about your area. It doesn't make sense to start an Airbnb and put all your time and effort into it if nobody wants to book in your neighborhood. Areas that have a high demand for tourism or business travelers tend to do better with Airbnb because there is a constant stream of people booking with you. Have a look to see how many other Airbnbs are in your area or how many other rental properties there are in general. Then see if they have a high occupancy rate. This just means how often the properties are booked out. That will give you a good idea about the viability of an Airbnb business in your current area.

SIGN #3: YOU'RE IN IT FOR MORE THAN JUST A QUICK BUCK

Building an Airbnb business takes some time. You are not going to be raking it in from the first moment you click publish on your listing. As with any business, it does take some patience in order to develop a successful long-term business. If you are not somebody who is able to put the necessary time and effort into your Airbnb business, this might not be the right option for you.

SIGN #4: YOU HAVE ENOUGH STARTING CAPITAL

An Airbnb business is not something that you can start up with absolutely nothing in your bank account. You need to have some start-up capital in order to get your property ready or purchase a new one. If you are looking to purchase a new property to start your Airbnb business, then you will need a good amount of start-up capital. Even if you are going to be hosting a property that you already own, you still need money to get your property Airbnb-ready.

Airbnb is not just about simply renting out an extra room in your house. You need to be able to create an experience for your guests. This means that you need to purchase new linen, furniture, and decor. You are trying to create a good experience for your guests, so you can't just use anything that you find in your house. You will need to purchase plenty of new things in order to get those good reviews from your guests. If you simply throw in the old lounge set from your 20s and the bed that you no longer use because it is now uncomfortable, you are not going to be able to run a successful business. Start-up costs are just part of the deal when it comes to running any successful business.

SIGN #5: IT'S ACTUALLY ALLOWED IN YOUR JURISDICTION

Not every area is going to be welcoming to Airbnb. There are various legalities, rules, and restrictions that might come into play depending on your area. You need to ensure that your Airbnb business will be legal. Make sure to check locally to ensure that you are allowed to run an Airbnb out of your property. You should also ensure that you understand the restrictions that apply if you are allowed to rent out your property as an Airbnb. This is definitely one of the biggest things that you should consider when getting into Airbnb. You might need to purchase a property outside of your current location in order to start up your business.

SIGN #6: YOU HAVE ENOUGH TIME AND ENERGY

It is definitely possible to start up your Airbnb as a side hustle, but you do need to have time to put into it. This is especially so when you are trying to get things off the ground. You'll need to make sure that your property is good to go, and this does take some time and effort. Once your property has been listed on Airbnb and is ready to receive guests, you need to have time to tend to your guests' demands and turn over the property for new guests. Maintenance and cleaning are all part of the deal when it comes to running an Airbnb, so you need to take this into consideration.

SIGN #7: YOU'RE OK WITH THE COSTS

It is so important that you are realistic about the costs involved with running an Airbnb. There are definitely one-time costs that need to be considered. However, the costs don't just stop once you have listed your home on Airbnb. There are recurring costs that need to be taken into consideration when you are running your business. For example, you would need to provide your guests with certain things in order to help them enjoy their stay. Perhaps you are providing them with a welcome basket, shampoo, body wash, basic cooking essentials, basic cleaning essentials, and similar items. All of these things will need to be replaced once they have been used.

You might also need to think about bringing in a cleaning or maintenance service to help you out. This is also going to incur costs. This is why it is important for you to sit down and make a budget for yourself so that you understand exactly how much money it is going to cost you to run an Airbnb business. This will help you prepare for the future and make sure that you have a realistic idea of how much profit you will be making.

SIGN #8: YOU HAVE ENOUGH RISK TOLERANCE

Like with any business, there are some risks to take into account when you are investing in an Airbnb business. There are financial and personal risks that come with this kind of endeavor. You need to be completely honest with yourself and sit down to discover what level of risk you are comfortable with and if this is the right option for you.

SIGN #9: YOU ARE COMFORTABLE WITH STRANGERS IN YOUR HOME

There are some people who are quite touchy about letting strangers into their personal and private spaces. This doesn't mean that you are not a hospitable person. It just means that you are uncomfortable with people invading your space. If this is the case, then Airbnb is probably not going to be the best option for you. Think about whether you are open to the idea of people you don't know using your facilities and sleeping under the same roof as you. It is completely understandable if this is not something that appeals to you. However, it is important that you be honest with yourself so that you don't start something that you, later on, find out that you just don't enjoy.

The truth is, being an Airbnb host is not for everyone. However, if you are willing to take the risk and if you have what it takes, the payoff can be huge. Running an Airbnb does have a monetary benefit, but the benefits extend far beyond this. You will be able to expand your knowledge and broaden your horizons based on the people that you invite to your home. It is truly an enjoyable experience if this is something you know you are well fit for. In the next chapter, we are going to cover the Airbnb framework that you can use to jumpstart your own Airbnb business.

THE "AIRBNB FRAMEWORK" FOR STARTING YOUR OWN SUCCESSFUL AIRBNB BUSINESS

You don't have to be a genius or a visionary or even a college graduate to be successful. You just need a framework and a dream.

— MICHAEL DELL

THE "AIRBNB FRAMEWORK"

The rest of this book is going to be organized into six separate parts. These parts are going to go through the framework for creating a successful Airbnb business. There will be a lot to cover in each of these sections, and when you put everything together, you will be able to run a very successful Airbnb business. In this chapter, we are just going to give a summary of what this framework is like for creating a prosperous Airbnb business.

Analyze (Chapters 6–8)

The first stage of this process is going to be analysis. Whenever you start a business, you need to have all the facts before you get going. This helps you to understand the environment and what your goals are. You will also need to look at the competition so that you can assess the viability of your business plan. Proper analysis is fundamental to any effective plan.

Insurance (Chapters 9–10)

When it comes to renting out a property, insurance is so important. If you do not have insurance, then you're putting yourself at risk of losing money and other valuable items. This is why we have to spend some time talking about insurance in general and what insurance you need to have.

Ready Your Property (Chapters 11–15)

The third step is all about getting ready for your guests. At the end of the day, an Airbnb business is all about the property and making your guests happy. If you are able to do this, you will encourage good reviews and get continuous business. This is an incredibly important part of the process and something that needs to be concentrated on. Another thing to note is that preparing your property is going to be a constant thing. You will always need to ensure that it is at its best at all times. This will make sure that every guest who steps through your doors has a great experience.

Booking Management (Chapters 16–19)

Being able to manage your bookings is an integral part of running an Airbnb business. You need to ensure that the process is easy to follow and efficient. This will remove a lot of stress from you and your guests and make it a lot easier to manage who stays in your Airbnb and all the details surrounding that process.

Get Noticed (Chapters 20–25)

Getting noticed is really important if you want to bring in as many new guests as possible. If your listing is not eye-catching and doesn't draw the attention of people scrolling through the platform, you will not be able to make a lot of money through Airbnb investing. This is why it is so important to do what you can to get yourself noticed. There are many strategies and tips that you can put into place, and in this section, you will be able to learn everything you need to.

Build Relationships (Chapters 26–27)

It is really important to develop good relationships with your guests. This will result in them wanting to come back and stay with you. If you have many returning guests, you will know that they will be taking care of your property, and you can trust them with your space. It also allows you to have more security in terms of bookings. You know that a few good people will be booking your property every once in a while. This is incredibly important to building a good business.

There are definitely many different paths that you can take when you are starting your own Airbnb business. The Airbnb framework is a very simple six-step process that will help you to start any Airbnb business from the ground up. It doesn't matter how much experience you have in hospitality or even building a business. In the next chapter, we are going to go over the first step of the process—analyzing the market.

STAGE 1

ANALYZING THE MARKET

HOW TO ANALYZE THE PLAYING FIELD

I n the US alone, there are over 660,000 Airbnb listings.[1] There are a ton of people who are making their dreams come true through real estate investing. There are different ways to identify who your competitors are and their place in the market. Not all of those 660,000 listings are successful. The ones that will be successful are the ones that put themselves in the most profitable position. This starts with being able to analyze what you are working with. Then you are able to make the right decisions for the current market.

TOOLS YOU'LL NEED

There are many different tools that you can utilize in order to help you with your analysis. These are easy to use and quite easy to access as well. Some of them might require you to pay some sort of fee in order to use them, but most of them are free.

AirDNA

The first tool we are going to be talking about is AirDNA. This platform provides research and analytics software. It helps you to understand how the short-term rental industry is changing over time. You will be able to dig deeper into the rental market using this tool. You can get trend reports and forecasts to help you make your decisions and understand exactly what is going on in your market. As a host, you will have access to granular insights that are behind the industry and the business.

AllTheRooms

This is a great tool that provides business insights and analytics. This is specific to the vacation rental industry. It includes multiple key features such as market intelligence, property intelligence, and competitive intelligence. This will help you to get a more in-depth look at what is happening in your area so that you are able to make better decisions regarding your rental property.

Facebook Hosting Groups

There are multiple Facebook hosting groups on the platform. You can join them and gain insight into what is going on in your market. It helps to connect with other Airbnb hosts so you can see what they're doing and what their strategies are. In most cases, other hosts are quite happy to share their knowledge and insights with people that are new to the market. If you can find a great community of people who are willing to give you one-on-one advice, this is going to be incredibly valuable to you. You can ask specific questions and get advice on what you are currently struggling with. It also helps just to have other people around you who are going through the same process. You will feel supported and most likely be able to develop better strategies for your Airbnb.

I have created a Facebook group for hosts to share, learn, get advice, and find support from other people who are going through the same thing. Everyone is welcome to join, so you can extend the invite to other Airbnb hosts you might know. This is a private group, so you can feel free to share, knowing that only the people who are going through the host journey will be able to see and respond. Please feel free to join. I would love to have you!

Here are the details:

Name: Airbnb Host Community

URL: www.facebook.com/groups/airbnbhostcommunity

QR Code:

FACTORS TO CONSIDER

When you are doing your analysis, before you start investing in Airbnb, you need to look at a few key factors. These factors will allow you to get a holistic view of how profitable your Airbnb will be. You will also be able to develop strategies that are specific to you, and that will let you know what will work for your area and your property.

Destination

When it comes to investing in property, location is key. Even if you already have a property that you want to turn into an Airbnb, you still need to understand the ins and outs of the location and if it's going to work for short-term rentals. If you think about it, people would rather stay in an average Airbnb that is located centrally to what they want to do and see than stay in an amazing property that does not allow them to see the sights they want to see or be surrounded by the environment they want to be in. This is why it is so important to think about the location. You can pretty much change anything about your property except for the location, so don't skip this step.

People often book holidays based on location and not on the accommodation that they're going to stay in. Once they decide on the location, they will then start looking for rentals in that area. This is not to say that the other aspects of your Airbnb are not important. It is just simply to note that location is typically the first thing that people consider, which is the reason why it is so important.

When you are looking at your current location or the location you want to invest in, you need to understand a few things. The first thing you should think about is seasonality. This means knowing when the high and low seasons are. When are people flocking to this area and when are people staying away? This will help you to understand the times of the year which will be the most profitable and why people are coming to the area at this time. It also allows you to price your properties appropriately at various seasons so that you can ensure you are making a good profit. Things like major holidays and events also impact how many people are coming to an area. If you live in an area that has big festivals or events, you know the people who want to stay at rental properties during this time.

Beyond simply understanding the important dates that guests are going to be coming to your area, you also need to understand what the place has to offer. Restaurants, sightseeing spots, landmarks, parks, and activities are all really important to the location. Guests will often look for local attractions and suggestions for things that they could be doing while they're in your city or your area. The better the facilities that surround your Airbnb, the more popular it will be. If your guest simply wants to relax and enjoy the time, it is reassuring to know that there are plenty of restaurants, stores, and activities around the property. This will result in a much better retention rate.

Target Market

The next thing to consider is your target market. This typically goes hand-in-hand with the location, as there will be a specific type of person that wants to visit a specific type of place. Not only that, certain people will gravitate toward certain types of properties as well. If you understand who your target audience is, then you will be able to tailor your property to meet their needs. You should be realistic about who this target market is as there are going to be some limitations based on your property.

Certain types of people will be more attracted to certain cities, areas, and properties. Your city's tourism website as well as active Airbnb listings will give you a good idea of the demographics. Think about whether your city attracts more leisure tourists or business people. If tourists frequent the area, you can think about whether these tourists are coming in groups, families, singles, or couples. Think about what kind of amenities they are looking for and what they are willing to pay for these amenities. All of this information will help you tailor your property to what your target guests need. This will help you with marketing as well as the general provisions of your property. You will also be able to understand what kind of people are going to be staying with you.

Local Regulations

Many cities and states have decided to regulate rental properties and alternative lodging in different areas. This means that every property investor needs to understand the regulations in the area they want to invest in. You don't want to be put in a situation where you get in trouble with your local government for not sticking to the rules. You also don't want to put all this money into your Airbnb, only to realize that you have to shut it down a few years or months later. It is a good idea to consult your municipality and HOA to get all the information that you need about your property and what you are allowed to do. Once you have this information, you might have peace of mind in your area, or you might need to look into investing in another city or state.

Competitors

Understanding your competitors in the area is really important. You can do this by finding a few similar properties and using them as a benchmark for yours. Make sure that the properties you look at are ones that are offering the same type of service that you are. It's not really going to make sense to compare yourself to a five-bedroom, self-catering house when you have a two-bedroom guest house. Look for properties that are going to be your closest competitors and go from there.

You will need to look for competitors in the same or nearby neighborhoods. The properties need to have a similar configuration to yours. This just means having the same number of bedrooms, bathrooms, and comparable amenities. Once you have found a few properties that are similar to yours, you need to do some investigation. Have a look at how many competitors there are in your area. If there are too many, you might struggle to get guests. If there are too few, it might be a good idea to find out why there aren't as many Airbnbs in that area. You can also have a look at the pricing and how much of the calendar is open. The pricing will give you a good idea of what people are charging. If you look at the calendar, you will be able to see how in demand the area and the type of property are. You can cross-examine the pricing and the calendars. This way, you can get a good idea of what pricing gets the most bookings.

It is also a good idea to have a look at the reviews that are on the properties. Try and find out why the reviews were good or bad. This way you will be able to avoid bad ratings and provide your guests with the things that they were missing in the other properties. Once you have evaluated your competition, you can have a look at your own strategy and see what you need to change. You might notice that your pricing is not optimal for the market, and you can tweak this a little. Perhaps you could look into providing a few more amenities for your guests to enjoy on your property. Simply having a look at your competitors and what they are offering is a really good way to help improve your Airbnb strategy.

Financial Considerations

When you're investing, it means that you have to put some money in order to get money out. Your investment needs to make sense for you, and you need to be sure that you will be getting a good return on your investment. It is definitely a good idea to take the financials into consideration before you start investing or start putting your plan into practice. You can calculate your potential rental income, but you also need to understand the expenses that come with running your own Airbnb. All the money you make from your daily rates is not going to be just for profit. You will need to use some of that money to keep your property running smoothly and for other business costs.

Your financial considerations are not just going to be limited to purchasing a new property or renovating the one you currently have. There are going to be some continuous costs that you will need to take into consideration. These are going to be your expenses. Any money you make through your rental needs to be able to cover your expenses and then have a bit left over for your project. Here are a few things that you should be considering in terms of expenses you might incur while running an Airbnb:

- Inspection fees
- Repairs
- Furniture
- Insurance
- Utilities
- Maintenance
- Property tax
- Rental income tax
- Cleaning fees
- Hosting fees

This is definitely not everything that you need to consider when it comes to your expenses. However, it gives you a good idea of what to expect.

When it comes to performing market analysis for your Airbnb, there are many things that you need to consider. The above factors will help you develop a plan and a strategy to better understand the market. You will find that making decisions is a lot easier when you have all the information in front of you. It might seem like a long and tedious task, but it is definitely worth it. In the next chapter, we are going to compare the different types of properties that you can rent out.

PROS AND CONS OF RENTING OUT DIFFERENT PROPERTY TYPES

Airbnb recently announced 56 new vacation rental categories for over 4.4 million of its listings.[1] This means that now, more than ever, it is important for first-time Airbnb hosts to think about their property and how they can make it stand out. Not only that, but it opens up the door of opportunity for you to rent out whatever kind of space you have. Some of the categories that have been opened up are camping, design, and amazing pools. If you have a property with a unique feature or that is in a unique area, you can definitely use this to your advantage and get noticed more.

Different types of properties will need different strategies to help them stand out. It is important to consider what type of property you have to purchase when you are getting into short-term real estate investing. In this chapter, we are going to take a look at the many different types of rental properties that are available. It will give you a good idea of the unique strengths and weaknesses of the various property types. This will allow you to make better decisions and create a better strategy for yourself going forward.

DIFFERENT TYPES OF RENTAL PROPERTIES

You might recall from Chapter 2 that there are four primary types of Airbnb accommodation. Along with this, there are more exotic types of accommodation available. With this being said, you will likely find similarities between unique stays and the four primary types of rentals that we are going to be talking about in this chapter.

Entire Place

The first option is to rent out the entire property. When doing this, your guest will have complete access to everything that is on the property. This might include the yard, pool, and all the other areas of the house. Renting out an entire property does not necessarily mean that it needs to be a house. You could also rent out an entire apartment, condo, or villa. However, there are some criteria that need to be met when renting out this type of property. Typically, a guest would be expecting a bedroom, cooking space, and a bathroom.

This is a great option for many guests because it allows them to have the amenities they need. If they are traveling in bigger groups or as a family, it is cheaper to book out an entire place and then prepare meals for themselves. It is also a good idea to book something like this if they are staying for a longer period of time. It can get pretty expensive to eat out or order in every single day. Providing a cooking space allows your guests to cater for themselves, and this brings down the cost of the overall holiday. Not only that, but your guests will be able to enjoy the privacy of having a property to themselves.

One thing to note is that this kind of property will be more expensive than others. You might be limiting your potential guests as single people or couples might not see the need to rent out an entire property. People who are looking to travel around and sightsee might also not want to book out this type of property as they will not be making full use of the amenities.

Private Rooms

A private room still offers privacy but on a budget. A private room will have a bedroom and usually a bathroom that is completely private. Other amenities, such as the living space or kitchen, will be shared with the other guests who stay on the property. If you have a spare room in your house that you are looking to rent out, offering a private room could be a good option. This way, you'll be able to make money from the spare space that you have and create privacy for yourself and your guests. If you are doing this, it might be a good idea to look into creating a separate entrance for your guests so they can come and go as they please, and it's not going to interrupt you and your life.

A private room is a great option for many guests. This is especially so when it is a single person or a couple who is looking to travel. They do not want to stay in their accommodation for long periods as they're looking to be out and about. They are also not too concerned with being able to cook and cater for themselves. Cooking might be an option if there is a communal kitchen available, but this is not necessary for many private room options.

Hotel Rooms

A hotel room offers a level of service that can be likened to traditional hotels. You might find these types of rooms available at lifestyle hotels, boutiques, bed-and-breakfasts, or similar properties. You will be able to charge a bit more for these types of accommodation since you will be offering a service that many other Airbnbs don't. Things like turndown service, breakfast, and cleaning would be expected. It is a great option if you have access to the property that would allow this and you have the funds to provide this or the time to do it yourself.

Shared Rooms

There are many guests who do not mind sharing space with other guests. These tend to be students and travelers who are on a budget. Essentially, you will be able to rent out your space, and the space will be shared amongst many different people. You can think of it more like a hostel or dorm-style room. There might be multiple beds and bunk beds in one room that people sleep in. All amenities on the property will be shared amongst the people who have booked with you.

It is important to note that many travelers might not want to use this option. Families and people who are older generally do not enjoy sharing rooms. However, you are opening up your side of the world to people who want to travel on a budget. This is a great option if you live in a more expensive part of the world that is known for its travel. People want to come to these areas and see them, but they might be on a budget. You'll be offering a place for them to sleep and store their belongings while they go out and see the sights and enjoy the activities.

The pricing for these types of rooms is much less than most other Airbnb options. However, since you will be having a lot more people booking with you since you have more space available, this will offset the cheaper nightly rate. It is likely that the people who book with you would not be staying for long periods of time as they will want to move on to the next destination. This means that the turnover time can be quite quick, and you would need to be ready to clean up and get the rooms ready for the next guest.

Each of the four different types of Airbnb accommodation has its own unique pros and cons when it comes to renting them out. Part of what should drive your decision on which type of listing to launch is also what's in your best financial interest. In the next chapter, we'll compare the profitability of different types of Airbnb listings.

WHAT'S THE MOST PROFITABLE TYPE OF AIRBNB LISTING?

On average, Airbnb guests tend to stay 2.4 times longer in Airbnbs than they do in hotels. This could be attributed to the fact that guests are looking for an experience rather than just a place to sleep at night. If you are able to create a really great place for your guests to stay, you will definitely attract them for a longer period of time and make more money. That being said, there are definitely some properties that are more profitable than others. Understanding which ones can help you make better decisions going forward.

CALCULATING PROFITABILITY

You need to be able to calculate your profitability for your future Airbnb. This will help you to understand how much money you can make with your property.

Key Variables

There are a few key variables that you should take into consideration when you're looking at how profitable your Airbnb could potentially be. Just remember that this is just going to be an estimation. Things might change over the years, so it is a good idea to regularly look at these variables and adjust your expectations accordingly.

Upfront Costs and Operating Expenditures

The first thing you're going to want to look at is the upfront costs and operating expenditures. These are the things that you will continuously be paying for throughout the life of your Airbnb business. This is the general cost of taking care of your property and ensuring that it is at its best. If you already live in the area, you should have a good idea of the maintenance and upkeep costs since you already own a property there. You can use it as a base point and then see if there are any additional costs that you need to include.

You also need to take into account things like taxes, insurance premiums, and platform fees. Your taxes will include property tax and the tax that you make from the profit of your business, so make sure you take both of these into consideration. We will be delving more into insurance in later chapters, but for now, you can just think of this as part of your operating expenditures. The next thing to look at is your platform fees. Every time you get a booking, you will be paying a fee for the platform to process the transaction. This could differ from area to area, so it is important to understand what applies to you.

Occupancy Rates

Your occupancy rate is going to be how often your property is booked out. It is almost impossible to have a 100 percent occupancy rate, so don't feel discouraged if you find that the percentage is lower than what you thought. You are in a good spot if you have around a 50 percent occupancy rate. You can work on increasing this as you see fit. It is pretty easy to work out an occupancy rate; all you need to do is take the days that your property has been booked out and divide that by the number of days it was available to be booked out. You can take this number and multiply it by 100 to get the occupancy rate as a percentage.

So, if your property was booked out for 62 days of the year and there were 120 days available for it to be booked out, your occupancy rate would be 51.7 percent.

62/120 x 100 = 51.7%

When working out your occupancy rate, it is important to take into consideration seasonal fluctuations. There will be times when people are just not going to be traveling as much and other ones where you are going to get an influx of people booking with you. Half of the year, your occupancy rate could be over 70 percent, and the next half could be 30 percent. This is something that you will need to gauge so that you get a good idea of your overall occupancy rate and how much you'll make on an annual basis.

Neighborhood Factors

There are multiple neighborhood factors that can increase or decrease the amount of money that you make through your property. Since Airbnb is a short-term rental service, you need to make sure that whatever area you are going to invest in is going to be best for short-term rentals. Long-term rentals are a completely different thing because people are looking for something different. When people are renting for the long term, they're looking for a place to settle down and be in a good neighborhood. However, this is not the same criteria as for short-term rentals. Short-term rentals are better in areas that provide experiences for the guests or conveniently meet their needs.

There are many tools you can use to help you do a neighborhood analysis. Here are a few that you can consider using:

- AirDNA
- Beyond Pricing
- Host Tools

- Price Labs
- Rate Genie
- Wheelhouse

EXPENSES BY ACCOMMODATION TYPE

Different property types will cost you more or less, depending. You'll need to work out your costs so that you can work out your profit based on the type of property you're looking to invest in. There are definitely pros and cons to the various types of properties you can choose from. It is all up to you, and you need to decide what is going to work best for you. Some of the costs we are going to be speaking about are going to stay the same regardless of the type of property, but most of them will change. You also have to take into consideration your area and other aspects that might impact the price of the listed expenses.

Business License

Certain jurisdictions and areas will require licenses, and you will also pay special taxes in order to run an Airbnb. The cost of these things will vary depending on your state and country. You can have a look at your local laws and regulations to make sure that you understand what you need to pay for and so that you don't incur any unexpected fees down the line.

Property Taxes

These are pretty much unavoidable regardless of where you live. Often, they are included in your mortgage payment, so it is easy to make the required installments. If it is not included in your mortgage, then you will need to make a big once-a-year payment. It is a good idea to save a little bit each month and then pay off your property taxes by the required date. This will make it a lot easier for you to pay, and it won't seem like you are just forking out a whole bunch of money once a year.

Housekeeping and Maintenance

If you are not going to take care of the cleaning and housekeeping yourself, then you'll need to pay somebody to do it. It is usually easier to have somebody come in and clean for you because you will free up time for yourself to work on other aspects of your business or continue working at your regular job. Housekeeping and maintenance are incredibly important because they allow you to get good reviews. Many people overlook how important a clean and well-maintained property is. If you do choose to clean it yourself, you will still need to cover the costs. Include the amount of money you will be spending on cleaning supplies in your expense list.

In terms of maintenance, you will need to put away some money just in case something happens that you need to take care of. If you own your own property, you already know that certain things always pop up. It might be an issue with the plumbing, or the home is in need of a fresh coat of paint. Regardless of what it is, sometimes these matters aren't visible until they actually need to be tended to. This is why it is a good idea to put aside a certain amount of money each month for maintenance costs. When something does happen that needs your attention, you will have the money to deal with it.

Insurance

Insurance is a really important part of running an Airbnb. There are always risks involved, so you need to be sure that you have good insurance and that all the important things are going to be covered.

Goods and Supplies

Typically, you are going to need to provide your guests with a few simple goods and supplies. When your guests live in your home, they are going to use these things. For example, toilet paper, soap, shampoo, coffee, tea, trash bags, and quite a few other disposable things. It would be a good idea for you to buy these things in bulk so that you lower the price of them, and you will always have them on hand so when you are turning over the property for the next guest, you can quickly replace what is needed.

Utilities

Water, gas, trash, sewage, electricity, and Wi-Fi are all important to any kind of rental property. All of those can be quite a big chunk of your expenses, so make sure that you have prepared for them. You don't really have a choice but to pay for these items, and there really isn't much you can do about it, so make sure you have the money available.

Airbnb Fees

Airbnb charges around 3 percent commission on all bookings. Sometimes this can differ based on area, so it is a good idea to check and see. However, you should expect a certain fee to be charged in addition to your booking fee. If you take this into consideration, then you will be able to charge a rate that will offset the fee so that you're not losing too much money.

There are many factors that you need to consider in order to find the most profitable way to rent out your property. You need to think about things like location, the type of property you have, the type of guest that is going to stay at your property, and a number of other things. Taking the time to understand your property and what you will be paying for is a really good way to estimate how much money you will be making from your Airbnb. In the next chapter, we are going to be diving into getting the right insurance for your Airbnb business.

STAGE 2

AIRBNB INSURANCE

AIRBNB INSURANCE—WHICH TYPE OF POLICY SHOULD YOU GET?

If you are just signing up for Airbnb, you might've heard that you can get automatic protection when you activate a listing. Many people believe that because of this, they do not need to get their own insurance. This is not necessarily true. This is why it's important to understand what kind of protection is included in Airbnb's insurance policy.

AIRBNB INSURANCE: WHAT EVERY HOST NEEDS TO KNOW

What exactly is covered by Airbnb AirCover? The main goal of this type of insurance cover is to protect the hosts from damage caused by guests. AirCover is completely free for every Airbnb host who signs up on the platform. Some of the things that are included in this insurance coverage are as follows:

- $1 million in liability insurance
- $3 million in damage protection
- Auto & boat
- Art & valuables
- Pet damage protection
- Deep cleaning protection
- Income loss protection

This may sound amazing, and you might feel pretty secure with this type of offering. However, this does not thoroughly protect your property. It definitely does reduce any out-of-pocket expenses for things like cleaning and damage, but the truth is that it is simply not comprehensive enough to replace regular insurance. In fact, it is not insurance at all. It is simply an alternative to insurance and was created as an incentive to use the platform.

The topic of insurance can be a complicated one, but it is something that you will need to be well versed in if you are going to be in the property business. There are multiple different types of insurance out there, and you need to know which one you should be getting. We are going to go through a few of the different types of insurance out there, and then you can decide which one is going to be the best one for you.

Homeowner's Insurance

Let's first start with homeowner's insurance. If you own a property, then it's very likely that you have this type of insurance. A homeowner's insurance policy will cover damages that are caused by natural disasters and other unforeseen circumstances. Things like fire, lightning, and hail are covered under homeowner's insurance. These things are not covered by Airbnb AirCover, so you can already see the difference here. The issue with homeowner's insurance is that it does not include any kind of business activity. Since most Airbnb hosts do not live at their rental properties, this will apply. If you do live on the property that you are renting out as an Airbnb, then there might be an exception to this, but it is important to check.

If you have homeowner's insurance and are renting out property that you do not stay at, it could be pretty risky. If your insurance company finds out that your home is not used by you and there is some damage that occurs, they will almost always reject your claim. This means that you will have to pay out-of-pocket for all of the damage that has taken place. If you are not living on the property, then homeowner's insurance is simply not going to be enough to cover your property.

Landlord Insurance

The next type of insurance that you can consider is landlord insurance. This includes casualty insurance and property insurance. This protects you, your tenants, and any other employees of the business. The biggest difference between homeowner's and landlord insurance is that the landlord insurance will offer income protection. What this means is that if your home is not fit for renters due to an unforeseen circumstance, like a natural disaster, your insurance policy will pay you your rental income. Landlord insurance does not cover things that are personal to your property, such as furniture, art, and appliances.

You will need to have a conversation with your insurance provider because many landlord insurance policies don't actually cover short-term rentals. If you are planning on renting out your Airbnb for more than a month, then landlord insurance could be a good option for you, but if it's less than 30 days, it's not going to be of many benefits. However, you can consider something like home-sharing insurance if you are just renting out one of your rooms on the property while you are still living in the main house.

Commercial Property Insurance

Commercial, home-sharing, or vacation rental policies are good options if you are choosing to rent out your property as a true Airbnb with consecutive short-term guests. A commercial property policy is also known as a business property policy. This is definitely one of the most common options. If you do not live on your property and are only using it for short-term rentals, it is possibly your best option. This type of insurance will cover liability and property. This means that damage to your property or any damage or injuries that happen to your guests will all be covered.

Umbrella Policies

An umbrella policy is simply an extension of liability coverage that is typically offered in homeowner's or landlord policies. These will reimburse you for any damages incurred above what has been outlined in the underlying policy. For example, if one of your guests gets injured due to a fault on the property and then decides to sue you, your homeowner's or landlord insurance will pay the initial claim. Anything over and above that will be covered by the umbrella policy. A blanket umbrella possibly covers properties in multiple cities or states. This makes it a really good option for any Airbnb investor who has properties in more than one place. You should make sure that you understand what will be covered by your umbrella policy and how it will all work. Not all of them will work exactly the same, so doing research is of the utmost importance.

There are definitely many things to consider when you are choosing an insurance policy for your Airbnb business. Although you will automatically get AirCover, it only provides certain types of protection for the host. This is simply not enough and should be supplemented with additional insurance coverage. In the next chapter, we will discuss some practical safety tips you can apply as an Airbnb host to help minimize any damage incurred.

SAFETY TIPS FOR HOSTS

While you might've heard that it can be dangerous for guests, the truth is that less than 0.1 percent of all stays result in serious safety issues.[1] This is quite a small statistic, so is it something to worry about? The truth is, it is the host's responsibility to make sure that nothing bad happens to the guest. Even though there is a very small chance that anything will happen, it is good to be prepared and make sure that you put in place the best safety practices that you can.

MOST COMMON PROBLEMS THAT HOSTS FACE

There can definitely be some unexpected situations that pop up when you are a host. However, you can prepare for the most common ones so that you're not completely caught off guard if they do happen.

Payment Disputes

Payment disputes tend to be quite common when you are renting out your property to short-term visitors. However, when you're using the Airbnb platform, these are not things that you would typically have to worry about. Since all payments are handled through the platform, it is a lot safer than dealing one-on-one with the customer. Both the guest and the host are protected in terms of payments.

Physical Injuries to Guests

If a guest gets injured on your property due to negligence or there is an issue with a facility that is on your property, they can sue you. This is why it is so important to have insurance to cover this and to make sure that your property is safe. Doing an inspection of your property every few months will help minimize the risk of this happening.

Theft of Personal Belongings or High-Valued Possessions

As much as you would like to believe that everybody who stays on your property is going to take care of your possessions and not steal them, this is definitely something that can happen. It's a risk you take when you are an Airbnb host. This is why it's best to not leave any kind of high-value possessions or personal belongings at the rental property. Do your best to ensure that anything that you deem valuable is not going to be there. This way, you can have peace of mind when your guests stay with you. Insurance usually covers theft and loss of belongings, but make sure that your insurance policy does include this.

Property Damage

Property damage is also a common risk that you have to think about. If you have a good insurance policy, then this will be covered. It is important to screen your guests as best as possible to make sure that they are responsible. With this being said, there really is only so much that you find out about your guests. There will always be a risk of property damage when other people are using your facilities.

BEST SAFETY PRACTICES FOR AIRBNB HOSTS

Even though there are plenty of risks that come with renting out your property to strangers, there are things that you can do to keep yourself and your property safe. If you stick to these safety practices, then you will significantly minimize the risk of having to deal with any unfortunate situations.

Only Interact Using Airbnb's Platform

It might seem beneficial to take all your business dealings off the platform because you would be able to skip the Airbnb fee and do things the way you want to. However, this is typically not the best idea because it can leave you vulnerable to certain situations. The platform has been designed in such a way as to protect both the guest and the host. When a guest puts in a request to book certain dates, you have the opportunity to look at their profile and find out more about them. If you take things off the platform, you do not have access to profiles, reviews, or references. Everything is simply left to chance.

Be Clear with House Rules, House Manual, and Expectations

The Airbnb platform will allow a host to create a house manual and rules and then upload them. This is completely visible to the guests, so they know what is going to be expected of them if they stay with you. This allows you to hold your guests accountable to the expectations that you set. You know that they have access to the rules and manual, so there really isn't an excuse for them to misuse any of your items. You can put in any type of rule that you deem fit. Your rules can include things like smoking, quiet hours, wearing shoes in the house, or Wi-Fi usage.

Even though setting these rules is really important, you have to be mindful of not overdoing them. If you set unnecessary rules, then people are going to be turned off from booking with you. At the end of the day, people still want to enjoy their holiday, and they don't want to be thinking about whether or not they can do certain things at home. You still want to make them feel comfortable and welcome in your home, but set a few guidelines so that it protects you both.

Have the Right Insurance

As you already know, insurance is of the utmost importance. Make sure that you do thorough research and get the right insurance for you. It is also a good idea to shop around for insurance. You don't want to pay more than you actually need to because insurance can be a costly expense. If you compare quotes from various insurers, then you can be sure that you are getting the best deal and the best coverage.

Get a Security Deposit for Every Stay

It is definitely in your best interest to ask for a security deposit from your guests. In the event of some minor damage, you will be able to dip into the security deposit and pay for it. Some damages don't really warrant an insurance claim, so collecting a security deposit means that you are not going to be expected to foot the bill for damages that were caused by the carelessness of the guest. If there was no damage, then the guest gets the security deposit back. Doing this actually helps keep the guest accountable because they want to get their money back, so they aren't going to be as careless.

Have a Security System Installed

A security system is a great investment for both your protection and that of your guests. You will be able to protect your home even when you are not there. It also helps you to keep tabs on everything that is going on. You will be able to automate things like the thermostat, locking up the doors, and the lights. One thing to note is that you will not be able to install security cameras in certain places that would be considered to be an invasion of your guests' privacy. If there are cameras on the outside of the property, then make sure you have notified your guests about this and understand the laws that surround things like this.

Add Smoke and Carbon Monoxide Detectors

Adding these two things helps give your guests peace of mind, and it also protects your property investment. It really doesn't cost that much to buy and install them, so it's not going to put you out a lot of money. You'll be able to add these features to your listings so that it builds trust and shows your guests that you take their safety seriously. You should test these detectors often so you can ensure they are still working properly.

Use Proper Cybersecurity Measures

There are risks from cyberattacks, and many people do not think of this. Home network security devices will alert you of any threats or Wi-Fi attacks. You will also be able to set a limit on how many people can connect to the device. This means that if your guests invite more people to your home and connect them to your Wi-Fi, you will be able to keep tabs on them.

You can also consider getting a VPN router that does not track your online activity. This means anything your guests do will remain private and cannot be traced back to your home's Wi-Fi. This means that you will not be held liable for any of their actions. This creates privacy for them and protection for you.

Even though insurance is really important, you do not want to be put in a position where you have to use it all the time. Insurance claims can be tiresome, and property damage will cause a lot of hassle for you. This is why you need to put things in place to prevent this from happening in the first place. If you do everything in your power to ensure that your property is safe and that you've created a safe environment for your guests, then you will likely not have to deal with insurance companies very often. In the next chapter, we are going to be looking at things that need to be done before you can list your property on Airbnb.

STAGE 3

READYING YOUR PROPERTY

THE ULTIMATE CHECKLIST FOR
ITEMS TO BUY FOR YOUR PROPERTY

New hosts that joined Airbnb since the start of the pandemic have collectively earned over $1 billion.[1] This is just the new hosts, so as you can see, it has been quite profitable even throughout a time when people traveled at a limited capacity. This being said, you need to ensure that you have everything in place in order to cater to your guests' needs. Creating checklists is going to help you in this regard. It allows you to keep tabs on what you need to provide your guests and what has run out. This ensures that you're not missing out on anything and that every guest will get the same experience.

BATHROOM(S)

- Bath Towels
- Hand Towels
- Toilet Paper
- Hand Soap
- Shampoo
- Conditioner
- Body Wash
- Toothpaste
- Floss
- Additional Toiletries
- Body Lotion
- Disposable Razors
- Disposable Toothbrushes
- Shower Caddy
- Towel Rack
- Hair Dryer
- Bath Mat
- Plunger
- Garbage Can

BEDROOM(S)

- Bed Linens
- Pillows
- Tissues
- Safe for Valuables
- Bedside Table and Lamp
- Garbage Can
- Notepad and Pen
- Hangers for Clothing
- Alarm Clock

KITCHEN

- Tea and Coffee
- Tea Kettle
- Sugar and Spices
- Dishes
- Pots and Pans
- Silverware
- Cups
- Wine Glasses
- Ice Trays
- Coasters
- Tupperware
- Cleaning Supplies
- Dishwashing Liquid
- Hand Soap
- Trash Bags
- Mop
- Broom
- Dustpan
- Oven Mitts
- Dish Towels

LIVING ROOM

- Coffee Table Reading Items (Books, Magazines, Travel Guides)
- Pens and Pencils

APPLIANCES

- Washer and Dryer
- Television
- Cable and/or Subscription Streaming Service
- Clothing Iron and Ironing Board
- Wi-Fi

SAFETY EQUIPMENT

- First Aid Kit
- Smoke Alarm and Carbon Monoxide Detector
- Fire Extinguisher
- Contact List for Emergency Services
- Wi-Fi Thermostat
- Childproofing
- Disaster Kit
- Anti-slip Mats

CLEANING SUPPLIES AND EQUIPMENT

- Cleaning Spray
- Paper Towels
- Gloves
- Duster
- Powdered Cleanser
- Magic Eraser
- Drain Cleaner
- Broom and Dustpan
- Vacuum

When it comes to listing your property on Airbnb, the small details really do matter. These are the things that will help you get those 5-star reviews. Creating a list and structure for yourself will make sure that you're not letting any of these things slip or fall through the cracks. In the next chapter, we are going to go over how to establish effective house rules so that you can ensure the safety of your property and your guests.

TOP 10 TIPS FOR ESTABLISHING EFFECTIVE HOUSE RULES

One of the easiest ways to keep yourself from getting into heated disputes with the guests is to set clear expectations from the start. In order to do this, you can utilize house rules. This will make sure that your guests understand exactly what you expect from them, and you can hold them accountable if they do not follow the rules.

WHAT ARE AIRBNB'S HOUSE RULES?

Your house rules are exactly what they sound like. You'll be setting rules for your guests to adhere to during their stay. This sets expectations and prevents misunderstandings. It also allows you to hold guests accountable for anything that happens. There are already some built-in house rules that are on the Airbnb platform. You can go through these and then add to them to ensure that you are covering all your bases. Some house rules are going to be specific to your type of property, while others are just going to be about general aspects of rental properties.

TOP TIPS FOR SETTING HOUSE RULES

Well-structured house rules allow both parties to understand what is to be expected. The goal is to make your rules clear and understandable for your guests. This will minimize any miscommunications and misunderstandings.

Tip #1: Be Specific and Clear

The first tip is to be specific and clear. You want to make sure that there is no room for misinterpretation. Even if it means that you have to use very simple language, try not to use any big words or unnecessary language, as this can confuse guests. You have to take into consideration that many people who are staying on your Airbnb might not be native English speakers or might not know the local terms that you use. This is why it's so important to be as simple as possible so that your rules are as clear as possible.

Tip #2: Be Reasonable

It can be very easy to go overboard with these rules. Please remember that you want guests to have fun and not feel like they are being extremely restricted. This is why it's so important to be reasonable with the rules that you set. Think about your guests' experience when you are setting the rules. Guests will look at the rules before they book, and if you have too many restrictions, they might not want to book with you. It might be a good idea to have a friend or family member look over your rules and give their opinion on them. This way, you can get an outside view of it and tweak it from there.

Tip #3: Tailor Your Rules to Your Target Guest

When you're writing your rules, take into consideration your target guest. You need to make sure that the rules are relevant to them. Try and read your rules from the point of view of your target guest. Think about whether you would appreciate all the rules or points given to you if you were in their shoes. You can remove all the irrelevant points and change your language based on who your guest is. This will help you communicate better with them and make sure that your rules are actually relevant.

Tip #4: Keep It Friendly

While it is important to be extremely clear with your rules, it is advisable to be friendly and polite as well. You don't want to come off as demanding and rude. All guests would like to be treated nicely and not be spoken to as children. Check the tone in which your rules are coming across. You can write it in a commanding tone, but remember not to be arrogant. In order to do this, you can add a few friendly touches here and there. You can add a few lines before the start of the rules list to set a friendly tone for what is to come. A guest should feel pretty comfortable when they read the rules, but also understand how important it is to do so.

Tip #5: Communicate Your House Rules Early On

From as early on as possible, make sure that your guests understand and respect the house rules. You can make it very easy for your guests to view your house rules even before they book. Once they have booked, you can email them a list of the rules along with the other information that you want to give them. Another helpful tip is to have a list of the house rules in your welcome package when the guests arrive. All of these will solidify the rules in your guests' heads and make sure that they aren't missing anything. They will already know what you expect of them before they get to your property and will be reminded of it at various intervals.

Tip #6: Keep It Concise

Once you've decided on all the important points of your house rules, you need to make sure that it's not too long and tedious to read. Each rule should be short and not consist of more than around ten words. This will allow your guests to quickly move through the rules and not feel like there's too much information to take in. Stick to one sentence for each rule. For example, instead of saying, "we highly encourage that you do not smoke on our premises as this can lead to an unpleasant experience for the next guests who arrive," you can simply say, "no smoking allowed." It is short and simple, and it gets your message across with no miscommunication.

Tip #7: Use Bullet Points

Bullet points are your friends. Bullet points make things a lot easier to read. When everything is in one long paragraph, it can be difficult for your guests to move through it. Bullet points will allow your guests to skim through the rules at a quick pace, and it just seems a lot more inviting and easier to read. It also helps them see how many rules there are at your property.

Tip #8: Prioritize Your Rules in Order of Importance

When you are creating a list of rules for your guests, make sure that they are in order of importance. As your guests read through the list, it is pretty likely that they will get bored by the time they come to the end. This is why, if you have the most important ones at the beginning, you know that these are definitely going to be the ones that are followed and taken notice of.

Tip #9: Have Your Rules Online and at the Property

Make sure your guests can access your rules online and have a physical copy at your property. If the rules are online, your guests will know what is expected of them before they get to the property. They will also be able to ask you any questions they might have about the rules. Then you can create a physical reminder for them if you have this printed out and at the property. This way, it is easy for them to have a look at them when they need to.

Tip #10: Use an Appropriate Structure

When you are writing out your rules list, make sure that you have structured it in a way that is easy for them to read and understand. You can create a poster with all the rules on it so that it is easy to understand. Feel free to add visuals to the printed copies of your rules so that they are more eye-catching and not dull. The main point about these rules is that they are easy to understand for your guests.

Establishing house rules is an important part of not only building a solid relationship with your guests but also automating your Airbnb business, so you have fewer problems to deal with in the future. It is one of the most important things you can do when you are renting out your property. In the next chapter, we'll look at using your house rules to create your house manual.

13

HOW TO CREATE YOUR HOUSE MANUAL

A simple key to setting yourself apart from other Airbnb hosts and delivering a memorable experience for your guests is providing a comprehensive house manual that thoroughly details your home. House manuals should be easy to access for your guests and provide easy-to-use instructions for everything they need. You can guarantee that your guests will have a much better experience when they understand how to use everything available on the property.

WHAT IS A HOUSE MANUAL?

You might be thinking that you do not have to create a manual because you already have the house rules. However, the house manual is something a bit different. It is basically like a how-to guide for your home. There might be things in your home that need a bit more explanation in order for your guests to understand how to use them. It will allow your guests to have a reference guide if they encounter any problems during their stay.

The house rules are basically like the do's and don'ts of your home, but the house manual shows your guests how to use things properly. You can add things to your house manual, such as how to use certain appliances, where to find amenities, and how the guests can make the most of their stay with you. The content and purpose of house rules versus house manuals are completely different. Your house manual does not show up on your Airbnb listing page. Instead, you will leave a copy of your house manual in the home when your guest checks in, and you can send a copy to them once the reservation has been confirmed.

WHAT DOES A HOUSE MANUAL LOOK LIKE?

There are many different formats in which you can structure your house manual. It really doesn't have to be rocket science, and you can definitely show your personality through it. The first thing that you're going to need is a short welcome message. This is a personal welcome message that you will write in order to establish a connection with your guests. This is especially important if you are not meeting your guests at check-in. Remember not to go overboard with your welcome message. Short and sweet is typically best. Here is an example of a good welcome message:

Dear Guest,

Welcome to [insert house name here]. We are so excited to have you stay with us!

This home is incredibly special to us, and we have made so many memories in it. We hope that you will be able to create many amazing memories as well.

Over the past few years, we have really enjoyed renting it out to travelers such as yourself. This home is a great starting point to discover the city and its surroundings. There is so much to do and see, and I'm sure you will fall in love with the city just as we have.

In this manual, you will find tons of important information. This will help you to make the most of your stay. There are instructions on how to use appliances, recommendations for delicious food places, and much more.

We truly hope that you have a magical stay!

Sincerely,

[Insert your name]

As you can see, this welcome note is personal and welcoming. It seems very friendly and shows the guest that there is a person behind the rental property. It also isn't long or drawn out because most of the information is going to be in the manual anyway.

After the welcome message, you can include some property information as well as contact information. This will be your contact info, emergency contact details, and if you are using a property manager, then include their contact details as well. You can also include the Wi-Fi password and any other codes or passwords they would need in order to utilize things in your house. This can be just after the first page so that it's easy to find.

You can attach your house rules to your manual so that everything is in one place. Then you give a general walk-through of your property's essentials. This can be how to use the various appliances so your guests understand how to operate everything in a way that is safe. This will prevent your guests from breaking anything because they are confused or simply don't understand certain aspects of your home. Even if you think it is common sense, it is really best to have these instructions. If your guests are coming from other countries, it is likely that they would do things differently and might not have the same types of appliances as you.

Other important details that you should include are check-in and check-out times. This is just a reminder because they should already know the times beforehand. If you provide parking for your guests, then include some parking information and instructions. This will prevent them from parking in a spot that obstructs other vehicles and people who live in your area. Also, include some local transport information so your guests can easily get around town. This is especially important if they are not arriving in their own car.

A page with some information about the local area is always welcome. You are the expert on the city or area in which your guests are staying. You want to ensure that they are going to have a good time, so give them a few recommendations for amazing restaurants, sightseeing spots, or local treasures. There might be things you know that are not common knowledge, and you can share this with your guests so they have a good experience and stories to tell.

You should also include an emergency page. This page will have emergency contact details for the local services around you. The fire department, police station, and other emergency services are important. It is highly unlikely that your guests would need to use these emergency services, but it is a good idea to have this information. You can also include information as to where the fire extinguisher and first aid kits are. This should be the last page of your manual, as this will make it easier for your guests to find if they do need it.

Even though this might seem like a lot of information, it really isn't. When you are structuring your manual, you will see that the information doesn't fill more than a few pages. When we think of manuals, we can think of thick books, but this should not be the case. Your guests are not going to be reading through a hundred-page document when they are on vacation. Your manual should not be more than a few pages long and just cover the necessities.

A house manual is like a comprehensive guide for living in your home. Making a detailed house manual goes a long way to helping form a clear understanding of the expectations between guests and hosts. It also allows the guest to understand how to utilize the property correctly so they have the best stay possible. In the next chapter, we will be going through legal and compliance issues you may have to consider before starting your own Airbnb business.

LEGAL REGULATIONS TO CONSIDER

The average host in the US earns the highest in the world per year, at over $18,000 annually.[1] In most cities and states, it is going to be easy for the average US citizen to take part in Airbnb. However, it is important to understand the legal regulations so that you don't have to pay any penalties or fees later on. This helps you to be better prepared and understand what your government requires from you in order to start an Airbnb business.

COMMON LEGAL RESTRICTIONS RELATED TO AIRBNB

When you are an Airbnb host, it is really important that you understand the laws in your city, country, state, or territory. The platform doesn't actually provide any legal advice, so it is a good idea to get this advice directly from your government or municipality. However, there are some considerations that could help you to understand the laws and regulations in your jurisdiction.

Business Licenses

There are many jurisdictions that require business owners or operators to apply for a license. You will need to do this before you can start operating your business. You will be able to find up-to-date information on this on your local government website. Most government websites have sections explaining the business licensing process and provide you with all the forms and relevant information that you will need.

Building Codes

Most governments have certain rules and regulations that specify minimum construction, design, and maintenance standards for buildings. These can also include health, safety, and habitability regulations. There are also certain rules that will apply to residential and non-residential uses of a property. Furthermore, certain jurisdictions might require that you take part in an inspection to make sure that your property meets the minimum requirements and standards. Only then will you be able to utilize your property as an Airbnb. Not all jurisdictions or areas will have such strict rules, so it is important to know what applies to you by going on the government website or contacting your local government.

Zoning Rules

There could be many rules or laws that dictate how you use your home. These can be found in a zoning code, city ordinance, or planning code. You can consult these rules and regulations to find out if your listing is consistent with the current requirements or uses definitions.

Special Permits

You might be required to get a special permit in order to rent out your home. You'll need to contact your local government or municipality to see if this applies to you. You will also be able to get some information on how you can get this permit.

Tax Laws

Most states and jurisdictions will require an Airbnb host to collect tax for each stay. You will then need to pay this tax to the city or to the jurisdiction where it applies. There are certain jurisdictions where Airbnb will automatically collect and remit certain taxes on your behalf. You will need to find out if this applies to you so that you have the relevant tax information.

Landlord-Tenant Laws

If you are hosting longer stays, you might be subject to landlord-tenant laws. This varies by jurisdiction and may impose more strict legal obligations on you and provide your guests with additional legal rights. It is a good idea to consult a lawyer that specializes in landlord-tenant law in order to learn more and see what applies to you.

WHERE TO LOOK FOR APPLICABLE LAWS AND REGULATIONS

The laws and regulations can seem a bit confusing, but it is quite easy to get the information that you need in order to make the right decisions going forward. You can log on to the Airbnb help center and see what kind of regulations apply to your city. This might not provide all the information you need, but it can provide a guideline.

If you are in North America, then you will most likely be required to obtain permits and business licenses before you can operate your Airbnb. The exact requirements will vary depending on many different factors. You can start off by going onto your local government website to see what kind of permits or licenses you would need in order to start a short-term rental business. In most cases, you will find a comprehensive guide and the steps that you need to take in order to obtain the permits. You would likely be able to fill out all the forms you need online and then submit them. If you are confused, you can call your government offices and see if they can help you with any of your queries.

Once you have determined exactly what permits and documents you need in order to start your business, you need to make sure that your property is in compliance. Each location will have its own safety regulations for the tenants. If you need to make any renovations or improvements to your property, then do so. Also, obtain proper insurance to ensure your guests' and your safety. You will also need to make sure that you comply with any requirements your insurance company might have in order to insure you for certain things.

It is so important that you consult your local laws and rules to make sure that you are not violating any regulations when you start an Airbnb. It is better to seek clarification and ask as many questions as possible, rather than assume that everything is going to be fine in the end. You don't want to be struck down with heavy fines, end up being sued, or possibly end up being evicted just because of a technicality that could have been avoided. Rather, do all the necessary homework now so that you can avoid any unpleasant situations in the future. In the next chapter, we are going to be talking about keeping your property clean and well-maintained in order to get those 5-star reviews.

A CLEAN PROPERTY LEADS TO 5-STAR REVIEWS

Many negative reviews come from the fact that the property has not been cleaned properly or is unkempt and untidy. Your guests might stay at an amazing property with beautiful amenities, but if it is not clean, they are going to complain. Would you like to stay in a hotel or guest house that is not clean? We all have higher standards of cleanliness when we are paying for a vacation rental. This means that you have to put a lot of emphasis on making sure your property is clean and neat.

TURNING OVER YOUR PROPERTY

Cleaning your property between stays is called turning over the property. It is not just about doing a quick clean and then welcoming the next guest. When your guests check in, you want them to feel that they are in an absolutely pristine boutique hotel. When you are doing a turnover cleaning, it is going to require a bit more energy and work than a regular house cleaning. It is a good idea to clean up your property as soon as your guest leaves. This will allow you time to discover if there are any damages or problems so you can process a claim as soon as possible. If there are any damaged items or items that need to be replaced, you have time to do this before the next guest arrives.

Turning over your property requires consistency. You need to create a system for yourself so that each guest gets the exact same experience. This actually makes it a lot easier, and you'll find that you can turn over your property a lot quicker as time goes on. It's a good idea to use a checklist so that you understand what needs to be cleaned and you don't miss anything. Later on in this chapter, we are going to give you an example of a checklist that you can use and tweak depending on your property.

Many first-time hosts underestimate the amount of time they need to clean their property. Of course, the size of your property definitely comes into play when it comes to how long you will spend cleaning. When your guests check out, you will only have a specific amount of time in order to clean it and get it ready for the next guest. You should have at least a four- or five-hour cleaning window so that you can do things thoroughly and make sure that everything is up to standard.

You might have to consider hiring a cleaner if you are not going to be available to turn over the property or if the work is going to be too much for you to handle on your own. If you are going to hire a professional team, make sure that you have cleaned your own property before and know exactly what needs to be done. This allows you to set the standard so you can communicate effectively with your team about what they need to get done. You will then need to provide them with a checklist as well so that the standard remains consistent.

It is also important that you do a thorough inspection when you are turning over the property. A guest might have broken something, or there might have been some sort of malfunction. It is a good idea to test all the appliances and the plug points to make sure that everything is still working fine. Also, check through the glassware and other commonly used items to make sure that nothing is chipped or broken. It is a good idea to bring a few extras with you when you come to turn over your property. You will need to replace anything that is broken so that the next guest gets a good experience.

REMEMBER TO RESTOCK AND RESTAGE

The turnover time also needs to include restocking and restaging your property. As your guests use your property, things are going to be moved around and finished. You need to make sure that you have reverted the property back to default settings so that your next guests are able to enjoy it just the same. Using the checklist that was given to you in Chapter 11 is a great starting point. Make sure that you bring all the items that could be used up with you. Things like toilet paper, shampoo, conditioner, tissues, and pantry items, will all need to be replaced. If you have these with you, then it's going to make it a lot easier for you to simply replace them. You can take any extras back to your storage.

Restaging simply means moving all the furniture and other items back to how they were before your guests checked in. It is a good idea to take a few pictures of your ideal property setting. This way, you can use the picture as a reference when you are moving everything back. It'll make things a lot easier until you are used to restaging your property. When you are cleaning, it is going to be a good idea to move the furniture so you can get underneath, just in case your guests have dropped things or lost things under the furniture. Then you can move things back into the ideal position.

Have a look at your decor items and make sure that they are all clean and in the proper position. When guests stay at a property, they might move things like artwork, decor, and similar items. You can simply wipe them down and move them back to where they are supposed to be. Since you are restaging for the next guest, candles are a good idea to add some ambiance to your property. Check to see that all the candles are not completely burned down or finished. You can replace them as needed. If you have any other disposable decor items, then you can also replace these and make sure that they are in the right position.

Your guests are going to expect the property to look like the listing photos. This is why it is so important to make sure that you are resetting your property to how it was in those photos. If you have cleaners that are working for you, then make sure they have access to these photos so they have a reference to how the furniture and settings should look.

Your guests' welcome package is something that you're going to have to restock every time. You can actually create a few welcome packages and keep them with you. This way you can just replace the old ones each time you turn over the property. You can provide these to your cleaners and your property managers so they can do the same for you.

CREATE A CHECKLIST

A checklist is really helpful to make sure that you are providing each guest with the exact same service. Here is an example of a housekeeping and turnover checklist that you can use on your own Airbnb.

Kitchen:

- Wash and put away the dishes.
- Wipe and sanitize all surfaces.
- Wipe and disinfect sink and backsplash.
- Clean inside and outside of fridge, freezer, and oven.
- Wipe down all small appliances like coffee maker and microwave.
- Refill all kitchen cleaning supplies like dish soap and sponges.
- Clean windows and dust the windowsills.
- Mop the floor.
- Take out trash, clean the garbage can, and put a fresh trash bag in.
- Ensure all kitchen supplies are arranged nicely.

Bedrooms:

- Remove sheets, pillowcases, blankets, and mattress protectors. Make sure they are laundered properly.
- Wipe down all surfaces including ceiling fans and decor.
- Remove smudges from windows and mirrors.
- Disinfect high-touch items like remotes and light switches.
- Check for any personal belongings that have been left behind.
- Check for damage on furniture and bedding.
- Vacuum the floors.
- Empty trash cans.
- Restock with fresh linen.
- Remake the bed with a clean and fresh set of bedding.
- Arrange all decor and artwork correctly.

Bathrooms:

- Remove all dirty towels and bath mats; have them laundered correctly.
- Look in the drawers and cabinets for any personal items left behind.
- Wipe down mirrors and windows.
- Disinfect countertops, sinks, faucets, and backsplashes.
- Scrub down the bathtubs and showers.
- Clean and sanitize the toilets thoroughly.
- Dust all windowsills, fans, and vents.
- Sweep and mop the floors.
- Replace and refill all amenities such as hand soap and toilet paper.
- Check bathroom for signs of wear and tear and damage.
- Place clean towels and bathmats appropriately.
- Ensure all the bathroom items are arranged neatly.

Living Room:

- Wipe down all tables, shelving, and furniture.
- Dust appliances such as the TV and radio, as well as decor.
- Wipe down windows, doors, and windowsills.
- Dust lighting fixtures such as lamps and ceiling fans.
- Sanitize frequently touched items like light switches and remotes.
- Wipe down and refresh couches, throw pillows, and chairs.
- Launder any blankets and replace them with new ones.

- Sweep and mop or vacuum the floors and carpets.
- Ensure any additional items such as books, board games, decor, or art are arranged neatly.
- Arrange throw pillows and blankets neatly on the couch.

Dining Room:

- Wipe down tables and chairs; make sure there are no crumbs in any hard-to-reach places.
- Check underneath table to make sure there is nothing stuck underneath it.
- Wash tablecloths and runners.
- Clean centerpieces.
- Wipe down all decor and replace in appropriate areas.

Outdoor Areas:

- Remove any branches and dead leaves from the lawn.
- Ensure all the bushes are trimmed and neat.
- Remove any debris or weeds.
- Wipe down all outdoor furniture.
- Clean railings.
- Sweep the patio or deck.

Laundry:

- Check for clothes left behind in the washing machine or dryer.
- Clean out any washing detergent left in the washing machine compartment.
- Wipe down all surfaces.

It is so important that you take the time to turn over your property correctly. If you have a look through Airbnb reviews, you will see that one of the most common things that people complain about is cleanliness. You can easily get marked down two or three points just because your property is not clean. In chapter 16, we will be moving on to setting up your booking system.

Your Secret Superpower as an Airbnb Owner

If you have knowledge, let others light their candles in it.

— *MARGARET FULLER*

In Chapter 25, we're going to look at the power of good reviews – and how you can get them. Think back to the last time you booked travel accommodation for yourself. I'd hazard a guess that reviews are one of the first things you looked at. Although we'll delve into this in more detail later on, it's worth having in the back of your mind at all times that positive reviews are your secret superpower as an Airbnb owner… which is why I'm planting this seed in your mind now.

Your property is a place people want to feel safe and comfortable while they're away from home, so it's clear that reviews are going to be very important for you. They let other travelers know exactly what they're getting for their money, what their experience will be like, and ultimately, whether they're making the right choice for them. Positive reviews give customers faith in your property and influence their decision to book.

I want to help other business owners like you because I truly believe Airbnb can be a lucrative and fulfilling business for anyone – and reviews are just as important for authors as they are for business owners. So, as you might have guessed by now, I'd like to ask for your help.

Simply by leaving your honest review of this book on Amazon, you can help the Airbnb business remain the goldmine it is today.

Just as reviews tell guests which property is right for them, they tell readers which books will provide them with the information they need. As a result, more business owners like you will see success… and *that's* how Airbnb will remain the lucrative business it is today, serving you and your fellow hosts well into the future.

Scan the QR code to leave a review

Thank you for taking the time to help me here – and I hope it illustrates just how important those reviews are going to be for you. Keep reading to find out more!

STAGE 4

SETTING UP AND MANAGING BOOKINGS

BOOKING POLICIES TO CONSIDER

Before you can even think about creating your listing on Airbnb, it is important to give some thought to the policies you want to enforce for guests staying on the property. Thinking about these things before actually publishing your listing helps you to be prepared, and eliminates any unnecessary issues down the line. Prevention of problems is always better when it comes to dealing with other people. This will be a lot less stressful for you and your guests. It will also help your guests to understand exactly what is expected from them.

COMMON BOOKING POLICIES THAT GUESTS ASK ABOUT

When you're running a short-term rental property, there are a few booking policies that guests are going to be concerned about. The Airbnb platform allows space for you to communicate what your booking policies are like so that it is clear and your guests understand it from the get-go.

Cancellation Policy

The first kind of policy that we are going to be talking about is the cancellation policy. It is also arguably one of the most important policies that you should think about. The Airbnb platform gives you a few options to choose from, and this is all going to be based on your preferences and what you deem as the best fit for you. These are the most commonly used policies.

Flexible Cancellation

The flexible cancellation policy allows your guests to cancel their booking and get a full refund up until 24 hours prior to check-in. In that case, you won't get paid. If they cancel after that, you will be paid for every night they stay plus one additional night.

Many guests like the flexible cancellation policy because it allows them to get a full refund. With this being said, it might not benefit you as it is difficult to find somebody who wants to book in their place within a day. When the cancellation can be done so close to the actual check-in time, it might result in you losing money. This is definitely something to think about when you are renting out your Airbnb.

Moderate Cancellation

A moderate cancellation policy allows the guest to cancel the booking and get a full refund up to 5 days before check-in. If the guest cancels after this, you will be paid for every night they do stay plus an additional night. You will also get 50 percent for all unspent nights. Using this kind of cancellation policy allows you to have a bit more security and it holds the guest a bit more accountable. They will not be able to cancel and get a full refund unless they cancel at least 5 days in advance. This might give you some extra time to find someone else to book in their place and still make money.

Strict Cancellation

A strict cancellation policy will allow your guests to receive a full refund if they cancel within the first 48 hours after they have made the booking. This needs to be at least 14 days prior to check-in. If the guest cancels between 7 and 14 days before check-in they will receive a 50 percent refund on the nightly rate, but will not be refunded for the service fee. If they cancel within 7 days of arrival, there is no refund. A strict cancellation policy means that if a guest books with you, they need to be sure that they can stick to the commitment. The issue with this type of policy is that it can put a lot of guests off. They might not want to book too far in advance just in case they have to cancel, and this means they would be looking for another property that would be a bit more flexible.

If you are new to running your own Airbnb, then it might not be a good idea to have this kind of cancellation policy. Since you have not yet built up your reputation and probably don't have that many reviews, there is no guarantee for your guests that your property is going to be worth it. As you build up your reputation and more people start to know you and your property, it would be a better time to implement this kind of cancellation policy. Properties that are very popular and have back-to-back bookings tend to do better with this kind of cancellation policy because people will do their best to ensure that they get a spot and keep the commitment to this day.

Flexible Long-Term Cancellation

If you are going to rent out your property on a long-term basis, 28 days or longer, it overrides the standard cancellation policy. The guest would need to cancel 30 days prior to check-in in order to receive a full refund. If they cancel after this time has elapsed, you will receive full payment for the nights they stay and for an additional 30 nights. If fewer than 30 days remain on the initial reservation, you will be paid for all remaining nights. This is done to protect you, as a host, since you will find it very difficult to find a new guest for a long-term stay in a short period of time.

Super Strict Cancellation

The super strict policy is not available to every host. Only experienced hosts who Airbnb has invited can select this option. There are also two options: super strict for 30 days and super strict for 60 days. The 30-day option means that if a guest cancels at least 30 days before check-in they will receive 50 percent of the total nightly rate. The service fee is non-refundable. If you choose the 60-day option, the guest would need to cancel 60 days before check-in to receive a 50 percent refund on the total nightly rate. The service fee for this option is also not refundable.

Non-refundable Option

If you are concerned about guests canceling their booking, you can set up a non-refundable policy. To do this, you would need to offer a discount of 10% off your base rate. Guests can then choose under which policy they book with you. If they choose the discounted rate, the booking will be non-refundable, and in case of a cancellation, you will get paid for all nights booked. The reservation will be subject to your cancellation policy if they choose the standard rate.

Cleaning Fees

There is an option to add a cleaning fee on top of your regular nightly rate. This helps with expenses that will go toward the maintenance and upkeep of the property. Guests will see the total that will include the cleaning fee as they browse through the site. When they get the bill, the fees will be listed separately, so your guests will know exactly what they are paying for. Bear in mind that if the cleaning fee brings up the total nightly stay price significantly, this might deter a few guests from wanting to stay with you.

Security Deposit

Airbnb will not charge a security deposit. Instead, Airbnb will inform every guest at the time of booking that they may be charged if they cause any damage throughout their stay, although there is one exception. You can still charge guests a security deposit if you manage your listing with API-connected software. It is completely up to you whether or not you want to charge a security deposit, but if you are worried that your guests may damage or break something, it is a good idea. It helps keep the guests accountable for your property because they know that they will not get their money back if they damage something.

Over and above your house rules, there are other booking policies you'll need to consider and decide on prior to publishing your listing. Thinking about these policies is really important because it helps protect you and your property. It also allows the guest to understand exactly what is expected of them so that there are no miscommunications and misunderstandings. The policies have been put in place to help the hosts keep themselves and their properties safe and in good condition. In the next chapter, we will go over effective pricing strategies for your Airbnb listing.

THE PRICE IS RIGHT—STRATEGIES FOR MAXIMIZING PROFITS AND INCOME

The average price per night for an Airbnb around the globe in 2021 was $137. In the US, the average was $208 per night.[1] This is due to multiple factors, but as you can see, the US Airbnb market brings in quite a bit more money. You need to understand how to price your property well to bring in the most amount of money. Your pricing strategy really does matter because this will either help you to maximize your profits or end up not working for you at all.

HOW TO FIGURE OUT YOUR AIRBNB PRICING STRATEGY

Airbnb hosts are always trying to figure out how much their place is worth. I'm sure you want to be able to make the most amount of money from your Airbnb rental. In order to do this, you need to understand how much people are willing to pay for your property. You do not want to underprice your property. Even though you might get a lot of bookings, you will be losing out on money. You also don't want to overprice your property, because then people will be turned off from booking with you.

It is a good idea to have a look at your competition to see what they are charging. This way, you can get a good idea of what people are willing to pay in a similar area and for a similar property with the same types of amenities. When you are researching your competition, it is a good idea to put together at least six similar listings and take note of different types of information. You will want to record rates for the weekdays in the low season, the high season, weekends in the low season, and weekends in the high season. All of these will have different prices because of what people will be willing to pay for each. This is why it is important to not just "set it and forget it" when it comes to your pricing. A dynamic pricing strategy will allow you to attract more guests and maximize your profit.

You also want to check out the pricing on peak dates. School holidays and public holidays such as Christmas, New Year, and Easter will be priced higher because there will be more demand. Special events like local sporting events, concerts, and conferences will also attract more people to your area and this means the pricing will go up. If you live in an area that has seasonal work like harvesting, prices tend to go up as well. Basically, anything that's going to draw people to your area who will need accommodation is going to drive up the general market price of an Airbnb stay. This means that you will be able to charge a bit more for your nightly rates since the demand is going to be higher.

EFFECTIVE AIRBNB PRICING STRATEGIES

There are multiple Airbnb pricing strategies out there. You will need to pick the one that's going to work best for you and ensure that you make the most money from your pricing strategy. Maximizing your profit means that you have more money left over to enjoy, and you will also have more money to invest back into your Airbnb if you choose to do so.

Maximum Fill Rate Strategy

The first strategy is called the maximum fill rate strategy. In order to implement this strategy, you will need to follow along with your competitors' pricing. You need to attempt to offer the best experience in your city or area. The main goal is to ensure that you have the maximum occupancy rate that you can have. This means that you will need to offer even more value than your competitors in your region. You will then set your nightly rate slightly lower than average to continuously attract guests. Even though your nightly rate is going to be lower than average, your income will be pretty stable since people would rather choose your property over another property that is similar but charges more.

Maximum Rate per Night Strategy

For this strategy, you will be setting a higher rate for your nightly charges. This will allow you to increase your net profit from each individual booking. You should expect that the number of bookings will be fewer because not everybody will want to book at this higher rate. However, your income will be sufficient because you will be getting a maximum profit from the least amount of effort possible. Your occupancy rate will be lower than average but you can look at this as an advantage because you're dealing with fewer guests and will have to spend less time and money turning over the property. It is important not to go overboard with this kind of strategy, as it could lead to nobody wanting to book with you. You also have to ensure that you are in an area where people want to book. If you are in a remote area and people are not interested in booking in that area or there is not a lot of demand, this strategy is going to be very difficult to implement.

Long-Term Rental Strategy

Another strategy that you could implement is the long-term rental strategy. In order to do this, you will be setting your pricing according to long-term rentals, which means monthly rates instead of nightly rates. You will likely need to provide a rental agreement and conduct a house tour before confirming the booking. It is a lot more work beforehand because you have to do additional paperwork as well as promote your listing a bit more than just on Airbnb. However, once you have found somebody who is going to stay at your property for a longer period of time, you can be completely hands-off for the most part. You will not have to turn over your house until the rental period has elapsed. So it ends up being a lot less work for you in that sense.

You will also have a much more stable income because you will be paid per month rather than nightly. You will have to take into consideration that you will have to bring down the monthly rate so that it is manageable for people to pay. While people might be happy to pay $200 per night if they are staying for a long weekend, they are definitely not going to be happy to pay $6,000 for a 30-day stay.

Balanced Airbnb Pricing Strategy

This type of pricing strategy is an integrated strategy. You will combine all three pricing strategies that we have already mentioned in order to efficiently manage your Airbnb business. This is more of a dynamic approach, so you will not just be leaving your price stagnant. You will continuously be changing your pricing strategy according to the demand and the season you are in. For example, in seasons where the demand is not high, you can choose to employ a long-term rental strategy so that you reduce the risk of leaving your property vacant. Then, during seasons where the demand increases, you can use the maximum fill rate or maximum nightly charge strategy to ensure that you get a maximum profit.

The Flexible Strategy

A flexible strategy is one way you will determine how much you will be charging for different seasons and different dates. This is also called a "dynamic pricing strategy" because it's always changing. One option that is available on Airbnb is the smart pricing tool. This sets your rates based on the current market. Many people like to use this tool, and there is definitely some appeal because it means that it is less work for you. However, it can end up losing you money since it is an algorithm that sets the price and not you. If you understand the market that you are in, it is going to be better and more profitable for you to focus on your own pricing strategy.

The flexible strategy that I am going to mention now is one that I have implemented in my own Airbnb business and had amazing results from it. The highest-yielding exercise is going to be to fill up your weekdays. This can be tricky, especially in the low seasons. In order to do this, you are going to need to drop your prices from Sunday through Thursday, if they are not already booked. You will need to drop your prices in order to get bookings at the start of this pricing strategy. I know it can be hard to drop your pricing because you've put a lot of work into your Airbnb and want to get paid fairly for it. However, being tied to the nightly rate as the overall value of your property is a mentality that will not allow you to increase your income. Your goal should be the bigger picture and you should look at ways to make more money annually rather than just focusing on how much you'll be making each night.

Let's look at an example to show you how you can utilize this kind of strategy to earn a lot more money over a 4-week period than just focusing on a nightly rate. Let's say your rate is set at $350 per night. This would be on your weekends, so Friday and Saturday, and you booked out all 4 weekend dates, so 8 nights. Let's also say you booked 8 nights on the weekdays at a rate of $250 per night. Let's calculate your earnings:

	Nights Booked	Average Nightly Rate	Total Earnings
Weekdays (Sun to Thu)	8	$250	$2,000
Weekends (Fri to Sat)	8	$350	$2,800
Total	16		$4,800

Now that you have your earnings for the month, you can calculate how many nights you're not booked. This will help you to see that the rates that you had were not successful for those days. In this example, you would've missed out on 12 weekday nights and no weekend nights. So your missed earnings would be calculated as follows:

	Nights Not Booked	Average Nightly Rate	Total Missed Earnings
Weekdays (Sun to Thu)	12	$250	$3,000
Weekends (Fri to Sat)	0	$350	$0
Total	12		$3,000

Now that you have this information, you need to calculate how many nights you could have booked and what rate would have worked. Now, it is not realistic to believe that you can get 100 percent occupancy throughout the year. Let's estimate it instead at about 80 percent occupancy. You would then need to discount 80 percent of the nights that were not booked. We can discount these nights up by 50 percent so that you can get 80 percent of them booked out. 80 percent would be ten nights.

	Nights Not Booked at 80% Capacity	Average Nightly Rate at 50% Discount	Total Earnings
Weekdays (Sun to Thu)	10	$125	$1,250
Weekends (Fri to Sat)	0	$350	$0
Total	10		$1,250

By reducing the rates, you were able to increase the number of bookings and get 80 percent of your available dates booked. This means that instead of not getting any income on those days, you have now made an additional $1,250 in the month. Most people do not want to do this because they would lose out on the full rates on the discounted night. This is actually completely true. This is why you should not discount your rates if the dates are far out. You should only discount your rate as the dates start creeping closer and they're still not booked out. When dates are far away, you can keep your rates higher so that you can make the most amount of money from fewer dates. As you get closer to the dates and you see that your desired occupancy is not being reached, this is when you start thinking about discounting your rates. Your discounted rate will start getting booked up a lot quicker so that you can make that additional money. It is much better to have your property occupied at a discounted rate rather than not have it occupied at all.

Another benefit to discounting your Airbnb is that you are getting more guests into your property. If a guest really enjoys staying at your property, they are likely to want to come back. They might not mind paying an increased amount of money for a weekend stay. They might also recommend your property to their friends and family, and this will improve your reputation as well as the number of people that are staying with you. As you can see, running an Airbnb is about a lot more than simply setting a nightly rate. You have to be willing to change up your strategies and look into the long term as well.

ONLINE TOOLS

There are so many helpful online tools available to you that make things a lot easier. If you utilize these tools, you will find that creating pricing strategies becomes a lot easier. You'll have access to a lot more information than if you just rely on your own physical research. You might find it helpful to try out a few tools to see which one works best for you. Here's a list of some to do some additional research on:

- Wheelhouse
- Beyond Pricing
- PriceLabs
- Host Tools

Finding the right pricing strategy for your Airbnb can be really tricky. Picking the right one depends on multiple factors that are constantly changing. Making use of software tools can really help you to adjust and optimize your price to maximize your earnings. You also should think about adopting a dynamic pricing strategy rather than just setting one price and leaving it there. Doing this will allow you to increase the amount of income you make per month. In the next chapter, we will take a closer look at how you can deliver a smooth and effortless booking experience for your guests.

STREAMLINING THE BOOKING PROCESS—HOW TO FIND GREAT GUESTS

Over 500 million guests stay in Airbnbs every year. In order to capitalize on the number of people that are willing to stay at Airbnbs you need to be able to streamline your booking process and find the right guests. There are certain tweaks that you can make in order to optimize your online booking experience for your guests. This will help you to avoid any horror stories happening to you.

WHAT IS INSTANT BOOK?

There is a feature on Airbnb called Instant Book. You can choose to select it or not, depending on what you prefer. If you choose to use it, then it will remove the approval process for you. Typically, a guest will request to book with you, and this will then be sent to you for approval. You can do some research on the guest and find out whether you want to approve this booking or not. Once you have approved it, the booking process will continue and payment can be made. This process can take a bit longer for the guest because you might want to find out more about them, their dates, and other situations. If you turn on Instant Book, the customer is completely in control. This will apply to all available nights in your calendar and they will be able to book as long as they have met the requirements that you've already ticked off.

Selecting the Instant Book option really does make your life easier because it is one less thing that you have to do. It also makes the guests' lives a lot easier because they can make bookings quickly. If they have a delayed flight or an emergency trip somewhere, they can simply book for the next day and know that their booking will be quickly confirmed. Guests who like this will use the filter on Airbnb so they can find Instant Book properties. You also increase your chance of getting the Superhost status because, in order to get this badge, you will need a 90 percent response rate. Your chances of achieving this are much higher with the Instant Book option.

On the downside, it removes the barrier between you and your guest. This means that you are giving up some control and don't really know who is walking through the front door. If you are not too concerned about this, then Instant Book could be a really great feature for you. If you are a new listing, then Instant Book can really help you. Your goal as a new Airbnb owner is to get as many people to book with you as possible. If you remove as many barriers as possible, then your chances of people booking with you increase. You will also show up on the Instant Book filter so that you have more guests interested in your property. With this being said, when you have the Instant Book option set up, you will need to be prepared for anything. Somebody could book today and arrive tomorrow, or even book to arrive at your property five hours from now. This option typically works better if you live close to your property or have property managers who are there to handle your Airbnb. You will also need to ensure that your property is always ready to receive guests because you simply do not know when they are going to walk through the door.

HOW TO SCREEN GUESTS WHEN THEY INSTANT BOOK

It is still a good idea to do some sort of screening even when your Instant Book option is on. The good news is that you can set conditions under which guests can book with you. For example, you can choose to only accept guests who have provided a government ID or who have been recommended by other hosts on the platform. This means that the guests have been pre-screened, and there is more information about them available. People who have ID verification on their accounts are a lot more reliable than those who do not. It also shows that they have used the platform a few times, so they are aware of the process and the etiquette that is involved with Airbnb.

It is also a good idea to have a look at the guests who have booked, even if the Instant Book function is on. You can still look through their social media and Airbnb profile to ensure that they are reliable. This will help you to have peace of mind and be prepared for whoever comes walking through your door.

STORY TIME

When you are an Airbnb host, you can't have full control over your guests and what they will be like. Even if you do extremely strict reviews, you might still end up with a bad one. On the other end of the spectrum, there are so many stories of people who have accepted guests that have no reviews on their profiles and they have been amazing. Sometimes it is just the luck of the draw and it is the risk that you take when you are running an Airbnb.

A few years ago, I decided to turn on my Instant Book function. This was just on a trial basis to see if my bookings increased. I noticed that for one of my listings I would receive last-minute bookings every now and then. The guests wanted to arrive within a few hours of booking. Once I saw this, I figured out that I may be missing out on many more of these bookings if people only search for listings that have Instant Book activated. This led me to turn on Instant Book, and I never looked back.

My last-minute bookings increased for this listing by a huge margin. I also decided to stop lowering my rates at the last minute in order to attract more people. This was because I knew that, come 5 p.m., someone would make a reservation to arrive very shortly after. In fact, I decided to increase my rate and just focus on the last-minute traveler demographic—I tried the strategy with another one of my properties, but I didn't see any positive results. For that property, I decided to leave the Instant Book function off. I learned that Instant Book doesn't work for all properties. However, if you are in a location where lots of travelers are booking at the last minute, give it a trial run. For my Instant Book property, I had around 25 percent of people who didn't have any reviews. This was either because they were new to Airbnb or they were not regular users. Personally, I cannot recall a single instance where a guest who didn't have any reviews caused me any trouble. With this being said, I know of friends who are renting on Airbnb and have had very different experiences.

All the positive experiences I had with my guests prompted me to write some glowing reviews for them. Here are a few examples of the reviews I left:

Stacy and her friends came to stay over at my property for the weekend. They left it in great shape and even did a good cleanup of the place. It was an amazing experience hosting them, and I would definitely recommend them to other hosts.

Walter was an amazing guest. He communicated effectively throughout the process. I was incredibly happy to host him and his fiancée. Both of them treated the place with the utmost respect, and it would honestly be a pleasure to host them again.

The names of the guests have been changed here, but I think you get the point. These are just a few of the examples of great reviews that I left for Instant Book guests. This just goes to show you that it is definitely possible to have an amazing guest experience even if you do not get to approve them before they book with you.

With all of that said, it is important that you have a balanced view of what can happen with Airbnb. I'm going to share the stories, not to scare you, but to make you aware. You might even have a few laughs along the way. The truth is that becoming an Airbnb host is truly a journey and an experience like no other. You really don't know what kind of people you are going to meet, and even in the moment, if you have to deal with a horrible guest, it could always turn into a funny story that you can tell later on. This is not to make light of any of the bad experiences that people have gone through, but to simply reframe them in a way that is not completely negative. When you start off with any kind of business, you need to expect that there will be a risk of something bad happening. Have a look at these two stories and hopefully find some humor in them.

Justin was fairly new to running his own Airbnb, so he was quite open to allowing any kind of guest to book with him. There was a guest who wanted to pay cash rather than use the website system. In hindsight, this should definitely have been a red flag, but Justin just wanted to make some extra money. He did a quick Google search of the guest's name and discovered that this person was actually a high-profile escort. It was too late to cancel the booking because the guest had booked with the Instant Book function for that evening. All Justin could do was wait it out and see what the property looked like the next day. Once he arrived at his property, he was met with empty wine bottles all over the floor, condom wrappers in the bin, and a whole host of other gross things. Let's just say that Justin was a lot more careful about who he let into his property from that day on. He also got the entire place deep-cleaned. Good choice, Justin!

Cory Tschogl simply wanted to rent out her property in Palm Springs, and two brothers decided to rent it for six weeks. Everything seemed normal, and the booking process went quite smoothly. However, a big surprise took place when it was time for them to check out. These two brothers simply refused to move out of the property. They decided to cite California's tenant rights, which makes it a lot more difficult to evict them after 30 days (remember we spoke about this in an earlier chapter?). There was a lot of publicity on the story, and with the help of a couple of lawyers, they left after two months and didn't leave any damage. However, Airbnb did offer to pick up the legal fees, which was pretty decent of them, I must say.

Finding great guests for your Airbnb starts with doing some specific research on who you want to attract to your property. I've already gone over how important it is to choose a target audience and target market so that you can construct your Airbnb experience around that type of guest. This is also going to help you with the booking process. The people who would be interested in your property would most likely be those who fit into your target market. It'll make it a lot easier for you to understand who is going to be booking with you and allow you to be a bit more trusting to use the Instant Book option. You should also ensure that you are investing some time into screening your potential guests so that you can filter out any problematic people. Even if you are screening your guests to the tee, you might still get a few unpleasant ones. It is best to mentally prepare for this so that you understand how to handle them if the situations do occur. If you follow a good process from the start, then you will lessen the likelihood of any of these negative experiences actually happening to you. This is why every step of the process is so important. In the next chapter, we are going to look at how you can use a channel manager to help manage bookings.

RENTAL CHANNEL MANAGERS

While Airbnb may be one of the more popular online vacation rental sites, there are at least a dozen other sites where Airbnb business owners can list their properties and gain more exposure. It actually makes a lot of sense to use multiple platforms in order to broaden your potential customer base. This will result in you getting more bookings for your property.

WHAT IS A CHANNEL MANAGER?

While advertising a property across multiple different platforms might sound like an amazing idea, it is not as simple as that. When you list properties on different sites, you have to be able to manage this property. The risk of double-booking is definitely high since the platforms are not all connected. This is where the channel managers come in. A channel manager is basically a software platform that makes it incredibly easy for a host to manage rental listings across a number of different platforms. They will be able to do this from one interface, so it makes life a lot easier for the host.

Not every host is going to benefit from using a channel manager. One thing you have to take into account is that this is a paid service. So you need to make sure that it's going to be beneficial to you before you sign up for one. The type of host that would benefit from a channel manager would be somebody who is managing their listings across various different platforms. It definitely does help to increase your exposure and minimize the risk of double-booking when you are doing this. It also allows you to communicate with your guests in an easy way, as you don't have to keep switching between multiple platforms. On the other hand, if you are a host who is perfectly happy with just using the Airbnb platform, there's no need to get a channel manager.

WHAT TO LOOK FOR IN CHANNEL MANAGER SOFTWARE

Not all channel managers are created equal. There are definitely some scams out there, so you need to make sure that when you invest in good channel manager software, that it is legit. The first thing you need to do is make sure that it is from a legitimate company. You can find this out by doing a Google search and seeing what people are saying about the software. The more people that are talking about it, the more likely you can trust the company. Have a look at the company's website and ensure that it looks reputable. You should also have a look to see if they are official Airbnb partners. You can do this by going onto the Airbnb website and checking out the software partners. If the system that you were looking into is not on the list, then there's a good chance that the technology is weak and it's probably not going to be of great benefit to you.

You can also visit a software evaluation website like Capterra to find reviews from past and current customers. This is a really good way to find out what people like and don't like about certain software. This will help you to make a more informed decision. If the channel manager software that you are looking into comes from a company that is integrated with a bigger booking website such as Airbnb, Booking.com, TripAdvisor, or Vrbo, then you know it's a good option.

Top Channel Manager Software Options

There are many different channel manager software packages out there. It is definitely worth it to do your research to find out which one is going to be best for you. To get you started, here is a list of the top channel manager software options:

- Avantio
- Hospitable
- Hostaway
- Hosthub
- iGMS
- Lodgify
- OwnerRez
- Rentals United
- SiteMinder
- Uplisting
- Zeevou

One way to help you scale up your Airbnb business or maximize occupancy for a listing is to use a channel manager. This can help you to get your listing on many other rental platforms that are similar to Airbnb. Getting more exposure is always a good thing because it means an increase in revenue. You will also get your name out there on multiple different platforms so people will recognize you and your property. In the next chapter, we will start looking at what goes into high-performing listings. This way, you can start to replicate that in your own business.

STAGE 5

GETTING NOTICED

HOW TO CREATE YOUR
FIRST AIRBNB LISTING

Nobody counts the number of ads you run; they just remember the impression you make.

— BILL BERNBACH

HOW TO LIST ON AIRBNB

Understanding how to list your Airbnb property on the website is really important. The good news is that it is pretty easy to do so. The platform basically guides you through the whole process as you progress. This means that it is incredibly user-friendly and you are not likely to mess up or miss any important information.

The first step is going to be to create your account. Once this is done, you can start to add your listing. You will select the "add a listing" option that's on the top right corner of the homepage. From here, you will be directed to a form that you will need to fill in with the general criteria of your property including:

- **Home type**: This is basically whether your property is an entire place, a private room, or a shared room. We have already discussed this in detail, so you should know the type of property that you have.
- **Number of guests**: This is the maximum number of people that can be accommodated by your listing.
- **City**: This one is pretty self-explanatory. Once you select your city, Airbnb will give you an estimate of what you can expect to earn per month based on the information you have already provided.

Once you have filled in all of this, you can click over to the next part of the process. On this page, you need to provide some specific details about your listing and property. You will be given a selection of descriptions to choose from, and you will choose the most accurate type.

Then you'll have to further specify the description from a drop-down menu. As you move along in this process, you will be guided to add more information about your listing, including things like the address, amenities, number of beds, and number of bathrooms. This is quite a lengthy list of things that you are going to need to check off, but make sure that you are choosing the right options. You will be able to edit it once you are finished, so you don't have to stress about it being final.

You will also need to include high-quality photos, a description, and an amazing title. We are going to get more in-depth into these things in the later chapters, so for now, just know that these are things that are required of you. Make sure that you are filling out your profile completely so that your guests have as much information available to them as possible. This makes you seem a lot more trustworthy and you'll definitely get a lot more bookings and interested guests for your property.

OTHER SHORT-TERM RENTAL PLATFORMS

As I mentioned before, there are plenty of other short-term rental platforms that you can use. You can definitely do some in-depth research on these different platforms to see what they offer and if you would like to list your property on them. I'm going to give you a quick overview of the best ones so that you can understand them better.

Vrbo

This stands for vacation rental by owner. It only offers apartments and private homes, so if you have other types of properties, you would not be able to use this platform. If you list your property here, then you will also be listed on Expedia since there was an acquisition that brought them all under the same umbrella company.

Vrbo works on a 5 percent booking fee plus a 3 percent credit card processing fee. The policies that deal with cancellation and payment will vary depending on the property. One thing to note is that a host is unable to delete any reviews, whether they are negative or positive.

Booking.com

Booking.com is definitely a guest-friendly and easy-to-navigate platform. There's also an instant book option, just as there is on Airbnb. Since guests enjoy using the platform, it is quite a good option for you to increase your occupancy rate. There are more flexible cancellation options, which also encourages its use. Additionally, there are no booking fees for users. One thing to note is that there is a 15 percent host fee on all completed bookings for most hosts. The fee can vary slightly depending on location, so it is best to check this out for yourself. This will be charged upon the guest's arrival, so if there is a cancellation or if the guest does not show up, then the fee will not be charged.

Expedia

This is typically not the first vacation rental platform that comes to a guest's mind. This platform seems to be overlooked by hosts, but this can actually be an advantage because you can get ahead of the competition. When you list your property on this platform, it will also appear on a few other travel sites. You will be paying a 15 percent fee on each booking. Last-minute bookings are also available on the site, and things like flights and car rentals are all in one place, which makes it very convenient for guests who are looking for the best deals.

TripAdvisor

One of the most prominent features of this platform is the ability to provide feedback from the travel community. Guests love using this platform to search for places to stay. Since it was founded in 2000, a huge number of reviews have been collected. This means that most travelers will trust it. All property listings will be translated across 26 languages and appear on all 26 TripAdvisor sites. This definitely helps expand your reach so you can attract more travelers from international locations.

The host fee per booking on this platform is 3 percent. This is on the total rent, which includes any optional fees or required fees that have been specified for the property. The guest can also book car rentals and flights through the platform, which makes it very user-friendly and a favorite amongst tourists from all over the world.

Creating a listing on Airbnb is an incredibly straightforward process. It doesn't take too much work and it's really difficult to mess it up. The platform makes sure that the process is easy to follow and the prompts allow the user to be guided through the process step-by-step. There are definitely similar processes that are involved with other short-term rental platforms. Some are better than others, so it is a good idea to do trials with these platforms so you can get a better feel for them. In the next chapter, we are going to be looking at what you should optimize in your listing to get the best chance of attracting guests on Airbnb.

HOW TO OPTIMIZE YOUR LISTING TO MAXIMIZE BOOKINGS AND INCOME

You cannot get anybody to do something if they're not paying attention to you.

— BRIAN CARTER

HOW TO RANK ON THE FIRST PAGE SEO

Airbnb SEO will determine your position among other listings with the same search results. You want to be able to get to the top of the page so more people will recognize you and book with you. Think of it like Google. When you search for something on Google, you are far more likely to click on the websites that are listed on the first and second pages. Anything after that usually calls for a new search to be typed in the search bar so you can find something that you truly are looking for. The same thing happens with the Airbnb platform. If you are ranked at the top, you will definitely get more bookings because more people will see you. The good news is that there are plenty of things that you can do to improve your SEO ranking.

Getting Back to Guests Quickly

The first thing that the platform is going to take into account is how quickly you respond to your guests. There are a few metrics that are used to measure your response to potential guests. Your response rate is the percentage of inquiries that you have responded to within a 24-hour period. Your response time indicates the average amount of time that it takes you to respond to each new message. These metrics will be based on data from the previous 30 days.

One thing you can do to help yourself out is to have a few common responses typed out. Most guests will ask very similar questions so this is a really good tip to help you feel less overwhelmed and so that you can spend less time typing. All you need to do is paste the relevant answer or guidance and send.

Avoid Cancellations

In order to be in the algorithm's good books, you need to avoid any kind of cancellations. You can do this by ensuring that your calendar is updated so you can reduce the chances of having to cancel on someone. Rejections also play into this, so you need to be sure that you are only rejecting people if absolutely necessary. The platform will compare you to other hosts, so you just need to make sure that you are not rejecting more guests than other hosts.

Enable Instant Booking

By now, you already know all the benefits and technicalities that come with Instant Book. At the end of the day, using the Instant Book option means that the Airbnb platform will push your listing to the top.

Leverage Your Top Reviews

Getting good reviews: It's so important to rank high on the Airbnb SEO. It will look at how many guests you've hosted and then how many have left ratings. You want to be able to get the best reviews possible but the good news is that a few bad reviews won't really affect your ranking if you have a lot of good ones. After your guests have stayed with you, why not email them and ask them for any feedback to improve your service. If they come back with positive reviews then you can also review them on the platform in a positive light. If they have given you negative feedback and are not happy with the stay then do not review them.

Optimize Photos

Taking good photos is really important to improving your Airbnb SEO. We are going to talk more about this subject in a later chapter, so hold on tight.

Choose a Great Title

The importance of your title cannot be underestimated. This is what's going to grab your guests' attention, so it needs to be good. There is a whole chapter dedicated to this because it is so important.

Write an Excellent Description

Your description is such an important part of your Airbnb listing. It is what allows your guests to understand what you offer and if you use the right type of words then the Airbnb SEO will push you to the top. We also have an entire chapter dedicated to this since it is such an important topic to cover.

Use Social Media

You can help get more interaction with your Airbnb profile if you post on your other social media platforms. Not only that, but Airbnb will notice this and boost your rankings immediately. Any kind of external link is very useful to help you climb in the search results.

Update Your Airbnb Profile

If your host profile is updated and complete, then you are more likely to rank well with Airbnb SEO. The host looks more trustworthy when the profile is up to date and all the information is filled out.

Showing up at the top of the Airbnb search results is a matter of fine-tuning your listing and getting every detail right. You will not regret doing this because there are so many benefits to ranking high with the Airbnb SEO. You'll be able to get more visibility and therefore get more bookings. In the next chapter, we will go into more detail about how to get attractive photos for your property.

HOW TO CAPTURE ATTRACTIVE PHOTOS OF YOUR PROPERTY

In one study, better quality photos lead to a 17.5 percent increase in bookings. This simple statistic shows how important taking good quality photos is. At the end of the day, most guests will not be able to take a tour of your property before they book with you. The photos are the only things that they will be able to use as a reference for what they will be paying for.

GETTING A PROFESSIONAL VS. SHOOTING YOUR OWN PHOTOS

One thing you should consider is getting a professional to take some quality photos of your property. This is an expense that you will have to consider, but you should think of it more as an investment. When you have professional photos taken, it will make you stand out from the crowd. Your property will look so much better than the other properties that are listed. You will look a lot more professional and like you truly care about putting your best foot forward. This says a lot about you and it builds trust with your potential guests.

You have about eight seconds to grab the attention of your potential guests. This number is even lower for the younger generations. This is really not a lot of time to make an impression. This is why having exceptional photographs is so important. You need to utilize that eight seconds of attention to work for you. Having professional photos taken will allow you to showcase your home in the best possible way. There is a lot of knowledge that comes with a professional photographer, and they will know exactly how to highlight the best features of your property. Things like lighting and angles can be difficult to understand, so a professional is a good option.

You might also be able to set a higher price if you have better quality photos. Listings that have photos that have been taken by professionals can command a premium of around 26 percent higher than listings that don't have this. Even though hiring a professional photographer is an upfront cost, it would likely make up for this with the number of bookings you get and by being able to charge a bit more than your competitors because your property simply looks better.

TIPS FOR TAKING AMAZING PICTURES OF YOUR PROPERTY

If you have decided that hiring a professional photographer is not for you, then there are a few things that you can do to enhance your photos. It is really important that you take the best photos that you possibly can. It is possible to get really good quality photos by using a smartphone that has a good quality camera and by implementing the tips that we are going to be speaking about now.

Organize and Tidy Everything Before You Shoot Photos

When you take your photographs, you need to put your best foot forward. This means that you need to clean and declutter your entire property. Make sure that everything is organized exactly the way you want the guests to see your property. Do your best to make things beautiful and ensure that there isn't too much clutter in the pictures.

Prep and Inspect Rooms Beforehand

Before you plan on taking pictures, ensure that you have prepared each room and that it has been inspected. You should do this even if you are hiring a professional photographer. This will just make everything go a lot smoother. You can use the checklists that have been provided for you in the previous chapters to help you prepare your home as if a guest is arriving the next day.

Use Natural Sunlight Where Available

There is just something about natural light that makes everything look 100 times better. This is why you need to prepare to shoot your photos in natural daylight. Natural light will help to enhance your property and increase the contrast, depth, and colors of your photos. Make sure that all of your blinds and curtains are completely open to allow the natural light to flow in. You should also switch on all your lights, even in the daytime. This will prevent any shadows or dark corners from showing up.

Shoot into a Corner

This might seem like a strange tip, but it is much better to face your camera toward a corner than down a straight wall. The corners will add some dimension to your photo, and you will get a much bigger space in the picture. Your room will look a lot more inviting and open. Test it out for yourself and you'll be able to see the difference.

Look at All the Small Details

The small details truly matter when it comes to your pictures. It's so easy to get caught up with all the big items and major amenities, but the smaller things could be make or break. The little things are what complete the picture for the guests, so do consider these things. Your property should be filled with personality and make your guests feel welcome. Try not to make it look too clinical; otherwise, it's not going to be very appealing.

Use Panoramic Shots

Using panoramic shots is one of the best ways to show off your entire room in one photo. If you are unable to take a panoramic picture, then try using a wide-angle lens. This will give the guests a better idea of the size of the space.

Try Different Angles and Perspectives

Taking pictures from just one angle is going to look very one-dimensional and boring. Guests will not want to scroll through 100 pictures that are taken from the exact same perspective. Add some variety by changing up the angles every now and then.

Use Post-editing Software

There are so many different photo editing software and apps out there. Many of them are completely free and will help you enhance your pictures. You can use these apps or software to crop and edit your photos to make them look their best. Small adjustments can really help make your pictures stand out.

If you can't afford a professional photographer or would rather take photos yourself, there are so many things that you can do to help you take amazing pictures. Just make sure that you are implementing as many tips as you possibly can. Your pictures are really important for the guests to get a true idea of what your property has to offer. In the next chapter, we are talking about how to write compelling listing titles.

LISTING TITLES THAT GET CLICKS

Lots of Airbnb hosts make the mistake of overlooking the title of the listing. The problem with this approach is that they're not focusing on what every guest is going to see when they find the listing: The title! It is one of the first impressions that your guests will get of your property, and that's why it's so important. It also helps the guest understand what your property is all about and what it provides. Remember, you only have about eight seconds to make an impression, so a catchy title is really important. If you have a good title, then you will have a better chance of a guest clicking on your listing and then converting that into a booking.

SECRET TIPS AND FORMULAS FOR WRITING TITLES THAT INCREASE BOOKINGS

There are many tips and tricks that can help you write an eye-catching title. The payoff is going to be huge when your title really draws in the guest.

Secret 1: Focus on What Makes Your Property Unique

You want a title to stand out from the crowd, so make sure that you focus on what makes your property unique. Use descriptions and adjectives that highlight the unique aspects of your properties. If you have a pool, make sure this is in your title because it's something different. Perhaps your property is in an interesting location or it has an amenity that guests are looking for. These unique features can be added to a title so guests know exactly what you are offering them.

Secret 2: Take Up All 50 Characters in the Title

Airbnb allows up to 50 characters in a title. Make sure to use up all of these characters so you can give an accurate description of the property. With this being said, there has been an update to the guidelines. Even though you are still able to use all 50 characters, only 32 characters will appear on mobile phones. This means that the first 32 characters are going to be the most important. Most guests will be searching using their phones because it is just simpler.

Secret 3: Be Specific with Your Words

Generic words simply don't get you anywhere. If you are too vague, you will just get lost in the crowd. Try and choose words that are unique and really speak to your property and describe it properly. You don't want to use words that people have never heard before, but you want to make sure that you are avoiding words like "nice," "good," and "pretty." Even though these words are technically descriptive words, they basically tell you nothing about the property. Since you only have a limited number of characters to use in your title, you should make sure that you are utilizing them well.

Secret 4: Name Your Property

A really cool thing to do is to name your property something unique. Instead of referring to it as a house or apartment, you can give it a distinctive name. The name of your property should be descriptive and provide an insight into what it is. It also speaks to your target guest so that you can grab their attention.

Secret 5: Tailor It to Your Audience

You want your target audience to be grabbed by your title. This is why you need to understand who your target guests are and then tailor your title to them. If your target audience is couples who are going for romantic getaways, then you can make your description more romantic and describe it in a way that's going to appeal to that group of people. If you are targeting large families with small children, then you can make your title more fun and family-friendly.

Secret 6: Use Abbreviations Where Possible

Since you have only a limited number of characters to use, it is wise to utilize abbreviations where possible. Just remember that the abbreviations you use should be ones that people actually understand. You don't want your guests to be completely confused about what you are trying to say.

Secret 7: Stick to Proven Title Formulas

There are a few formulas that help you create very effective titles. These ones have been proven time and time again. It will allow you to draw attention to your listing and also convey accurate information that the guest wants to know.

- Formula 1: [Specific Adjective] [Property Type] w/ [Unique Features]
- Formula 2: [Specific Adjective] [Property Type] Perfect for [Experience Type]
- Formula 3: [Adjective] [Property Type] Near [Landmark]—[Distance]
- Formula 4: Enjoy [Unique Feature] at [Specific Adjective] [Property Type] in [Location]

Your listing title might seem like such a small thing or a minor detail, but it is one of the first things that your guests will come across. This means that you want to make sure your title gets them to click and hopefully book with you. In the next chapter, we are going to talk about what makes for a perfect listing description.

WRITING LISTING DESCRIPTIONS THAT MAKE GUESTS INSTANTLY BOOK WITH YOU

I f a strong title is what catches your guests' attention, then a powerful description is what gets them to book with you. The description is not a place for you to simply summarize your listing. It is an opportunity for you to sell your guests on why they should book and stay at your property over the other options they have. You want to highlight the most significant and unique features and benefits of your property and convince them to stay with you. This should be your top priority. Writing a good description is something that can truly get you many more bookings.

WHAT MAKES A LISTING DESCRIPTION EFFECTIVE?

In order for your description to be effective, it needs to draw the attention of your guests. Instead of being too salesy and sounding like a car salesman, you need to tell a story. Something that's going to make the guests want to continue reading to find out what else your property has to offer. Your description also has to be eye-catching. Something that makes guests want to learn more about your property. This is why it shouldn't be a sales pitch but rather an effective description.

Now, it can be easy to get carried away when you are describing your property. Just make sure that you are being accurate and telling the truth. Stretching the truth in your description is not going to be of any benefit to you. Sure, you might get the booking, but when they come to your property, they will see that it does not match the description. This will result in you getting negative reviews, and you just don't want that.

Your description needs to be targeted and tailored to your target audience. This is why it is so important for you to know who your target audience is. The way you would describe something to a family looking to go on vacation is completely different from the way you would describe something to a businessperson coming into town for a meeting. Regardless of who your target audience is, your description needs to be easy to read. People do not want to read lengthy descriptions of things that aren't going anywhere. Make sure that it is specific and concise but still conveys the message you are trying to get across. Try not to use language that is too complicated for people to read through. It's really not going to benefit you if your guests can't even understand the words that you are using in your description.

THE BASIC STRUCTURE OF A TOP-PERFORMING DESCRIPTION

You can follow a basic structure in order to create a great description. Here are a few things that you should definitely include in your description:

- Interesting introduction.
- Description of all the rooms.
- Describe outdoor spaces.
- Discuss the location and nearby attractions.

Your main goal when writing your description is going to be to answer the questions before your guests even ask them. A few things that guests would like to know about are as follows:

- How close is your property to the nearest landmarks and public transportation?
- How many rooms, beds, and bathrooms are available on the property?
- Is the property kid-friendly and what is the pet policy?
- What are the unique features of your property that others do not have?
- What amenities and items do you provide?
- What is available in the surrounding areas and some things to do?

People will likely skim through the description and not read it word for word. This is why it is a good idea to segment the description into separate sections. You can use paragraphs and bullet points for this. You will start off with the introduction, then in the next paragraph, you can move into the different living spaces. You can use bullet points to describe the amenities you provide. Then in the final paragraph, you can review the general location and sign off. You can also use headings within your description so that you can break up the different sections. This does make it a lot easier to read, and your guests will be able to easily find the information they are looking for.

AN EXAMPLE OF HIGH-PERFORMING DESCRIPTIONS

Title: <u>Newly Renovated Romantic House with Ocean Views</u>

What You Will Love

- Complete renovation was done in 2022, so everything is brand new.
- Breezy coastal decor.
- Gourmet, fully equipped kitchen with stainless steel appliances.
- Beach access is just one block away.
- Private outdoor space with barbecue.
- Beautiful deck to enjoy the ocean views.
- Can use as a remote workstation with Wi-Fi.

About the Property

This beautiful house is steps away from the gorgeous coastline, so you can smell the salty air every time you take a breath. It is located in a peaceful area, so you will not be disturbed when you enjoy your morning coffee on the deck.

The lounge and living spaces display works by local artists and coastal decor that has been designed by local woodworkers. With three bedrooms and two full bathrooms, there is space to comfortably accommodate six people. The primary bedroom has a king bed and an en suite bath. The second bedroom also offers a king, and the third, a queen. Both of these bedrooms will share a large bathroom situated in the hallway.

The outdoor amenities are simply spectacular. With a large deck that offers a lounge and dining area, you can enjoy breakfast, lunch, and dinner with views of the ocean and the sound of the waves crashing against the shore. Feel free to sit out on the deck in the evening with a glass of your favorite wine and gaze over the ocean or stargaze to your heart's content.

Getting to Know the Area

The property is conveniently located close to many natural amenities. You are steps away from the ocean and just a short walk away from a beautiful recreational park. A stunning golf course is a simple five-minute drive away.

The town is an artist's paradise with art galleries, spas, boutiques, and restaurants. You will find craft beer, farm-to-table cuisine, and delicious cocktails around every corner. The town draws all manner of explorers, so if you are looking to meet some interesting people, then one of the many bars is the place to go.

This is simply a tiny treasure of the region that everyone will come to love and enjoy. There is truly something for everyone, and it draws you in with its quiet and charming vibe.

THE POWER OF WORD OF MOUTH —GETTING PROFITABLE REVIEWS

Without integrity, no company can have positive word of mouth.

— JAY ABRAHAM

TIPS FOR GETTING TOP-RATED REVIEWS FROM GUESTS

Getting good reviews is incredibly important when you're running your own Airbnb business. Reviews mean credibility. People are far more willing to book with hosts who have a lot of positive reviews. It shows that people have been happy with the service that they received and are willing to come back. This is one of the best ways to increase your revenue and bring in more guests. With this being said, it can be quite tricky to get these good reviews when you're first starting out. However, there are many things that you can do to get these reviews and ensure that they are good ones.

Tip #1: Underpromise and Overdeliver

The first step to getting amazing reviews is to exceed your guests' expectations. This means that you need to underpromise and overdeliver. Now, there is definitely a balance to this because you still need to convince your guests to book with you. So if you are too humble with your descriptions and your title then you will not get any bookings. The key is to deliver what you promised and then a little bit more.

Your guests' expectations are going to be set by what you have mentioned in your listing. If you provide something that is even better than that, they will be delighted. It's all about adding something special and a bit different. You don't have to change around your whole property, so the guests are completely shocked when they walk through the door. In fact, this is probably a bad idea. Instead, look at a few small things that you can do that will be a happy surprise to your guests. For example, include a welcome note in your welcome basket with a few local snacks and suggestions of where they can go to enjoy their stay. This is a small cost to you, but it leaves a huge impression.

If there are any pitfalls at your property, ensure that you let the guests know about this in advance. You can mention it in your listing but frame it in a slightly positive way. For example, if the street on which your property is located can be quite loud in the mornings, you should mention it in the listing. If you don't mention it and you get a guest who is a light sleeper, they will absolutely hate the experience and give you a negative review. If you put this in the listing, they will have already expected this and the light sleeper would probably not have booked with you in the first place. This is just better for everybody involved.

Tip #2: 6-Star Service Leads to 5-Star Results

You should do your best to go the extra mile for your guests. Start thinking about how you would like to be treated on your own property. The things you would like to have done for you are the things you should provide for your guests. Perhaps you can contact them a few days before they arrive and ask if they have any special requests. You can also follow up with them during longer stays and ask if they would like a complimentary cleaning service.

Tip #3: Pick the Right Guests to Stay with You

Making sure you pick the right guests is so important. One of the biggest reasons hosts should background check their potential guests is to see their ratings and identify whether it is a good choice to allow them onto their properties. If you see that other hosts have enjoyed the guests, then there is a good chance that these are good people.

Tip #4: Take Care of Issues Right When They Happen

It is very common for issues to arise when a guest stays at a property. Even if you have meticulously planned things down to the tee, slipups sometimes happen. In many cases, it's not even going to be your fault. If some of these incidents do happen, don't panic. All you have to do is handle them as soon as possible. Most guests are not too worried if something small happens, they just want to know that the issue will be resolved quickly.

It really does help if you have procedures and steps in place to help you address any potential issues quickly. For example, if you know that power cuts occur in your neighborhood, then have a plan to mitigate this issue. You can also notify guests of common issues that might occur and how they can go about dealing with them. As long as you provide them with the resources to deal with any potential problems, they will usually be OK with it.

With all of this being said, you must remember that the guest will always be right. If they come to you with an issue, it needs to be resolved, even if you don't think it's a big deal. Guests will be coming from all different places and backgrounds. This means their standards are going to be different from yours. Being gracious with your guests is a good way to establish a relationship with them and ensure that their needs are met. If you want to get good reviews from your guests, then you need to take care of them in the way that they want to be taken care of. You must show them that you are on their side, and whatever the problem is, make sure that you apologize sincerely and take action as quickly as possible. You will definitely see this pay off in your guest reviews.

Tip #5: Try to Be Flexible with Things Like Check-In Times

Being flexible with your check-in and check-out times is a good way to get good reviews. Guests really do appreciate it when they can arrive and leave whenever they please. Sometimes plans simply do not go according to plan, and it is not possible to check in at the regular time. Perhaps a guest has arrived earlier than expected or is going to arrive much later. Having a flexible check-in time allows the guests to set their own schedules for what is going to be best for them.

The best way to implement this is to have electric locks, so your guests won't have to arrive only when you can let them in. You can set a personal code for the guest, and they can use this to unlock the doors. This is actually an added safety measure because it can be set to lock automatically after a certain period of time and it will prevent guests from losing their keys or leaving your home unlocked when they go out. A cheaper option would be a key safe lock box if electric locks are not possible. You can place the key in the box and set a code to open it so the guests have access to the key. Since you don't have to be there when they check in, it allows you to have more flexibility as well.

Tip #6: Overcommunicate

Communication is key when you are dealing with other people. It is much better to overcommunicate than to undercommunicate. Your guests are going to be dependent on you for a good experience. This is especially so if they are new to the area or have not used the Airbnb platform before. It is a good idea to be accessible to your guests so they can contact you if they have any questions or need a helping hand. Remember, it can be scary to be in a place that you do not know or are unfamiliar with. Having somebody that you can communicate with really puts you at ease.

With this being said, it can be quite inconvenient to have somebody call you for simple things. This is why it's important to predict any common issues that might arise in your home. If you know you have a very old type of coffee machine that guests could have trouble using, stick some instructions next to it or include it in your house manual. This way, your guests will have all the information they need and they will not need to call you unnecessarily.

Tip #7: Stay on Top of Upkeep

Maintenance issues can cause an undesirable experience for the guest, and this is not going to lead to a good review. This is why it is a good idea for you to take some time to turn over the property and ensure that everything is still working well. It only takes a few minutes to do a quick scan of the property to ensure that everything is as it should be. You should also schedule inspections every now and then to ensure that all of your plumbing and electronics are working well. This way, you won't be surprised by any issues down the line because you've already taken preventative measures.

Tip #8: Keep It Seasonally Themed

Different seasons will bring out different aspects of your property and the location in which you are. If you decorate your property according to the theme, it will really bring out the best in the location. You can pull the theme from the outdoors and bring it indoors. For example, in the winter you can turn your property into a cozy feeling place. In most cases, people love to feel warm and cozy when it is cold outside. In the summertime, you can go for more fun and coastal decorations to bring a summer vibe to your property. It is no secret that every season brings its own feelings and vibes to an area. You can use this to add an extra level to your property.

Tip #9: Seek Out Feedback from Guests

Getting your guests' input is the best way for you to continuously improve your services and your property. Your guests know exactly what they expect and what you are missing. Most guests are very happy to give you some constructive feedback so you can make things better. Once guests have checked out, consider sending them an email to get some feedback from them. If the feedback you received is positive, then you can go ahead and ask them to leave a review for you. If you have received some negative feedback, then you don't necessarily have to prompt them to give you a review. Also, let them know that you are going to do your best to implement the feedback that they have given, so the next time they come to your property they will have a better time.

Getting 5-star reviews is a simple matter of being diligent and conscientious as an Airbnb host. Understanding what your guests need is so important to their overall experience and to make sure that you are becoming the best host that you can be. In the next chapter, we are going to touch on what it takes to create the ultimate guest experience.

STAGE 6

BUILDING RELATIONSHIPS WITH YOUR GUESTS

20 ESSENTIAL QUALITIES OF EVERY SUCCESSFUL AIRBNB BUSINESS OWNER

Strive not to be a success, but rather to be of value.

— ALBERT EINSTEIN

20 QUALITIES OF SUCCESSFUL AIRBNB BUSINESS OWNERS

We have already spoken about all of these qualities throughout the book. This is more to remind you of the qualities that you can work on. You'll be able to find information about most of these tips throughout the book, so feel free to go back and find the information that you're looking for. More likely, you will be reminded of what you have already learned so it is solidified in your brain. You will also realize that every step of the process makes you a better host. These 20 qualities are things you already know based on what you have learned.

1. Invest in high-quality photos of your property.
2. Have enough time to devote to being an effective and attentive property manager.
3. Create lasting first impressions, especially at the start.
4. Personalize every guest's experience.
5. Be as prompt as possible when responding to customers.
6. Buy back your time by outsourcing smaller tasks.
7. Success is in the details.
8. Be willing to go above and beyond.
9. Reach out personally before your guests arrive.
10. Offer some guidance for the local area.
11. Add a personal touch to every interaction.
12. Decorate your space tastefully and thoughtfully.
13. Don't overcomplicate the process.
14. Always be clean.

15. Keep supplies stocked.
16. Leave snacks for guests.
17. Price yourself competitively against hotels in the areas, not just competitors.
18. Always abide by your local laws.
19. Proactively collect 5-star reviews.
20. Don't think, just do it.

Arguably, anyone can become an Airbnb host. But there are only a select number of hosts that are able to deliver top-notch experiences that have guests constantly raving about them. This is the type of host that you should strive to become. In the next chapter, we will look at ways to automate the booking process to make operations for both you and your guests more efficient.

WHEN AND HOW TO USE AUTOMATION FOR YOUR AIRBNB RENTAL

Automation has been regularly shown to increase efficiency in companies across industries. For example, setting up automated processes in your Airbnb business can increase occupancy rates by as much as 80 percent.[1] That is a big payoff for reducing the amount of work that you have to do.

THE BENEFITS OF AUTOMATING YOUR AIRBNB BUSINESS

Running an Airbnb rental, or just a rental property in general, requires an investment of both time and money. If you have a busy life or you have multiple Airbnb properties, then it is a good idea to start thinking about automation as an option. As you scale your business, you will need to free up your own time because you simply can't be everywhere at once. In most businesses, automation is something that they integrate, and the rental industry shouldn't be any different.

There are plenty of benefits that come with Airbnb automation. Firstly, you will be able to work remotely and still have control over your properties. This gives you flexibility and saves you time. Routine tasks that can be automated mean that you do not have to spend time doing them. You can allocate your extra time to more important things in your business and your personal life. You'll also be able to take on more work because the smaller things have been taken care of.

Automation means that everything will run a lot more efficiently and you can increase your revenue because of this. You'll be able to speed up communication with your guests, the booking process, and cleaning procedures. Automation allows you to scale and grow your business without complicating anything. There are many different ways in which you can automate your business, and we are going to go through a few of them.

Smart Home Automation

Smart home technology is the way to go. You can invest in things like smart locks, smart televisions, and noise monitoring systems. If you have smart locks on your property, then you do not need to be there in person in order to do key exchanges or to welcome your guests to the property. All of these things can be done by themselves, and all you need to do is give your guest a unique access code. Smart TVs are just a really good way to simplify the check-in process. Anybody can figure out the smart TV, and you can schedule a welcome video to play as soon as they walk in or switch on the TV. Noise monitoring is a great way to go if you have fussy neighbors. You will be notified if noise levels exceed a reasonable level and can take action to ensure that all parties are happy.

Guest Communications

Communicating with your guests is of the utmost importance when it comes to renting out your property. You need to make sure that your guests are always kept in the loop, and there are things that they will need to be reminded about. If you have a lot of guests staying in your various properties, then it can become overwhelming to try and keep in contact with all of them. You can automate this by setting up automated messaging, automated notifications, and an email welcome series. All of this allows the guest to have the communication they need, but you are not doing anything.

Pricing Strategy

We have gone quite in-depth about pricing strategy in a previous chapter. From there, you know that it can get a bit complicated. This is where pricing strategy tools can be incredibly helpful to you. You can use dynamic pricing tools and automated pricing to help you out if you do not have the time to sit and manually work on your own pricing.

Automated Task Management

If you are not the one who is performing maintenance or cleaning services at your property, then having an automated task management service is a really good choice. This will automatically notify your cleaning service when the guests have checked out. Then they can come in and turn over the property for the next guest. Maintenance contractors can also be alerted when repairs need to be made to certain aspects of the house. You do not have to be involved in any of this, and you know that your home is going to be well taken care of.

A Channel Management Solution

We have already gone quite in-depth with channel management services, but these are also a great way to automate many different aspects of your property management. Things like promotion, distribution, and booking of your listings can be handled across multiple platforms all from one window. This simplifies everything for you so that you are not jumping from platform to platform.

You might not yet be at a point where automation is necessary for your business. However, it's never too early to start thinking about ways you can make your operations more efficient so you can spend your time on more important things and get back some of your free time.

CONCLUSION

Getting into the Airbnb business is truly a journey like no other. You are creating a way for yourself to make extra income while doing something that is really enjoyable. You open up your home or property to other people so that they can have some amazing experiences. Not only that, but you are also creating a way to make more money and possibly start a business so you no longer have to work your regular 9-to-5 job.

By now, you should have a good grasp of what you can expect from the process. You will also be able to put together a workable strategy so that you can move forward. At the end of the day, none of the information that you have learned from this book is going to be of any use unless you start implementing it. I would suggest that you start from the beginning and slowly work your way through the book. See where you can begin implementing things to make your current Airbnb business better or start on this journey from scratch.

I would urge you to commit to taking some sort of action. This could be in the form of research or writing out a list or plan. The more you take action, the more momentum you will build for yourself. Once you have reviewed everything in the book about two times, it will be time to start going through each phase of the Airbnb framework. You can start by performing a market analysis. From here, you can just continue to take action. You will start to see things take shape the more you make moves in the right direction.

If you have found the information in this book useful and valuable in your Airbnb journey, would you consider leaving me a review? This will really help me connect with more people to help them achieve their Airbnb dreams.

Customer Reviews

⭐⭐⭐⭐⭐ 2
5.0 out of 5 stars ▾

5 star	████████	100%
4 star		0%
3 star		0%
2 star		0%
1 star		0%

See all verified purchase reviews ›

Share your thoughts with other customers

Write a customer review

Scan the QR code to leave a review

REFERENCES

Airbnb Automation: 7 Ways To Put Your Business on Autopilot. (2021, June 01). iGMS. https://www.igms.com/automate-airbnb/

Airbnb hosting: 6 ways to protect yourself and stay within the law. (2019, May 13). LearnBNB. https://learnbnb.com/airbnb-hosting-laws/

Airbnb house rules: Actionable tips and templates. (2020, September 7). Hospitable. https://hospitable.com/airbnb-house-rules/

Airbnb pricing strategy. (n.d.). Renting Your Place. http://rentingyourplace.com/airbnb-101/pricing/

Airbnb rules: 6-step checklist to stay within the law. (2019, November 27). iGMS. https://www.igms.com/airbnb-rules/

Airbnb SEO: 10 proven tips to boost your ranking. (2020, February 28). iGMS. https://www.igms.com/airbnb-seo/#

Airbnb statistics. (2022, May 4). iPropertyManagement. https://ipropertymanagement.com/research/airbnb-statistics

Airbnb supplies: A complete checklist for hosts to help you exceed your guests' expectations. (2018, October 16). iGMS. https://www.igms.com/airbnb-supplies/#

Airbnb titles: Proven formulas that attract 5x more bookings. (2020, April 27). iGMS. https://www.igms.com/airbnb-titles/

Arrojado, C. (2022, May 11). *Frank Lloyd Wright homes, farm stays, glamping sites—Airbnb's new search categories feature these cool listings.* AFAR. https://www.afar.com/magazine/airbnb-unveils-56-new-vacation-rental-categories

Average Airbnb prices by city: How much should you charge for your Airbnb? [2022] (2022, May 2). AllTheRooms. https://www.alltherooms.com/analytics/average-airbnb-prices-by-city/

Best Airbnb listing descriptions: Our top examples. (2022, March 9). GuestReady. https://www.guestready.com/blog/best-airbnb-descriptions-examples/

The best Airbnb pricing tools in 2022—maximize your profits with dynamic pricing. (2022, July 9). Floorspace. https://www.getfloorspace.com/best-airbnb-pricing-tools/

Best vacation rental channel managers 2022. (n.d.). Hostaway. https://www.hostaway.com/best-vacation-rental-channel-managers/

Carville, O. (2021, June 15). *Airbnb is spending millions of dollars to make nightmares go away.* Bloomberg. https://www.bloomberg.com/news/features/2021-06-15/airbnb-spends-millions-making-nightmares-at-live-anywhere-rentals-go-away

Clark, R. (2021, October 28). *15 Airbnb horror stories you won't believe are true.* Lodgify. https://www.lodgify.com/blog/airbnb-horror-stories/

Clarkson, A. (2021, January 12). *Airbnb cleaning checklist | 5-star turnover success.* Mamma Mode. https://mammamode.com/airbnb-cleaning-checklist-5-star-turnover-success/

Comprehensive list of Airbnb host expenses. (2020, December 1). Unbound Investor. https://www.unboundinvestor.com/comprehensive-list-of-airbnb-host-expenses/

Daly, A. (2021, March 12). *25 insanely useful Airbnb tips that will make you a better host.* BuzzFeed. https://www.buzzfeed.com/anniedaly/pro-tips-from-airbnb-superhosts

Dar, S. (2022, February 23). *What kind of insurance do you need for an Airbnb property?* Baselane. https://www.baselane.com/resources/what-kind-of-insurance-do-you-need-for-an-airbnb-property/

Davis, G. B. (2022, June 27). *How to be an Airbnb host: 14 tips for fast success.* SparkRental. https://sparkrental.com/airbnb-host/

Deane, S. (2022, January 4). *2022 Airbnb statistics: Usage, demographics, and revenue growth.* Stratos Jet Charters Inc. https://www.stratosjets.com/blog/airbnb-statistics/

Debunking Airbnb myths | Top 10 Airbnb hosting misconceptions. (n.d.). Hostaway. https://www.hostaway.com/airbnb-hosting-misconceptions/

Deciding to list your place on Airbnb—legality and regulations to consider. (2022, July 18). Padlifter. https://padlifter.com/free-tips-and-resources/deciding-to-list-your-place-on-airbnb/airbnb-legality-and-regulations-to-consider/

Dendinou, J. (2021a, August 20). *How to a create a listing on Airbnb.* Hosthub. https://www.hosthub.com/guides/how-to-create-a-listing-on-airbnb/

Dendinou, J. (2021b, August 20). *How to create a listing on booking.com.* Hosthub. https://www.hosthub.com/guides/how-to-create-a-listing-on-booking-com/

Drew, R. (2022, June 13). *21 critical Airbnb house rules examples (& templates) for hosts.* Rental Recon. https://www.rentalrecon.com/host-advice-and-ideas/airbnb-house-rules/

Duckworth, P. (2018, October 7). *Private room vs entire place.* Bnb Duck. https://bnbduck.com/airbnb-private-room-vs-entire-place/

Filippousi, M. (n.d.). *How to write an awesome description for your Airbnb listing.* Hosthub. https://www.hosthub.com/blog/how-to-write-an-awesome-description-for-your-airbnb-listing/

5 tips to earning a 5-star review on Airbnb. (2019, December 11). LearnBNB. https://learnbnb.com/earning-a-5-star-review-on-airbnb/

Fok, R. (2020, May 21). *300 days of hosting on Airbnb.* Medium. https://reneefok.medium.com/300-days-of-hosting-on-airbnb-adb48f38b0a9

A full guide to listing your vacation rentals on Vrbo. (2020, November 30). IGMS. https://www.igms.com/vrbo-listing/

Griffiths, C. (2020, February 18). *How to conduct an Airbnb market analysis.* Lifty Life. https://www.liftylife.ca/airbnb-market-analysis/

Griffiths, K. (2019, October 10). *How to rank #1 on Airbnb—the best Airbnb SEO advice.* Lifty Life. https://www.liftylife.ca/how-to-rank-on-airbnb/

He, S., & Svetec, J. (2022, March 17). *Airbnb for Dummies: Baseline pricing for your Airbnb.* John Wiley & Sons. https://www.dummies.com/article/home-auto-hobbies/travel/baseline-pricing-for-your-airbnb-271329/

How picture-perfect Airbnb photos increased bookings by $2,521. (2021, April 29). Rankbreeze. https://rankbreeze.com/airbnb-pictures/

How to ask Airbnb guests for 5 stars. (n.d.). Hostaway. https://www.hostaway.com/how-to-ask-airbnb-guests-for-5-stars/

How to automate my Airbnb in 2021—5 easy tips. (n.d.). Hostaway. https://www.hostaway.com/how-to-automate-my-airbnb-in-2021-5-easy-tips/

How to find the best Airbnb pricing strategy. (2020, October 30). Hosty. https://www.hostyapp.com/how-to-find-the-best-airbnb-pricing-strategy/#:~:text=If%20you%20offer%20less%20value

How to identify your target Airbnb guest—pro tips. (2020, July 27). LearnBNB. https://learnbnb.com/target-rental-audience-on-airbnb/

How to screen Airbnb guest in three simple stages? (2021, March 19). Hosty. https://www.hostyapp.com/how-to-screen-airbnb-guest/

How to start an Airbnb business? (n.d.). Hostaway. https://www.hostaway.com/how-to-start-an-airbnb-business/

How to take great Airbnb photos: An essential guide for success. (2020, November 24). IGMS. https://www.igms.com/airbnb-photos/#How_to_Take_the_Best_Airbnb_Photos_9_Helpful_Hints

Hrovat, J. (2021, May 24). *Our proprietary 3 step pricing formula to earn an additional $1,250 every month.* Beyond BNB. https://www.beyondbnb.io/post/3-step-pricing-formula

The inside story behind the unlikely rise of Airbnb. (2017, April 26). Knowledge at Wharton. https://knowledge.wharton.upenn.edu/article/the-inside-story-behind-the-unlikely-rise-of-airbnb/

Is Airbnb safe, reliable, and legal? (2022, March 11). TechBoomers. https://techboomers.com/t/is-airbnb-safe

Kelsey, K. (2019, September 15). *Finding a profitable Airbnb property.* AirHost Academy. https://airhostacademy.com/finding-airbnb-property/

Kidd, S. (2022, April 19). *Ultimate Airbnb cleaning checklist + free template.* TurnoverBnB. https://turnoverbnb.com/airbnb-cleaning-checklist/

Kovachevska, M. (2022, March 18). *28 amazing Airbnb statistics you should know before booking.* CapitalCounselor. https://capitalcounselor.com/airbnb-statistics/

Krones, T. (2020, July 3). *How to automate your Airbnb rental & increase efficiency.* Host Tools. https://hosttools.com/blog/short-term-rental-automation/automating-airbnb-rental/

Krones, T. (2020, August 7). *Airbnb house rules template: 15 examples of essential house rules for every listing.* Host Tools. https://hosttools.com/blog/short-term-rental-tips/airbnb-house-rules/

Krones, T. (2020, November 13). *The best Airbnb pricing tools for small hosts in 2021.* Host Tools. https://hosttools.com/blog/short-term-rental-tools/best-airbnb-pricing-tool/

Krones, T. (2021, March 2). *Is Airbnb profitable for hosts? Everything you need to know.* Host Tools. https://hosttools.com/blog/airbnb-rentals/is-airbnb-profitable-for-hosts/

Krones, T. (2021, July 5). *Airbnb photography: 8 tips to taking the perfect Airbnb photos.* Host Tools. https://hosttools.com/blog/short-term-rental-tips/airbnb-photography-guide/?swcfpc=1

Kutcher, J. (2020, January 31). *10 tips for running a successful Airbnb.* Jenna Kutcher Blog. https://jennakutcherblog.com/10-tips-for-running-a-successful-airbnb/

Lake, R. (2021, August 31). *Does your homeowner's insurance cover Airbnb?* Investopedia. https://www.investopedia.com/articles/insurance/120816/does-your-homeowners-insurance-cover-airbnb.asp

Lang, L. (2018, January 25). *23 things to do to prepare your home for Airbnb guests.* The SpareFoot Blog. https://www.sparefoot.com/self-storage/blog/20259-23-things-to-do-to-prepare-your-home-for-airbnb-guests/

Lara, J. (2021, April 24). *How to start an Airbnb. Ask yourself these 8 questions first.* Short Term Sage. https://shorttermsage.com/how-to-start-an-airbnb-business/

Lauzon, A. (2022, March 3). *Is Airbnb profitable in 2022?* Mashvisor Real Estate Blog. https://www.mashvisor.com/blog/is-airbnb-profitable/

Leonhardt, M. (2019, July 8). *82% of people think Airbnb-ing their home is a good money-making strategy—here's what you need to know.* CNBC. https://www.cnbc.com/2019/07/03/is-running-an-airbnb-profitable-heres-what-you-need-to-know.html

Manage multiple channels at scale. (n.d.) Guesty. https://www.guesty.com/features/channel-manager/#:~:text=A%20channel%20manager%20gives%20yous. (n.d.). Guesty.

Must-have Airbnb tools & apps. (n.d.). Hostaway. https://www.hostaway.com/must-have-airbnb-tools-and-apps/

Nix, D. (n.d.). *The ultimate insurance guide for Airbnb hosts.* Steadily. https://www.steadily.com/blog/airbnb-insurance-guide

O'Connell, C. (2022, June 9). *Best Airbnb descriptions to drive more bookings.* Guesthook. https://guesthook.com/best-airbnb-descriptions/

Plus vs Luxe: Comparing different types of Airbnb rentals. (2019, November 7). GuestReady. https://www.guestready.com/blog/airbnb-rentals-overview/

Protect your investment: Airbnb safety tips for hosts. (2018, November 7). Hosty. https://www.hostyapp.com/protect-investment-airbnb-safety-tips-hosts/

Responsible hosting in the United States. (n.d.). Airbnb. https://www.airbnb.ca/help/article/1376/responsible-hosting-in-the-united-states?locale=en&_set_bev_on_new_domain=1655368744_ZDBhODY1ZGUyODc0

Russell, T. (2019, November 12). *15 tips on how to automate your Airbnb property.* Short Rental Pro. https://www.shortrentalpro.com/15-tips-on-how-to-automate-your-airbnb-property/

Safety tips for hosts of places to stay. (n.d.). Airbnb. https://www.airbnb.ca/help/article/231/safety-tips-for-hosts-of-places-to-stay

Screening Airbnb guests. (n.d.). Renting Your Place. http://rentingyourplace.com/airbnb-101/airbnb_property_management/screening-guests/

7 tips for staying safe and secure as an Airbnb host. (2018, March 16). Fing. https://www.fing.com/news/7-tips-to-staying-safe-and-secure-as-an-airbnb-host

A step-by-step guide on how to list on Airbnb. (2018, November 26). Guesty. https://www.guesty.com/blog/step-by-step-guide-how-to-list-on-airbnb/

Suknanan, J. (2021, March 18). *Airbnb hosts shared 19 of their best tips for getting a five-star rating.* BuzzFeed. https://www.buzzfeed.com/jasminsuknanan/airbnb-five-star-review-hosting-tips

10 things to consider before hosting on Airbnb. (2020, July 27). LearnBNB. https://learnbnb.com/10-things-to-consider-before-hosting-on-airbnb/

3 biggest Airbnb myths busted. (2018, June 3). HelpHost. https://www.helphost.com/chicagoairbnbblog/3-biggest-airbnb-myths-busted

Tips on how to write Airbnb house rules. (2020, July 2). MasterHost. https://masterhost.ca/airbnb-house-rules/

Top 12 Airbnb competitors and alternatives for hosts. (2020, July 3). iGMS. https://www.igms.com/airbnb-competitors/

289+ great Airbnb host review examples (July 2022 update). (2022, July). Eat, Sleep, Wander. https://eatsleepwander.com/host-review-example/

Types of places to stay. (n.d.). Airbnb. https://www.airbnb.ca/help/article/5/types-of-places-to-stay#section-heading-0-0

The ultimate Airbnb host checklist: Everything you need to host successfully. (2022, August 17). Floorspace. https://www.getfloorspace.com/airbnb-host-checklist/

An ultimate guide to Airbnb automation. (2021, July 18). Zeevou. https://zeevou.com/blog/an-ultimate-guide-on-how-to-automate-airbnb-management/

Wade, T. (2018, September 27). *Airbnb home insurance—what you need to know*. Ratehub. https://www.ratehub.ca/blog/airbnb-home-insurance-what-you-need-to-know/

What are Airbnb's policies? (n.d.). Guesty. https://www.guesty.com/vacation-rental-guide/airbnb-policies/

What is a channel manager and why it's important. (n.d.). Hostaway. https://www.hostaway.com/what-is-a-vacation-rental-channel-manager/

What is Airbnb and how does it work? (n.d.). Airbnb. https://www.airbnb.ca/help/article/2503/what-is-airbnb-and-how-does-it-work

What regulations apply to my city? (n.d.). Airbnb. https://www.airbnb.ca/help/article/961/what-regulations-apply-to-my-city?locale=en&_set_bev_on_new_domain=1655368744_ZDBhODY1ZGUyODc0

When (not) to use Instant Book on Airbnb. (2018, March 1). GuestReady's Airbnb Hosting Blog. https://www.guestready.com/blog/airbnb-instant-book/

Why professional photography is important for Airbnb bookings. (n.d.). MadeComfy. https://www.blog.madecomfy.com.au/blog/professional-photography-a-deciding-factor-in-booking-short-term-stays

Yes, you need insurance to be an Airbnb host. (n.d.). Six Figures Under. https://www.sixfiguresunder.com/insurance-to-be-an-airbnb-host/

Zaidi, T. (2022, March 24). *Airbnb's cancellation and refund policy (flexible, moderate, strict)*. TRVLGUIDES. https://trvlguides.com/articles/airbnb-cancellation-refund-policy

Zaqout, K. (2017, November 30). *What's the best property type for short-term rentals?* Mashvisor Real Estate Blog. https://www.mashvisor.com/blog/airbnb-apartment-vs-airbnb-house/

Zaragoza, R. (2021, November 26). *Conducting accurate Airbnb rental market analysis in 7 steps*. Mashvisor Real Estate Blog. https://www.mashvisor.com/blog/airbnb-rental-market/

IMAGE REFERENCES

Bezanger, J. (2021, June 5) [Image]. Unsplash. https://unsplash.com/photos/9k_gCYLoH2g

Carstens-Peter, J. (2017, Feb 6) *If you feel the desire to write a book, what would it be about?* [Image]. Unsplash. *https://unsplash.com/photos/npxXWgQ33ZQ*

Cottonbro. (2020, July 11) *Group of friend inside a dormitory*. [Image]. Pexels. https://www.pexels.com/photo/group-of-friend-inside-a-dormitory-5158945/

Dancre, R. (2020, October 27) *People signing documents for a wedding*. [Image]. Unsplash. https://unsplash.com/photos/doplSDELX7E

Glenn, K. (2018, March 18) [Image]. Unsplash. https://unsplash.com/photos/xY4r7y-Cllo

Gudakov, Z. (2021, August 10) *Red house*. [Image]. Unsplash. https://unsplash.com/photos/faBWQt9i7dg

Hendry, A. J. (2019, February 2) [Image]. Unsplash. https://unsplash.com/photos/KNt4zd8HPb0

Karpovich, V. (2020, March 21) *Woman working at home using laptop.* [Image]. Pexels. https://www.pexels.com/photo/woman-working-at-home-using-laptop-4050291/

Kayden, R. (2021, August 5) [Image]. Unsplash. https://unsplash.com/photos/FARBiTC4Bm0

Lach, R. (2021, December 20) *Bottles of cleaning products standing on metal shelf.* [Image]. Pexels. https://www.pexels.com/photo/bottles-of-cleaning-products-standing-on-metal-shelf-10558189/

Mallorca, T. (2019, June 14) [Image]. Unsplash. https://unsplash.com/photos/NpTbVOkkom8

Nickson, R. (2020, January 10) *The Juniper Room, Whisper Rock Ranch, Joshua Tree, California.* [Image]. Unsplash. https://unsplash.com/photos/emqnSQwQQDo

Perkins, P. (2017, August 13) *Airbnb.* [Image]. Unsplash. https://unsplash.com/photos/3wylDrjxH-E

Picjumbo. (2016, October 24). *Person holding blue ballpoint pen writing in notebook.* [Image]. Pexels. https://www.pexels.com/photo/person-holding-blue-ballpoint-pen-writing-in-notebook-210661/

Pixabay. (2014, February 13) *Security logo.* [Image]. Pexels. https://www.pexels.com/photo/security-logo-60504/

Schaffner, A. (2021, June 1) *Taking some pictures with my youngest daughter.* [Image]. Unsplash. https://unsplash.com/photos/n5OqZ-sDbSI

Scholz, S. (2019, May 16) *Nuki smart lock.* [Image]. Unsplash. https://unsplash.com/photos/IJkSskfEqrM

Spacejoy. (2021, April 12) [Image]. Unsplash. https://unsplash.com/photos/vOa-PSimwg4

Tankilevitch, P. (2020, May 1) *A person cleaning the table with cleaning cloth.* [Image]. Pexels. https://www.pexels.com/photo/a-person-cleaning-the-table-with-cleaning-cloth-4440608/

Terry Magallanes. (2019, February 7). *Four Brown Wooden Chairs.* [Image]. Pexels. https://www.pexels.com/photo/four-brown-wooden-chairs-2635038/

NOTES

1. AIRBNB BASICS

1. *Airbnb Statistics iPropertyManagement, 2022*
2. *The inside story behind the unlikely rise of Airbnb.* (2017, April 26)

3. THE TRUTH ABOUT AIRBNB HOSTING—MYTH VS. REALITY

1. *2022 Airbnb statistics: Usage, demographics, and revenue growth*
2. *Airbnb statistics.* (2022, May 4). iPropertyManagement.

4. 9 SIGNS STARTING AN AIRBNB BUSINESS IS RIGHT FOR YOU

1. *Airbnb Statistics iPropertyManagement, 2022*

6. HOW TO ANALYZE THE PLAYING FIELD

1. *2022 Airbnb statistics: Usage, demographics, and revenue growth*

7. PROS AND CONS OF RENTING OUT DIFFERENT PROPERTY TYPES

1. (2022, May 11). *Frank Lloyd Wright homes, farm stays, glamping sites—Airbnb's new search categories feature these cool listings*

10. SAFETY TIPS FOR HOSTS

1. 2021, June 15). *Airbnb is spending millions of dollars to make nightmares go away.* Bloomberg

11. THE ULTIMATE CHECKLIST FOR ITEMS TO BUY FOR YOUR PROPERTY

1. (2022, March 18). *28 amazing Airbnb statistics you should know before booking.* CapitalCounselor

14. LEGAL REGULATIONS TO CONSIDER

1. (2022, March 18). *28 amazing Airbnb statistics you should know before booking.* CapitalCounselor

17. THE PRICE IS RIGHT—STRATEGIES FOR MAXIMIZING PROFITS AND INCOME

1. *Average Airbnb prices by city: How much should you charge for your Airbnb? [2022]* (2022, May 2).

27. WHEN AND HOW TO USE
AUTOMATION FOR YOUR AIRBNB RENTAL

1. *Airbnb Automation: 7 Ways To Put Your Business on Autopilot.* (2021, June 01

HOW TO UNLEASH YOUR AIRBNB'S FULL POTENTIAL

THE COMPLETE STEP-BY-STEP GUIDE TO MAXIMIZING BOOKINGS, RENTAL INCOME, SETTING UP AUTOMATION AND OPTIMIZATIONS FOR YOUR SHORT-TERM RENTAL BUSINESS

INTRODUCTION

There are currently over 6 million Airbnb listings on the platform (Woodward, 2022). It is crazy to think that there are so many. This means there is a lot of competition when it comes to short-term rentals. The positive side is that business is booming, and it is a good time to be on the market. The downside is that it is very competitive, and you need to be innovative if you want to stand out from the crowd. You need to prove why your Airbnb is better than any of its competitors. This way, you can maximize your booking potential and make sure that your calendar is always full.

You may be someone who is just starting out on Airbnb, or perhaps you have been a host for quite some time. Either way, there are definitely some challenges when it comes to ensuring you meet your Airbnb's potential. Perhaps there are some seasons in the year where bookings are not as good as you would like them to be. You might've noticed a dip in your bookings, or perhaps you struggled to get your Airbnb off the ground in the first place. You may be part of a completely different group of people who have decided to increase their capacity when it comes to Airbnb and are struggling to balance everything. All of these are valid struggles. The good news is that there are solutions to all of them.

In my personal experience, all it takes is a few tools to help take your Airbnb business to the next level. I have managed to grow my short-term rental business to the point where I am making a sizable income. I started my journey small, like most of us, and by implementing the tips and tricks I will share in this book, I have increased my capacity and productivity. On top of that, I am able to deliver top-quality service to all of my guests, and I've made the entire process a lot easier for myself as well. This is what I would like to share with you—it is not something that is only possible for a few people. Every person who is in the short-term rental industry is able to maximize their growth and income.

In the world of short-term rentals, there can be a lot of confusing information. It can seem like there are always new tools and technologies that come out. This makes it difficult to decide which ones are actually going to be beneficial for you. In this book, we will go through all things Airbnb and make sure that you can choose the right avenues to increase your income and profitability. You can also make your life much easier by using technology to automate many areas of your Airbnb rental business.

This is a very exciting time in the Airbnb industry. There is a lot of growth, and if you use the right tools, you'll be able to beat the competition and make your Airbnb stand out from the rest. Eventually, you'll grow your business to the point where you have multiple vacation rentals booked out like crazy. Some strategies are incredibly simple and don't take a lot of work to implement, while others do take a bit of elbow grease to get moving. However, all of them are valuable and can add something to your Airbnb business. All you need is to know the right information so you can get moving. There has never been a better time to start, so we are going to dive right in.

1

UNDERSTANDING THE MARKET

Building a successful Airbnb business hinges on understanding the market. Finding out what your guests really want means you can cater to their needs and ensure they leave happy with their stay. Understanding the market allows you to predict their wants and needs, so you are always one step ahead. This leads you to outperform your competitors, setting you apart from the pack.

CONDUCTING MARKET RESEARCH

Market research is the backbone of understanding the market. It is like studying before the big exam. You need to take steps to find out the relevant information. After doing this research, you will have a much better understanding, so you can make informed decisions on your pricing, listing, and any other important aspects of running your Airbnb.

Find Out More about Your Competition

Running an Airbnb is a competitive business. Hundreds of Airbnbs near yours could offer similar benefits to guests. This means you are competing for the same pool of potential guests. Knowing as much as you can about the competition puts you in a better position to beat them. As they say, knowledge is power.

When you are looking for your direct competitors, those will be the ones in the area where your property is located. Look at the Airbnb platform to get an idea of the properties in your area. See what they are offering to guests and how they advertise themselves. You may notice a few commonalities between them, and this gives you an indication of the trends. The properties with the highest ratings and the most bookings will be the ones that are doing something right, so pay special attention to those Airbnbs. It is also a good idea to take note of their unique selling points and anything extra they offer guests.

To help keep track of all this information, you can create a spreadsheet. Fill in all the information so it is easy to read. You will be able to organize it so you can see your direct competition and the strategies that are bringing in the most money.

Compare the Pricing Models

Pricing is one of the most important things to consider when you run an Airbnb. Even if you have the most amazing property in the world, nobody is going to book with you if it is way overpriced. You will also end up losing out on a large amount of profit if you underprice your property. Understanding the pricing of the Airbnb competitors in the area will give you insight into what you can charge. When comparing, make sure you are only comparing your prices to those of similar properties. It isn't going to work if you try to match prices for your one-bedroom apartment with a four-bedroom house. Look for direct competitors and develop your pricing model from there.

Look at the Reviews

The reviews of your competitors' Airbnbs give you a ton of information. You will find out what guests liked and didn't like. There is a chance that those same people would book an Airbnb in the same area, and if you can provide something that your competitors could not, you can attract new guests. For example, you might notice a few guests were upset by the lack of clean towels and sheets in one of your competitor's Airbnbs. You can make sure you have enough of these items in an easy-to-find closet. It would also be a good idea to highlight this in your listing so guests know they will not face this problem if they book with you.

Understand Your Guests

Knowing who your guests are goes a long way when it comes to understanding their needs. It can be tempting to try to cater to a wide variety of guests, but the problem with doing this is that you risk missing the mark for *all* guests. It is very difficult to cater to a family with small kids the same way you would to a group of friends in their early 20s looking for a good time. You will need to make compromises, and it is risky. Focusing on one type of guest will help you zero in on what you should be providing them, and you will end up with happier customers.

Your property's location, size, and amenities will have an impact on the type of guests you attract. Make sure you consider all of this before you decide on your target market. Any reviews or feedback you receive needs to be looked into. Your guests are a wealth of information. Try not to get upset or defensive if you do get a negative review. Rather, look into it and let the guest know you will fix it for their next stay. This is especially important if the review is on public platforms. People will look at how you handled the feedback before booking with you. If you have addressed the concern, then this should not impact your bookings, and it will show that you are really concerned about meeting your guests' needs.

RECOGNIZING PEAK SEASONS AND EVENTS

Understanding your area's peak seasons and popular events helps you plan and set your prices accordingly. When accommodation is in demand, you have the opportunity to raise your prices since more people want to book. In slow seasons, you can reduce your prices to encourage people looking for a deal to book your Airbnb. Different areas will have different peak seasons. If you have a beach bungalow, summer is going to be when people want to book with you to enjoy the beach. A mountain cabin might have its peak season in winter because it's cozy, and the snow will be a fun experience for families.

Peak seasons can shift from time to time. This is why it is important to keep an eye out for what is happening in the travel world. After all the lockdowns from the pandemic a few years ago, there has been an uptick in shoulder-season travel (the period of time between a region's peak season and offseason). This means the traditional peak seasons have shifted slightly to include the few weeks before and after them. We don't know how long this trend is going to last, and there could be even more shifts in peak seasons in the future. It is a good idea to do your research on this each year so you are fully prepared.

An event can be anything that brings people to the area. There may be festivals, conferences, or showcases. It is important to stay connected with the community where your Airbnb is located, even if that is not where you live. Connecting with community groups in the area is a great way to know what is going on. When there is an event that will draw a crowd, you can raise the prices to match the demand and maximize profit.

At points in time when demand is low, you have to be a bit more aggressive when it comes to your marketing strategies. Making a few changes to your listing and requirements can make a huge difference. If you offer a discount, it is important to make this known. You can change the title of your listing to include the word "discount." This will make people more aware of the price drop. You can also reduce the minimum night requirement and change your cancellation policy to be more flexible. These small changes remove barriers and make it easier to draw people in when it's normally more difficult.

CONNECTION WITH LOCAL TOURISM OPERATORS AND BUSINESSES

Running an Airbnb is a great way to improve the community if you do it right. You are bringing more people into the area, which means you can bring in new business. Many small businesses miss out when it comes to tourism because visitors are not aware of them. As an Airbnb host, you have a unique opportunity to bring attention to these small businesses and create a stronger community.

When people go to a new city or area, they rely on the recommendations of their Airbnb host since they do not have any previous knowledge of the place. You can establish yourself as a trustworthy place by making good recommendations that are not as common and well-known. This will add to your guests' experience, and the small business owners will benefit as well.

A great way to do this is to incorporate some local treats and flavors into a welcome box for your guests. You can connect with local businesses and vendors to see if they would like to collaborate with you to get some exposure. This means you could get a discount on the items in your welcome box or get them completely free if the business owners agree. You may be able to access discounts for your guests. Perhaps free coffee or drinks with a meal are offered at certain restaurants. Another option is asking for "buy one, get one free" cards from business owners.

Incorporating the local vibe into your guests' packages is a great way to create an entire experience for them. This can be an optional add-on for them to purchase when they make the booking. Perhaps have an option for local fresh flowers to be added to the room or a local meal to be delivered to them on the day of arrival.

The options are truly endless when it comes to incorporating local businesses into your business. You get the added benefit of word of mouth. Anyone who shops at a local business you have partnered with will hear about you. This could drum up more bookings for you and make you more known among locals and those living in neighboring towns.

STRATEGIC PRICING 101

You have an amazing Airbnb in a wonderful location, but it isn't making as much money as you thought. Ever wonder why that is? Your pricing strategy could be the culprit. Sometimes, it's not about the physical Airbnb but about other factors, such as price. Price plays a huge role in whether people want to book with you. It also influences whether you make the most profit from your Airbnb.

THE BASICS OF DYNAMIC AND STATIC PRICING

There are two main strategies when it comes to pricing: dynamic and static pricing. When you are thinking of a pricing strategy, these are typically the two that would be suggested that you would think of. One tool that can be used is called Airbnb Smart Pricing. This tool will adjust your pricing depending on many different factors. It helps you keep your rates competitive without having to change the prices manually all the time. Your pricing will be automatically updated depending on what is going on in the market. If there is more demand in your area, the price will automatically go up, and in seasons where the demand is lower, it brings the prices down. This gives you a better opportunity to get bookings based on what people are looking for and is more of a dynamic pricing strategy.

Before going any further, let's discuss dynamic and static pricing. Dynamic pricing is when the price of an Airbnb listing changes as time goes on. Sometimes, people are willing to pay more for an Airbnb, and there are others when they will be looking for cheaper deals. Let's say you have a beach bungalow as your Airbnb. People will probably want to book with you in the summer when they can enjoy the beach and the sunshine. Your peak times will be during the summer holidays and weekends. Your off-peak times will be in the winter and during the week. Understandably, people are not as drawn to the beach in the colder months as in the summer months. You can charge more in the summer because people want to go on vacation. They are willing to pay more, and places will quickly get booked. In the winter months, people won't be as likely to book, so in order to draw them in, the price will need to be lower. Changing the prices depending on demand is a dynamic pricing strategy.

There is a lot to consider regarding a dynamic pricing strategy. There are plenty of ways to do it, and it sometimes takes trial and error to figure out what is going to work for you in your specific area and market. Another way to incorporate dynamic pricing into your pricing strategy is to look at the dates you have available. The most popular date could be booked up, and you have a bunch of random dates here and there that are not getting booked. This is pretty common, and it might be a good idea to use a dynamic pricing strategy to draw in some potential guests. If you bring the price down for those specific days, people are more likely to want to book with you. You would end up beating out the competition, who are all vying for a very small number of guests. In a competitive market like this, it is going to work in your favor if you do your best to beat the competition with your low prices. Just remember that you don't want to put it so low that you aren't making any profit at all.

If you use a dynamic pricing strategy, you may want to consider a few tools. These will help you access the data needed to make better choices. Many of the tools can also change the prices based on what is happening in the market, which makes things easier for you. There are quite a few tools on the market, and they are constantly being updated. Keeping up-to-date on the development of the tools in this space will allow you to choose the ones that will benefit you most. A few to look into are Airbnb's Smart Pricing, AirDNA's Smart Rates, Beyond, PriceLabs, and Wheelhouse.

Then, we have a static pricing strategy, which just means the price stays the same. You will decide on a price that suits you and leave it for the duration of your Airbnb business listing. It is much easier to handle static pricing since you do not have to change it all the time. However, the problem with this is that you are potentially missing out on revenue because you're not using a pricing strategy that changes with the market. Your pricing might work in the summer months, but it would be too expensive for people to pay in the winter months. You are now losing out on all potential guests in the winter, so your property stands vacant for a longer period of time than it should.

You can use static pricing to your advantage if you also consider adding discounts for longer stays. It is usually more beneficial for your property to be booked for a longer period of time. If someone is simply booking for one day, it can get in the way of other people being able to book. For example, somebody could book for one Saturday, and this means that any potential weekend holiday-goers will not be able to book your property. It gets in the way of them potentially booking a Friday to a Sunday, which would bring in more money. Encouraging longer booking stays helps you maximize your profit, even with a static strategy. For example, you could keep your booking price at a higher rate and then start offering discounts with more days booked. I would start with your high rate for a one-night stay, which will probably discourage people from booking one night. Then offer a 10 percent discount if the person books for two nights and a 15 percent discount if they book for three. Now, you have created the opportunity for potential guests to think about whether they can book for longer, which would discourage one-night stays. This leaves your property open for longer bookings and increases your overall revenue.

GENERAL PRICING GUIDE

Before you decide whether to use a dynamic or static pricing model, you can use a general pricing system to help you set your prices.

This will help you get the most out of your pricing without having to constantly change it or put in as much active work. Using a general pricing guide is a good idea to get your base pricing right so you know what to charge, even if you are looking to implement more dynamic strategies.

The first thing you will need to do is start researching your competition in the local area. Almost every area already has Airbnbs. This means there is already a general price that people are willing to pay in order to stay there. You can take a look at your competition to find out how much they are charging and what they are offering. If you charge too much, you risk your competitors getting all the guests, but if you charge too little, you end up losing money. Remember to only compare your property to ones that are similar to yours so you can understand what price you should use and what your potential guests would be willing to pay.

To discover the general pricing in your area, you will need to jump into the shoes of a potential guest. Log into the Airbnb platform as a guest and then start searching for properties in your area. Put in the filters that are applicable to your Airbnb and see what shows up. The next thing you will do is click on the price range filter, which will show you the average price for the date range you selected. This filter only gives you the average price, which means that any excessively expensive or cheap outliers will impact the price you are seeing. You need to exclude these outliers since they skew the average and don't give you an accurate view of what people are willing to pay. All you have to do is move the minimum price up and the maximum price down so that you remove all the outliers, and it should give you a better idea of the average price people are willing to pay.

Also, look at the number of available listings for the criteria and filters you have placed. This will give you a good idea of how many rentals are offering the same thing as you and how big your competition is. It is a good idea to check both types of information for every single month of the year, as they can change. You can create a spreadsheet for yourself to note the average nightly price and the number of listings for each month. You can then set different prices for each month, taking advantage of the changes in season. For example, in months when fewer listings are available, you can increase your price by 10 to 20 percent, as there is less competition in the area.

PRICING STRATEGIES FOR DIFFERENT PROPERTY TYPES

It is so important to fully understand your property type before you choose a pricing strategy. This is because the type of property will play a direct role in how much people are willing to pay to stay there. Someone who is just looking for a room with a bathroom is going to pay a lot less than somebody who is looking for a fully furnished apartment. When looking at your competition, you have to take into account the types of properties they have, as well as the amenities they offer. You will need to identify your direct competition in order to price your properties correctly.

When you create a listing on Airbnb, you'll be asked for your arrangement type, and there are four basic types to choose from. These are an entire home, a hotel room, a private room, and a shared room. An entire home would be the most expensive of the arrangements, while a shared room would be a lot cheaper. However, with a shared room, if you do have an entire property, it means that you can have multiple guests who stay in one home. This could result in you ending up with more profit due to the way you are listing your property on Airbnb. However, it is important to note that each arrangement type targets a specific type of guest. That is why it is important to know who your guests are and what they need so you can cater to them directly.

Amenities are such an important part of creating a pricing strategy or a price base point. Some Airbnb hosts provide the bare necessities, and others go over and above to provide more amenities for the guests. A property that has amazing amenities will be able to charge more because it offers more. Some great examples of amenities that people are willing to pay more for include hot tubs, swimming pools, gaming rooms, or even fantastic views and easy access to things like the beach.

When you are trying to figure out how much you should charge for your property, you will need to use the filters so you can see the properties that offer similar amenities to yours. It is a good idea to do a deep dive into the pricing of all the properties in your area so you can get a better idea of what they offer and how you can be different. Adding an amenity that most properties do not have in your area can be a huge benefit because it makes you stand out from the rest of the properties. Not only that, but you can start charging slightly higher rates because you are adding more value to your guests.

Now that you have a solid understanding of the basics and the most fundamental aspects of Airbnb pricing, it is time for us to dive a little deeper. In the next chapter, we are going to explore more advanced pricing strategies. These are the tools the top Airbnb hosts use to optimize their income.

ADVANCED PRICING STRATEGIES

Not long ago, the keywords "Airbnb collapse" were trending on Twitter. It's usually not a good idea to get your information from social media, but it was interesting to see how many people jumped on the bandwagon to say that Airbnb was going down and the prices would need to start dropping. It is no secret that many Airbnb hosts feared this becoming a reality, but the truth is that much of this can be avoided by using the right pricing strategies. Like other businesses, Airbnb goes through highs and lows in terms of average revenue. Knowing how to preempt this and ensuring that your pricing strategy matches what is going on in the market will lead you to create a sustainable and long-lasting business. Not only that, but you will be able to create an Airbnb business that brings in the maximum amount of profit possible.

Before diving into the different scenarios for changing your Airbnb pricing strategy, let's talk about it as someone who is new to the Airbnb market. When you first start out on Airbnb, you are not going to have any reviews on your listing. Reviews are the lifeblood of an Airbnb. The more reviews you have, the more people trust you and the more bookings you'll get. Someone who is new to the platform will need to focus their energy on getting positive reviews before they can start to maximize their profit. In order to do this, you need to set your price quite a bit lower than your competitors. This is so you can start attracting people to your Airbnb. Since you cannot win on reviews at this point, you will have to win on price. It does mean that you will lose out on profit, but the truth is that you need to build a base before you even have a chance to make a sustainable and long-term profit.

After you have a good number of reviews, you can start to slowly increase the price of your listing. You don't want to keep the price low for too long. Otherwise, you will be missing out on potential profit. It is usually best to make it a gradual increase rather than slapping a doubled price tag on your Airbnb. Over the course of the next few months, you will slowly increase the price until you are happy with the amount that you are charging and are sure this will bring the maximum amount of profit for you. At this point, you should have a good number of reviews, which means that you have more credibility in the market.

STRATEGIES FOR WEEKDAYS AND WEEKENDS

Setting up different prices for weekends and weekdays is pretty crucial to maximizing your Airbnb profits. Most people go away on vacation on the weekend, and if your property is a vacation rental, this will be your most in-demand time. Also, people who want to stay in the Airbnb during the week usually do so for work and are not planning to relax or enjoy the accommodation. This means they are more likely to choose the cheapest option than the option that is going to offer them the most amenities.

Many Airbnbs change their price depending on the time of the week, so you can have a look at your competitors to see how they price. This will give you a good idea of what your base price should be, and then you can work from there—on weekends when there are events happening in your area, you can increase the price even more since accommodations in that area will be in demand.

STRATEGIES FOR ORPHAN DAYS

An orphan day or an orphan period is a day or a number of days that are in between bookings. If you have a minimum night's stay on your bookings, this can create an unbookable day in between. For example, someone could book from Monday to Wednesday, and another guest could book from Thursday to Sunday. This leaves Wednesday night open. If your minimum night's stay is set to two days, then nobody will be able to book out the Wednesday, and you will essentially be losing money due to this.

One of the easiest things to do for an orphan day is to reach out to either one of your guests and ask if they would be willing to book an extra night. You can offer a good discount for this night and not issue any additional fees, such as the cleaning fee. This way, it makes booking the extra night a lot more attractive, and you don't have to worry about having a random day open that is not bringing you any money. If one of the guests says no, then you can reach out to the other guest to see if they are willing to. You would be surprised at how many people are willing to extend their stay for a discount.

If neither of the guests wants to book the orphan night and your minimum night's stay is set to two nights, you will have to change it and allow a one-night stay for that date only. You may think a one-night stay is not worth it, especially if you have set a two-night minimum and are used to multi-night stays. However, you may be surprised at how much extra profit you can make by filling the gaps in your calendar.

Earlier, I mentioned how to filter search pricing on the Airbnb platform and find out what your competition is charging. You can use this method to search your area for similar listings on the date of the orphan night. When you search for the date that the orphan night occurred, you will most likely find that most of your competition is booked for this date. If that's the case and competition is low, you can increase your price for a single night, especially if it falls on a weekend. If the orphan night occurs in a slow season or in the week, many other listings will be available, and you should create a discount to attract a booking.

STRATEGIES BASED ON LEAD TIME

A booking lead time refers to the period between when the guest makes the reservation and the day they check in. For example, your guest could make a booking on November 5 and only check in on November 25. This means the booking lead time is twenty days. You can easily find out what your average booking lead time is by using Airbnb's professional tools option. While this information is definitely accurate, it would be better for you to track your bookings to find out when people are booking your Airbnb. Remember that average booking takes into consideration outliers, and it doesn't give you accurate information that you can actually work from.

The best thing you can do is create a small spreadsheet for yourself. In one column, you will put the different booking lead times in spaces of five days. Your first column will have zero to five days, your second six to ten, and so on. You will then fill in how many bookings you get within those lead times throughout the year. This way, you have an accurate idea of when people will commonly book and when they will not. This will give you better information so you can make more informed decisions about your pricing strategy.

If you notice fewer bookings as it gets closer to the day, you can start offering discounts to encourage people to book with you. The closer you get to the actual day, the more discounts you can offer until you reach the minimum booking price that you have set for yourself. However, the opposite could be true, where you get most of your bookings closer to the stay, and most of your guests do not book in advance. Having this information on hand means you are not going to panic when you are a few weeks away from a specific open date. You know that your guests typically book with shorter notice, and you can trust that information, so you don't have to bring down your prices or offer discounts, since you can still make a maximum amount of profit even with shorter booking lead times. You can adjust your prices based on the information you have gained from your booking lead time data.

Having a deep understanding of the market and your competitors will help you make better decisions when it comes to pricing. It is also important to know what is happening in your area, in terms of events and the booking patterns that your typical Airbnb guest displays. All of this allows you to have as much information as possible when it comes to setting your prices. Being able to set strategic prices can be the difference between being profitable and struggling.

TRANSITIONING AND DIVERSIFICATION

It is important to be flexible when it comes to your rental property business. There can be shifts and changes in the market that will render your current strategy ineffective. When this happens, many property investors get disheartened and sell up. Rather than looking at these situations as negatives, look at them as an opportunity to shift into something different. You will be able to maximize your profits, which will lead you to becoming more successful. A little bit of flexibility can lead to a much more stable property business year-round.

SHIFTING FROM SHORT-TERM RENTALS (STR) TO MID-TERM RENTALS (MTR)

I have personally found success using this strategy. A few years ago, after a busy summer season, I noticed that my bookings started to slow down. This was common for most hosts in my area. Weekend bookings remained strong, but fewer bookings came in during the week. Ultimately, prices started to decrease as most hosts competed for the same type of guest who stayed from Friday to Sunday.

This prompted me to start renting out my properties weekly or monthly to get through the slow season. I was happy to reduce my rate to attract longer-stay bookings. The idea of having a nearly 100 percent occupancy rate with fewer turnovers sounded good. I knew that construction had begun on a new Correctional Center that, when completed, could hold 1700 inmates. This project lasted several years. The prison was located in the middle of nowhere, and the nearest town with motels, shops, and pubs was about a twenty-minute drive away— exactly where my accommodation was situated.

There were some workers who moved to the area and rented permanent, unfurnished houses, but many companies also came for shorter periods to work on the construction site. Their workers had to stay in motels, which was costly. Airbnb listings in the area were not an option, as most hosts' calendars were already booked out for future weekends, making a month-long stay impossible in those Airbnbs.

One day, I drove to the prison's construction site, and the plan was to stick business cards on all car windshields, advertising my houses as fully furnished mid-term rentals. Unfortunately, the car park was gated, and security didn't allow me onto the construction site. Determined, I spent the next six hours parked in my car outside the construction entrance, taking note of all trucks and vans that entered or exited the site. Most of these vehicles had advertisements or company logos, so I collected their names and phone numbers. I called each one and inquired if they needed furnished mid-term accommodation. And you know what? It worked!

I managed to secure a group of temporary workers from out of town. They were initially staying in a motel, paying premium rates. We agreed on a minimum stay of six weeks with one week's notice before moving out. This group ended up staying for three months. As they left, they passed my number on to the next group of workers, who also booked with me for several weeks. This cycle continued, and those six hours spent in my car at the construction site turned out to be the best time investment for finding new guests. I accommodated carpenters, concreters, painters, electricians, plumbers, and fitters, all working on the same construction site.

Opportunities to increase business for your Airbnb are everywhere if you are willing to think outside the box. I had four solid years of mid-term bookings that brought in a steady income in the slow seasons, so those six hours in my car were totally worth it. Mid-term rentals are simply rentals that are longer than traditional short-term rentals. It bridges a gap and attracts a completely different type of guest. Many hosts do not even think of this as an option, and that means you will be one of the few who use this strategy. You will probably attract more guests and don't have to worry about not making an income in the slow periods.

Filling the Calendar with Monthly Bookings

After hearing my story, you might be thinking that shifting your strategy is a great idea—or maybe you need a little more convincing. The mid- to long-term market is increasing, and there is a definite need for more of these accommodations. The way people travel and live is changing, and this means people need places to stay on a mid-term basis. There is a rise in people who travel for work, are digital nomads, and are remote workers. These people want a place to stay so they can explore the area and don't have to worry about furnishing an apartment or staying in a hotel for a long time. Renting out your Airbnb on a long-term basis is the answer to this.

There are tons of tangible benefits that you can access when you change your strategy. One of the biggest risks associated with a short-term rental is the low turnover rate. This means it may take weeks or months before you are able to get another guest into your rental. In this case, you will have lost revenue because your property is standing empty. If you know there is a slow season coming up, it is the perfect time to start thinking about a mid-term strategy. This way, you don't have to lose out on revenue. You have the freedom to change the rates as demand increases and decreases to maximize your profit. This is not something that can be done with a long-term rental. With a mid-term rental, you get the flexibility of a short-term rental and the stability of a long-term one.

Another benefit is that it is simply easier to manage. You don't need to turn over the property every weekend. Since it is a longer stay, they will likely handle everything for themselves, and you just have to be on call in case of emergencies. You also don't have to replace items that have been used up because the guest will do their own grocery and toiletry shopping. This helps you save both time and money.

You will have peace of mind knowing that your property is bringing in money, but you don't have to do as much work. When the peak seasons roll around again, you can switch your strategy back to a short-term one so you can get the best of both worlds. Overall, you will increase your profits throughout the year and meet the needs of various types of guests.

When moving into a mid- or long-term strategy, the needs of the guests do change. Many short-term guests look for novelty and something different because they are on vacation. This is why you can attract them with themes, activities, and novelty products. However, it is not the same for mid-term and long-term guests. They are after more practicality since they are going to be calling this place home for a few weeks. You can highlight your property's more practical elements when marketing it to a new group of people. For example, you don't have to mention a welcome box or additional amenities like board games and other fun items. Rather, focus on bringing attention to Wi-Fi, a desk or office space, a quiet neighborhood, storage space, and other things that would be more attractive to someone who may be working from the location or in need of some rest after a long day at work.

INCREASING OCCUPANCY

Now that you have decided mid-term rentals are the way to go for the slower seasons, it is time to think about how you are going to increase your occupancy rates. These strategies can work with either short- or mid-term rentals; you just have to target the right audience. If you remain fluid with your approach, you will have a better chance of increasing your occupancy.

Work on Your Listing

Your listing is the most important part of attracting guests to your property. It is the first impression they get, and it will help them understand if your property is a good fit or not. Bookings are won and lost with a listing. You will need to make sure it is consistently updated and that you have all the relevant details in it. Since you are renting it out using different strategies, you should highlight when mid-term rentals are available so people are prepared for this.

In the peak seasons, your rental will target vacationers. This means your strategy will be focused on making the experience unique and enjoyable. Highlighting why potential guests should book with you is essential. There is more competition when it comes to short-term rentals, so you really need to sell it. Make it engaging and draw people in.

When you switch over to long- or mid-term rentals, people look for something different. They look for convenience and comfort. They don't want an overbearing landlord checking on them all the time and usually prefer to be left to their own devices. They will be bringing their own food and personal care items, so you will not have to worry about that. Instead, highlight what makes your property comfortable and feel like home. For example, if you have an extremely comfortable couch, you can highlight this and let them know there is nothing better than sinking into your plush sofa after a long day's work. Think about what you would want in your home away from home, and that should give you a good indication of what you should be highlighting.

Offer Discounts

Everybody loves a discount. If you offer one, you will get more people interested in your property. When moving to a mid-term strategy, you can highlight the discount guests will get if they book for a longer period of time. This will reel them in. Look at other discounts you can offer at specific times of the year, or even combine experiences with your booking. If you work with local vendors, you can get discounts for your guests for meals and activities. All of this is a huge draw.

Use Social Media

Social media is a great way to market your property. Many people just focus on the Airbnb platform, but this is a mistake. Even though you are hosting your listing on the platform, you should still market using whatever is available to you.

There is a large group of people who do not use Airbnb to find their rentals. This means you are missing out on this market. Using social media allows you to connect with them and show them what you're offering. You also have the benefit of short-form marketing, where you can make a post highlighting one aspect of your property at a time. It makes it easier for people to digest.

In today's world, people always go to social media to do research. Places with a social media presence are a lot more reputable and of better quality. This is why having this aspect of your property business really does help. It does take work, and you must be consistent with your posts to ensure you are getting the most out of social media. One of the best things you can do is plan your posts for the month. That way, you have everything ready to go. You can create and save drafts and only post them when you are ready. Set a reminder on your phone to post at specific times and days so you don't forget. All you have to do is click "post," and it will go live. It makes posting on social media a lot more manageable.

You will also need to engage with people in the comments and if they send you private messages. This boosts your credibility, and communication is always key when you are working with social media. You would be surprised at how many people get their information from the comments section of a post.

Increasing Your Airbnb's Capacity

One of the reasons someone may want to book an Airbnb rather than a hotel room is because it is bigger and more flexible. One of the best things you can do to attract more guests is to increase the capacity. All you need to do for this is add more sleeping spaces. This is an easy and cheap way to get more bookings. There could be a family with small children that needs an extra space or two.

You don't need to add an extra room to your property in order to do this. It is a simple fix. Adding a sofa bed or a bunk bed does not take up any extra space, and you get more sleeping space out of the deal. You increase your guest pool and allow more people to find you. Your listing can sleep more people, so you can add this to the listing. If you had a four-sleeper, you now have a five- or six-sleeper and are appealing to more people.

ADDITIONAL REVENUE SOURCES

There is plenty you can do to increase your revenue when you are renting out your property. This is a business, so it is important to think like a business owner. This helps you get into the mindset of finding more ways to increase revenue. The more revenue you create, the more profit you have and the more you can do with it.

Send a Questionnaire upon Booking

It is a big win to find out what your guests actually want and need. If you can give them additional services, you can make them happier and earn some extra money as well. The questionnaire does not ask them about their experience but rather creates a better one for them. You will also have the option to upsell certain things to them.

Remember to be transparent with this questionnaire and put the additional prices on it. Not every guest will want the additional services, but some will. Some ideas for additional services are a full fridge stock, airport pickup and transfers, daily cleaning, and taxi or transportation services. You can also include things like asking for their favorite wine, food, or snack in their welcome box. What you offer and ask with this questionnaire will depend on your capacity.

Customized Check-In and Checkout Times

Many guests would like to check in or check out at a different time than what is regularly stated. It takes very little effort from you to offer early or late check-in or check-out. Most guests are happy to pay extra for this. It does give you less time to turn over the property to the next guest, so bear this in mind.

Tours

If you are a resident of this area and know it well, you can offer tours. Many guests love to tour the local area and learn more about it. You could also hire a tour guide or affiliate yourself with a tour company.

Events and Celebrations

There are a huge number of guests who book an Airbnb because they are celebrating something. You can offer specific services for these celebrations. Offering a custom cake for birthdays, graduations, and anniversaries is something many guests will want. Depending on the occasion, you could also offer a celebration basket that includes champagne, a special meal, snacks, flowers, and balloons. There are tons of ways to make this work. You can add the price to the list so they are aware of it. Since many guests will be looking for places to get these items for their celebrations, you would be making their lives a lot easier.

Partner with Businesses

There are probably tons of small businesses around your Airbnb. Partnering with them will help you offer your guests unique experiences, contribute to the economy of the area, and make you some extra money. Most guests will look to you for guidance on what they should do, see, and eat in the area. Offering a custom package in which you plan their trip and guide them to all the different spots in the area helps them and you. Many businesses will be happy to offer discounts to you and your guests. Just make sure to reach out to these businesses first so you can work out a deal.

By following these transition and diversification strategies, you can ensure consistent income. But do note that successful implementation relies on understanding your performance and the market, which brings us to the next topic: data analytics and metrics.

DATA ANALYTICS AND METRICS

According to *Analytics Comes of Age* (2018), 36 percent of companies indicated that data and analytics have changed the competition in their industry. Also stated was that 32 percent of companies have changed their long-term strategies based on what they have learned from data and analytics. There is so much that can be learned. It helps you improve your strategy and takes your business to the next level.

THE POWER OF DATA ANALYTICS

More information is always going to be better when you are making decisions and building strategies for your business. It allows you to know what is actually going on in the market so you can react appropriately. So much can change over the years that simply using the same strategy is not going to work in the long term. In this business, it is important to remain flexible throughout the process.

When you go in blind, you risk making mistakes. Using data and analytical tools means that you don't have to take that risk. You have the information in front of you, so your strategies can be based on facts and real-time data. You no longer have to use the trial-and-error approach because you can learn from what is already happening. It is like learning from other people's mistakes rather than making the same ones yourself. You know what is most effective and what is causing the most growth for others, and it will probably do the same for you.

You will find that you are far more confident with your decisions, which means you can make them a lot more quickly. When we are unsure, it takes us longer to actually get going. There is a lot of beating around the bush because we are not confident in our actions. With data, you will be more proactive and can make choices more quickly. Data will be available to you in real time so you can be more effective in your strategies and ensure they are implemented almost immediately.

Using these tools means that you can also monitor yourself and your own business. You will be able to quickly notice if there is something different with bookings or revenue. The sooner you are aware of problems, the faster you can fix them. This means you are better prepared and more aware.

There are so many tools on the market that you are spoiled for choice. You can do your own research to find one that suits you best. Just remember to look at reviews and check what they offer so you can compare them properly. Most of the good ones require you to pay a fee to use them, so you want to ensure you are paying for quality. AirDNA is one of the best tools and has been around for quite some time. It collects and provides short-term rental data for the host so they can make more informed decisions. It has access to data from over 10 million rentals, so the information you get will be well-analyzed and true. AllTheRooms and KeyData are also good options to look into.

DIFFERENT METRICS TO TRACK

Many different metrics can be tracked to help you make better decisions. A good program will have all or most of these available. Make sure to check what is offered before you buy or subscribe to data and analytics software so you can be sure you are getting what you need.

Revenue per Available Room (RevPAR)

This is an essential metric, and almost all hotels and rental properties will use it. It helps to fully understand the performance of the property at any given point. You can easily recognize any gains or losses. This metric allows you to see how well your pricing strategy is working for you. It also allows you to see your overall profitability. It is very easy to work this out. Here is the formula:

$$\text{RevPAR} = \text{Average Daily Rate (ADR)} \times \text{Occupancy Rate}$$

Let's say your rental is booked 60 percent of the time, and your average daily rate is $100. This means your RevPAR is $60. You can track this to make sure you aren't dipping too low. If the overall number increases, then you know you are doing something right.

Average Daily Rate (ADR)

We used ADR to work out the previous metric, so you are probably wondering about it. This metric shows you the average amount your guests are paying per day at your rental property. Since it is common to offer discounts and there may be one-time fees applicable for a multiday booking, the nightly rate is not always accurate. Here is the formula:

$$\text{ADR} = \text{Total Revenue} / \text{Number of Booked Nights}$$

You will be using the total revenue, which means if you charge a cleaning fee or any other fee, this will need to be included. This way, you get a more accurate idea of your ADR.

Occupancy Rate

An occupancy rate can be measured using a percentage or simply by stating the number of days booked in a year. The occupancy rates are important because they affect the revenue your Airbnb makes. The more bookings a property gets, the more money it will make. Working out the occupancy rate is simple. Here is the formula:

$$\text{Occupancy rate} = \text{number of booked nights} / \text{total number of nights available to be booked} \times 100\%$$

You will get a percentage amount, so you can see how much of your total available bookings has been taken. If it is less than 50 percent, you will need to work on increasing your bookings in some way.

Response Rate and Acceptance Rate

This is important to understand because if it is low, then you are likely not getting many bookings. Your response rate shows you how often you respond to guests within 24 hours of them reaching out. Clear communication is essential when you are running an Airbnb. Guests will be looking at multiple potential bookings; usually, the ones that respond first have a higher chance of being booked. Your acceptance rate refers to how often you accept or decline booking requests and reservations. There could be many reasons you decline a reservation, but it is not a good thing to do this for no reason. It actually reflects badly on you on the Airbnb site.

These two metrics are easily located on the platform. The acceptance rate can be found in the performance tab under "Basic Requirements." This will show you your acceptance rate for the past 365 days. Only formal booking requests count towards this, so any messages and inquiries will not count.

Cancellation and Rejection Rates

These affect how successful you are on the Airbnb platform. Airbnb only wants to suggest reliable hosts, and this means if you are rejecting and canceling too often, it will affect how often you show up in search results. If you cancel too often, your account could be suspended, which is definitely not something you want. You should not cancel more than three times a year; otherwise, suspension could be the result. You will be able to find this information under the performance tab on the platform. If guests cancel with you, then your cancellation rate will not be affected. It is best to aim for zero percent, as this means you are the most reliable.

Now that we've explored the world of data analytics and metrics, it's time to apply this knowledge to the core of your Airbnb business—your listing.

OPTIMIZING YOUR AIRBNB LISTING

An optimized listing is your ticket to more bookings. Think about it: The first thing your guests will see is your listing. It is the first impression. In the first few seconds, your guests will decide whether your Airbnb is an option or if they should keep scrolling. You need to make your listing as appealing as possible so you can attract as many guests as possible.

WHY A COMPLETED LISTING MATTERS

Let's say you are looking to buy a house. The first place you look is on a property listing site. As you are scrolling through, you notice one that meets most of your requirements and is in your price range. Jackpot! You click on the listing, and there are only two pictures, one from the sidewalk. On top of that, the description is just one sentence. Do you bother messaging the agent? Probably not. This listing is incomplete, and that is an immediate red flag. The person who posted it clearly does not care about what they put forward, and this means that their house is not likely to be well cared for. You immediately click out and continue scrolling.

This is the same thing people do when looking at the Airbnb platform. At the end of the day, perception matters. Even if your property is the best priced and meets all its requirements, if your listing is incomplete, any potential guests will not trust you. A complete and well-done listing shows that you care about what you put out into the world, and it shows guests what they can expect. You can have all the best marketing strategies in the world, but it isn't going to matter if your listings are horrible.

The more detailed your listing, the better. Not all guests will go through every detail, but there are some who will want to. The guests who just want the basics can skim through, but at least the information is there for them should they want it. Before your guests even click on your listing, they will have a look at the cover photos. These need to draw them in, so your property's selling points need to be showcased here. Make sure all photos are of good quality. You will put the most important ones first, and then you can add all the rest after. Many guests don't read the description, but they will all look through the photos. Even if you need to hire a professional photographer, it is worth it. In my first book, *How to Set Up and Run a Successful Airbnb Business,* I go into more detail about getting the perfect pictures for your listing.

Your description is the next thing your guests might go through. It needs to be around 175 words. This is short enough not to bore them, but it also gives them enough details. Highlight key points that actually matter and that they would care about. You can also speak to the type of guest you are looking to attract. For example, if you want families to book with you, you can highlight how kid-safe and family-friendly your property is.

If you already have an Airbnb set up on the platform and have reviews, make sure you take a look at them. They might indicate things that the guests really loved and areas you can improve on. If you have taken the feedback on board and added amenities, make sure to add this to your description. These are things that your guests want, so it is important to showcase that you do have them. If your guests suggest something that would make the experience better, make sure to listen to them and do your best to get it in the future. You will be able to add the new updates to the listing. Sometimes, the smallest things make the biggest difference.

IMPROVING TITLE, DESCRIPTION, AND AMENITIES

Taking the time to craft your listing is essential. Even though they say a picture is worth a thousand words, your words also matter. Ensure you have the right title and description because this gives your potential guests the information they need. The title is what will draw them in and allow you to show up in the right search results. If the title is not appealing, you will get very few clicks. Use words that make the guest want to click rather than simply explaining the basics. Let's say you have a small property in the forest. A great title would be: Cozy Forest Hideaway. It shows the guests exactly what they can expect, but it also draws them in and allows curiosity to take over.

Your title will lead into the description, so you will need to carry the same energy over. It is so easy to just list out information, but nobody is excited to read a list. Try to tell a story with your words. This is the best way to get your point across and engage the potential guest. Your photos will give the guest a good idea of what you offer, but you need to describe the things that make your property stand out from the rest. The basics will already be listed, so you don't have to indicate the number of rooms, bathrooms, and amenities. Use this space to tell your guests about the surroundings, additional amenities, and any other unique selling points.

The additional amenities you mention should be things your guests would actually need. Knowing your guests helps you target them specifically. It is all about knowing their wants and needs before they do. If your ideal guest is someone with young kids, you must know what they would want from a vacation rental. If you have a pool or body of water close by, you could provide toys for the kids to play with, flotation devices, and canoes. If your ideal client is a businessperson, they would want an office space with quiet surroundings and good Wi-Fi.

Make sure you are able to provide these things, and you will have a better chance of landing quality guests.

TIPS FOR INCREASING VISIBILITY IN SEARCH

The Airbnb platform is competitive in nature. It has been designed to help guests find the perfect place to stay. This means all the properties are fighting for attention. Making it on the platform means you need to stand out from the crowd. Your property needs to show up among the first results in the search. How many times have you scrolled to the second or third page of Google's results? Probably never. The same works for the Airbnb platform. It functions like a search engine, and you need to show up high in the search results to make an impact and get the best chance of being seen.

Airbnb SEO

SEO stands for search engine optimization. This is key when using the platform because you want to rank highly in searches. Even if you have the perfect property, it isn't going to matter unless people can actually find you. You need to know what people are searching for, and then put that in your title and description. This comes back to identifying your ideal guest and then marketing to them directly. You will still appear in search results for other people, but knowing who your target market is makes it much more effective.

A great way to find out what words you should be using is to look at the most popular properties on Airbnb that are similar to yours. Look at how they describe their properties, and look at their reviews as well. Since you are offering something very similar to them, you are going after the same guests in the area. Knowing what has made them popular will give you some ideas for doing the same.

Be Reliable

Part of Airbnb SEO is using various techniques to be more reliable and show up more in searches. The right words are important, but so are many other factors. Airbnb wants its users to make the process smooth for their guests. This is to encourage people to keep coming back to the site. If guests have a terrible time on the site, then it will affect the platform and all the hosts. That is why they focus on rewarding reliable hosts who help guests have the best experience possible.

Replying to guests and making sure you do not cancel are two ways of doing this. You will be notified when you get a message, so you will be able to answer it as soon as possible. If you don't want to be active all the time, you can set a few times in the day when you handle messages and inquiries. This way, you are still able to answer all the questions and inquiries, but you are not stuck. As long as you are responding within twenty-four hours, you should be okay, but the faster and more responsive you are, the better.

Competitive Pricing

Again, Airbnb is a competitive market. This means everyone will be pricing their Airbnbs in order to attract as many guests as possible. Believe it or not, your place on the search page is impacted by the price you charge. Airbnb will not put the most expensive properties first because this might dishearten guests looking for an affordable stay. Have a look at the prices of the Airbnbs in your area that offer the same thing, and then price from there. This way, you know you're being fair, but you're also not undercharging. Charging too little might get you a spot on the first page of the Airbnb search engine, but you are going to be losing potential revenue. It is a balancing act.

Increase Available Booking Dates

The calendar on your Airbnb page is essential. It shows when your property is available to be booked and when it is full. If you do not have the Instant Booking function enabled, then you will need to log on and refresh your calendar manually every so often so that Airbnb knows that your calendar is accurate and updated.

Instant booking makes it much easier because guests can book without your approval. It makes things a whole lot easier for everybody involved when your calendar is updated automatically. You also have a higher chance of becoming a Superhost because your response rate will go up. You will find more guests interested in your listing, and you will show up more on their radar since many guests use the Instant Book filter.

After building an irresistible and visible listing, it's time to focus on building a strong reputation that draws guests in and keeps them coming back.

BUILDING A STRONG REPUTATION

"But brand is simply a collective impression some have about a product."

— ELON MUSK

Your reputation will follow you throughout your short-term rental journey. You will get repeat guests, and people will recommend you to their friends and family. When you have met all your guests' wants and needs and they have had an amazing stay, you will be surprised at how often you get referrals from them. It is a great way to continue getting your Airbnb booked as often as possible.

BECOMING A SUPERHOST

Becoming a Superhost is one of the best things you can do for your Airbnb business. It takes a while to become a Superhost, so it's not something that you can just start off with. Knowing how to become a Superhost is essential because you can start working on it from the beginning. It requires consistent work because even once you've gotten your Superhost status, you must continue working to ensure you retain it.

Let's first start by defining what a Superhost is. A Superhost is basically like a badge or award given to a host who is recognized for having great reviews and giving excellent guest experiences. You will get an orange badge on your listing to make sure people know that you are a Superhost. There are so many benefits to becoming a Superhost. You will get increased visibility as well as more trust from your guests. There is a filter on the search engine that allows a guest to filter out anyone who is not a Superhost. If they are looking for reliable and high-quality bookings, they will do this, and you will appear in a search.

You will need to hit a few milestones in order to become a Superhost. Your response rate will need to be above 90 percent, and you will need to have hosted guests ten times in the year or have 100 nights booked with three separate reservations. Your rating must be above 4.8, and

80 percent or more of your reviews must be five stars. The final criterion is that your cancellation rate be 1 percent or lower. Airbnb will assess and grant Superhost status every few months. Be patient because even if you don't get it, you can always try again. You can check your status on the Superhost tab of the platform. It makes it easier to see how far away you are from becoming a Superhost.

COLLECTING FIVE-STAR REVIEWS

Getting those five-star reviews is essential to becoming a Superhost. The more five-star reviews you have, the better your chances are of becoming a Superhost, and you will attract more guests. Once you become a Superhost, it is easier to maintain it because you are used to putting in the effort. The first thing you need to do is make sure that your Airbnb is of good quality, comfortable, and clean. Many people get bad reviews because of the inferior cleanliness of their Airbnb. You are in direct competition with hotels, so you need to make sure that it is justified for people to book with you rather than a hotel with professional staff. You might want to hire a professional cleaner who can look over the property and clean it well. If professional cleaners are not in your budget right now, you can create a cleaning checklist for yourself to make sure that you do not miss anything.

One of the biggest mistakes that Airbnb hosts make is that they oversell their listings. If you make your property seem so amazing that meeting those standards is unrealistic, then you will not get good reviews. You need to put your best foot forward when it comes to your listing, but you also need to be honest and accurate. This way, when your guests check-in, they know what to expect, but it's also easier for you to exceed expectations and get a better review. For example, you don't have to mention there will be a welcome box or basket waiting for them. However, they will have a welcome surprise when they see this waiting for them when they check in. This enhances their experience and makes it more likely that they will give you a good review.

At the end of their stay, make sure to ask them for a review. Many guests have a great time but don't leave a review; this is a missed opportunity. Sometimes, just asking is the push they need to give you that review. If you are there when they check out, you have a better chance of connecting with them. You can ask them if they have any feedback or if there is anything negative you need to change for the next time. This way, there is a lower chance of them simply leaving a bad review if they aren't happy with something. You can reassure them that you will make the changes. You can also offer them a discount on their next stay or something similar to apologize. Explaining to them that good reviews are essential for your business means you are more likely to get their review. If they were unhappy with their stay, do not suggest they give you a review. Otherwise, it could turn out badly for you.

On the Airbnb platform, you can review your guests. This will let other Airbnb hosts know whether they should allow a booking from this type of guest. This is also a great way to prompt your guests to review you. If a guest has been a good guest, make sure you give them a positive review. For guests whose experiences were less than ideal, it's important to provide an honest and appropriate review reflecting their stay.

ENCOURAGING REPEAT GUESTS

Getting some repeat guests is really going to help with your profit, as well as make your property management easier. When you have a trusted repeat guest, you know that your property is going to be in good hands, and there will be lower marketing costs. You don't have to worry about trying to fill empty spaces because you know your guests are going to come back. This leads to a more secure and stable income, and you can build relationships and trust with your guests.

Welcome Them

First impressions really do matter a lot when you are running an Airbnb. If they have booked with you, it means that you have made a good first impression online, and now it's time to carry this through by making a good impression in person. Meeting your guests and introducing yourself is a great way to do this. It helps to establish a personal relationship with them. You can show them around and let them know that you'll be available for whatever they need.

It makes many guests feel secure to know that they can put a face to the name they have been communicating with. Don't worry if you can't be available in person to meet your guest at check-in. We will cover remote check-in in the next chapter.

On the property, make sure that you have provided the basic necessities, but also try to go above and beyond. Surprising your guests with small things can really go a long way. A bottle of wine and some homemade treats can make all the difference. Also, make sure to stock things like toilet paper, fridge essentials, and other bathroom essentials so they don't have to worry about going out to find and buy these items. If they have forgotten something at home, it is already taken care of, and they can enjoy their vacation. Think about what your hotel or Airbnb offers you when you stay over. What would've made your stay smoother and more enjoyable?

Keep in Touch

Once they are ready to check out, make sure you meet them and receive the keys, so you can have a conversation with them and wish them well on their way. If you are unable to meet with your guests, don't worry too much about it now. We will cover other ways to stay in contact a bit later in the book.

This is also a great time to get any feedback and reassure them that you will be implementing it in the future. This way, it instills some excitement, so they will want to come back to see how you have improved your Airbnb.

You can also send them an email the day after they check out to thank them for staying with you. At this point, you may want to ask for a review. Once you get the review, make sure that you reply to it, whether it is positive or negative. For a positive review, you can simply thank them and let them know you are excited for the next time they stay with you. If it is a negative review, you can address the points they are concerned about and let them know that you will make the changes accordingly.

Give a Discount

Everybody loves a discount. One of the best ways to encourage people to rebook with you is to give them a discount for the next time they stay. Your discounts don't have to be for busy times. You can set these discounts or specials for times when you know bookings are typically slower. This way, you encourage people to book at those points, but you also offer them a discount, so they are incentivized to do that. They will be happy, and you will benefit from it as well.

You might even consider creating some sort of loyalty program, if it works for you. You can create an email list of all of your previous guests during the slow period. Simply send out an email with the discount exclusive to them. You would be surprised at how many people will jump at the chance to stay at an Airbnb they truly enjoy for a cheaper rate.

Your reputation is essential when it comes to building a sustainable Airbnb business. The good news is that if you do these few things, you can get there. Having established a strong reputation, let's now turn to one of the fundamental notions that underlies everything we've discussed so far: communication.

Leveling Up Airbnb Properties Across the Board

"Alone we can do so little; together we can do so much."

— *HELEN KELLER*

Take a moment now to think about yourself as a guest rather than an owner. If you were thorough in your research, you probably stayed in a good number of Airbnbs before you started listing yours… How many did you see had room for improvement?

Of course, every Airbnb owner wants their property to stand out from the crowd… But we also want to raise the quality of Airbnbs across the board and make our own stays (and booking experiences!) as guests more enjoyable – and this is part of my hope with this book.

So while your brain is busy thinking through all the ways you can maximize your property's potential, I'd like to ask you to take a moment to help other Airbnb owners level up their game.

That's as easy as leaving a short review – just as you want happy guests to do when they leave your property.

By leaving a review of this book on Amazon, you'll show other Airbnb owners where they can find the guidance they need to get the most out of their property – and, in the process, you'll help raise the standard across the board.

Simply by letting other readers know how this book has helped you and what they'll find inside, you'll show them where they can find everything they need to make sure their property is fulfilling its true potential as an Airbnb destination.

Scan the QR code to leave a review

Thank you so much for your support. Now, let's get back to it!

MASTERING GUEST COMMUNICATION

One study found that 72 percent of complaints on Twitter were the result of poor customer service (Kemmis, 2022). Another 22 percent were related to scams, but we are not in the business of running scams, so this should not happen. A lot of poor customer service or unmet expectations come down to communication. If you communicate to your guests exactly what they will be receiving and everybody's on the same page, then there will be a much lower likelihood of complaints. Knowing how to properly communicate with your guests is a valuable skill when running any kind of property rental business.

AUTOMATING GUEST MESSAGES

When it comes to communication, there are a few very standard questions and concerns that are always brought up. Sometimes, this is specific to your Airbnb, and other times, it is a general question. As you spend longer in the business, you will realize what the most common queries and concerns are. This makes it a lot easier for you to develop a communication standard because you know exactly what is going to be asked.

When you are communicating with your guests, it is so important that you be transparent and available to talk to them. Many hosts want to sell their property as the best place on earth. That is understandable, but the truth is that you are setting up your guests to be disappointed. If they tell you they want a quiet location because they want to rest and relax, you might have the urge to sell your property as the perfect place for that. However, if your property is right next to a highway or close to an amusement park, you know that it's not a quiet area. While you may reassure the guests that your property is perfect for their needs, when they get there and realize there are children running around or cars driving past every five minutes, it's going to be an issue. You may get a negative review and some very unhappy guests.

Most guests are pretty forgiving when they know what to expect and when you are honest with them. Communicating well helps protect you and manage their expectations. If you have communicated something to them, then you can always go back to the conversation and show them what was agreed upon. Any important communication should always be done through email or some other kind of written medium. This way, there is a trackable history, so either of you can go back and ensure the other one is holding up their end of the bargain.

Some guests will want to communicate all the time, and others won't bother with it. Either way, it is important to make sure that the line of communication is open. There are specific moments when you should make yourself available to communicate with your guests. Firstly, it's going to be when they make an inquiry about booking with you. This is when they will have the most questions, and you should be available to answer them. Once they have booked, it is a good idea to send a message thanking them for booking with you and letting them know you are available to answer any questions or address their comments if they have any. The day before or the day of their arrival, you should send them a message to make sure they know the basics, such as the directions and check-in details, so everything goes smoothly for them. After they have checked in and are settled, you might want to check in after the first night to ask if everything has gone well and if they need anything. Once they have checked out, you can continue communication a few days after they depart to make sure they enjoyed their stay.

If you are the one who initiates most of the communication, it means that you have more control over what is going on. It is much better to be the one in control of the conversation because there is a lower likelihood of arguments and misunderstandings on your end. Sometimes, guests forget to communicate until the last minute, and then it is very difficult for you to meet their needs.

Being on point with communication can be quite difficult, especially if you are busy. This is where automated messages come in handy. You only have to create message templates, which you can copy and paste into your message field. Airbnb has a saved message feature, which makes it a lot easier. You can create as many saved messages as you would like for every occasion. You can create templates for the most commonly asked questions, booking confirmations, and welcome messages. This means that you can effectively communicate without actually having to do much.

Another option is to use a third-party site where you can completely automate the messages. This means that you don't even have to click and send the messages since it will be done on your behalf. You will have a saved message template on the software, and when specific events pop up, the right message will be sent to your guest. You could have messages for check-in and checkout, booking inquiries, booking confirmations, and cancellations. This way, the information is sent to your guests, and everybody receives the same type of communication. If there is something specific that the guest contacts you about, they can do so, as there will always be this option. Remember that even automated messages cannot cover every situation. Sometimes, speaking to your guest is going to be the best way to understand what they need or what their concerns are. Automated messages make your life a little bit easier because you don't have to continuously communicate the same thing repeatedly.

CHECK-IN OPTIONS: IN-PERSON OR REMOTE

When it comes to checking into an Airbnb, there are typically two options. The first is an in-person check-in where you, as the host, will go to meet your guests and check them in. This allows you to connect with your guests face-to-face and meet them. You will be able to show them the Airbnb and guide them through any rules or expectations, or even assist them with certain things if needed. Many hosts prefer an in-person check-in because you get to build this personal connection. They feel as though it gives them a better chance of receiving a higher review.

Remote or self-check-in options have become more popular since they are more convenient for both the host and the guest. With self-check-in, you would need to install a key lock box or smart lock on your Airbnb. A key lock box is simply a box in which you place the key that you lock using a code. You would then give the guest the code so they could access the key. With a smart lock, they would use a code to open the door of the Airbnb in order to get access. You would change the code for each new guest to enhance safety. Once the guest checks out, you can change the code so they no longer have access to the property.

This is definitely a less personal way to check in. However, there are many benefits to it. Doing an in-person check-in means that you have to be available at a certain time to check the guests in. This can be incredibly inconvenient, and if the guests are late or something unexpected happens, then you could potentially be wasting a lot of time. From the guest's perspective, it means they are limited to a specific time when they can check in and check out. Only when you are available to come and check them in and out will they be able to do so. This lack of flexibility makes the process a bit more difficult for everyone involved.

When using the self-check-in option, you need to ensure the communication is on point throughout the whole process. You will not have the opportunity to talk to your guests when they check in. This means you should send your guests a message or an email with detailed check-in instructions to smooth the process. Make sure they know what the code is and how to unlock the lock box or use the smart lock. You should still be on standby, just in case something goes wrong and they need your assistance. No technology is fully proven, so it is important to be available should something happen.

On top of all of this, you also need to make sure your guests know how to use the items in the home so they are not confused about anything. Things that you may think are common knowledge might not be for them. Since you are not there to answer their questions, having detailed instructions is really helpful. Make a book or pamphlet with instructions for the different technologies and electronics in the house. You might also want to place instruction sheets next to the relevant electronics and appliances. This does not have to be in an email since this can be in the actual home and will make it easier for them to know what instructions are for what thing.

You would also want to send them clear checkout instructions. You can do this with the check-in email you sent them, but you can also remind them when they check out. This should make things a lot smoother for them since it is easy to forget when on vacation. You will definitely have to be more intentional with your communication when you allow self-check-in, but it does make things a lot easier. You also have the opportunity to get better reviews because your guests can handle the process smoothly. As long as the communication before and during this day has been good, you don't have to worry about getting negative reviews for not being there in person for check-in. In fact, many people prefer a self-check-in, as it is a lot quicker and allows them to check in early in the morning or late in the evening if they need to.

DEALING WITH PROBLEM GUESTS

The dreaded problem guest! If you have been in the Airbnb business for a while, you have probably had a run-in with a problem guest. This is someone who is just a bad Airbnb guest and causes unnecessary issues for you. The good news is that most Airbnb guests tend to take care of the property and obey the rules. However, a small percentage of them can cause huge difficulties for you.

Learning how to deal with these guests is essential to running your Airbnb business. At the end of the day, a guest is a guest, and you want to handle the situation properly so you don't get any negative reviews. On top of that, you want to deliver excellent service as much as is within your control. This may mean you have to go a little above and beyond what you normally would to de-escalate the situation and make sure your guest is happy.

Instant Book is a great function because it allows a guest to book without you needing to confirm. It makes the whole process a lot easier, but there is a catch. When you manually confirm an Airbnb booking, you get to check their profile to see if there are any red flags. Instant Book does not allow this. If you are worried about getting a problem guest, you might consider turning off the Instant Book function and just making sure that you are on point with guest inquiries and confirming bookings. It is also important to note that reviews tend to be subjective, which means that you have to use your discretion. Sometimes, a host might give a guest a bad review that wasn't warranted in the first place. However, it is a good idea to be cautious of guests who do have negative reviews.

The next thing you need to do is make sure that your house rules are clearly laid out. Indicate that by staying at your Airbnb, they agree to the rules and terms of doing so. This means you can hold them liable for not following the rules you have established. In many cases, it is not that the guest is disrespectful, but you must remember that you could get people from various cultures, cities, and countries. The way they do things may be completely different from the way you do them. This is why you need to make sure that your expectations are clear so that everybody's on the same page. The rules that you sent out should be easy to understand and simple so there is no miscommunication. You will need to communicate this upon booking and then again when checking in. If they do not agree or don't like the rules, they simply will not stay with you, and you have avoided a bad situation.

If you encounter a situation where a guest is breaking the rules or causing a problem, you will need to deal with it directly. Many times, it could be a case of miscommunication or them simply not understanding. It is always best to communicate directly with your guests rather than getting other people involved. In many cases, you will be able to come to some agreement and move past the situation. In a dispute or disagreement, it can be easy to go on the defensive, but it's important not to blame or judge a guest. That could turn out badly for you, so handling the situation diplomatically is essential. Understand where they are coming from and what they need. It is usually best to be flexible to find a solution to the issue a guest is facing. You can offer solutions, and usually, you will come to some sort of middle ground or agreement. The main goal is to make sure your guest does not get overly emotional or upset. This could lead to irrational behavior that can be difficult to de-escalate. You need to be the calm and stable one, and if you feel that things are getting out of control, it may be best to take a step back and come back to the conversation in a few minutes. You can always talk to someone else if you need to vent, but make sure that this does not happen when you are with the guest.

If you end up in a situation where there is no middle ground and the guest is simply not listening, then you can escalate it to Airbnb. They are usually good at handling these situations. If it is a terrible situation where there may be legal issues, then you could possibly get the authorities involved. However, this is a very rare case, so you shouldn't be too concerned about that. Just remember that having the guests' best interests in mind is going to help you deal with any situation that arises in the most constructive way possible. It gives you the best chance of having a happy guest while still sticking to your standards. It might be a good option even if you have to make a few compromises until the guest leaves. You can then never allow that guest to book with you in the future, so you will not need to deal with the situation again.

Mastering communication is just one aspect of running a successful Airbnb. It allows you to make sure that you and your guests are on the same page. This will give your guests a better experience and ensure your standards are met. But how can you manage all these tasks without consuming your entire day?

AUTOMATION AND TIME MANAGEMENT

Automation is the future of Airbnb because it makes the entire process a lot easier for the host. When you are an Airbnb host, you will have to do quite a few things on repeat. This can get quite tedious and, frankly, annoying. Finding ways to automate these aspects makes the process easier for you so you can focus on other things. Automation is especially important for those who have multiple properties.

AUTOMATING RULESETS

When you have multiple listings on Airbnb, you can access certain Pro Tools features. This allows you to create pricing and availability rules that can be saved and applied to all or some of your listings. It makes it a lot easier to run your Airbnb business because you don't have to keep doing the same things over and over again. Let's dive a little bit deeper into rule sets and how they work. A rule set is basically a set of parameters and rules for a specific action or thing. You will be able to name your rule set and then set the rules for how you would like things to change based on those rules.

Let's say you want to create a rule set for your nightly price. You could set a rule for adjusting the price per night based on the time of year. Your price could decrease by 10 percent during the weekdays or during low travel seasons. You may also want to create a rule set where a discount is automatically applied if the guest stays longer than a certain number of days. Other rule sets you could use are to give last-minute discounts as the day draws closer or an early bird discount if they book well in advance. You can also set things like check-in and checkout requirements, where you choose the days that a guest is able to do this. You can then apply your rule set to one or all of your listings, and it will change your current pricing and availability settings based on that.

The rules will only be applied when needed. If you have set a rule that there is a 20 percent discount on last-minute bookings, the 20 percent discount will automatically be applied to your pricing as the day draws nearer. You won't have to do anything; it will just automatically change on the Airbnb platform. When somebody books at the last minute, they will get this discounted rate. You don't have to worry about manually changing the pricing.

Using rule sets makes things so much easier. When you have multiple properties, it becomes very difficult to track exactly what is going on. You will have bookings for certain days and times based on the property, so this means there are multiple calendars to manage. You will probably be using a similar strategy across all of your properties, so using a rule set means that you don't have to be actively involved. You can develop your strategy and then just implement it across the board. You can also set rules for specific properties if you have different strategies for each one.

SCHEDULING AND AUTOMATING GUEST CHECK-INS

We touched on self-check-in in the previous chapter. This is a form of automating guest check-ins, so you don't have to be available in order for your guests to check into the Airbnb or check out when their stay is done. First, you will need to ensure you have the right equipment to automate the check-in process. This means you'll need either a smart lock, keypad, or lock box so your guests can get into the property.

The type of tool you use for self-check-in depends on your budget and what you feel is going to work best for you. Lock boxes are a pretty inexpensive way to do the self-check-in process. You'll just need to purchase a lock box and mount it on the wall near the property entrance. You will then program the lock box with a specific code that you will give to your guest on the day of check-in. They will enter the code and access the key when they arrive.

Another option is a smart lock, which is very secure and convenient. You do not need physical keys in order to use a smart lock, so it means you will have to replace the current lock with a new one. There are some smart locks that will attach to the lock that's already on the door. You will provide your guests with a passcode, and they can just enter it in order to access the house. This is actually a great option because it also eliminates the risk of the guest losing a key. These locks are great because you can integrate other software into them, such as being sent an automated message when guests check in. This message can be used to welcome guests to the property and give them relevant information about whatever is in the home.

Once you have your automated check-in set up, you just need to ensure the process is smooth for your guests. You are not going to be there to take care of them, so making sure the process is smooth is essential. You can set up a welcome box so they can easily find it as soon as they enter the Airbnb. This can be everything they need for their stay. You can have a guidebook or a house manual. This will have all the relevant information they need on this day, as well as how to use the electronics and appliances. You should also add things like the rules, Wi-Fi details, emergency contact information, and recommendations of things they can do in and around the area. This will make the guest feel a lot more at home and at ease.

Since you are not going to be there, it is important to make the welcome feel personal to them. Adding a few personal touches always goes a long way toward making them feel special and welcome. Providing a bottle of local wine or fresh flowers in the vase are nice touches that really add to the welcome experience. If the area is well known for a specific type of food or snack, then you can place these in a basket or on the counter so they can get the full experience of the area.

It is always a good idea to send your guests a checkup message at some point during their stay. This can be done in the morning after they check in because they will be settled. At this point, they might have a few questions, and you would be able to provide them with the answers. It helps them connect with you and shows you are an attentive host, even though you have not met them personally. You can automate this messaging process as well so you do not forget.

AUTOMATING OR OUTSOURCING CLEANING AND MAINTENANCE

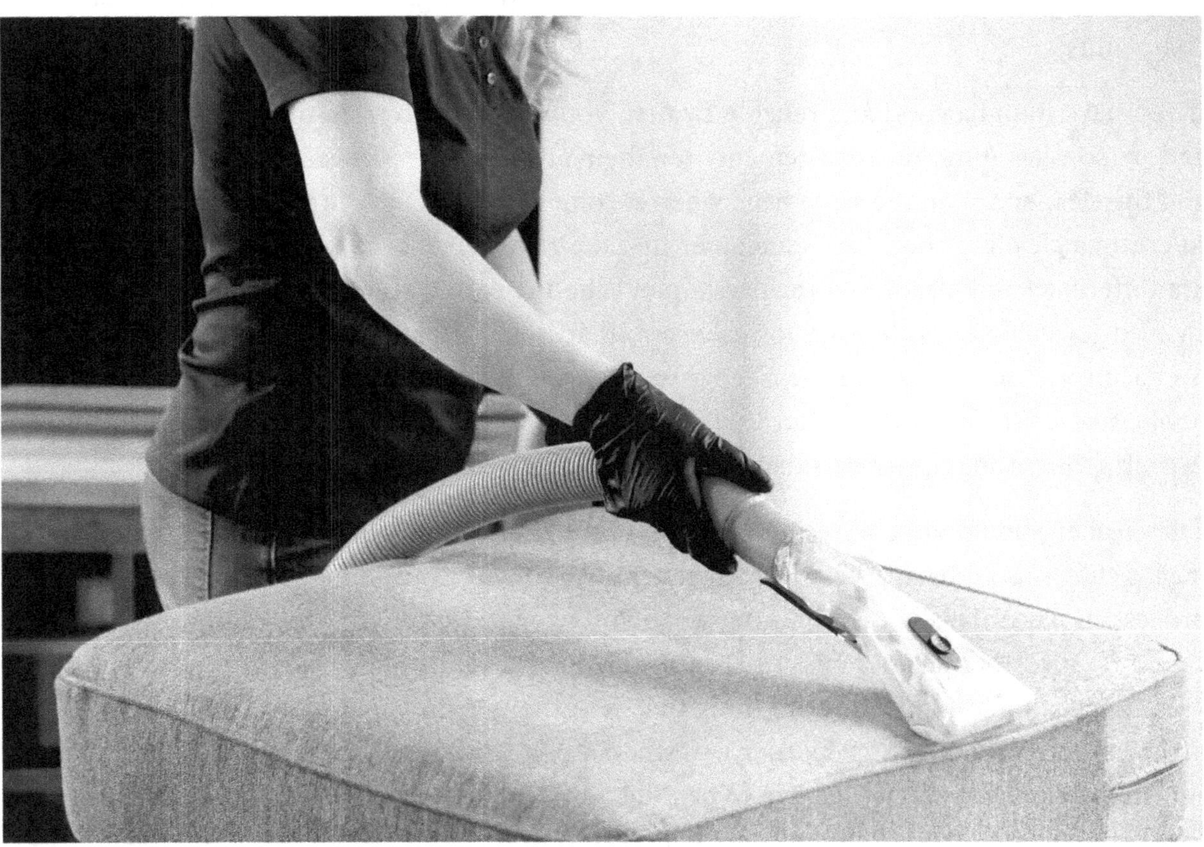

Keeping your Airbnb clean and well-maintained is crucial if you want your guests to have a good experience. If you look through reviews on Airbnb, most of the negative ones come because the house has not been well-maintained or is dirty. Cleaning and maintenance should always be at the top of your priority list, and they need to be done thoroughly so that every guest has an amazing time at your rental. If you have ever stayed at a dirty hotel, you know how uncomfortable it can be. You do not want your guests to feel the same way when they stay at your Airbnb.

As far as we have come with technology, we do not have automatic or robot cleaners just yet. Even if you do try to use some sort of robot or technology to clean, there's no guarantee that it will get everything done. You still need a human being to go in and check to make sure the property is clean and up to standard. The good news is that you have many tools at your disposal when it comes to automating your Airbnb cleaning and maintenance.

The first thing you want to do is hire a professional cleaner who will be able to get into your Airbnb and clean regularly. You can hire one from a company or go online to find one. You might even know a few professional cleaners personally, and it will make it easier to trust them if you do. It is important to get a reliable cleaner who is going to do the job well. The whole point of automating your cleaning processes is that you don't have to be involved. You want to be able to trust the cleaner, as you don't want to be called on by your guests with complaints.

If you have found a good and reliable cleaner, you will need to train them. Every Airbnb host and person has different requirements for their properties. You need to make sure that you and the cleaner are on the same page when it comes to this. One of the best ways to do this is to create a cleaning checklist. Remember that the requirements for cleaning a vacation rental are different from cleaning a regular home. When it comes to an Airbnb, it is best that the cleaner goes above and beyond to make sure that it is completely spotless. Create a checklist for each room so it's easy for the cleaner to go through it and get things done. In my previous book, *How to Set Up and Run a Successful Airbnb Business*, we go through exactly how to get your Airbnb spotless and the aspects that many people overlook.

The cleaner should also be responsible for restocking the property for the next guest. This means they should have access to your inventory, so you need to have an inventory tracking process in place. This way, you know when you need to go out and buy more inventory and can make sure nothing goes missing. You can create a checklist on an app or even use a spreadsheet. You can make a list of everything that is in the inventory, as well as how many of each product there are. When the cleaner is restocking, they will simply update the spreadsheet to show the current number you have. When the numbers start getting low, then it's time for you to go shopping to replace the inventory. It is best to leave all the products in a place on the property where your guests cannot reach them, but your cleaner can easily access them. A locked cupboard or room tends to be a good option.

Now that you have all of this set up, it is important to make sure that the cleaner knows exactly when they need to go in and clean. This means they need access to your booking calendar. This way, they're able to see when people are checking out and when they're checking in. Make sure the booking calendar is as detailed as possible and includes the times your guests will be checking in and out. On the day of checkout or the day after, the cleaner will go in and clean the property as instructed. If there are any changes, you can communicate directly with the cleaner, but for the most part, the process should be completely automated.

On top of regular cleaning, you should also schedule deep-cleaning. This is especially necessary when you have many guests staying back-to-back at your property. Regular cleaning may not suffice, and there are always things that you need to get into. You can schedule this deep-cleaning when there is an empty space in the calendar. The cleaner can go in and take care of a few in-depth things related to cleaning and maintenance. This is actually incredibly valuable because it will help identify anything that needs to be replaced or maintained. Your cleaner can communicate with you if something has broken or is perishing. You will then have the information to go in and replace or fix it. These deep-cleaning sessions should happen once every few months, depending on how busy your Airbnb has been.

There is specific software that deals with this entire process to make things easier for you. It can automatically connect you with a cleaner and update your calendar on both ends so everybody knows what needs to be done. One of these apps is called "Turno," and it will handle everything for you. It is worth looking into.

Even though the entire process is going to be automated, it is still important that you be involved at some level. You will need to go in and check the property to make sure that the standards have remained the same. You don't have to do this often, especially if you trust your cleaner. However, doing spot checks every few weeks or months is always a good thing. If something needs to be changed or you want the cleaning strategy to shift a little, then you can do that or identify the problem when you are there. Overall, automating your cleaning makes everything so much easier and gives you a lot more time to focus on building a business and doing other things.

Automation and efficient time management are the backbone of a successful Airbnb business. Knowing how to do this effectively will make your life much easier. You will be saving so much time and effort. Another crucial aspect is making smart financial decisions, which we will cover in the next chapter.

FINANCIAL CONSIDERATIONS

Regardless of the type of business you have, it is very important to have a good financial strategy. This will help you take your business to the next level and ensure that your profit margins are as large as they can be. If you don't have a financial strategy, you can end up losing money in areas that you weren't even thinking of. A simple plan allows you to keep yourself organized and make sure that you are taking steps to reach a specific goal.

CHOOSING THE RIGHT CANCELLATION POLICIES

Multiple cancellation policies are available on the Airbnb platform, which is great. Choosing the right cancellation policy can have an impact on your finances. If you allow your guests to cancel up until the day they check in, this means that they do not have to pay, and it is highly unlikely that you will get somebody else to fill in that spot. This results in a loss of income. Another thing to consider is that if your cancellation policy is way too strict, people aren't going to want to book since there is no flexibility. Again, this could result in a loss of income.

Let's talk a little bit about your options when it comes to cancellation policies. Once you set up your listing on the Airbnb platform, you'll be asked to choose a cancellation policy, and there will be a brief description of what it would entail. Airbnb can change how they set up their cancellation policies, so it is always best to make sure that your information is up-to-date. However, we are going to go through the basics here so that you fully understand and can start thinking about your cancellation policy strategy.

The cancellation policies are divided into two categories. These are standard and long-term policies. You will use the standard policy when you are using your Airbnb to allow people to stay for short-term reservations. This would be less than twenty-eight consecutive nights. Long-term policies would be anything more than that, and they would override standard policy.

Underneath the category of standard policies, you have four cancellation policies. The first is a flexible cancellation policy where a guest can cancel up to twenty-four hours before the day and time of check-in. If they do that, then they will get a refund. If they cancel less than twenty-four hours before check-in, then you will be paid for the first night, but if they cancel after the check-in day, you will be paid for every night plus an additional one.

The moderate cancellation policy allows the guest to cancel up to five days before they check in. If they do this, then they will get a full refund, but if they cancel after that, you will be paid 50 percent for all nights booked that they didn't stay, plus an additional night. If they decide to stay for part of the booked nights, you'll get paid in full for each night they stay.

The firm cancellation policy entitles the guest to a full refund if they cancel more than 30 days before check-in. If they cancel between seven and thirty days before, then you will get 50 percent for all nights they have booked. If they cancel less than seven days before they are required to check in, you'll get 100 percent of the rate for every night. They are entitled to a full refund if they cancel within forty-eight hours of booking, but this only applies if they do so at least 14 days before they check in.

Next, we have a strict cancellation policy, which means that you will get 50 percent returned for all booked nights if they cancel between seven and fourteen days before they check in. If they cancel after that, you will be entitled to 100 percent of the nights. If they want a full refund, they will need to cancel within forty-eight hours of booking, which needs to be done at least fourteen days before the check-in date.

For long-term policies, you have two different cancellation policies. This is a firm, long-term cancellation policy where the guest can receive a refund if they cancel a minimum of thirty days before the check-in date. If they fail to do this, then you will get 100 percent for every night they spend at your Airbnb, plus thirty additional nights. If fewer than thirty nights remain on the reservation at the time and the guest decides to cancel, you'll get 100 percent of the remaining nights. The next policy is a strict long-term cancellation policy where the guest can be refunded if they cancel the reservation within forty-eight hours of booking, but this must be at least twenty-eight days before the date of check-in. If the guest does not abide by this, then you will get paid for every night booked, plus thirty additional nights from when they canceled. If the guest decides to cancel with less than thirty days remaining on the reservation, then you'll still get paid 100 percent for the nights remaining.

The type of cancellation policy you choose is totally up to you, but you should bear in mind that it has consequences. You will definitely attract more people with a more flexible cancellation policy. People won't feel like they are locked into something they are not sure they can commit to. Many Airbnb hosts choose a flexible cancellation policy since that generally attracts more guests. However, if you notice this does not work for you, then you can bump it up to a strict cancellation policy. This will protect your finances and make sure that you have enough time to fill the spots should someone cancel.

UNDERSTANDING THE ADDITIONAL FEES

There are multiple additional fees that can be added on when you have an Airbnb. This means there are other sources of income besides the accommodation rate you will be charging. This is a really important concept because you want to make sure you are maximizing your profit. Now, you don't want to just charge without a purpose. That can be really annoying for a guest. However, you should look at what you can charge or what additional services you can offer to your guests.

Cleaning Fees

This is a fee that you add on for the cleaning and turning over of your Airbnb. It is a one-time fee that the guest will pay. Typically, it will be included in the price the guest pays when they book. Since this is a one-time fee, it will be split over the days your guests book. So if your guests book for four nights, then the cleaning fee will be divided by four and added to each night's rate. This means that your guests will not be shocked when they go to pay and notice a fee added on.

Since the fee is added to the overall price, guests are able to filter the listing by the overall price, including fees. It gives them a more accurate idea of what they will be paying for their stay. You can charge whatever you would like as a cleaning fee. Just make sure you are not going overboard. Recently, Airbnb guests have not been happy about the cleaning fee. It is a good idea to keep an eye out on social media to see what people are saying so you know if there is a change to be made.

Some hosts prefer not to charge a cleaning fee and simply increase the nightly rate. This can work, but if you get shorter stays, you might not make enough to cover the cost of the cleaning. You also don't want to increase your nightly price so much that it becomes unreasonable for most people. A cleaning fee is just a one-time expense, so there is no danger of that.

You will need to decide how much to charge based on your property. A bigger house with multiple rooms and bathrooms should have a higher cleaning fee than a one-bedroom apartment. The average is about $50–$75, but averages can be misleading. Rather, have a look at the competition and see what they are charging. Remember to only look at properties similar to yours. This will give you an accurate idea. Another way to work out the cleaning fee is, if you use a cleaning company, to determine the company's fee. All you have to do is charge the company fee plus a little more for supplies, and that will be the cleaning fee.

Additional Guest Fees

When you set up your Airbnb listing, you get to set the initial prices and how many people it will sleep. However, you can also charge for an additional person. Sometimes, there is an unexpected guest joining them, or they have a small child who doesn't need that much space. It is important to note that your property will still have a maximum capacity and cannot accommodate more than a certain number. Sure, a person could potentially sleep on the couch, but when a guest is paying a fee, they may not be happy with that.

An extra person is an extra cost for you. Even if you don't have to add any extra furniture to accommodate them, there are utility costs, the use of toiletries, and more wear and tear. It is important to consider these things. You also don't want to charge too much for an additional person. The guest is already paying for the Airbnb. You can have a look at what your competitors are charging before you decide on your price. If you notice that the majority of your competitors are not charging this fee, it might be best to skip it. When people go to book and see a fee has been applied, they may be turned off and look for another place to stay. The fee is added to the price they see, so they should be happy with how much they are paying before they go to checkout. However, there is a breakdown of what they are paying for at the end, and this can simply turn people off when they see fees.

Pet Fees

It is becoming more common for people to travel with their furry friends. This means that if you do not allow pets at all, it could end up hurting your bottom line. This is especially true if you have an outdoor type of property where dogs are able to get out and explore, or people can take them for walks. It is important to note that you will not be able to collect fees on service animals. In most cases, a service animal does not include emotional support animals, so you are able to charge for them. Make sure you check the laws in your area. For example, New York and California prohibit charging for emotional support animals.

You will be able to charge a flat fee for the pet. This will cover additional cleaning and maintenance due to having a pet in the home. You can charge per pet or have one fee for all. It is up to you. You will need to decide what fee is going to work for you, but remember to not charge too much. Around $25–$100 seems to be the average, but it depends on your property. Bigger properties can charge more since there is more to clean.

There are risks to allowing pets. Not everyone has well-trained pets. On top of that, people have different rules for their pets. If you are allowing pets in your Airbnb, then it is a good idea to have some rules and guidelines for people to follow. Mention any areas or rooms that pets would not be allowed to enter, and if you don't want pets on the furniture, make sure to mention it. With this being said, it can be difficult to enforce since you just don't know what goes on when you are not there.

By now, you've gotten a firm grasp on the financial aspects of running an Airbnb business. Yet, maximizing profits isn't just about getting your pricing and fees right; it's also about ensuring you attract enough bookings in the first place.

INNOVATIVE STRATEGIES FOR BOOSTING BOOKINGS

"Innovation distinguishes between a leader and a follower."

— STEVE JOBS

Figuring out how to boost bookings is incredibly important. It can help you increase your income, possibly even double it. The good news is that many of these strategies do not even require that much effort or more money. You will need to put in some additional work, but the profit you can get from this is definitely worth it. You don't have to do everything in this chapter. Rather, look at what is realistic for you and what you can actually maintain. You still want to give the best service and quality to your guests.

SWITCHING TO PER-ROOM LISTING

Last-minute bookings can really help you increase your overall income. There are many people who choose to book at the last minute because of unexpected circumstances, so you can take advantage of this. In most cases, people who are booking last minute are not coming in large groups or large families. When a family or a group of people go on vacation, they typically have to plan in advance so everybody's schedule matches up. If you have a large property that can hold multiple people, you might be missing out on the last-minute booking market.

Thankfully, there is a way to still get into this market without buying an entirely new and smaller property. All you have to do is switch from renting out an entire home to a per-room listing. You have the option to divide up your property so that more people can stay at your Airbnb. If you have four bedrooms in your Airbnb, you can rent it out to four people. A single person or a couple who is looking for a last-minute booking would be happy to stay in this kind of arrangement since it would be cheaper. You would need to make your nightly rate lower than what it is for an entire property. Have a look at what people are charging in the area for one-bedroom apartments or per-room listings.

PET-FRIENDLY PROPERTIES

As mentioned in the previous chapter, there are many people who love to bring their furry friends along with them when they go on vacation. When you have an Airbnb, your main goal is to try to appeal to as large a population as possible. This will help you find a large number of guests who are willing to stay with you and pay your rates.

People who want to bring their pets are usually willing to pay a little more since fewer pet-friendly places are on the market. They are more likely to stay in an Airbnb rather than a hotel because there is more space. It is also usually cheaper to bring the pet along rather than book them into a kennel or hire someone to go to the house to feed and take care of it.

When you offer a pet-friendly listing, you'll need to make sure that the home is pet-proof. Just as people babyproof their homes, the same applies to pets. If you have any fancy little trinkets and delicate items in the home, it is best to remove them, as you don't want these things to break. You may also need to change your house rules to include pets. There might also be limitations on the type of pet that is allowed. For example, if you have a small apartment, someone would not be able to bring a large dog. You can put weight and size restrictions on the type of pet that you allow on your property. You should also stipulate that the pets who stay should be well-trained and housebroken. This should minimize the number of accidents that happen.

It is also important that you highlight the type of pet that is allowed on your property. Even though cats and dogs are the most common pets, not everybody has them. There are some exotic pets and some that are not traditional. If you're not happy to have these in your home, then stipulate the type of pet that will be allowed. In general, if you just allow dogs, you should cover most of the people who want to bring their pets along with them.

Having a specific section for pet rules in your guest book and on your listing is a good idea. This will help the guests know exactly what is expected of them and add some security for you so you can protect your property. Things that may seem common sense to you might not be for other people, so it is important to be very specific with your rules. Highlight areas where the pets may not be permitted to enter, and state whether you allow them to be on the furniture. Make sure you have stipulated how to get rid of dog poop and cat litter. You will also need to indicate how they should keep the property clean.

Next, you need to move on to making your rental pet-friendly. When you advertise as a pet-friendly place, you need to make sure that the pets feel just as comfortable as the people. You can provide things like food and water bowls, a dog bed, toys, and a litter box or litter pick-up bags. If there are areas that are off-limits to pets, then install some fencing or gates to cordon off these areas. Another good idea is to have removable and washable covers for the furniture. This is important because even if dogs and cats are not allowed on the furniture, there is no guarantee they won't be. On top of that, they could easily rub against the furniture and cause stains and smells to stick. If the next person to check in has allergies or dislikes animals, they might be offended and unhappy with dog hair on the furniture. Easily removable and washable covers mean that you can keep things clean. Remember, you are trying to include a lot of different guests and not isolate yourself to just a pet-friendly Airbnb.

Another thing you can do is charge a higher security deposit and cleaning fee when people bring their pets along. The risk of breakage is a lot higher when there are pets, and most pet owners are aware of this. Charging high-security deposits means you are protected and will have the money to replace something if it breaks. If nothing happens, you can simply give back the security deposit, and nothing is lost on the guests' part. You can only charge a security deposit if connected through an API. We will talk more about this later on.

It is also really important that you get the property thoroughly cleaned after pets have been in it. Even if you only allow families with pets to stay at your Airbnb, making sure it's clean for the next person is essential. Animals can get worked up if too many scents of different dogs and cats are on the property. Invest in some good cleaning products that will help remove any odors. These can be a little bit more expensive, and that's why you charge a slightly higher cleaning fee.

RENTAL ARBITRAGE

Airbnb continues to expand. This means that more people do want to get into it. Whether you are thinking of getting into Airbnb or you already have a property, you can take part in rental arbitrage. It allows you to get into property rentals without actually owning property. It makes it a lot cheaper to get started, so you can increase your income.

The basics of rental arbitrage are to simply rent a property and then sublet it on the Airbnb platform. We all know that purchasing a property can be incredibly expensive, and it is becoming less and less realistic for people to do so. Growing your Airbnb business in this way means you can build a mechanism to increase your cash flow without actually owning your property and putting down a huge amount of money to get started.

You will essentially be using the income from your Airbnb to pay off the rent every month. If you play your cards right, you will be able to make quite a big profit from doing this. Now, you have to make sure that your landlord is happy for you to do this. Some landlords are quite strict and may not allow it. You don't want to sign a lease only to realize that you are not able to rent it out on Airbnb. Being completely transparent with your landlord is going to save you a lot of time and stress. You will also need to ensure that you have insurance and are protected for things like damages and injuries that take place on your property. This is part of the

Aircover that Airbnb offers, but it is a good idea to get additional insurance to make sure you are completely covered.

If you have decided that rental arbitrage is something that you want to do, you need to start convincing your landlord to allow it. It is usually easier to find a property with a landlord that will allow subletting than to convince an existing contract to change. One thing to remember is that rental arbitrage is completely safe and legal, and if you follow the short-term rental laws in your state, county, or municipality, there is nothing for them to worry about.

Many landlords are under the false assumption that it is not allowed. If you come up with facts, then you'll have a better chance of succeeding. You should also show the landlord your strategy for how you plan to start an Airbnb. The risk is that they would want to do it themselves. That is why it is important to show why this is going to be beneficial for both of you since you will be handling all the work.

For example, you can let the landlord know that you will need to take much better care of the property than if you were living there. The goal is to make the most profit through Airbnb, which means giving your guests high-quality service. You will need to ensure that the amenities are working well and that your home is completely presentable, neat, and clean. On top of that, you can assure your landlord that they will be paid on time every month because you'll be running a lucrative business through the property. Since your income comes from renting out space, it will be easy for them to understand that you always have money to pay on time.

Your landlord may be concerned about the noise due to guests being in and out. They do not want to deal with this kind of disruption, so you need to reassure them that there will not be noise or parties happening in your Airbnb. There are ways that you can monitor this, such as by using noise tracking technology or stipulating there should be no noise past a certain time at the Airbnb. You will be able to enforce the rules with your guests to make sure they stick to them. Otherwise, there could be consequences.

You are presenting a strategy that will be a win-win for everyone involved. If they are already renting out their property on a long-term basis, they likely do not want to be as involved. Short-term rental means that you will need to be involved all the time to turn over the property and ensure the guests are happy. The landlord does not have to worry about any of this because you will be taking care of everything and making sure the property is well cared for.

While these innovative strategies can certainly boost your bookings and revenue, they can also introduce new risks to manage. In the next chapter, we will delve into risk management and policies to ensure your Airbnb business is not only profitable but also secure and sustainable in the long run.

RISK MANAGEMENT AND POLICIES

When you have an Airbnb, it is important to manage risk. There are many situations that can pop up that could cause you direct and financial harm. You don't want to be put in that position, as it can be demotivating. You can avoid most of it if you put the right measures in place.

SETTING HOUSE RULES AND SECURITY DEPOSITS

Let's first talk about house rules. This is mission-critical when you run an Airbnb. You want your guests to clearly understand what they are allowed and not allowed to do. What may be second nature to you might not be to others. Remember that people will be coming from all over the country and the world. There are different cultures and ways of doing things. If you leave things unexplained, there is no telling what will happen.

The type of rules you set will also determine the type of guests you attract. Every guest will be different, and it is important to consider why they are coming to stay with you. What might attract one guest to your Airbnb could repel another. It is also about respecting your guests. If your rules are too strict, then people will not want to stay with you. When someone is on vacation, they do not want to have a curfew, be unable to relax, or feel too restricted. You will need to filter your house rules so you stick to the ones that are actually important. If the list of rules is too long, they will likely not bother reading it. Then, they will not stick to the rules, which can cause problems. Your house rules should not be pages and pages long. Understand what matters and what you can just skip.

What you can do is set a few categories for your rules and then simply explain them within those categories. It will make it more manageable, and they will know the basics even if they do not read the full rules. Let's review a few categories and what can fall under each one. The first would be off-limits areas. There will be areas on your property that you might not want your guests snooping around. You would lock these, but it is also good to put a note in your rules. If the guests are bringing along pets or children, you might want to stipulate specific areas that should be restricted to them for their safety. You might also have storage areas, areas under construction, or general places you just don't want your guests in. Make a list of these areas under the heading of prohibited areas.

The next category would be smoking. It is up to you whether you allow smoking on your property. If you do allow it, it would be best to have designated smoking areas so your guests don't smoke anywhere they want to, which could ruin your furniture or worse. Remember that the smell of smoke is a turn-off for guests who do not smoke, so you do not want the smoke to stick to your furniture. Smoking areas should always be outside. Another category to consider is social events and parties. These can get out of hand very quickly and lead to injuries and damage to your property. If this is a big concern for you, then you can ban them entirely. You could also set rules and parameters if you do allow gatherings or parties.

Further categories would be extra guests and noise. An extra guest is an extra cost to you since they will be using the utilities and amenities. If extra guests are allowed, there should be an additional cost for them to stay the night. You can also set a limit on how many visitors can come by in a day. For noise, it will depend on where your Airbnb is situated. If it is in a remote area, it may be okay to be more easygoing. However, in a busy or residential area, there will be noise restrictions. You can set quiet hours if necessary and give general guidelines to keep the noise down.

The final category is trash. Every area and country has a different way of handling trash, which is why it is important to have guidelines and rules set out. There may be specific recycling rules in your area, so make sure your guests know about them and are able to follow them. You might also want to indicate that trash should not be left inside the property and should be properly disposed of in the designated trash containers.

There are plenty of other rule categories that you can highlight. It all depends on you and what you think is necessary. For example, specifying rules for appliance usage could be a good idea if you have specialized appliances that require specific handling.

You don't have to make these rules too long, as wordiness confuses people. Clear and concise instructions will serve you best.

Let's move on to security deposits. These are taken to cover any potential breakages or damages. The guest pays it to you, and you give it back to them in full if no damage has occurred. You cannot take a security deposit on the Airbnb platform without using API-connected software. This allows you to access the offline fee option on the platform. In other scenarios, you will not take a security deposit but instead request reimbursement for the damage caused by the guest. This will be done through the platform, and the guest's payment method will be charged. Then you will get the money for it.

Regarding damages and breakages, it is important to ask the guest first. Blindsiding them with a reimbursement request could end badly. You should always check the property as soon as you can after checkout. Make sure everything is there and accounted for. Having an inventory list for your property and all the rooms really helps. You will be able to keep track of all your items. You will be able to figure out if something is missing or broken quite quickly and can send in the reimbursement request. If you have taken a security deposit, you will check the room or home and then send the money back to them if there are no issues. If there was a problem, you could take the amount needed and send back the rest. It is a good idea to send the guest a message or email highlighting why you have issued the reimbursement or taken from the security deposit so that everyone is on the same page.

AIRBNB'S AIRCOVER

Insurance is an important part of every business, and even more so when you have a rental property. Accidents or issues can happen, and then you will need to foot the bill. This can be really expensive. Many businesses have gone down in situations like this. Most people simply do not have the money to cover large problems. Insurance steps in to help cover costs and protect you.

With Airbnb, every host has access to AirCover. It covers both liability and property damage and is automatically applied to every host. This means there are no extra steps involved. You can also get other types of insurance on your own, but AirCover will always apply. You will need to file a claim in order to get paid. The team at Airbnb will review this, and you will get a response in due course.

The property damage protection is called Airbnb Host Damage Protection. You get up to $3 million in protection for any damage caused by your guests, their visitors, or pets. The damages need to have taken place during the time between check-in and checkout. This protection also includes loss of income if the damage caused by the guest forces you to cancel future bookings. It is quite comprehensive, and it does get updated every so often. It is a good idea to go onto the Airbnb website and have a look at what it covers so you are fully prepared when the time comes. It is always best to submit a claim as soon as possible after the incident.

Getting additional insurance to cover the areas that AirCover does not cover might be a good idea. For example, AirCover does not cover damage caused by natural disasters. This means that if there were an earthquake and your property was damaged, you would have to pay cash for the repairs. In this case, it is best to get additional insurance so you are fully covered and don't have to worry about it.

Under AirCover, you also get Host Liability Insurance. This insurance program helps cover any legal responsibility you have as a host and also covers anyone who helps you, should there be some sort of issue on the property. This includes a guest or third-party getting hurt on your property or something of theirs being damaged or stolen during their stay. This insurance program gives you liability coverage for up to $1 million.

This type of insurance has been recently updated, and there are specific things it will cover. Just as with the previous type of insurance, it is important to have a look at the Airbnb website to see exactly what is covered and what is not. In general, any kind of bodily injury to the guest or other people on your property, or damage to their property while they are checked in at your Airbnb, will be covered. On top of that, it will cover damage that your guest has caused to a common area of a neighboring property. If damage has been caused but not by accident, this will not be covered. Any purposeful damage that is caused to your property by the guest is not covered. However, this is covered by the previous type of insurance.

When it comes to AirCover, it is important to understand exactly what is protected and covered. Many people get upset with AirCover simply because they do not understand the rules or what it will cover. In general, it works like many other types of insurance you can get from an insurance company. However, there are limits to what it does protect you from and what it doesn't. Remember that when you put in a claim for coverage, someone will go through the claim, do some research, and make sure that they reimburse you the necessary amount. This amount is decided based on many factors. This can mean that you don't get the results you want. For example, if you bought an antique lamp for $500, and the guest breaks it by accident, you may want to make a claim with AirCover. In your eyes, the lamp has appreciated in value, which means it has increased in value and is worth more now. However, the insurance team isn't going to take that into consideration. Instead, they will look at what you paid for the lamp and how long you've had it and then give you an amount based on that. You might only get $100 or $200 for the lamp. Sentimental value and potential value are not considered when it comes to almost any kind of insurance.

This is why knowing what to keep in your Airbnb and what you shouldn't is essential. Any sentimental or important items should be taken out, as you'll never receive the amount you believe is owed to you if something were to happen. At the end of the day, your guests probably don't even care about the antique lamp in the first place, so it's not going to add too much to your property. It is important to be smart with how you handle the layout of your property so that you can diminish the risk of accidents in the first place. Now that we have covered how to manage risks and safeguard your property, it's time to think bigger and go beyond the Airbnb platform.

EXPANDING YOUR REACH

Airbnb is a wonderful platform where you can get many benefits and tons of exposure. However, your rental property is a business first. Even if you want to be loyal to Airbnb, this might not be the best strategy for growing your business and seeking out more profit. Many different tools and platforms on the market could be really beneficial to you as you continue to grow. Considering these options could take your business to the next level.

LISTING ON MULTIPLE OTAS AND CREATING A DIRECT BOOKING SITE

Airbnb is definitely one of the larger property rental platforms. However, it is definitely not the only one. This means that just using Airbnb is costing you a few good opportunities. The goal is to reach as many people as possible so you can fill up your booking calendar. Many people prefer other platforms to Airbnb. They could be loyal to their preference, and the only way to hook them in is to be where they are.

OTA stands for online travel agency. Using multiple OTAs has tons of benefits. You get the chance to maximize your income and increase the number of bookings you get. This is the goal for most people in this business. While there are all these benefits that you can access when you use multiple different sites to promote your property, there can also be a few challenges. It is important to understand these challenges so you can navigate through them and make sure that you aren't caught off guard. You will need a good plan in place to manage the bookings for multiple sites and not get overbooked and confused. If you do not manage this properly, it can lead to some very unhappy guests who will not want to stay with you again. The good news is that there are many strategies and tools. You can use them to navigate these problems so you can get the most out of your property rental.

Different sites may need different strategies in order to be successful. There are very different requirements across the channels, so knowing what you need from each is important. You will need to optimize your listing. The better your listings are, the more clicks you will get in there, and more guests will want to book your rooms. If you spend time optimizing your listing, then you don't have to keep doing this. Great photos, SEO, an amazing title, and a compelling description are all going to play a huge part in making your listing look desirable and credible.

You also have to be prepared for the specific challenges that come with using each of the sites. Not all of them are going to be built as well as you would wish. You might notice there are things you like about each one, as well as things you dislike. It's never going to be perfect, and that's why it's best to learn how to navigate the issues instead of simply giving up. One thing you will have to consider is that you will be paying a commission on each of the websites you use. Placing a listing is usually free, but almost all of them will charge a commission for every booking made. The amount will vary; some can be up to about 20 percent. You will have to keep in mind the different commission fees that will be taken out of your nightly rate. Navigating this can be a bit tough, but you must understand the financial aspects of hosting on various platforms such as Airbnb, Booking.com, Expedia, and VRBO.

Once you have decided that this is the route you want to take because of all the benefits, you can start looking into getting a channel manager. This is a great tool because it allows you to easily host on multiple sites. It allows you to do everything from one dashboard, so you don't have to keep switching between sites, which would make the process more complicated than it needs to be. You will be able to publish your listings on as many OTAs as you would like. Since everything is available on one dashboard, it is easy for you to keep track of things. That means there is almost no risk of double booking across the various sites. You will have a calendar that you can see, and it updates on all the sites, so if somebody has booked through site one, the same dates will not be available on-site two. You will need to pay a fee to use this type of tool, but it is really worth it if you are trying to scale your business. With that being said, you don't have to jump in right away. It is easy to manage your listings if you are only posting on one or two rental sites, in which case you might not need a channel manager. Once you get to a point where you want to accelerate the growth of your business, you can consider signing up with a channel manager.

A Direct Booking Site

A direct booking site is something slightly different from what we have discussed already. With this, you'll create your own website so potential guests can go there to find all the information they need about your rentals. You will be able to market your property as well as accept direct bookings from your website. Instead of your guests using Airbnb or another site to book with you, they just need to go onto your website, and in a few clicks, they will be booked. This is how hotels work. With hotels, you can go to the actual hotel site and book your room from there. They have direct booking sites. If you want to see how this looks or works, you can go onto any hotel website and have a look.

There are many benefits to doing it this way, and it doesn't mean you cannot use Airbnb or other rental sites either. When you have your own website, you have full control over what you put on it. It becomes part of your brand, and your guests are able to see what you stand for and the quality of service you provide. If you have multiple properties, this is a great way to cross-market. Someone who had an amazing time staying at one location might want to book at another location as well. All they have to do is go onto the website and see all the different locations that you have properties in. They would expect the exact same type of service and quality each time they stay with you.

You can also use your website as a marketing tool because you get to use SEO, which helps people find you. You can use techniques such as creating blogs, newsletters, and social media to help build your brand through your website. You can put as much information as you want about your property and business on your website. When people search the internet, they will put in a few keywords. If you have these keywords on your website, you'll have a higher likelihood of showing up on the first or second page of the search results. This means that anyone looking for a property to stay in that is similar to yours would be able to find it easily.

Another benefit is that you do not have to worry about booking fees. With all other sites you post a listing on, you have to consider the commission you owe them. Since this is your own site, it's not a concern. All the money that is paid to you goes directly into your pocket. You can end up saving quite a bit of money this way.

You can hire somebody to create the website for you, but there are easy ways to do it using a website hosting provider. Typically, they will offer you all the support you need to easily build your website. You get to design it the way you want to, and you can get support as you need it. There are a few things that you have to ensure that you have. One of the most important things is a secure payment gateway. Whenever you purchase something online, you are usually redirected to a secure payment gateway. This ensures that both parties are protected, and that the money is transferred from one bank to another safely. It is also a good idea to make sure that your website is mobile-friendly because most people use the internet on their mobile phones. If the site is too difficult to navigate on a mobile device, they will probably click out and look for something else.

USING SOCIAL MEDIA FOR MARKETING

Social media is another powerful marketing tool at your disposal. Social media is also completely free. This means you can build your brand and market yourself without any monetary investment. With that being said, as you get more comfortable on social media, you can start looking at paid options that can boost your marketing strategy. Almost all successful businesses are on social media. That is because they all recognize how powerful a tool it is. Most people spend at least a few hours on social media every single day. Using it means that you get the attention of people you may not be able to connect with simply through a website or various property rental platforms.

There are different requirements that come with each type of social media platform. This means you'll need a different strategy for each one. On top of that, each social media platform shows a different kind of content and has different audiences. If you stick to only one type of social media, then you will only target a specific type of person. However, you want your reach to be as wide as possible. The good news is you can repurpose content and use it across multiple social media platforms. You might need to make a few tweaks here and there, but it is quite simple to post on various platforms.

When running social media pages for your business, you must ensure you have a plan. Pages that post consistently are the ones that get the most traction and attention. It also gives you a sense of credibility when you are constantly posting on social media. It can get overwhelming to post all the time, so one of the best things you can do is take some time to create lots of content. You can create posts and images and then simply save them as drafts. Then, once or twice a week, you can post on your social media channels. This should only take a few seconds, so it doesn't take much of your day. The best times to post are usually during the day on a workday. The truth is that there are far fewer people on social media on the weekend because everybody is busy doing things with their friends and family. People are more likely to be on social media during lunch hours and after work, which means your posts will get more views when you post at those times.

Facebook

Facebook is the original social media platform that people remember. Sure, there were definitely other social media platforms before Facebook, but Facebook has stood the test of time and continues to stand strong over the years. You can post your Airbnb listings on Facebook to generate more traction. You can easily connect your Facebook account to Airbnb, so it is easy to post your listings on Facebook. All you will need to do is go onto your Airbnb account and click on a feature called social accounts. Here, you can easily connect your Facebook account and be walked through all the steps to create a secure connection. You can also disconnect your account in the same manner if you find you no longer want it.

The first thing you want to do is create a business page for your Airbnb on Facebook. You can share information on your personal page, but that means the only people you'll be reaching are your direct friends and family. You want to reach a wider audience, so creating a dedicated page will help you do that. If you make a business page, you can also share that page on your personal social media if you want to. Having a social media page for your Airbnb means that you put forward a sense of professionalism to your potential guests. It is straightforward to set up a page. All you have to do is click "Create a page" and then follow the instructions.

Speaking about Facebook, I have created a Facebook group for Airbnb hosts to connect, share their experiences, and learn. There is so much to learn, and you can pick up some great tips from others. If you would like to join, here are the details:

Name: Airbnb Host Community

URL: www.facebook.com/groups/airbnbhostcommunity

QR Code:

Instagram

Instagram and Facebook are linked social media platforms. This means whatever you post on Instagram, you can also immediately post the same thing on Facebook. All you have to do is link the profiles, and you are good to go. That's a great advantage, as it requires minimal effort on your part. Instagram is a photo-based social media platform. Make sure you are taking high-quality pictures that you can post. You can then give a little description at the bottom and click "Share."

The great thing about a platform run with pictures is that there is a never-ending supply of content. You can give people a tour of your house, show your guests having a good time, and advertise other businesses in the area. The options are basically endless. With the new update to Instagram, you can also post video content in the form of reels. These get quite a lot of visibility if you can create content that people want to engage with. You can use the same content that you create on TikTok to post to your Instagram reel, so you're not doing double the work. We will talk about TikTok shortly.

LinkedIn

LinkedIn is a professional networking site that can also be used to market your Airbnb. Since LinkedIn is a more professional network, it is definitely more trusted, and you are more credible when you have a LinkedIn profile. It can also help you connect with people who are in the same industry as you. This can help you be part of a community where you can share ideas and grow your business in a completely different way. You can connect with other businesses that inspire you and that you want to follow. This helps you get other ideas so you can continue learning and becoming better in your field. While this may not be a strictly Airbnb marketing or social media platform, you can use it to grow your brand and connect with people who can help you build your business in the future.

TikTok

TikTok is one of the newer social media platforms, but it has grown so fast in its 7 years of existence that it is actually crazy.

With TikTok, you can post short-form video content. This takes a little more work than posting photos or status updates on other social media platforms. However, TikTok has the unique ability to make things go viral. If one of your posts goes viral, it means that thousands or even millions of people will see it. This is great exposure for your business. And don't worry, TikTok is not just for teenagers; there are millions of adults who are also on the platform.

When you have a vacation rental, you have access to travel content. Travel content is some of the most popular and watched content on TikTok. The younger and even the older generations love to travel and see various locations. If you are able to break into the niche market on TikTok, you will quickly gain a lot of traction and possibly go viral. It does take a bit of practice to learn what kinds of videos get the most views. However, a quick hack is to look at the songs that are the most popular on TikTok. If you use these songs and put them in the background of your TikTok posts, then you will have a higher chance of going viral and being seen. You can also post your TikTok videos on Instagram reels, which means you get more use out of them.

X (Twitter)

X, which was formerly known as Twitter, is another platform that you can use to market yourself on social media. The landscape has changed slightly since Elon Musk took over. There are a lot of changes taking place with the platform, which means that it may change the way brands use it to market themselves. With this platform, you will need to post short text content. This allows you to share information and your opinions on various aspects. You can post tips and tricks for traveling and staying at Airbnbs. This way, the content you post is valuable to a wide audience, and you have a higher chance of people connecting with it. You can also post pictures and videos onto the platform, so you're not just limited to text. However, it is a good idea to always include some sort of text, even if you post a video or pictures, since this is a text-based platform.

BECOMING A CO-HOST FOR OTHER AIRBNB OWNERS

Perhaps you are at a point in life where you cannot afford a property to post on Airbnb on your own. There is another option: You can become an Airbnb Co-Host. The owner of the Airbnb can decide what you have access to and can manage your payouts as well. Many Airbnb hosts do not have the time to do the work, which is why they would want a Co-Host to come in and handle most of the work for them. You will then get paid through the Airbnb platform because the host will decide on the payment split that works best for them. You can definitely negotiate if you need to.

It is important to remember that Co-Hosting is quite a bit of work. The reason you are becoming a Co-Host is to handle all the nitty-gritty aspects of renting an Airbnb. Each host is going to be completely different, so it is important to find out what they expect from you when you are Co-Hosting for them. If they give you full access to their Airbnb platform, it means that you will have access to the calendar, listings, messages, and transaction history. There are other options that allow you much less access. Some of you will only have access to the calendar; others will have access to the calendar and can message guests.

You will need to have a conversation with the host of the property so you understand exactly what your tasks will be. It is a good idea to create a resume for yourself so you can start applying for these jobs. Becoming a Co-Host is a great way to understand what is required to run your own Airbnb. It gets you a foot in the door so you can gain experience for when you host your very own property. You also get additional income from this job, which you can put towards saving for a property. In most cases, this can be a part-time job, depending on how many properties the owner has and how much work they want you to put in.

With all of this being said, you could also get a Co-Host on board for your Airbnb. If you find the work too much for you to handle, you can get a friend, family member, or someone else to become a Co-Host on the platform for you. It may make things a lot more manageable, and you will have a lot more free time and not have to worry about messaging guests and organizing the calendars.

We've explored some innovative ways to expand your reach and boost your income. But with increased scale comes increased complexity. In the next chapter, we'll delve into selecting the right management tools to help streamline operations, save time, and reduce stress.

CHOOSING THE RIGHT TOOLS FOR MANAGEMENT

Many people are getting into Airbnb and vacation rentals because they are so profitable. The industry is absolutely booming. However, this means there is way more competition now than ever before. In order to set yourself apart from the rest, it is beneficial to look into technology-based tools. Most property managers tend to rely on these tools to help them become more effective in their jobs. Knowing which tools to use can simplify the process and make you much more productive. This results in more income and easier management of your property.

PMS AND PRICING MANAGERS

In a previous chapter, we mentioned channel managers. These tools help you manage your listings on various platforms from one dashboard. In this section, we will be talking about two other tools that could be incredibly useful in your Airbnb journey. The first one is Property Management Software (PMS).

Making sure your property is up to standard can be a difficult task. It is even more so when you have multiple properties to worry about. Using property management software makes things so much easier to keep track of. It also allows you to incorporate automation into your property management. You'll get to manage things like maintenance tasks, revenue, guest communication, and channels, all wrapped up in one box.

Maintenance management is one of the most important things when it comes to running your own Airbnb. This is something that many people forget to do because it's not at the top of their priority list. However, this results in a loss of income when something happens that needs to be repaired. This is not something you want to happen to you, so having a maintenance schedule is so important. When you have proper maintenance management software, you'll be reminded to do various maintenance tasks that directly impact the quality of your Airbnb. It allows you to streamline your tasks and automatically assign tasks to different people and vendors. This means you know the schedules are being kept and that your property is well cared for.

Another important feature of property management software is that you get access to accounting features. Money management is one of the most important things to consider when running your own business. You need to pay for things, as well as make sure you have a good profit margin. Doing this without proper software can be really difficult, especially when you have multiple properties and sources of income to consider. An accounting system will allow you to have everything in one place so you can easily see it and work from there. Your financial decisions will be much more balanced, and you can make sure you have enough money for important things.

This leads us to pricing managers, which are great tools when running an Airbnb or any vacation rental. This tool helps you automatically price your vacation rentals to optimize your pricing strategies. This way, you can make the most money with the least amount of effort. It will take into account various metrics as it works out the ideal pricing strategy for you. So many programs have this feature; some of the best include Beyond, Wheelhouse, and PriceLabs. These can be fully integrated into most property management software, and that's why it is important to choose a good one.

Here are some PMS to consider:

- Avantio
- Hostaway
- Hospitable
- Hosthub
- Hostfully
- iGMS
- Guesty
- Lodgify
- OwnerRez
- Uplisting
- Zeevou

It is always important to do your own research and make sure you have picked the one that's going to work best for you. If you want to read and compare reviews, you can go to www.-capterra.com. You also have to consider the fees that come with using this technology and pick one that suits your current budget. You can always make changes later on when you have different needs. Plus, so many new types of technology keep coming on the market that you can consider.

INSTANT BOOK AND SMART PRICING

Instant Book and Smart Pricing are tools that are available on Airbnb. You can use them to help improve your property management and ensure you are getting the most out of the platform. Airbnb allows its hosts access to amazing tools that can really assist in their profitability. However, there are always advantages and drawbacks when it comes to this type of thing. You will need to decide for yourself whether these options are good for you, or if you need to seek out something else.

Let's start by talking about the Instant Book function. We have already mentioned this briefly in a previous chapter. With Instant Book, your guests can simply click and book without you confirming first. This is an amazing feature for last-minute bookings because it gives the guests security that they will have a place to stay when they book with you, and you don't have to worry about confirming before then. Not only that, but there is a filter guests can use to filter out properties that do not use Instant Book. This means your pool of potential guests will be smaller when you do not use this function.

As a host, you can receive same-day bookings when this feature is on. Someone can easily book a stay at your accommodation on the day they are going to arrive. You are able to specify when same-day and instant bookings are no longer available for that day. This means you can set a cutoff time, which makes it easier to manage. If you do not want to use same-day bookings, you can still use the Instant Book function; however, you will need to add an advance notice to your Airbnb listing. If you are using same-day booking, you may want to consider a self-check-in process so you do not have to be there to check your guests in. It'll make things a lot easier for you, and you'll still have flexibility.

Smart Pricing is another tool you can use to optimize your pricing strategy on the Airbnb platform. If you struggle with pricing, then this could be a useful tool. The tool evaluates relevant data from the property listings on Airbnb and then prices your property accordingly. It will automatically update the price depending on what is going on in the current rental market. This means if your area is in demand, you can increase the price to make more profit, and if there is a slow month, you can lower the price to still attract travelers who want a cheaper option.

It is important to note that Airbnb's smart pricing tends to set the price too low. This means you will end up losing income even though pricing is much easier to manage using the system. If this is your first time on the Airbnb platform and your property is new to the platform, then using this tool is great because you can attract people at a lower price. However, once you have gained some credibility on the platform, you may no longer want to use the smart pricing tool. There are a lot of gaps in this technology, so it is important to recognize that. It is definitely not one of the best pricing tools on the market. However, the better ones tend to be slightly more expensive. You will just need to weigh the pros and cons of using this technology versus another one. On top of that, you could manually do your own pricing and work on your pricing strategy. With all that being said, Smart Pricing is a good option for those just getting started with their Airbnb. Just make sure to monitor and check so that you know when it is time to move on to something different so you can make more profit.

This brings us to the end of our journey through the intricacies of running a successful Airbnb business. However, this is just the beginning of your own journey. In the book's conclusion, we will review our journey together, summarize key takeaways, and, most importantly, talk about your next steps to make your Airbnb business not just survive but thrive.

Help Another Airbnb Owner Out

As a fellow Airbnb owner, you know how difficult it can be when you're first getting started – and this is your chance to make the road a little easier for someone else.

Simply by sharing your honest opinion of this book and a little about your own experience, you'll show new readers where they can find the guidance they're looking for to see success with their property listing.

Thank you for your support. I wish you the best of luck with your business.

Scan the QR code to leave a review

CONCLUSION

A great way to make a huge amount of money in the rental industry is by using effective strategies. There are so many tactics to increase your profitability and ensure your business is as successful as possible. Whether you have just started out on your Airbnb journey or you have been in the industry for quite a while, the tools you have learned will help you increase profitability and make sure you are as productive as possible.

Even implementing one or two of the things you have learned in this book will greatly help you increase your bookings. Can you imagine what would happen if you used them all? I'm not suggesting that you jump in and try to do too much at once. It is usually best to try one thing at a time so you can implement it properly before moving on to the next. The truth is that many of these tactics require time and money. You will need to plan in order to implement them properly. That way, you can ensure you are getting the most out of the tools and tricks you have learned.

As you turn the final page of this book, you're not just closing a chapter—you're opening the door to a new era of growth. Take the first step, the next, and the one after that. Ponder the area you want to improve upon, and then create a step-by-step plan to implement your decision. Start taking actionable steps toward your goal. At the end of the day, if you do not practice what you have learned, then it won't do anything for you. Taking the right steps will always yield the best results.

I wrote another book, *How to Set Up and Run a Successful Airbnb Business: Outearn Your Competition with Skyrocketing Rental Income and Leave Your 9 to 5 Job Even If You Are an Absolute Beginner*. I started this book with a powerful quote, and I will use this same quote to sign off this book.

"The longer you're not taking action, the more money you're losing."

— CARRIE WILKERSON

REFERENCES

1Angel17. (2022, November 11). *Switch to LTR?* Reddit. https://www.reddit.com/r/realestateinvesting/comments/ys49hd/switch_to_ltr

6 creative ways to collaborate with local businesses at your airbnb. (2021, August 24). Mama Mode. https://mammamode.com/6-creative-ways-to-collaborate-with-local-businesses-at-your-airbnb/

7 steps to an unbeatable airbnb pricing strategy. (2023, February). Guest Ready. https://www.guestready.com/blog/airbnb-pricing-strategy-tips/

10 key benefits of market research. (2018, June 26). Turquoise. https://thinkturquoise.com/blog/market-research/10-key-benefits-of-market-research/

16 actionable ways to increase bookings during off season. (2022, August 14). Hostfully. https://www.hostfully.com/blog/more-bookings-airbnb-off-season/

70 relevant analytics statistics: 2021/2022 market share analysis & data. (2019, October 7). Finances Online. https://financesonline.com/relevant-analytics-statistics/

A step-by-step guide to pricing your place on airbnb. (n.d.). Padlifter. https://padlifter.com/free-tips-and-resources/pricing/a-step-by-step-guide-to-pricing-your-place-on-airbnb/

Airbnb automated messages: A guide to guest communication. (2020, October 23). Host Tools. https://hosttools.com/blog/short-term-rental-automation/airbnb-automated-messages/

Airbnb cleaning fee: Everything you need to know. (2023, February 2). Hospitable. https://hospitable.com/airbnb-cleaning-fees-heres-everything-you-need-to-know/

Airbnb cleaning fee: Facts and figures you should know. (2022, December 28). IGMS. https://www.igms.com/airbnb-cleaning-fee/

Airbnb co-host: Beginner's guide. (2023, May 9). Hospitable. https://hospitable.com/airbnb-co-host/

Airbnb house rules: Best examples and free template. (n.d.). Lodgify. https://www.lodgify.com/guides/airbnb-house-rules/

Airbnb instant book: Useful information for hosts. (n.d.). Lodgify. https://www.lodgify.com/guides/airbnb/instant-book/

Airbnb pricing strategies to boost your profit [master class summary]. (2020, February 3). IGMS. https://www.igms.com/airbnb-pricing/

Airbnb rental arbitrage [and how to succeed at it]. (2021, November 17). Hostfully. https://www.hostfully.com/blog/airbnb-rental-arbitrage/

Airbnb self check-in: 5 steps to automating the check-in process. (2021, February 23). Host Tools. https://hosttools.com/blog/short-term-rental-automation/airbnb-self-check-in/

Airbnb self-check-in: How it works and how to set it up. (2021, January 29). IGMS. https://www.igms.com/airbnb-self-check-in/

Airbnb smart pricing – should you use it? (2023, March 29). Floorspace. https://www.getfloorspace.com/airbnb-smart-pricing/

Airbnb tools: The complete list (2021 update). (2020, July 3). Airbnb Smart. https://airbnbsmart.com/airbnb-tools/

Amadebai, E. (2020, December 10). *13 reasons why data is important in decision making.* Analytics for Decisions. https://www.analyticsfordecisions.com/data-is-important-in-decision-making/

An in-depth guide to airbnb smart pricing [+ alternatives]. (2022, June 5). Hostfully. https://www.hostfully.com/blog/airbnb-smart-pricing-and-alternatives/

Analytics comes of age. (2018). In McKinsey Analytics. https://www.mckinsey.com/~/media/McKinsey/Business%20Functions/McKinsey%20Analytics/Our%20Insights/Analytics%20comes%20of%20age/Analytics-comes-of-age.ashx

Average airbnb prices by city [2022]. (2022). AllTheRooms. https://www.alltherooms.com/resources/articles/average-airbnb-prices-by-city/

Average daily rate (ADR) vacation rental metrics. (2018, November 26). AirDNA. https://www.airdna.co/blog/vacation-rental-metrics-adr

Average daily rate (ADR) vacation rental metrics | ADR calculation. (2018, November 26). AirDNA. https://www.airdna.co/blog/vacation-rental-metrics-adr

Booking lead time | vacation rental metrics. (2019, February 2). AirDNA - Short-Term Vacation Rental Data and Analytics. https://www.airdna.co/blog/vacation-rental-metrics-booking-lead-time

Caravitis, A. (n.d.). *How to build a direct booking website for vacation rentals for under $100.* Hosthub. https://www.hosthub.com/guides/how-to-create-your-own-direct-booking-website/

Cariaga, V. (2023, July 9). *Housing market 2023: Viral tweet says "airbnb collapse is real" — is now the time to buy a home?* Yahoo. https://finance.yahoo.com/news/housing-market-2023-viral-tweet-113009741.html?

Channel manager partners. (n.d.). Airbnb. https://www.airbnb.com/help/article/3304

Choose the right cancellation policy for you. (2020, February 5). Airbnb. https://www.airbnb.com/resources/hosting-homes/a/choose-the-right-cancellation-policy-for-you-19

Clark, R. (2021, June 28). *How to advertise your airbnb on facebook in 7 easy steps.* Lodgify. https://www.lodgify.com/blog/advertise-airbnb-facebook/

Consider your area and circumstances when pricing. (2023, May 25). Airbnb. https://www.airbnb.com/resources/hosting-homes/a/consider-your-area-and-circumstances-when-pricing-589

Dasgupta, N. (2023, July 7). *Importance of improving your quality on your airbnb listing featured.* Staah. https://blog.staah.com/featured/importance-of-improving-your-quality-on-your-airbnb-listing

Dynamic pricing strategy: Definition, types, benefits & examples. (n.d.). Paddle. https://www.paddle.com/resources/dynamic-pricing-model

Elon musk quotes. (n.d.). BrainyQuote. https://www.brainyquote.com/quotes/elon_musk_567298

Everything you need to know about the airbnb search algorithm. (n.d.). Hostaway. https://www.hostaway.com/airbnb-search-algorithm/

Freeze, P. (2022, September 20). *How to encourage repeat guests in your vacation rental.* Bay Property Management Group. https://www.baymgmtgroup.com/blog/how-to-encourage-repeat-guests-in-your-vacation-rental/

Fuchs, J. (2022, July 9). *Dynamic pricing: The complete guide.* Blog.hubspot.com. https://blog.hubspot.com/sales/dynamic-pricing#f

Hollander, J. (2023, February 16). *The 6 best airbnb pricing tools in 2023.* Hotel Tech Report. https://hoteltechreport.com/news/airbnb-pricing-tools

How do rule-sets work? (n.d.). Airbnb Help Centre. https://www.airbnb.com/help/article/2061

How does airbnb dynamic pricing drive revenue growth? (2021, May 21). IGMS. https://www.igms.com/dynamic-pricing-airbnb/

How does the airbnb cancellation policy work? (2019, March 29). Medium. https://medium.com/@airgms/how-does-the-airbnb-cancellation-policy-work-e5333b9541b2

How hosts on airbnb help support small businesses. (2020, November 25). Airbnb Newsroom. https://news.airbnb.com/how-hosts-on-airbnb-help-support-small-businesses/

How smart is airbnb smart pricing and should you be using it? (2021, March 19). IGMS. https://www.igms.com/airbnb-smart-pricing/

How to automate airbnb cleaning: 6 simple tips for hosts. (n.d.). Turno. https://turno.com/automate-airbnb-cleaning/

How to charge extra fees for services: A community help guide. (2016, June 3). Airbnb Community Center. https://community.withairbnb.com/t5/Help-with-your-business/How-to-Charge-Extra-Fees-for-Services-A-Community-Help-Guide/td-p/101736

How to get good reviews on airbnb | 5-star vacation rental reviews. (n.d.). Vacasa. https://www.vacasa.com/homeowner-guides/how-to-get-good-reviews-airbnb

How to get more airbnb bookings during the off-season. (2023, January 10). Hospitable. https://hospitable.com/get-airbnb-bookings-during-off-season/

How to prepare your airbnb for peak season. (2023, May 12). AirDNA. https://www.airdna.co/blog/how-to-prepare-your-airbnb-for-peak-season

How to set a pricing strategy. (2020, December 1). Airbnb. https://www.airbnb.com/resources/hosting-homes/a/how-to-set-a-pricing-strategy-15

How to set up an effective listing page. (2020, November 18). Airbnb. https://www.airbnb.com/resources/hosting-homes/a/how-to-set-up-an-effective-listing-page-12

How to supercharge your airbnb listing with instagram. (2019, October 14). GuestReady. https://www.guestready.com/blog/airbnb-hosts-instagram/

How to switch from entire home to private room. (2018, February 12). Community.withairbnb.com. https://community.withairbnb.com/t5/Hosting/How-to-switch-from-entire-home-to-private-room/td-p/614322

How to turn your short-term rental properties into pet friendly paradises. (n.d.). Guesty. https://www.guesty.com/guide/turn-your-short-term-rental-properties-into-pet-friendly-paradises/

How to use social media to advertise airbnb property. (2021, November 24). Hosty. https://www.hostyapp.com/social-media-and-airbnb-property/

InternationalPirate. (2022, February 3). *Any positive experiences with "aircover?"* Reddit. https://www.reddit.com/r/AirBnB/comments/sjusx2/any_positive_experiences_with_aircover/

Is linkedin helpful for your vacation rental? (n.d.). Hostaway. https://www.hostaway.com/linkedin-for-your-vacation-rental/

Johnson, D. (2020, February 24). *Why and how to do market research for your vacation rental.* Simple Vacation Rental Management Software. https://your.rentals/blog/market-research-for-your-short-term-rental-business/

Kemmis, S. (2022, May 3). *Unpopular opinion: Airbnb has become terrible.* NerdWallet. https://www.nerdwallet.com/article/travel/airbnb-terrible

Krones, T. (2023). *What is an orphan period pricing rule?* Host Tools Help Center. https://help.hosttools.com/en/articles/5105363-what-is-an-orphan-period-pricing-rule

Lauzon, A. (2022, November 29). *How to research an airbnb market and quickly find a good place to buy rental property.* Mashvisor Real Estate Blog. https://www.mashvisor.com/blog/how-to-research-airbnb-market/

Leavy, J. (2020, June 17). *How to deal with bad airbnb guests (5 tips).* AirHost Academy. https://airhostacademy.com/how-to-deal-with-bad-airbnb-guests/

McClymont, A. (2023, June 19). *Boost your airbnb success with strategic market research: Choose the perfect property to maximize....* Medium. https://medium.com/@astrid.mcclymont/how-to-choose-the-most-profitable-airbnb-property-through-market-research-b9f95a63fc61

Must-Have airbnb tools & apps. (n.d.). Hostaway. https://www.hostaway.com/must-have-airbnb-tools-and-apps/

NoPressureLife. (2021, August 9). *All the automation ideas. give me some time back!* Reddit. https://www.reddit.com/r/airbnb_hosts/comments/p0q9w9/all_the_automation_ideas_give_me_some_time_back/

Peña, R. (2022, June 25). *The ultimate guide: How to find rental arbitrage properties.* Airbtics | Airbnb Analytics. https://airbtics.com/how-to-find-rental-arbitrage-properties/

Ribbers, J. (2019, December 10). *7 ways to boost your bottom line with airbnb add-on services.* Get Paid for Your Pad. https://getpaidforyourpad.com/blog/additional-revenue-airbnb/

Rodriguez, A. (2022, February 20). *How to find out the airbnb demand in my area.* Mashvisor Real Estate Blog. https://www.mashvisor.com/blog/airbnb-demand-in-my-area/

Rogers, C. (2022, August 9). *Off-Season airbnb tips for higher bookings.* DPGO. https://www.dpgo.com/go/off-season-airbnb-tips-for-higher-bookings/

Scott, R. (2023, May 19). *Airbnb data and analytics to optimize your listing.* Beyond Pricing. https://www.beyondpricing.com/blog/airbnb-data-and-analytics-to-optimize-your-listing

Security deposits. (n.d.). Airbnb. https://www.airbnb.com/help/article/140

Seven ways airbnb hosts can increase revenues with a directory website. (2023, February 24). GeoDirectory. https://wpgeodirectory.com/seven-ways-airbnb-hosts-can-increase-revenues-with-a-directory-website/

Shirshikov, D. (2023, April 19). *Airbnb occupancy rate: What to expect for your property.* Awning. https://awning.com/post/airbnb-occupancy-rate

Should you list your vacation rental on multiple channels? Or stick to airbnb? (n.d.). Hostaway. https://www.hostaway.com/should-you-list-your-vacation-rental-on-multiple-channels/

Six ways that short-term vacation rentals are impacting communities. (2017, April 15). Granicus. https://granicus.com/blog/six-ways-that-short-term-vacation-rentals-are-impacting-communities/

Static vs. dynamic marketplace pricing - how to choose. (2022, July 1). StoreAutomator. https://www.storeautomator.com/blog/static-vs-dynamic-marketplace-pricing-how-to-choose/

Steve jobs quotes. (n.d.). BrainyQuote. https://www.brainyquote.com/quotes/steve_jobs_173474

Succeed at airbnb long-term rentals: Strategy and tips. (n.d.). Hostfully. https://www.hostfully.com/blog/airbnb-long-term-rentals/

Tamplin, T. (2022, May 2). *What is a financial strategy? | importance, types, and steps.* Finance Strategists. https://www.financestrategists.com/financial-advisor/financial-plan/financial-strategy/

The advantages of outsourcing airbnb cleaning to a professional service in toronto. (2023, January 25). UpMaid. https://www.upmaid.com/the-advantages-of-outsourcing-airbnb-cleaning-to-a-professional-service-in-toronto/

The basics of communicating with guests. (2020, January 8). Airbnb. https://www.airbnb.com/resources/hosting-homes/a/the-basics-of-communicating-with-guests-33

The best airbnb pricing tools in 2022 - maximize your profits with dynamic pricing. (n.d.). Floorspace. https://www.getfloorspace.com/best-airbnb-pricing-tools/

The importance of airbnb cleaning: Why a clean property is essential for providing a positive guest experience. (2023, January 3). Turnify. https://www.turnify.com/the-importance-of-airbnb-cleaning-why-a-clean-property-is-essential-for-providing-a-positive-guest-experience/

TikTok for vacation rentals: Fad or marketing opportunity? (2021, June 24). Rentals United. https://rentalsunited.com/blog/tiktok-marketing-vacation-rentals/

Top 5 property management software for airbnb [2023 guide]. (2022, September 21). Door Loop. https://www.doorloop.com/blog/property-management-software-for-airbnb

Understanding airbnb market research. (2023, June 22). IGMS. https://www.igms.com/understanding-airbnb-market-research-for-vacation-rental-hosts-a-guide-to-success/

Understanding response rate and acceptance rate. (2021, April 21). Airbnb. https://www.airbnb.com/resources/hosting-homes/a/understanding-response-rate-and-acceptance-rate-86

Understanding your market. (2023, May 25). Lloyds Bank. https://www.lloydsbank.com/business/resource-centre/business-guides/understanding-your-market.html

Using social media to market your airbnb. (n.d.). Hostaway. https://www.hostaway.com/using-social-media-to-market-your-airbnb/

van Eyk, L. (n.d.). *A landlord's guide to mid-term rentals.* Steadily. https://www.steadily.com/blog/guide-to-mid-term-rentals

Wahi, U. (2022, December 13). *How to craft authentic guest experiences by partnering with local businesses | rental scale-up.* Rental Scale Up. https://www.rentalscaleup.com/how-to-craft-authentic-guest-experiences-by-partnering-with-local-businesses/

Welcoming guests in person vs self check in - will it impact ratings? (2018, May 11). Airhostsforum. https://airhostsforum.com/t/welcoming-guests-in-person-vs-self-check-in-will-it-impact-ratings/22558

What airbnb aircover is and how it works. (n.d.). Hostaway. https://www.hostaway.com/airbnb-aircover/

What are short term rentals? (n.d.). Lodgify. https://www.lodgify.com/guides/business/short-term/

What is airbnb superhost status and is it worth getting? (2021, March 15). IGMS. https://www.igms.com/airbnb-superhost/

What is RevPAR? (2019). STR. https://str.com/data-insights-blog/what-is-revpar

What is the average airbnb pet fee? What is reasonable? (2023, April 15). BnB Facts. https://bnbfacts.com/what-is-the-average-airbnb-pet-fee-what-is-reasonable/

What to do when you receive a bad review on airbnb. (2014, March 21). Guesty. https://www.guesty.com/blog/handle-getting-bad-review/

Why you NEED airbnb dynamic pricing - expert tips. (2015, June 16). LearnBNB. https://learnbnb.com/airbnb-supply-demand-dynamic-airbnb-pricing/

Woodward, M. (2022, August 16). *Airbnb statistics [2023]: User & market growth data.* Search Logistics. https://www.searchlogistics.com/learn/statistics/airbnb-statistics/

Your airbnb pricing strategy SUCKS. (2014, August 2). LearnBNB.com. https://learnbnb.com/airbnb-pricing-strategy-sucks/

Image References

Distel, A. (2019, July 24). *Person using laptop and smartphone* [Image]. Unsplash. https://unsplash.com/photos/tLZhFRLj6nY

Dole777. (2020, January 24). *iPhone with social media icons* [Image]. Unsplash. https://unsplash.com/photos/EQSPI11rf68

Fauxels. (n.d.). *Group of Friends Making Toast* [Image]. Pexels. https://www.pexels.com/photo/group-of-friends-making-toast-3184193/

Fewings, B. (2018, August 8). *Colorful welcome sign* [Image]. Unsplash. https://unsplash.com/photos/6wAGwpsXHE0

Firmbee. (2015, May 29). *Person writing on paper* [Image]. Unsplash. https://unsplash.com/photos/gcsNOsPEXfs

Forseck, R. (2020, September 10). *Black and white dog laying on dog bed* [Image]. Unsplash. https://unsplash.com/photos/Mlrc9NwoZFk

PhotoMIX Company. (2016, Mar 17). *Documents on Wooden Surface* [Image]. Pexels. https://www.pexels.com/photo/documents-on-wooden-surface-95916/

Muza, C. (2016, April 17). *Laptop on table* [Image]. Unsplash. https://unsplash.com/photos/hpjSkU2UYSU

Trovato, G. (2023, June 8). *Woman vacuuming ottoman* [Image]. Unsplash. https://unsplash.com/photos/5TXz228u4eo

THE ULTIMATE REAL ESTATE INVESTING BEGINNER'S BOOK

ACHIEVE FINANCIAL FREEDOM WITH RENTAL PROPERTIES USING PROVEN FINANCING STRATEGIES AND WEALTH-BUILDING TECHNIQUES

INTRODUCTION

When you think about real estate investing or simply purchasing a property, it can seem like something only rich people do. However, this is definitely not the case, and one man's story highlights this. Shaun Conlon was a pretty average guy from Ireland. He came from humble beginnings and decided to move to Chicago to earn some money. He started working as an assistant janitor, which didn't pay much. He painted apartments at night to make some more money and kept up with his routine for a few years. He saved up as much money as he could and bought an apartment after a few years. He then sold his apartment and made a profit, which was highly motivating for him. He got a taste of real estate investing and decided that this was what he wanted to do. He kept his job, but he invested in real estate and began selling real estate as a side job. He did this for over three years and became a top real estate broker. Then, he landed his first job at a brokerage and continued to hone his skills. About four years later, he was able to open his own real estate investment firm. He now uses real estate as his primary source of income, and it all started from a humble beginning.

"I was an ordinary person who did some fairly extraordinary things. It's America. You can still do those things."

— SEAN CONLON

The story simply highlights that anyone can get involved in real estate investing. It doesn't matter if you have tons of money to play with or just a few dollars in your piggy bank. There are strategies and ways in which you can dip your toes in the wonderful pool of real estate. Before moving on, it is important to understand what real estate investing is in the first place. When you invest in real estate, you are essentially investing in properties. You are using real estate as an investment vehicle to gain profit. There are many ways to generate a profit through real estate, and throughout this book, we will dive into each one of these methods and topics so you can fully understand how diverse real estate can be.

The two major categories of real estate are residential and commercial. Residential real estate is the type of property people live in, and commercial real estate is typically used to generate income on a larger scale. We are going to dive more into these two types of real estate, and many others, in the first chapter of this book. Real estate is multifaceted, and it's important to understand all the different types of real estate as well as all the ways you can invest. The reason anyone can invest in real estate is that there are so many options out there. You can tailor your investment strategy to suit your needs and goals.

Another common concern that people may have about investing in real estate is that it seems too risky. Property is expensive, and if you're putting a lot of money into something, you want to have a guaranteed positive outcome. I would love to say that you are guaranteed to make a lot of money through real estate, but we must realize that any kind of investing comes with its own level of risk. That being said, real estate tends to be one of the most stable forms of investment since property has a trend of increasing in value over time. Now, there are a few things that you have to consider, such as the location, amenities, and type of property, but this rule rings true if you do your research and choose the right property to invest in.

You don't have to be a homeowner first or choose the perfect time in the market to start investing in real estate. Your property investment journey can start right now, and it can be fruitful and rewarding. In fact, the longer you take, the more you delay the potential benefits of real estate investing. While there may be many excuses that you can make to not take the plunge into real estate investing, it simply means that you are delaying your potential wealth-building. Real estate is a cornerstone element for building your wealth, and it's a tool you can use to help reach your financial goals and additional stability in your life and future.

By the end of this book, you should have all the tools, tricks, and knowledge you need to confidently invest in real estate. The goal is to give you a comprehensive understanding of real estate investing as well as practical and actionable steps. This book is not just theory; there are also actions that you can take to help push you toward the right real estate investments. Interactive learning tools have been incorporated throughout the book to assist you with grasping concepts and give you practical aid along your real estate investment journey. All of this will help you have confidence in your decision-making so you can forge a path to financial freedom.

This book has been designed on a three-part framework. This way, you can first build a foundation and then work your way up into other aspects of real estate investing. The first part is going to be building the base. This essentially means that you will be building a firm foundation for your real estate knowledge. In this part, there are two chapters, and the overarching topics discussed will be the types of real estate investing and how to finance your real estate investments. Part two is about mastering the fundamentals and has three chapters within it. These three chapters cover the metrics of valuation, risk assessment, and actually purchasing your property. Finally, we have part three, which is about making a profit and prospering on your real estate journey. In this phase, there are five chapters, and the topics covered are tax benefits and legal considerations, passive income, short-term rentals, long-term success, and wealth building.

All of these parts are essential to investing successfully in real estate. They will give you all the knowledge you need to walk into your real estate investment journey with full confidence. By the end of this book, you should be well-equipped and ready to go. So many people wish they had started their real estate investment journey earlier in their lives. Regardless of your current life situation or your financial standing, you are in a good position to start investing in real estate. Simply picking up this book and taking the first step in the process already puts you on the right path. This is exactly where you need to be to find success when investing in real estate.

I have guided people through the process, and none has ever regretted it. Investing in real estate is one of the most fulfilling, exciting, and rewarding journeys you will ever go on. You don't have to make all the mistakes other people make because you now have the handbook and the directions away from all the pitfalls. I have already written books on Airbnb and how to use short-term rentals to build wealth. I have done it myself and, through these best-sellers, have guided others along the process. If you are interested, you can add to the knowledge from this book with guidance from my other books. This could be essential reading should you want to become an Airbnb host. Here are the titles:

- ***How to Set Up and Run a Successful Airbnb Business:*** *Outearn Your Competition with Skyrocketing Rental Income and Leave Your 9 to 5 Job Even if You Are an Absolute Beginner*
- ***How to Unleash Your Airbnb's Full Potential:*** *The Complete Step-By-Step Guide to Maximizing Bookings, Rental Income, Setting Up Automation and Optimizations for Your Short-Term Rental Business*

If you have ever wanted to invest in real estate but were unsure how to do it, you are in the right place. From here, we will build the base with Chapter 1 so you can fully understand the different types of real estate investing out there. Next, we are going to move on to two different topics that will build a robust framework for you to continue on your real estate investment journey. So, without further delay, let's jump into the first chapter.

PART ONE

BUILD A BASE

TYPES OF REAL ESTATE INVESTING

Ninety percent of all millionaires invest in some form of real estate (Red Oak, 2022). This is an incredibly high number and demonstrates that real estate is a viable option for building wealth and creating financial security. If nine out of ten millionaires choose to add real estate to their investment portfolio, then this is something that a beginner investor or somebody looking to build wealth should also look into. It is clear that real estate is a fantastically valuable asset in your overall investing portfolio.

An individual investor can invest in many types of real estate. This makes real estate investing even more attractive because you can find a type of real estate investment that is going to fit you and your goals perfectly. In order to make the right decision, it is important to understand the different types of real estate that you can invest in.

RESIDENTIAL REAL ESTATE

The first type of real estate we are going to be talking about is called residential real estate. This is one of the most popular types of real estate investments since it is accessible to the average person. On top of that, any person who has purchased a property, rented, or is in the housing market would have some experience with residential real estate, making it much easier to transition into this investment vehicle. Under the umbrella of residential real estate, you can purchase different kinds of properties, and each has its benefits and things to consider before investing.

Single-Family Homes

When it comes to residential properties, a single-family home is definitely one of the most popular and most common varieties out there. Not only are plenty of single-family homes currently on the market but there are also many constantly under development. This means there will be even more being brought onto the market. As the name implies, a single-family home is designed to meet the needs of a family. There are many varieties of properties that can fall under the category of a single-family home, and these include freestanding homes, cottages, villas, and even mansions.

These types of properties are incredibly popular with couples who have a family or are looking to establish a family. The reason for this is that there are key features in a single-family home that benefit the traditional family lifestyle. This includes having a garden, yard, or outdoor space for kids to play or adults to use for recreational and outdoor activities. These types of properties, specifically detached homes, also offer privacy because the homeowner would not be sharing space or walls with neighbors. The other benefit is that the homeowner has almost complete control over what they do with their property and can design and change things up as they see fit.

Multi-Family Homes

A multi-family home is more like an apartment or a duplex. With these types of properties, the people living within it will be sharing space and walls with their neighbors. From an investment standpoint, purchasing a multi-family home could be a good option because you can have multiple renters in one property, which means you are collecting multiple streams of rental income. Something that investors are doing with multi-family homes is called house hacking. This is when you stay in a portion of the property and then rent out the rest to a tenant. The tenant contributes to or covers the entire cost of the mortgage payment, which means you, as the investor, get to stay on the property for a fraction of the cost or completely for free.

Multi-family homes have a different target audience than single-family homes. Since there are communal living spaces such as gardens, lounges, and other areas, it may not be as attractive for larger families. These properties can be quite convenient to stay in, as many multi-family homes or apartments are close to city centers.

Condos

A condo or condominium is very similar to an apartment or a multifamily home, but these are typically situated in a larger building. Condos often offer more space than apartments and come with distinct ownership; each condo unit is individually owned, while apartments are usually rented. These types of properties have some shared amenities, but they do offer individuality, which means they are a blend of single-family and multi-family homes. There is a sense of community since many of the living spaces are shared, and you live in close proximity to your neighbors. On top of that, most condominiums are in desirable areas such as urban centers and cultural hubs, meaning the location is advantageous to many people, which can bring up the property's price.

Townhouses

With a townhouse, you are looking at a semi-standalone building attached to a collection of other houses or buildings. In many cases, a townhouse will offer a small yard, and you can think of a townhouse as a smaller version of a single-family home. There will be some shared amenities if the complex has a pool or communal gathering area. However, everything else is more private. Sometimes, a townhouse will share a wall with a neighbor but offer the separation of a standalone house. These properties tend to be more affordable because they are smaller than single-family homes and are usually lower maintenance.

Mobile Homes

When considering investing in property, a mobile home may not be the first thing that comes to mind, but it is definitely an option. A mobile home is essentially a living space that is movable. To move these types of homes, you need to attach them to a specialized trailer or truck. It will have wheels so it is easily movable from place to place. It is also important to consider that a mobile home is designed differently, so you must understand the ins and outs of your particular mobile home to know how to move it and take care of it.

A mobile home is definitely more affordable than other real estate options, and it offers the flexibility of moving from place to place. These days, you can get some pretty advanced mobile homes with different rooms and living spaces that offer a lifestyle similar to that of a traditional home. There is also the option of permanently placing a mobile home on a support system that will act as a foundation. To do this, you need to rent or purchase the land on which you place the mobile home.

COMMERCIAL REAL ESTATE

The next category of real estate investment property is commercial real estate. For a property to fall under the category, it needs to generate profit through rental income or capital gains. It typically does not include properties that people live in from day to day.

Retail Spaces

The first category of commercial real estate is retail spaces. If you go to a shopping mall, you will see many stores, and the shop owners have to rent out these rooms or spaces in order to sell their products there. A restaurant or any other business that you might find in a shopping mall is also located in a retail space. There are also retail spaces that are a lot bigger and stand-alone. For example, if you visit a huge store like a Walmart or Costco, it may be a big center that stands alone without other stores around it. These still count as retail spaces.

Office Spaces

Offices are another option for commercial real estate buildings. This still generates income, even though there is no direct buying and selling of items from the office space. These spaces may be small suburban office buildings where only one company works or an office park where multiple companies rent the spaces. From an investor's point of view, these types of properties can be a lot more expensive to purchase, as an office building is quite a large investment but also generates a large amount of profit.

Industrial Properties

An industrial property is typically located outside an urban or suburban area. These types of properties are used for manufacturing, assembly, warehousing, and a mixture of all of these. These types of buildings need to be customized for the type of operations that will be running within them. Industrial property needs to be quite large because of the nature of the work occurring within the property. Some special licenses and permits may be needed for an industrial property due to the type of activity that is taking place.

Hotels and Motels

Even though people stay in hotels and motels, they are still categorized as commercial property. This is because they provide a service, and there may also be restaurants, boutiques, and shops within it. There are many different types of hotels and leisure properties out there. These could include ones that are full service, which means there is room service and a restaurant on site, whereas limited service means it is likely just going to provide the room for the guest to stay and may not have room service or a restaurant on site. There could also be extended stay rooms or options, such as an area equipped with a kitchen so guests can stay for longer periods. Resorts are also in this category, and they offer both full service and a large amount of land where people can take part in many recreational activities.

REAL ESTATE INVESTMENT TRUSTS (REITS)

A real estate investment trust is a great option for those who are looking to dip their toes into the water of real estate investment. The truth is that many forms of real estate investment come with a hefty price tag. It can take months or even years to save up enough to invest in real estate or build up your credit so that you can take out a loan to invest. A REIT helps you invest in real estate without having access to a large amount of funds. On top of that, you don't have to physically buy or manage property in order to invest.

The aim of a real estate investment trust is to create a liquid investment out of an illiquid asset. A REIT will combine the contributions from multiple investors to invest in property. Then, the profit from these investments will be shared among all who have contributed. REIT can invest in various kinds of properties, including complexes, townhouses, hotels, infrastructure, office buildings, shopping centers, warehouses, and residential real estate. This means an investor can diversify their real estate investment portfolio by simply investing in one thing. On top of that, investors do not have to put a lot of money into getting started with real estate investing. This makes real estate investing a lot more accessible and allows you to invest and get used to the real estate market as soon as possible. Since this type of investment is managed by somebody else, not all your money will be invested in real estate. Some of your money will be put toward a fee for the management of your investment.

There are three main types of REITs: equity, mortgage, and hybrid. Equity REITs are the most common and are equity-based, meaning that revenues are typically brought in through rent charged to tenants. Mortgage REITs will lend money to property owners through loans or invest in mortgage-backed securities. Revenue is primarily generated from the interest earned on these loans and securities. Finally, hybrid REITs mix both of the above strategies into one portfolio.

DEVELOPMENT AND LAND INVESTING

Investing in land means purchasing the raw land that property can be built upon or used for other purposes to generate revenue. There are many types of land investing out there, so interested investors should understand what they want to do with it and what type of investment they are trying to make. Regardless of how you choose to use the land, if it's an investment, you must choose the right location. A terrible location will not have much value and will, therefore, be a poor investment.

Whether the location is good or bad depends on what you will use the land for. If you want to build a house on the land, then you need to choose a location that is convenient and close to everyday amenities that the average family would need. If you want to build a warehouse or some sort of commercial property, you need to ensure that the land you purchase is an ideal location. For example, if you are looking to use the land for commercial purposes, you need to ensure that it is easy to get to so that people can either shop, live, work, or participate in recreational activities there. Other uses for the land could be farming practices, such as raising livestock or growing crops.

It is also possible to purchase a piece of land and not do anything with it besides basic upkeep and then sell it for a higher price later on down the line. Land appreciates in value, so it will continue to increase in value, especially if it is in a good location. If you are planning to build on the property, then it's important to budget accordingly. Building a house or other type of real estate costs a lot of money, and it also means that you will need to get the right people on board to help develop that land. It can also take quite a long time because you will need approval and paperwork in order to get started. This is why purchasing land to start a development may not be the best option for a beginner investor or somebody who wants to see their returns as soon as possible. However, if done correctly, this can be one of the best ways to make a large return on your investment.

HOUSE FLIPPING

House flipping is getting more popular, and for good reason. The goal of flipping a house is to purchase a property, renovate it, and then sell it as quickly as possible for a higher price than you bought it for. When trying to make the most profit from this, many investors choose to purchase undervalued properties. The property may not have been taken care of, or there might be something wrong with it that has caused it to drop in value. The investor will purchase the property and make the necessary repairs to bring the property price back up. The newly refurbished property can be sold for more, and the investor makes a profit in a short amount of time.

When investing in this way, it is important to research and ensure you understand the property you are purchasing. If there is too much damage or the renovations are going to cost you a lot of money, then it's not going to be worth purchasing. Any renovation or additional cost needs to be less than the potential profit you could make from selling the house. The positives to taking part in this type of real estate investment are that you get to diversify your real estate investment portfolio and have an investment with a quick turnaround time. When it comes to real estate investments, few options offer you a quick turnaround time so that you can get your profit soon after investing.

While flipping a house could be a wonderful addition to your investment portfolio, you also have to take into consideration that it is a risk. The goal of flipping a house is to sell it quickly, but there are no guarantees. You will be taking a risk of some financial loss or having to hold the property for longer than you might expect. You will also need to do your due diligence in terms of research when it comes to the renovations, as you need to make sure that you have enough finances available for the renovation costs. It is always a good idea to plan to spend more money than you think you'll need, as there may be unexpected costs along the way. Planning is always key in any kind of real estate investment, and flipping is no exception.

BUY, REHAB, RENT, REFINANCE, REPEAT (BRRRR)

While this acronym might be funny to say, this is a very legitimate method in real estate investing. It follows a very similar principle to house flipping, as you will purchase a distressed property and then rehab it to make a profit. However, instead of selling the property, you will rent it out. From here, you will then refinance the property by taking a cash-out refinance. With this money, you will buy other properties that need to be refurbished and rented out. The great thing about this method is that you use little of your money to invest. You are using the money from the refinancing to purchase a new property, and since you are renting out your properties, you are constantly making an income.

The goal is to build on the momentum and continue to repeat the process so that you can build a robust real estate portfolio. There are definitely risks when it comes to this method, as investing in a distressed property may not always be as easy as we would like. There could be damages and issues with the property that you cannot see at first glance, so you must get a professional to inspect the property before you make a purchase. This way, you are completely aware of what needs to be done and whether it's going to be worth it for you to purchase the property. You should also consider any legal limitations that specific areas or properties might impose for certain types of renovations or changes. Having a legal professional on your team is really going to help you and save you a lot of time and money. However, if you can find a good property to get started, then you can continue building on this and bring in a satisfying amount of income through this investment method.

VACATION RENTAL PROPERTIES

With the rise of vacation rental websites, such as Airbnb, it has become a lot easier for people to market their vacation or short-term rentals to the public. This can make you a lot of money if you are willing to open up your property to tourists and travelers. When you rent out your property as a vacation rental, it is essentially private accommodation for a short-term stay. It differs from a hotel, and you can decide what kinds of amenities you offer to your guests. Since this is a short-term rental property, it needs to be fully furnished so that people can have a comfortable stay. On top of that, you will need to ensure that you are giving your guests an enjoyable experience because they can rate your property and the service they get on many of the vacation rental websites. You must maintain an excellent reputation because word-of-mouth is a great marketing technique, and you want people to talk positively to their friends and family so you can get more bookings.

When it comes to a vacation or short-term rental, knowing what you are offering is important. Location is also really important, as you need to have a property somewhere where people actually want to stay—for example, a cottage on the beach or an apartment in a big city. If you have a property close to any popular tourist destination, then you are already a suitable candidate to have a vacation rental. If you want to purchase a property as a short-term rental, then make sure you choose the right location and pick somewhere where people will travel and want to stay.

Since there are people in and out of your property, you can make more money than if you rented out the property on a long-term basis. You could have multiple tenants or guests within a month and make a huge profit. With this being said, it is important to consider that there will be periods when people are not as willing to vacation or travel. For example, during the summer months, vacation homes and vacation rentals will be more popular since more people are traveling. However, when it gets to the colder months or when work tends to pick up, such as the financial year-end, it may be a low season when people are not traveling as much. In these seasons, you may not make a lot of money.

Another thing that you need to consider is higher maintenance requirements when it comes to vacation rentals since multiple people use the space. It is also your responsibility to ensure that the space is safe. Short-term rentals also mean having to turn around the property for your new guests so it is clean and ready for their stay. This means it is not a completely passive form of income since you will need to actively check up on the property, ensure your guests are fine, and make sure that the property is up to scratch for each one of your guests when they check in. If there are complaints or emergencies from your guests, then you will need to rush to their side in order to assist them. If you do not have the time to take care of a short-term rental, you can hire a property management company to do it for you. This does come at a cost, but it may be worth it since you do not have to handle the day-to-day running of the property. This is also a good option if you have multiple rental properties you are trying to manage.

INTERACTIVE ELEMENT: WORKSHEET TO DETERMINE PERSONAL INVESTMENT PREFERENCES

Asking the right questions is essential when determining your investment goals and preferences. Go through this worksheet to help you understand your preferences and investment style. Remember to answer the questions honestly.

What is your primary goal when it comes to real estate investing?

____

How much money do you aim to use as an initial investment?

____

How comfortable are you with high-risk investments that can potentially lead to higher returns?

____

Do you prefer:

1) A stable, lower-risk property with modest returns.

2) A higher-risk property with high earning potential.

____

Would you prefer to hire a property manager or take a more do-it-yourself approach?

____

List the properties discussed in this chapter in order of what interests you most to least.

____

____

____

There are many types of real estate you can invest in, and this is a good thing. You get to choose the types that best suit your needs and speak to you the most. This is an important decision, so take some time to think about it. We discussed the different ways you can invest in real estate and the strategies you can use. As a beginner, choosing one to focus on is best; from there, you can grow your investment portfolio.

Now that you have a clearer picture of the various real estate investment options and have assessed your personal preferences, it's time to explore how to finance these investments.

FINANCING YOUR INVESTMENTS

When it comes to investing in real estate, over 80 percent of buyers finance their investments (National Association of Realtors, 2018). This means that most people who own property or invest in real estate are not buying with cash but rather financing their investments. Financing means borrowing money from someone else, often a financial entity, in order to have the funds to make your investment. There are many ways to do this, so in this chapter, we will dive deeper into the topic.

FINANCING KEY TERMS

- **Interest Rate:** This is a percentage fee placed on a loan's principal amount.
- **Principal:** The amount borrowed without the addition of any interest.

- **Amortization:** A method of accounting used to distribute or spread loan payments over a specified period of time, in which each payment covers both principal and interest.
- **Loan-to-Value:** This is a ratio that is worked out by taking the loan amount and dividing it by the asset purchased or any collateral being borrowed against.
- **Lenders Mortgage Insurance:** A type of insurance that protects the lender. As the investor, you need to pay if you are borrowing over 80 percent of the value of the property you want to purchase.
- **Collateral:** A way to secure a loan is by pledging an asset, so if you default on the loan and cannot pay it back, the lender can take that asset to recuperate the money you owe them.
- **APR:** This stands for the annual percentage rate and is the yearly cost of a loan. This will include all charges, fees, and interest rates.

There are many different financing options available. This is a good thing because it means you'll be able to find an option that works best for you. Since every investor is different and has different strategies and a different amount of money, it is important to choose the financing option that is going to suit your needs the best.

Traditional Loans

The most common way to finance a property is through a traditional loan. There are a few different types of traditional loans, and you must consider the service provider. Each financial service provider will have their own terms and rules surrounding specific loans, so it is important to not only understand the type of loan you're taking out but also compare different service providers.

Fixed-Rate Mortgages

When the term fixed is used in financing, it means that there will be no change or movement. A fixed rate means there is a fixed interest rate for the entire duration of the loan. This interest rate is agreed upon prior to the loan being taken out, and it stays the same until you have paid off the loan in full or the loan term has ended. Many people choose this type of mortgage because the interest rate does not fluctuate with what is happening in the market. Since a mortgage or a home loan is a significant commitment that spans many years, having a fixed rate means more security and predictability.

Variable-Rate Mortgages

Conversely to a fixed-rate mortgage, a variable-rate mortgage has a monthly repayment that can change because the interest rate can change. This means it can either go up or down, and you pay either more or less. The benefit of this type of mortgage is that it allows you to overpay on your payments, which means you could potentially pay off your mortgage much more quickly. For example, if the rate moves to a lower percentage than what you usually pay, you could make your usual payment, meaning that you are paying over the required amount. This money is not lost but put toward your principal, helping you pay off your mortgage sooner.

The downside to this type of mortgage is that your payments will change over time. This will definitely affect how you budget and plan your future finances. You are also risking a higher interest rate than what you might have originally planned due to an uncertain economic situation. At the end of the day, the economic markets are unpredictable.

Interest-Only Loan/Mortgage

This type of mortgage is set up quite differently from the ones we have already discussed. With an interest-only mortgage, the borrower will only pay the interest required on the loan for a specified period of time. Once this time has elapsed, the borrower will owe the principal amount in a lump sum or based on an agreed-upon payment schedule. With other types of mortgages and home loans, you must repay the principal and the interest in your monthly repayments.

The benefit of this type of home loan is that you will pay back a minimal amount each month for the beginning portion of the mortgage term. This will help if you need some additional cash flow and expect your income to increase over the next few years. It may also be a good option for investors who are looking to flip the property or gain an income from the property in the coming years. This way, they are deferring larger payments to focus on their investments. However, it is a risk because you never know how finances are going to play out in the future, and once the interest-only portion of the mortgage term has ended, you will then be required to pay back the principal, and this means the overall monthly repayments are going to be much higher.

Balloon Mortgages

With a balloon mortgage, you will be required to make small payments for a certain period at the beginning of your loan term. This is followed by one large balloon payment once the term has ended. When taking out this type of mortgage, it is important to ensure that you will be able to afford the balloon payment at the end of the term. This type of mortgage can be tempting because the repayments are so low at the beginning. However, if you are not fully prepared to pay the balloon amount at the end of the mortgage term, it could result in you falling into a lot of debt, so ensuring that you have a plan in place is key if you are considering this type of mortgage.

Lease Options and Rent-to-Own

Let's first talk about a lease option, which is where you enter into an agreement with the current property owner to lease the property for a certain amount of time with the option to purchase it later down the line. This means that you have the opportunity to purchase the property once the lease is over. To have the chance to purchase the property, you, as the renter, will need to pay something called an "option fee upfront." This fee is included in your monthly rent and will also go toward the down payment of the property. This is not any kind of agreement to purchase the property, so the renter is not obligated to make the purchase after the lease has ended.

A rent-to-own agreement is exactly the same as a lease option but with a slightly different name. There is no obligation to purchase the house after the lease expires, but the current property owner can only sell after first giving you the option to purchase it as the renter. If the agreement is a lease-purchase contract, then you are required to purchase the property once the lease comes to an end. This option is good for those who are trying to save up for a bigger down payment or simply do not have the funds to purchase the house outright and would like to rent first. Once the lease ends, the renter is required to purchase the property.

Seller Financing

With a traditional mortgage, you must go to a financial service provider and apply for the loan. The service provider will pay for your mortgage, and you will pay them back in monthly installments. An alternative to this financing method is called seller financing. With this method, the seller of the property will act as the mortgage lender. All this means is that there is no intermediary, and you will pay your mortgage installments directly to the person selling the property. This is a unique situation, and you will need to find a seller who is willing to enter into this kind of financing agreement. If you find somebody willing, you get to skip a lot of the red tape associated with getting a mortgage and can handle all transactions directly with the seller of the property. In this case, the seller will set out the mortgage and down payment terms. You may also be able to negotiate better if you are doing it directly with the seller of the property.

Cash-Out Financing

If you are looking for a way to access the equity that is currently sitting in your properties, then a cash-out refinance could be a good option for you. Essentially, when you apply for a cash-out financing option, you are replacing the mortgage you have at that moment with a larger loan, and the difference is given to you in a lump-sum payment. You can choose to use this money however you would like, but from an investment point of view, most investors will use it to invest in other properties or their current property to increase its value. The rules for this type of financing will vary based on where you are and the financial service provider you decide to go with, but in most cases, you will need at least 20 percent equity in your home. This means you would have needed to pay off at least 20 percent of what you owe on the property before considering a cash-out financing option. It is also a good idea to ensure that the interest rate you are getting on the new loan is not much more than what you are currently paying; otherwise, this could be a bad financial move. These types of loans should only be taken out if you have a plan in place and know what you're going to do with the money.

Home Equity Line of Credit (HELOCs)

With this financing option, you can cash in on the equity you currently have on your property through variable-rate financing. HELOC is a revolving line of credit that works similarly to a credit card. When you take out this line of credit, you do not have to use it if you do not need it. You are free to borrow the money you need and repay it as you use it or whenever you choose to pay it back. Most people will use this type of financing to make improvements to their homes or other aspects of their property investments. It basically just gives you access to additional funds so that you can spend it in other areas.

GETTING PREPARED FOR FINANCING

The process of receiving financing for your property investments doesn't start when you are ready to make the purchase. It starts as early as possible in your life because having a good financial standing is incredibly important. You can prepare yourself for big purchases from the time you start earning your own money and building up your credit score.

Improving Your Credit Score

Your credit score is extremely important when it comes to making any kind of big purchase and getting a loan from a financial institution. The bank or other financial service providers will look at your credit score to determine whether or not you are responsible with your money and if they can trust you with a big loan. It is a risk for financial service providers to give out big loans at good interest rates, which is why they look at the credit score to mitigate this risk. When you have a good credit score, it's a lot easier for you to get financing. You will get a good interest rate and terms on your loan so that you do not have to pay more than you need to. You also have more financing options, so you don't have to go with whichever provider offers you any kind of loan.

You can check your credit score on any of the major credit bureaus, and this is completely free. Depending on how well you have managed your credit over the past few years, you will either have a good or bad credit score. A good credit score is typically over 620; anything lower can be considered bad or moderate. The goal is to get your credit score as high as possible so you can give yourself the best opportunity for your mortgage. It is always best to start off on the right foot with building your credit score, but if you have a lower credit score, you can also work to build it up. The tips we will talk about in this section will help you build your credit score from scratch or increase a low credit score.

The first thing you need to do is have a look at all of your bills and make sure you know when they need to be paid each month. Missing bill payments or paying them late has a negative impact on your credit score. If you have any debit orders, you also need to make sure there is money in your account when your debit orders are taken to ensure you are not missing those payments. It's helpful to move all your payment dates to the same day or week so it's easy for you to remember to pay them.

The next thing you need to do is look at all your credit card balances to see how much you owe on your credit cards. Then, you will need to work on reducing these balances as much as possible. Owing too much money on a credit card negatively affects your credit score. You should only use about 20 to 30 percent of your available credit at any time. This is a safe area to be in, but lowering it as much as possible will help you stay out of debt. This leads to the next point—making sure your credit utilization is also low. Credit utilization is how much of your available credit you are actually using, and when you keep it low, it shows that you can manage having this credit available.

While you are working toward building up your credit score, you must not add any additional debt. Try not to get any more credit cards or any additional loans. Building your credit score takes small steps. Every month is going to compound, and you will have a good credit score sooner if you stick to the plan.

Down Payment Requirements

An important thing to consider when you are looking into taking out a mortgage or other financing option for an investment property is your down payment. Most types of financing will require you to have a down payment ready. On top of that, the larger the down payment you have available, the smaller the mortgage loan you will need for your investment. In general, it is better to have a larger down payment, especially if this is your first investment. Typically, there is a 15 percent required down payment for most types of property financing, but it is advisable to save 20 to 30 percent of the property price as a down payment.

There are also some other requirements you should aim to hit before you start applying for mortgages and home loans. For example, having a credit score above 680 is going to be in your favor. If you can get it higher than this, you will put yourself in an even better position. You also want to make sure that your debt-income ratio is lower than 50 percent. This means that you are making twice as much as you owe on your debts. This just gives security to lenders, showing that you have the finances available to pay off your debts.

If you haven't started saving toward an emergency fund, this is a good time to start because having about six months' worth of reserve finances is essential in life. This is going to help protect your finances if unexpected situations occur in your life. On top of that, having these reserve finances shows lenders you are financially responsible and have finances available should you not have access to your salary or if there's some other unexpected emergency that needs to be taken care of. All these aspects play important roles when getting a home loan, as well as being able to manage one when you have it.

Saving for Your Down Payment

There are a few things that you can do to help yourself when you are saving for a down payment. This will take some sacrifice, but it will definitely be worth it when you can afford the property you really want to invest in. The first step when saving toward anything is to budget and cut down on unnecessary expenses. Most of us do not really know how much we are spending until we write it down and create a budget, and when you do this, it'll be a lot easier for you to see where your money is going and where you need to cut back. A budget will help you plan your finances in every area of your life.

Saving is incredibly important. There is only so much you are going to be able to save since you need to use your money for your daily expenses. Looking for ways to increase your income is essential when you are saving toward bigger purchases or any kind of financial goal. This way, you can create more revenue for yourself to work with, and you can save quickly. When it comes to saving, it is also important that you make it a priority. You can do this by creating an automatic transfer from your main account into your savings account. This way, you don't even have to think about saving; it is just done for you.

When you are saving toward a goal, it is important that you track your savings and see how you are progressing toward it. This will allow you to pick up on any potential saving pitfalls to resolve the issue as quickly as possible and get yourself back on track. You will also be able to recognize whether you are on track for your saving goals, and if you are not, then you can make a plan to adjust your current spending habits to align more with your goals. This is an excellent way to ensure that you put yourself in the best position to save money and reach your financial goals.

INTERACTIVE ELEMENT: CALCULATE YOUR LOAN-TO-VALUE RATIO

Loan-to-value is an important calculation to figure out if an investment will be a good choice or not. You can use this simple formula to work it out:

LTV% = (Loan Amount / Asset Value) x 100

When calculating your LTV, aim for a lower ratio. Lenders typically view lower LTVs more favorably, as they signify reduced financial risk for them. A lower LTV often results in better financing options, including lower interest rates, especially when the ratio is at or below 80%. However, achieving a lower LTV may require a larger down payment on your part.

You can fill out this worksheet to compare different properties and determine which will be the best investments.

LTV%	Loan Amount	Asset Value
35%	$140,000	$400,000

Financing is one of the most important things to think about when it comes to real estate investing. Since property is such an expensive asset, choosing the right type of financing could save you a lot of money or end up costing you in the end. It is always best to start preparing yourself as early as possible. In fact, you can start now, even before you have an investment in mind. With a solid grasp of financing options, it's time to go deeper into evaluating real estate investments. Next is Part 2 of our framework: Master the Fundamentals.

PART TWO

MASTER THE FUNDAMENTALS

UNDERSTANDING KEY METRICS

Alex became an accidental landlord very early on in his life. By the time he was twenty-five, both his parents had passed away, and they left him with a condo in California. He didn't really know much about property investment and actually thought about selling the condo quite a few times. However, he decided to keep it even though he didn't even live in California. He hired a property management company to handle the day-to-day business since he could not do it himself. It didn't make him that much profit, but it wasn't a liability at that stage either. You could say that he almost completely forgot about it, but it gave him a little insight into property management and what it entailed.

Over the next few years, he prioritized saving toward his retirement and building up a good portfolio for his future. However, these investments were not making as steady progress as he would've liked. This led him to think about other options. One day, he remembered his condo in California, and even though it wasn't making him a great profit, he recognized that property could be a wonderful investment. This is when he started doing more research. He figured out why his property wasn't making that much and decided to fix some of the issues—or at least not make the same mistakes with his next investment. For example, he knew California was a very expensive state and that the rent you could charge was really not worth it, based on the expenses needed to run a rental. With this information, he decided to invest in property in cheaper states, which would help him turn a bigger profit. He also looked at properties that would appreciate in value, which meant purchasing properties at a cheaper price so he could increase the value and make more profit. He also ensured the properties he was looking to invest in had lower operating costs so he could maximize his potential profits.

Having a strategy in place really helped him to aggressively start investing and grow his real estate portfolio. With the strategy in place, it took him about four years, and suddenly, he owned thirty-five rentals that were bringing in a massive income. This was helping him to save toward his retirement and other financial goals, ensuring he and his family had financial security for the future. While it took him a while to realize the value of real estate, once he did, he was able to put a plan in place that really helped him to increase investment opportunities and make real estate a viable investment choice.

CASH FLOW

When it comes to investments or running a business, it is important to have cash flow. Speaking of cash flow, you'll notice that people refer to it as positive cash flow or negative cash flow. When you have a positive cash flow, it means that you have cash left after you have spent money on all of your expenses. It basically means that you are turning a profit. However, if you have a negative cash flow, it means that your expenses are more than what you are making. When you have negative cash flow, it means you don't have any money to continue to grow the business. It is highly important to ensure that you do everything you can to maintain a positive cash flow, as this will result in you having money to put into your investments and continue to grow your overall investment portfolio.

It is very easy to work out cash flow, and it is one of the most important numbers when it comes to your investments. It's a simple way to see whether you are making a profit and whether you will be able to pay your bills when it comes to your properties. If you have a negative cash flow, it indicates that you may be overspending in certain areas or that the investment you made is not viable. In some cases, you have a negative cash flow for one month, and then the next few months have a positive cash flow. Therefore, it is important to track your cash flow over the course of a few months so you can get a better idea of how your investments are performing.

When you have multiple properties in your real estate investment portfolio, it becomes even more important for you to track your cash flow. You will need the cash for the individual properties as well as the overall cash flow in your entire investment portfolio. Your overall cash flow will give you a snapshot of how your portfolio is performing, and cash flow for individual property investments shows you which ones are turning the most profit and which ones you will need to reevaluate. Cash flow is also an indicator of where you need to put in more work or effort to increase the profit of certain properties.

PROPERTY APPRECIATION

Property appreciation takes place when the value of a piece of real estate gradually increases over time. There are many reasons for the value increase, including the general real estate market, the economy, and improvements or renovations to the actual property. Appreciation is one of the fundamental ways many real estate investors make an income through their real estate investments. When investing in a property, the goal is to choose one with the best chance of appreciation.

In order to figure out whether a property is a good candidate for overall appreciation, you will need to look at a few key points. These are the market demand, economic indicators, and location. Market demand simply means that more people want to live in a certain area or purchase the property that you have. If there are more people who want to purchase properties in the area that you have invested in, the overall property prices will increase. You can gauge future market demand by looking at areas currently being developed and where other investors are choosing to put their money. As a first-time investor, you can also look at places that already have a high market demand to see if you can purchase any properties within or close to that area.

Economic indicators have a tremendous impact on all types of investments, and real estate is no exception. These economic indicators could be job growth or creation, interest rates, and inflation. If the economy is moving in a positive direction, the price of real estate will probably increase. However, in the case of an economic downturn, the price of property might decrease. It is important to understand that there are always highs and lows when it comes to the economy, so it will never be completely stable throughout the lifespan of your investments. However, you may be able to use it to your advantage if you do your research. You could purchase properties when they are at a lower price, and then when the economy picks up again, these properties will appreciate in value and give you a larger profit.

Location is easily one of the most important aspects to consider when investing in property. People will pay a lot more money for a lot less if the location is good. We know this because properties in central hubs and big cities tend to be much more expensive to buy and rent than those on the outskirts or in inconvenient areas. You will probably pay double or triple the amount to buy an apartment in New York or London compared to what you would pay if you purchased a property of the same size in an outlying area. Location is so important because people want to live near employment opportunities, amenities, and safe neighborhoods and areas. This doesn't mean that you have to purchase properties in big cities, but you have to make sure that you are choosing the right location and that it is going to be somewhere where people want to live. Look for up-and-coming areas with good schools that are walkable, safe, and have all the necessary amenities nearby.

EQUITY

When we speak about equity, it simply represents how much of the property you actually own. It shows you how much money you would get from the property if you were to sell it immediately. To figure out your equity, you need to subtract the outstanding balance of your mortgage from the current market value of the property. If you sold the property immediately, you would need to pay off the mortgage before you could take any profit from it. This is why many investors do their best to pay off the mortgage as quickly as possible so they have more equity in their investments.

You can use or leverage equity in a way that is beneficial to your investments and overall profit. One way you can do this is by improving your property to increase the market value. Since the mortgage payments are already agreed upon and will not change, making improvements to the property to increase its value will not impact how much you owe on your mortgage but will impact how much the property is worth. When you sell the property, you will get a larger profit since the property is more valuable. You can make many types of home improvements, like adding new rooms and amenities and making the home more aesthetically pleasing.

You can also consider taking out a home equity loan, which allows you to get cash based on the equity of your current property. You will use that money to improve your current property or even invest in additional properties to continue growing your real estate investment portfolio. This needs to be done with caution, and you will need to ensure you do your research before taking out this type of loan. However, investments can increase your overall profit and make your investment portfolio more valuable.

NET OPERATING INCOME (NOI)

The net operating income is the income generated from operating your property after deducting operating expenses. This amount does not include your mortgage payments. However, it does include most other things that you will pay for when it comes to your property. This will include insurance, property management fees, maintenance, and property taxes. To figure it out, all you have to do is look at the total revenue your property is bringing in and measure it up to the total operating expenses. This is an important figure, especially if you are using your property to bring in some sort of income, for example, if you are renting out your property. However, if you are living in your property and not using it for any kind of current profit, then you do not need to work out NOI.

You never want to spend more money than you are making. If the net operating income is very low or is a negative amount, this is a good indication that you are either spending too much or charging too little. With this information, you will then change your strategy to either lower your expenses or increase the rent you are charging so you can make a good profit from your property. Remember that your total income is being considered when you are working this out, so ensure you include rental income and other sources of revenue that your properties are bringing in. This could be revenue from the use of amenities such as laundry machines or parking fees. You will then subtract the total expenses from your total revenue in order to get your net operating income.

CAP RATE

The cap rate, or capitalization rate, is the net operating income divided by the purchase price or current market value. This figure is calculated to help an investor measure the return on investment of a property. A cap rate helps investors estimate the return they may expect to generate on their investment property. It is important to recognize that this is not a set-in-stone number, and many things can affect a cap rate. This is simply a prediction or estimate that an investor can use when making decisions.

Many factors can affect a cap rate. These include location, the size of the property, market stability, growth potential, and capital liquidity. Many investors use a cap rate to compare potential investments and see which one will be the most profitable. They will take into account all the factors above and figure out which one of the potential property investments will be the most profitable for them. For example, imagine there are two properties that an investor has their eye on. They are very similar in every way, except they are in different geographical locations. The investor will need to take this into consideration. The geographical location affects the net operating income and the potential returns the property can make. One property could be in a remote location. That means profit will be lower. Operating expenses will also be lower. The property could be in a big city, but this means that the operating expenses will be more expensive, and the rent you can charge and the amount of money you can make through this property will be a lot more. From here, the investor can work out the cap rate to see which one is going to be more profitable and then decide which property to invest in. You can work out the cap rate with this formula.

Cap Rate = Net Operating Income / Current Market Value

INTERACTIVE ELEMENT: CALCULATE THE NOI FOR A SAMPLE PROPERTY

The best way to understand NOI is to do it yourself. This is easier than you may think. The first thing you need to do is work out how much your potential property will make. This includes rent and other income sources such as:

- Parking fees
- Cleaning fees—charges collected from guests or tenants for cleaning services
- Charges for amenities
- Vending machines
- Laundry

Next, you will need to determine how much the property's expenses will come to. Many expenses could come up; the most common are:

- Utilities
- Taxes
- Repair and maintenance
- Insurance
- Accounting fees
- Legal fees
- Property management fees
- Cleaning fees—costs paid by the landlord for cleaning services
- Marketing expenses

The next figure you will need is the Gross Operating Income. It can be worked out with this formula:

Gross Operating Income = Potential Rental Income – Vacancy Losses

After you have all three figures, you can plug them into this formula to find out the NOI of a property:

NOI = (Gross Operating Income + Other Income) – Operating Expenses

To practice this, you can choose a few properties currently listed for sale on a property website. Try to find out as much information about them as possible and follow the above steps to find out their NOIs. You can then compare to see the difference. You can use the template below.

Income

Name	Amount
Total	

Expenses

Name	Amount
Total	

After financial metrics, we now delve into property valuation and risk assessment. The next chapter helps you with these so you can make well-informed investment decisions.

PROPERTY VALUATION AND RISK ASSESSMENT

Camila decided she was ready to start on her real estate investment journey. She found a wonderful apartment that she believed she could rent out to bring in a significant income. The process was going smoothly, and she decided to make an offer on the property. While waiting for the final paperwork and the details to be finalized, she decided she wanted to get the property valuated by her property evaluation expert. Before this, she had simply trusted the seller on the value of the property. After a few days, her property evaluator came back to her and said that the property was valued at much less than she thought and much less than the offer she had put in.

She was quite surprised by this and went back to the seller to ask for clarification. The property owner was adamant that the original pricing was correct and that Camila's evaluator was the one who was wrong. Since Camilla had already made an offer, the property seller knew how much money was on the table and refused to bring down the price. After a few days of back-and-forth, Camilla was forced to let go of the property. This was a hard one for her because she really believed that this property would be the perfect investment. It took her six months to find another similar property that could offer her great investment benefits.

A lot goes into investing in real estate, and property valuation is one of the most important aspects. It's easy to look at a property and think it is valued at a certain amount, but once the property has been inspected, it could be a completely different result. Getting a property inspected will help to ensure that you are paying a fair amount for the property, and if you already own it, you will get a fair amount if you choose to sell it.

VALUATING PROPERTIES

Property valuation is simply the assessment that your property will undergo in order to determine its value based on various factors, including location, amenities, and size. Property valuation is an incredibly important step in any real estate process, not only for the people who are buying and selling but also for other aspects, such as property insurance and taxation.

During the property assessment, the property surveyor or inspector will look at all the space on the property. They will consider the condition, size, number of rooms, age, and any potential for future development of the property. It is highly important to get a reputable professional to do this so you can get an accurate property assessment. It is also a good idea to have your own property assessor look at a property that you are planning to buy. This will give you peace of mind and ensure you are not overpaying for a piece of real estate.

Home value can be broken up into three different categories. These are assessed value, fair market value, and appraised value. A tax assessor in your municipality determines the assessed value and is only used for tax purposes. If the value is high, then taxes will be high. Fair market value is the amount you would be expected to get if you sell your property. The appraised value is the price given to you after a professional appraisal has been done on the property and is a more accurate representation of the property's value and what the seller should expect to get for it.

CMA

CMA stands for comparative market analysis, and it is used to estimate a property's price based on similar properties recently sold in the same area. Real estate agents do this type of analysis and then give it to people who want to sell their properties so they're able to list at an appropriate price. Property buyers can also use this to make a competitive offer on a property they are interested in purchasing. While real estate agents use their own special tools to do this kind of analysis, you can also do a basic form of a CMA on your own. All you have to do is go onto property listing websites and see how much properties are going for, and this will give you a good idea of what you should expect to pay for a similar property or what you can expect other people to pay for a property that you are looking to sell.

You can expect a CMA report to include aspects such as location, size, square footage, age of the property, number of rooms and bedrooms, any special features, the date of the sale, and the terms of financing for the sale. If you're looking to do your own CMA, there are a few steps you'll need to go through to ensure it's as accurate as possible. First, you will need to have a look at the neighborhood and whether it is a pleasant neighborhood. A good neighborhood is typically identified through the amenities, cleanliness, safety, and proximity to transportation and other necessities.

Next, you have to look at the property and gather the relevant details. If you're looking to purchase a property, you can look at the online listing to get a general idea of what the property provides, but it is always best to do an in-person visit to ensure the listing details are accurate. When you do a visit, make sure that you look at the size of the home, style, age, condition, layout, and general livability of the space. You will then need to list three to five comparable properties in the same area. These properties should have been recently sold so you can get the closest comparison possible, as the price of real estate fluctuates quite quickly.

Once you have done this, you will need to adjust for any differences between the comparable properties you have used and the ones that you are interested in buying. Every property is going to have differences of some sort, so it is important to understand these and their monetary impact. Professionals have prices and values assigned to certain differences. For example, if the property you are looking to purchase has an extra bedroom compared to comparable properties, this will significantly impact the price, as an extra bedroom or bathroom adds value to a property.

CMAs are definitely not perfect, but they can give you a great idea of how much you should expect to pay if you purchase a property and how much you should expect to get if you were to sell your property. It allows you to plan and budget effectively before you make an offer or even start the purchasing process, ensuring you are not getting a bad deal when buying or selling your property. The CMA is essentially a base around which you can build your real estate investment pricing.

RISK ASSESSMENT

When it comes to investing in real estate, there will always be some risk involved. Typically, the more risk an investor is willing to endure, the higher the potential reward could come from the investment. With that being said, it is unwise to take risks without assessing the risk and seeing if the potential reward is actually going to be worth it. When we talk about risk, we're talking about losing the money that we have invested. When it comes to real estate, risk is more of a complicated topic because so many factors can play into a property's value. On top of the value, you also have to consider whether it would be easy to sell the property when the time comes or to rent it out to tenants.

When thinking about risk and how it affects real estate, there are several aspects to consider. The first aspect is the real estate market. We already know that this market is incredibly unpredictable, and while there are forecasts used for market prediction, in many cases, these are not completely accurate. When it comes to the market, things like supply, demand, government policies, and unforeseen national events can all play a huge part in the value of a property. It is a good idea to have a look at the market and see what the forecast is saying so that you can plan. Still, it is also important to recognize that unpredictability is the only thing that is predictable in the real estate market. With that being said, typically, the real estate market goes up over time, so even though there are pockets of time where the market will be in a downturn, it is highly likely that it will pick up again.

Structural risk is an important type of risk that must be considered when purchasing a property. Every property will have its flaws, but it is important to understand what these flaws are to make sure you are investing in something that will last for the long term and will not cost you a bundle to rectify. For example, something like a damaged foundation or mold within the building is going to cost you a lot of money to repair, and in some cases, it might be irreparable. However, smaller structural issues could be fixed and dealt with. Purchasing a property with some structural issues will probably be cheaper, but you have to consider the amount you will be paying to complete the repairs.

Location is easily one of the most important factors you need to consider when investing in any kind of real estate. With that being said, location can also be a risk factor, especially if the area is not good or goes downhill from the time that you purchased the property. It is highly important that you research the location before you make a purchase, as this will be one of the biggest factors to impact the value of your property.

Another risk factor to consider is liquidity and cash flow. When it comes to real estate, there is not a lot of liquidity available since all of your money is going to be tied up in the physical property. You won't be able to quickly pull out some money from your investment for an emergency or if you want to purchase something else. There is a long process to get your money out of a real estate investment, so it is important to understand that even though property increases your overall net worth, you might not have access to that money until much later on. Cash flow is another thing to consider, as a negative cash flow is an enormous risk to any investor. Ensuring you make the right investments and set yourself up for positive cash flow is essential. If you realize you are going through a period where you have a negative cash flow, it is important to figure out why this is so you can solve the problem before you lose too much money.

A huge factor when it comes to real estate investment is your tenants. If you rent out your property to other people, there will always be a risk that they will not pay or they will not take good care of the property. You can't control other people and what they do, but you can ensure you do your research beforehand and don't accept tenants simply because they have applied. There needs to be a screening process before you allow somebody to move into your property to ensure they will pay on time and take care of your property. If they don't, you will spend a lot of time, money, and effort trying to get your rent and fix any of the issues they may cause. In line with this, another risk is vacancies if you cannot find tenants for your property. If you have vacancies for long periods of time, it means that you are not making money, and your cash flow will go into the negative. There are many things that could cause vacancies, such as the economic market or the location of the property. In order to mitigate this, you will need to ensure that you have done your research to purchase a property that is in demand and that people will more likely want to stay in. You will also need to price your property competitively to attract more potential tenants. Marketing is also very important, and it may be worth it to get a real estate expert on board to assist you.

We always talk about how property tends to appreciate in value over time, but another risk is property depreciation. If the property loses value over time, it is depreciating in value. It is important to choose the property you are going to invest in very carefully. Researching real estate markets and statistics when it comes to the type of property and its location will help you ensure you are setting yourself up for success with your investment. It is also a good idea to monitor the market even when you already have a property you have invested in. If you notice a risk of depreciation, it may be worth it to consider selling to save yourself from losing a lot of money. When it comes to investing in real estate, it is not simply purchasing a property and leaving it there. You will need to constantly be doing market analysis to ensure that you mitigate any risks as early as possible.

INTERACTIVE ELEMENT: CALCULATE THE CAP RATE OF A PROPERTY

In order to get the CAP rate of a property, you will first need to have the NOI. In the previous chapter, you worked this out for a sample property. You can use those figures in this exercise as well. Here is the formula for the CAP rate:

Cap Rate = Net Operating Income / Property's Sale Price or Market Value

There is a lot that can go into defining what a good cap rate is. Typically, between 8 percent and 12 percent is good, but in some cases, lower than this is also favorable.

After valuation and risk assessment, you're now ready to move forward with purchasing a property.

PURCHASING THE PROPERTY

An interesting statistic is that 75 percent of recent homebuyers have regrets about their purchase (Zillow, 2022). This is a huge number, and it can make people wonder whether real estate is actually worth it if so many people regret it. The reason so many new homeowners tend to regret their purchase is that the property requires a lot more maintenance and work than they initially expected. Knowing this, it's clear that many people who purchase property do not do the research they need to. It is so important to do the relevant research before you make such a big purchase. This regret can definitely be avoided if people knew what they were getting into and were prepared for it from the start.

PREPARING TO BUY

Preparation is key when you are looking to make a large purchase, like when it comes to real estate. You definitely don't want to be part of the 75 percent of people who have regrets about their purchase. There are many steps to take when it comes to investing in a property. Ensure that you are going through the steps and taking your time to ensure you are making the right investment for you and your needs.

Make Sure You're Ready

The first rule of buying a property is to make sure that you are actually ready to do so. This means being financially and emotionally ready because buying a property is a huge commitment. You will also need to consider whether buying a property right now will fit into your goals for the future. Consider how buying this property is going to affect your finances and your life for the foreseeable future. You may even want to list out a few pros and cons to get a balanced idea of where you are when making this huge investment.

Get Your Finances in Order

As you already know, purchasing a property is a huge financial commitment. In fact, it is one of the biggest financial decisions you can make. You'll have to take some time to look at your finances to see whether you can afford a property right now. Have a look at your current finances, including your income, debts, assets, and liabilities. Consider whether you could afford a down payment on the property and the subsequent monthly mortgage payments.

After you have looked at your finances, you may conclude that you cannot afford a property right now. That's completely fine, and it's much better to be honest with yourself from the beginning. The next step from here is planning your finances so that you will be able to purchase a property in the future. This may mean cutting down on your expenses so that you can save toward a down payment. It may also mean that you should be looking for ways to increase your income so that managing the mortgage payments will be easier for you. Understanding your finances will help you plan for your future real estate investments.

The Down Payment

Once you know how much you can afford or whether you can afford a property at all, it is time to save for your down payment. It is advisable to save about 20 percent of the price of the property as a down payment. The reason is that a larger down payment will decrease your monthly mortgage payment and make it easier for you to pay off the mortgage quickly.

With that being said, you do not need to put down 20 percent. Many people choose to put down a smaller down payment and then increase their monthly mortgage payments in order to pay off the mortgage quickly. Whatever you decide, it is important to have some money saved for your down payment before you start aggressively looking for properties. Once you have the down payment, the purchasing process is going to happen a lot more quickly because you can put in an offer and then make the payments almost immediately. If you are looking for property now and don't have the money for a down payment, it may mean that all of this is wasted effort because you cannot put in an offer or get a mortgage.

Find the Right Mortgage

Many types of mortgages and home loans are offered by a variety of financial service providers. When you are looking for a mortgage, you must take the time to compare quotes from as many financial service providers as possible. You should also look at the different types of mortgages to see which one suits your needs the best. Applying for the right type of mortgage will significantly increase your chances of getting the mortgage and make the entire process easier for you.

Start Preapprovals

Once you have decided which mortgage and which mortgage lender you want to go for, you can start the preapproval process. Apply for mortgages with various lenders at the same time. This is an excellent strategy because even if you get denied by one lender, you still have others who could approve your mortgage. Just make sure that you are happy with all the financial service providers and types of mortgages you are applying for. You will need to gather financial paperwork and fill out multiple forms to start the preapproval process. However, it is a lot easier to do everything in bulk because once you have sent the documents to one lender, you can simply use the same financial documents for all the others.

Get a Real Estate Agent

Having a real estate agent on board is going to make the entire process of looking for the right property much easier. You can look on your own, but you will not have access to all the connections and options that a real estate agent does. On top of that, real estate agents can be a really important asset when it's your first time investing in a property, as they can guide you through things that you may not have thought of.

You don't have to go with the first agent you meet with. You can interview a few real estate agents and see which one suits your needs the best. Asking your friends and family members which real estate agents they have used is a great way to figure out which agents are reputable and professional. You always want an agent who will be on your side and will help negotiate on your behalf.

Go Shopping

Now starts the fun part of the process. You get to look for your property. Your real estate agent will guide you to different sites and send you properties that match your needs and budget. Have a look at a variety of property listing websites and just start scrolling through until you find properties that suit your needs. Once you have decided on a few different properties, you can actually visit and do walk-throughs of your ideal properties. When you visit the properties, take some photos and write a list of pros and cons so that you can keep track of which properties you like the most and why. If the market is hot and there are many people looking for real estate in that area, you may not have a lot of time to make your decision. This is why it is important to keep track of your thoughts so that you know exactly whether this property is for you if you need to put in an offer quickly.

Make an Offer

Once you have found the property of your dreams, it is time to make an offer. This is when you tell the current owner of the property that you want to make a purchase and then let them know how much you're willing to pay. You can go back to your real estate agent and ask how much they are expecting and how much you should be offering. Once you put in the offer, it is the seller's turn to accept or reject it. If they reject the offer, you have the opportunity to make a counteroffer that might be more appealing to them. This may start discussions between you and them until you can find an offer that both parties are happy with. Sometimes, the seller will not accept your offer; in that case, you have to move on and find another property to invest in.

Get a Mortgage

If the offer is accepted, then you move on to getting a mortgage. At this stage, you should already have preapprovals, so you can choose a lender who has preapproved you. This process involves a lot of paperwork, so it is a good idea to ask your real estate agent what is required in your area for a mortgage. This way, you can get everything collected, so when you apply for the mortgage, it is a much easier process. Some documents that you need are your W-2 forms, pay slips for the last two months, proof of income, tax certificates, bank statements, details on any loans, and your personal details, such as your ID and Social Security number.

Get Homeowner's Insurance

In some cases, mortgage lenders will not give you a loan unless you have homeowner's insurance. Even if the mortgage lender does not state this is a requirement, getting homeowner's insurance is a good idea to protect you and your investment. The policy should only become effective on the closing date or the date of sale. The insurer will help you along in this process.

Home Inspection

Before the deal is closed, it is important to do a home inspection to make sure you know exactly what you're getting into. Even if you have visited the property, you could have missed underlying problems that could end up costing you a lot of money once the house is in your possession. Getting a professional to do the home inspection is the best way to go. If you find anything that was not disclosed in the initial stage, then you can bring it to the seller's attention, and you might be able to negotiate a lower price, or you might decide that you no longer want to purchase the property. Regardless of the outcome, it is definitely better to know what you're getting into before you proceed with the purchase.

Have the Home Appraised

Home appraisal is different from the inspection that was done in the previous step. When you get your home appraised, you are figuring out how much it is worth. Typically, your mortgage lender will organize the appraisal even though you will be paying for it. The lender will need to know exactly how much the house is worth before they give you the mortgage.

Negotiate Any Repairs

You are now nearing the end of the process, so it is time to negotiate. This can be done face-to-face or through your real estate agents. If there are any repairs needed, you can start negotiating these with the property seller. Remember to be realistic, as the outcome of the negotiations will depend on the kind of market you are currently in.

Close the Deal

Once you're happy with everything, it is time to close the deal. This means that you and the seller have now agreed on the terms of the sale, and your mortgage has been approved. Some closing documents will need to be filled out. At this stage, you will probably be asked to do a final walk-through of the property. This is to make sure everything is as it should be. Once all that is done, you can close the deal, and you are now a property owner.

QUESTIONS TO ASK BEFORE BUYING

You are going to be putting down a lot of money when you purchase your property, so it is important that you ask the right questions. You are free to ask any questions you would like when negotiating or deciding whether you want to purchase a property. It is far better to ask more questions than fewer questions. Here are a few that you should consider before you make an offer or make a purchase:

- How old is the house?
- When were the major appliances installed?
- How long until these appliances need maintenance or replacement?
- Were any major renovations done, and if so, when?
- Do you have any paperwork on the house's repairs, appliances, and systems?
- Are there any water-related or electrical issues with the house?
- Has the property been bought or sold multiple times? If so, what were the reasons for this?
- Are there any negative aspects or history with this property?
- Is there anything else that I would need to know?

THE UNDERWRITING PROCESS

Underwriting is a very important part of the process when it comes to purchasing a property. This is not done by you but by the financial service provider. The process involves evaluating and assessing any financial and risk-related aspects of the investment. Essentially, the financial service provider is doing the due diligence to determine whether or not it is feasible to invest or lend you money. If you are a professional real estate investor, then you will probably have some underwriters on your team who do this for you to make sure the investments are viable and good options for your goals.

When the underwriting process is underway, a few different things are done. One of the first things is a financial analysis, in which all the financial aspects of the investment are looked into. This will include the potential for income, expenses, cash flow, and other financial aspects that need analysis. At the end of the day, when you are a property investor, you want to make sure that your property is going to bring in an income.

Risk assessment and cash flow analysis are also done during this process to make sure that no unnecessary risk is being taken and that the property will be in a good position to have a positive cash flow. Market analysis will also need to be done to consider the effect the current real estate market may have on the income potential and the general viability of a property investment. Finally, the underwriting process needs to do its due diligence to gather and verify relevant information regarding the property. This is just to ensure all the information and reports are accurate so that potential issues are dealt with as soon as possible.

As a real estate investor, you can use techniques from underwriting in order to analyze and evaluate your potential real estate investment deals. The basics of underwriting are to assess risk and ensure that your investments will be viable in the future. You can conduct your own underwriting analysis since you will have access to the majority of the data and information needed. You can also get a third party involved to assist you with the underwriting process. This can be done by a financial advisor or a broker who will identify any blind spots or issues that you may have missed when you did your own financial and risk analysis. The underwriting process is important because it allows you to plan your future and mitigate risk when investing in property. Investing in property is definitely exciting, but it is important not to get carried away with the process. If there are any red flags, you should definitely take a step back and think about whether it is worth it. Property investors will tell you that there are deals that you simply have to walk away from after you have done the necessary analysis. It is far better to walk out on a potentially risky deal than be stuck in a situation where you are hemorrhaging money unnecessarily.

Underwriting is part of the process in which you prepare to buy a property. Many of the steps we discussed in the first section of this chapter apply to underwriting. For example, you will need to gather all of your information and documentation, fill out the necessary forms, be responsive and available to your underwriters throughout the process, and ensure that any financial activities you participate in are relevant to purchasing this property. When you're going through the process of purchasing a property, it is important to be very cautious about what you are doing in the financial space, as opening any new lines of credit or taking out a loan could be a complication in the assessment that will be done. You don't want anything to impede the underwriting process or the property purchasing process.

DUE DILIGENCE

This is the time between your offer for the property being accepted and the closing of the deal. At this stage, it is important to ensure you review all the aspects of the deal and the transaction before you close. This stage is put in place to ensure that you are happy with the deal and that there are no red flags that you might have missed through the other steps of the process. If you find something that doesn't sit well with you, or there has been miscommunication or outright deception regarding the property, then you are free to cancel the deal. Just because the offer has been accepted does not mean that it has been finalized.

After the offer has been made, the true process of due diligence really starts. The first thing that happens is a home inspection. This is a more formal home visit than the one that you might've done before you made the offer. You will get a property inspector to come in and identify any issues with the property. If any major issues have been found, then you can back out, or you can negotiate with the seller of the property to bring the price down or have them resolve the issues before you move in.

Next comes a home appraisal, which will evaluate the property's market value based on various factors. Once this is done, a title check will need to be conducted. This is done to ensure there aren't any lawsuits or claims on the property that either you or the current owner are not aware of or have not disclosed. This is done to protect you from any potential legal expenses you may not be prepared for down the road. The next step in the process is a land or property survey. This is done in order to map out and locate features, boundaries, improvements, and corners of the land your property is on. The goal of this survey is to show you exactly where your property ends and another property begins. In many areas, this survey may already exist and can be passed on from seller to buyer.

Enlisting the service of a real estate attorney is necessary to review all contracts and legal documents related to the purchase. This is a complicated process, and you don't want to miss something or make a mistake that could cost you down the line. The lawyer takes care of things like examining the purchase agreement, disclosure statements, and any documents from the homeowners association (HOA) or zoning regulations. A real estate attorney is someone on your side to give you valuable insight into potential legal issues and ensure that your interests are always protected.

Another important part of the process is disclosures, in which the seller needs to disclose all information about the property in a written document. What they disclose will depend on the laws in the local area and those on a federal and state level. You can talk with your real estate agent or legal advisor about what exactly the seller needs to disclose to you. Certain things will always need to be disclosed, regardless of where you live, including any health and safety risks and the presence of potentially dangerous substances like asbestos and lead paint.

Every area will have its own rules, dependent on the neighborhood or area. This is where a homeowners association comes in. Not all properties are covered by a homeowners association, but if the one you are considering is, you'll need to know what they expect and any bylaws or covenants that you will be bound to if you decide to purchase that property. Some HOAs have restrictions on renting out your property, decorations, and even design choices, such as the color of your house paint. There are also fees attached to HOAs, which must be disclosed to you as soon as possible. The fees cover any public areas and protection that the HOA might take care of.

Next comes the zoning rules, which will show you what the property is allowed to be used for within the community. For example, if you are purchasing a property in a place where local flora and fauna are abundant, laws and rules may prevent you from building and encroaching on this flora and fauna. These zoning rules might be a deterrent for you to continue with the purchase of the property, so it is important to understand this aspect to make sure you know what you are allowed to do and what you are restricted from.

Finally, you will also have to consider insurance, as many mortgage brokers do not lend money to those who do not have homeowner's insurance. There is no law that suggests you should purchase homeowner's insurance, but it will impact your eligibility to get a mortgage or home loan. Homeowner's insurance is also important to protect you and your home. If anything major were to happen to your property, it would come at a hefty price, so having this insurance would cover these planned situations. The type of homeowner's insurance that you need will depend on the property location and risk factors. For example, if you live in an area where floods are common, then you would need flood insurance tacked on to your insurance policy. Speaking to an insurance broker is the best way to go about this process.

ESTIMATING COSTS FOR RENOVATION DURING PROPERTY ANALYSIS

During the property analysis process, certain areas of maintenance may arise that you will need to address. Your property assessor will look through all the different aspects of the property and then assess whether repairs or renovations are needed. In case you take on repairs, it is important to understand the common renovations when purchasing a property. This could help you mentally prepare should you need to do them. Some of these renovations include roofing, plumbing, electrical work, drywall, pest removal, garbage disposals, and HVAC (Heating, Ventilation, and Air Conditioning) systems.

It can be difficult to estimate the cost of renovations and improvements, but having a roundabout number to work with is important. This is going to help you budget effectively so you can ensure you are renovating properly and have the finances to do so. On top of that, estimating the renovation cost can also help you negotiate with the seller. If there are renovations that are going to cost you a lot and you're willing to do them, then you can negotiate down the price.

Many factors come into play when talking about renovations. The price of a renovation depends on various factors, including the scope of the project, the labor and materials needed, and the duration of the work. You will also need to consider the cost based on your area or region, as labor and supplies vary depending on where you are. The range for any kind of repair or renovation is incredibly wide, so it's not helpful to guess if you do not have specific numbers or know precisely what the renovations are going to entail.

When trying to estimate any kind of renovation, the first thing you need to do is know what renovations will have to be done. You can start researching labor and materials needed for the renovation. It is a good idea to start calling around and contacting the relevant professionals who will be taking care of the renovations. They will send you a quote based on the information you give them, and then you can start comparing quotes. If you have done a home inspection, then you should have a good idea of what needs to be done on the property and can then give this information to the relevant professionals. If you are doing these renovations as an add-on or addition to your property, then you will need to let the professionals who will be doing the renovations know exactly what you are planning to do.

The first person you should get in contact with is a general contractor, as they will be taking care of a majority of the processes. These are the people who have contacts with other relevant professionals in the industry. It may be difficult for you to know who to get into contact with if you do not know what is needed. The general contractor will come in and have a look at your vision and needs, and then both of you can work on a plan going forward and bring in other contractors, such as plumbers and electricians. You are under no obligation to go with the first quote you get, and it is definitely important to shop around so you can find the best deals for your renovations.

INTERACTIVE ELEMENT: DUE DILIGENCE CHECKLIST

Due diligence is an extremely important step when it comes to purchasing a property. You want to ensure you are doing your research to avoid any problems down the line. Here is a checklist you can use for this process.

Pre-offer

- Population growth
- Income levels of households in the area
- Vacancies in the area

- Average and median rent prices
- School ratings
- Property value
- Crime rates

Financial Due Diligence

- Potential gross rental income
- Any other income you could make from the property
- Expenses
- Cost of maintenance and repairs
- Taxes
- Insurance
- Contributions to an emergency savings account for property issues and improvements

Post-offer

- Home inspection by a professional
- Utilities and mechanical systems
- Overall condition of all rooms
- Outside areas, such as the driveway and garden
- Mold and termite inspection
- Flood zone verification

Financial Due Diligence

- Profit/loss statements for two years prior
- Previous owner's income tax return
- Current rent
- Lease terms
- Additional fees charged to renters
- List of repairs and capital improvements
- Existing service contracts
- Taxes

With the property purchase process and renovation planning covered, it's essential to understand the tax benefits and legal considerations of real estate investing. We now go into the third part of the framework.

TELL YOUR STORY TO INSPIRE OTHERS

"If you want to go somewhere, it is best to find someone who has already been there."

— ROBERT KIYOSAKI

The further you get into your journey with real estate investment, the more questions people will have for you. How did you do it? Is it really something that anyone can do? You'll be able to tell them your story and encourage them as they start considering whether they, too, could get started with real estate investment—but unless you decide to dedicate your life to guiding others through the process, you're probably not going to have the time to walk them through every little thing they need to do.

Guiding people through the process has become something of a passion of mine, and it's this that led me to write about both real estate investment and setting up an Airbnb business. I want to make this process as easy and accessible as possible for those with big dreams but little experience, and I want people to realize that this is a much more realistic option than they might have imagined. Essentially, I want to answer all the questions that you're probably going to be asked as you start seeing success with real estate investment… and that means you have a very easy way to help people who are inspired by your journey—all you have to do is point them in the direction of this book!

I'd also like to encourage you to share this book on a wider scale so that I can help more people through this process. All you need to do to make a big difference is leave a short review online.

By leaving a review of this book on Amazon, you'll show new readers exactly where they can find all the information they need to get started with real estate investment—and find a solid route to success.

Reviews are so helpful in connecting books with their intended audiences, and simply by leaving your feedback, you can help others find the information they're looking for quickly. This, combined with any friends or family members you pass this on, will make a huge difference to anyone interested in exploring real estate investment.

Scan the QR code to leave a review

Thank you so much for your support. I truly appreciate it.

PART THREE

PROFIT AND PROSPER

TAX BENEFITS AND LEGAL CONSIDERATIONS

When Brendon started his real estate investment journey, something that nobody told him about was the tax benefits. In his first year of running a short-term rental, he brought an accountant on board to help him with the general finances and his taxes since his financial situation had changed. He sat with the accountant, who explained to him the various tax deductions and benefits he could take advantage of through his investments. He was quite surprised as he worked through the list of tax-deductible expenses and items. He never knew that owning an investment property not only increased his income but also reduced his taxable income. This was a big win for him because, like most of us, he's not a big fan of paying unnecessary taxes.

TAX BENEFITS

Real estate investments can help you reduce your taxable income, which is one of the major benefits of investing in real estate. It is important to understand these tax benefits because you don't want to pay more tax than is necessary. Reducing your taxable income means that you have additional finances to put into other areas of your life and even back into your investments. You can speak to a professional accountant or tax advisor for some specific advice, but there are some key areas to be aware of when you are a real estate investor.

One of the most obvious tax benefits of real estate investing is the write-offs that you get with it. A write-off means that you're not taxed on the amount you spend in these areas, which lowers your overall taxable income and results in paying fewer taxes. These tax write-offs include property taxes, insurance, interest on your mortgage, property management fees, and any costs you have to repair or maintain your property. Those are the most common write-offs, but you can also get them if you run your real estate investment as a business since there are business expenses that can be tax write-offs, too. These include business equipment, travel, advertising, fees for legal services, and accounting.

Another tax benefit is depreciation, which is the loss of your property's value over time. If your property produces income, such as a rental property, you will be able to deduct depreciation as an expense and lower your taxable income. You will also have tax benefits through capital gains, which is the amount you will make if you sell your property. This can be divided into short-term and long-term capital gains. Short-term capital gains occur when you buy and sell a property within a year. Long-term capital gains are if you are in possession of the property for more than a year, and capital gains in this category have a much lower tax rate, which is more beneficial to you.

Another wonderful tax benefit that comes with real estate is that if you have rental property and are earning income, you effectively avoid the FICA tax. This payroll tax applies to self-employed individuals who earn an income. If you are self-employed and earn an income through most other avenues, the money you earn is taxed on payroll tax since this person will need to pay for both the employer and the employee portion of the FICA tax. However, if your rental property is considered passive income (as are most long-term rentals), it is not liable for this kind of tax, so you avoid it completely.

1031 EXCHANGE

A tax benefit that needs its own section in this chapter is called the 1031 exchange. This is a strategy in which you defer taxes when you take the profit gained from selling one property and invest in another property. When you take the money out of an investment, you are liable for capital gains tax, but with the 1031 exchange option, you can skip capital gains tax by investing the money from the old property into a new investment property. This is a great way for investors to lower their taxes or at least defer for a significant amount of time.

A process needs to be followed if you want to go this route. The first thing you will need to do is figure out which property you want to sell and which you are going to buy. You have to have properties in mind in order to make the exchange. On top of that, the properties you wish to make this exchange between need to be very similar, even if they're not the same quality and one is more expensive or has a higher value than the other. For example, you would not be able to use the 1031 exchange if you own a one-bedroom apartment and want to exchange it for a vacation home.

This is not the kind of thing that can be done on your own, so you will need an intermediary. This person acts as an exchange facilitator and will handle the transaction. The person or company needs to be qualified, and they will hold your sale in escrow until the exchange has been completed. They will handle most of the process, including coordinating with the seller of the property so they fully understand the implications of the exchange and the process going forward. They will also prepare all the documentation for you and the seller of the new property to make sure the exchange happens successfully and smoothly. The funds from the sale will remain in escrow until the sale is complete, which means the money will be out of your account and be held separately. If everything is successful, the money will be transferred to the seller, but if things don't go according to plan, you will get your money back. They will also guide you through all the paperwork, including the change of title on the deed and property.

There are many requirements for the 1031 exchange, and it is important to understand them before you go through with this process. Firstly, the properties being exchanged need to be of a like kind. You need to ensure that the properties are similar in nature and function for the exchange to occur. Another important consideration is that you will not have access to the proceeds from the sale of your property. If you take any proceeds from the sale, that will be taxable income, and you would not have taken full advantage of the 1031 exchange.

There are timeline requirements that need to be followed in order for this exchange to be successful. First off is the forty-five-day rule. This rule states that you have forty-five days after you sell your property to find a replacement property. You will need to identify this property in writing and include a description of the new property. Then there is the 180-day rule, which specifies you have to close the sale of the replacement property within 180 days of selling your relinquished property. If you do not meet this deadline, you will need to pay capital gains tax on the profit you made from the sale of the initial property you had in your position. Since these timelines are quite short, it may be a good idea to find the exchange property well in advance and start the conversation with the seller of the property. This way, things may go a lot more smoothly, and you will not be at risk of not meeting the deadlines for the 1031 exchange.

LEGAL CONSIDERATIONS

The legal aspects of investing in property are so important. While it might be tempting to skip legal considerations and just throw your money at investments, this is definitely not the most beneficial way to invest in real estate. There are many legal considerations that you will have to contemplate. Knowing what these are is going to help you put your best foot forward.

The first thing you want to do is understand the local regulations where you want to invest. Every city, country, and area is governed by different regulations. This means that what may be legal in one area is completely illegal in another. The local regulations dictate many things, including the type of property development, rental regulations, and zoning laws. Before you even consider investing in a property, ensure you fully understand all local regulations. You can easily find this on the municipality or state's website. If you are concerned about something, then it is worth getting a property lawyer involved to help explain things to ensure you have all the knowledge you need. You definitely don't want to be in the process of making a real estate investment only to realize that you cannot use it in the way you wanted due to overlooked legal considerations.

As you know from Chapter 5, doing your due diligence is essential when it comes to investing in real estate. Legal due diligence has many aspects, but they are all important. The first thing you will need to do is do a title search to make sure that the title is free and that you will be able to take ownership rights of that property. You also need to do a property inspection and survey the property to make sure that you are not being given false information. You want to ensure that you get exactly what you think you'll be getting when you purchase that property. Another part of due diligence is environmental considerations, such as hazards or contaminations. You may need to get a professional involved to evaluate any potential environmental risks currently on the property or that could arise based on what you want to do with your property once you've purchased it.

When you are ready to start negotiating and creating a contract, doing your due diligence in this area is important, too. You definitely don't want to be signing any documents without making sure that you are protected. There will be a lot of paperwork in the process of purchasing a property, and you don't want to overlook any important areas. You can get a real estate lawyer involved to help review contracts and negotiate favorable terms so you are not missing out. There may be potential risks in the contract negotiation that you could miss simply because you do not have all the knowledge. If you choose to go through the process yourself, make sure that you are doing the relevant research and reading through the contract meticulously. If you find a clause or statement that raises a red flag, ensure that you do your research about it and reach out if you need help. It is better to sort this out well in advance rather than being stuck in a contract that is unfavorable to you and your investments.

If your goal is to rent out your property and become a landlord, then it is essential that you understand tenant and landlord laws in the area in which you are investing. You must understand the world and responsibilities of a landlord before you take on that obligation. Being a landlord is not simply renting out your property and then never seeing it again. You have to take care of the maintenance, rental agreement, payments, structure, eviction processes, and any tenancy issues. It is a lot of responsibility, so it is important to understand what you are responsible for and what the tenant's part will be. Knowing this before you become a landlord is important so you can prepare yourself and decide whether you want to do this.

The legal aspects of owning and using a property as an investment are important. You must take the time to understand all legal aspects and do your due diligence in all areas. While this can take some time and effort, you will definitely be thankful that you went through the process. It will save you a lot of time, money, effort, and heartache in the future if you put in the effort now.

Now that we've covered tax benefits and legal considerations, let's discuss generating passive income through rental properties.

PASSIVE INCOME THROUGH LONG-TERM RENTALS

When you're using your real estate investment as passive income, long-term rentals tend to be one of the best options. There are many reasons for this, including the fact that you are making a rental income and earning money through capital growth, getting tax benefits, and diversifying your assets. Taking the time to understand this type of investment strategy is really going to help you see whether it is a good fit for you. Plus, you get to explore the world of rentals and understand the topic at a deeper level.

LONG-TERM RENTALS

A long-term rental is a rental property that you lease out to a tenant for a longer period. These leases can vary in length, but they fall under the umbrella of long-term rental if you are renting out your property to somebody for more than six months.

Benefits

There are many benefits to investing in long-term rentals. Many real estate investors choose to do this due to the benefits and stability it offers. In this section, we are going to talk about the many benefits that come from long-term rentals.

Monthly Rental Income

One of the most obvious benefits is the fact that you are getting a monthly rental income. Since you are renting out the property on a long-term basis, it means that you're making a passive income by getting rental income every month. This stable form of income is predictable and comes in at an agreed-upon date. It allows you to budget and plan, and you know that you are going to get your money.

Depreciation/Tax Deductions

When you own a long-term rental, you have some tax advantages, including writing off certain expenses. For example, you'll be able to write off the interest on your mortgage and depreciation of your assets on your tax forms. This effectively lowers your taxable income, and you will be paying less tax.

Building Equity

If you have a mortgage on your rental property, then you can use your rental income to put toward your mortgage and build equity into your investment. This means that you are paying down the amount you owe so that you own more of the property yourself. You can leverage this equity into other investments or leave it as is, so even if you do have to sell your property before you pay off the entire mortgage, the amount of money you can take out of the property will be a lot more.

Property Appreciation

When a property appreciates in value, it means it is increasing in value over time. Now, there is no guarantee that your property will appreciate in value; however, if you have made a good investment, it is highly likely that your property will increase in value. When you have a rental property, you are making an income from two different areas. The first one is your rental income, and then you're also making money through the property's appreciation in value. While property appreciation might not feel like it is bringing in an income at the moment, when it comes time to sell the property, you will get a lot more than what you purchased it for. You can sell your property for profit when you need to.

Leverage on Investment

If there comes a time when you want to start investing in more than one property or in different kinds of properties, then it is good to know that you can leverage your current properties to do so. You can get a mortgage or loan on a second property by leveraging your first property so that you can get more investments and increase your investment income exponentially. This needs to be done very carefully, as there is a risk when you leverage one property in order to buy more properties. However, if you can make the right investment choices and do your research, you will definitely put yourself in a position for success.

Tips and Tricks

Investing in real estate and rental properties has a learning curve. As you become a more experienced investor, you will learn the nuances that come with this type of investment. With that being said, you want to set yourself up for success from the beginning, so following a few tips and tricks may help you do just that.

Choose the Right Neighborhoods

The neighborhood of the property you want to invest in is going to be crucial for making the most profit. Before you even consider investing in a property, you should do some research on the neighborhood. Even a simple drive through the neighborhood can tell you a lot. An area that is safe and close to good schools, amenities, transportation, shopping centers, and recreational activities is going to be the best neighborhood to invest in.

People always want to live in areas like that, so there will be a demand. When there is a demand for property in an area, a real estate investor can make more money. You will find it a lot easier to find tenants who want to stay in the neighborhood for a long time. When your goal is to make a passive income, getting people who want to live in the neighborhood for an extended period is going to be incredibly beneficial. Many people are willing to rent for five, ten, or even twenty years if they like the neighborhood and want to put down roots there. In this case, you now have a passive stream of income for many years, and you don't have to go through the process of finding new tenants or taking care of a property. Most of the work is done for you, and you can just generate an income.

Locate Profitable Investments

The type of property that you invest in is almost as important as the neighborhood. The property type needs to make sense for the tenant you want to welcome into the home. Properties with more bedrooms and bathrooms will attract bigger families who typically have children. However, smaller properties may attract people who are single or who are just starting out in their lives. This means the amount of money you can charge for rent is going to change. On top of that, how you go about finding your tenants and managing the property is going to differ depending on the type of property you have.

For example, a luxury property will be a little more difficult to market and find tenants for. That is because there is less of a market for luxury properties. However, a single-family home is more appealing to the public, which means it will be a lot easier for you to find tenants. For a beginner investor, a single-family home tends to be the best option. This can be a standalone house, townhouse, or even an apartment.

Look at the Numbers

It is all good to find a beautiful property that you want to invest in, but it is essential that you look at the numbers before you make any kind of investment. The numbers are going to tell you whether the property is going to make a successful investment or if it's going to be a liability. If you have a few properties in mind for your investment, then you can compare the numbers to see which one is going to be the most beneficial investment.

In order to compare the numbers for the different properties, you will need to look at the expenses, cash flow, and potential income from those properties. This is great to assist you in making the best decisions regarding your property investments and ensure that you are not choosing something that will look good on the outside but won't bring in the returns you want.

PRICING STRATEGY

Your pricing strategy is an incredibly important part of your rental investment. If you price your rent too low, it means that you are leaving money on the table, and you might not be making enough to cover your costs. You don't put yourself in a position where you are essentially losing money when making a profit is possible. If you overprice your property, you may end up struggling to find people to rent the space, which will also end up costing you money since you will have vacancies. The goal is to find the sweet spot when it comes to pricing, where you can maximize your profits and ensure you can afford all your expenses.

Know Your Competition

You may have a number in mind that you think you deserve for your rental property, but it is important to know your competition and situate competitively. There is probably a range in which people in the area are willing to pay for property similar to yours. If you set your rent too high, you will put yourself in a position where it is difficult to find tenants. If you set your rent too low, it means that you'll either attract bad tenants or you will be losing money.

Knowing what is going on in your neighborhood will help you set a competitive rate for your rent to maximize your profit and ensure that you have people interested in renting your property. You can go onto property websites to see how much people are charging for rent on properties similar to yours. When doing this research, ensure that you are looking for properties with features and amenities similar to your property. That is what's going to give you the most accurate idea of how much people will pay.

Property prices tend to shift over time, so make sure you check at least every few weeks. This way, you can shift your rental rates to keep your property relevant and competitive in the market.

The 2 Percent Rule Is Just a Guideline

One rule that many landlords tend to stick to is the 2 percent rule. This rule states that you should be charging up to 2 percent of your property's value as rent each month. It makes it easy for you to set a price for monthly rent. This is definitely just a guideline and shouldn't be something that you follow strictly. There is so much to consider when it comes to setting rental prices that it's simply not beneficial for you to stick to this rule without doing any additional research.

Seasonality Matters

You may think that the weather has nothing to do with whether people are looking to rent a property or not, but that is not true. Depending on where you live, there may be differences in seasonality, but the general trend seems to be that people are more likely to move—and look for new properties to live in—during the warmer months. This is probably because it is easier to move when it is warmer. However, in very hot climates, extreme heat can also deter people from relocating. People are generally more willing to stay put in the colder months when they just want to stay indoors. This is especially so if you live in a very cold climate, as it can be incredibly inconvenient and unappealing to move houses in a snowstorm or when children are in the full swing of the school year.

Since the demand for property tends to be lower in the colder months, you may need to price your rent much lower in order to attract potential tenants. If you are going for a long-term rental strategy, this could have a huge negative financial impact on your overall income. If at all possible, you should spend most of your time marketing your property in the summer months so you can get your renters moved in and settled, so you do not have to worry about it in the winter months.

Consider Your Property's Amenities

The price you set for your rental property will not just be based on the property itself. The number of bedrooms and bathrooms is incredibly important, but there are other things that people look for. That is why it is important to consider your amenities, both on the property and in the surrounding area. There are many amenities that people look for and will pay a little extra for. One of these is safe parking. This could be in the form of a garage, assigned parking, or safe street parking. People do not want to park far away and have to walk down the street in order to get home. This means they will be willing to pay a little bit extra if there is safe parking on or close to the property, or if the property is conveniently located near public transit.

Another key aspect is the general safety of the property and the area. If there is some sort of added security, this will give your tenants peace of mind. This kind of security could be a gated community or even smart home technology and security systems installed in the home. People also look at the safety of the general area and whether it is walkable or not. Walkability means that the property is going to be close to local shops and services and that it's safe to walk on the streets.

Another highly beneficial feature that can increase a property's price is outdoor features and entertainment areas. A pool, patio, balcony, or any kind of recreational area is hugely beneficial. This doesn't have to be directly on the property. For example, if there is a tennis court or communal pool nearby or shared by the same cluster of properties, then this will increase your potential rent prices.

TENANT SCREENING

Once you have set up your pricing strategy and are ready to welcome new tenants, it is time to consider the tenant screening process. One of the biggest mistakes that first-time investors make is allowing anyone to rent their property just so they can get an income. Your tenants can make your life much easier or create huge difficulties for you. This is why it is so important to have a robust tenant screening process to ensure you are choosing the right tenants. You want to make sure that the people who live on your property are going to pay on time, take care of your property, and be responsible.

When you put out advertisements for your rental property, you are probably going to get some interest. You should take some time to research all your potential tenants, even though it may be a little more trouble. Certain things are essential to ask your potential tenants about so you can get some data on them to see whether they would be a good fit. With regard to paying their rent on time and being able to afford the rent, you will need their proof of income and creditworthiness. A good rule of thumb is to look for tenants who make more than three times the monthly rent you will be charging. This safe zone shows that your potential tenants can afford to live on the property. It is a good idea to ask for a three- to six-month bank statement to make sure that they have been earning a steady income. In order to check their creditworthiness, you will need to have a look at their credit history and their credit score. If they are good at managing their credit, it means that they are less likely to fall behind with their rent payments and have proven that they managed their finances well.

Next, you will need to check whether they are good people who live responsible lives. You can check their criminal background, eviction history, and their references. You definitely don't want somebody to live on your property who will put the neighbors in danger, so make sure you run a background check to ensure that the potential tenant did not participate in activities that could put your property or people living in the surrounding area at risk. Checking eviction history helps you to see whether this person is a good tenant. Always find out why the tenant was evicted. If it was because of a violation of the lease agreement or any kind of illegal conduct, damages, or missing rent payments, then you know this person may not be a good fit for you. Finally, you will need to have a look at their references, as these will give you a good indication of their character and whether they have been good tenants in the past. It is definitely a red flag if their references don't have anything particularly good to say about them. After the screening process, you will have a much better idea of whether this person is a good fit for you.

SELF-MANAGEMENT VERSUS PROPERTY MANAGEMENT

For managing your rental property, you have two choices. You can either choose to manage it yourself or get a property manager on board to do it for you. Let's start talking about the self-management method and the pros and cons that come with it.

PROS AND CONS OF SELF-MANAGEMENT

Pros

Saving on Fees

Property management comes at a fee, so if you are doing it yourself, you are saving money. You don't have to pay yourself to take care of the property, so you can put this money into other areas of your investment or simply save it for yourself.

Doing Things Yourself

There is something to be said for doing things yourself. You're able to do things your way, and there is no risk of misunderstandings or miscommunications with somebody else. If you enjoy taking on a challenge and doing things yourself, this could be a good route for you.

Choosing Tenants

Managing your property means that you get to be the one to choose the tenants. With a big investment like real estate, there is peace of mind when you make the decisions yourself and choose the tenants based on your own criteria. You can also build a relationship with your tenants that can lead to mutual respect.

Cons

Takes Commitment

Managing a property by yourself takes commitment and a lot of effort. It means you must be available should there be an emergency or if your tenants need you. Many smaller tasks that take up quite a bit of your time need to be taken care of consistently.

Legal Considerations

There are quite a few legalities when it comes to investing in real estate and renting out your property. A property manager will have all the necessary experience that a first-time investor may not have. It will take some extra work on your part to make sure that you understand all the legal processes and requirements so you don't end up in a sticky situation.

Requires Marketing

Doing things yourself also means you will have to market your property yourself. This can be challenging if you have never done it before. On top of that, many property managers have a network that can assist them with finding the right tenants for a property, and an individual investor may not have the same contacts.

Roles of a Property Manager

A property manager deals with many rules and responsibilities. This alleviates a lot of pressure from the investor. Understanding what a property manager does might help you decide whether this is somebody you want to bring onto your team.

Acquiring Tenants

A property manager will be responsible for acquiring the right tenant for the property. If a tenant's lease is up and they decide they no longer want to stay there, the property manager will start the process again and find a new tenant.

Collecting Rent and Handling Evictions

A property manager will also handle the strict tasks of collecting rent and handling any evictions that need to occur. If a tenant is not paying on time, the property manager will start the process of collecting that money and might need to get lawyers and other legal professionals on board. If this situation escalates, then the property manager will also need to handle evictions and all the necessary processes that follow.

Managing Tenant Requests

When you rent out your property, you become a landlord. This means that if anything were to go wrong on the property, the tenants could call you and request that you attend to the issues. If you have a property manager, your tenants will call them should they need anything or have any requests.

Taking Care of Accounting

Accounting is a very important part of managing a property and ensuring that it is running smoothly. Your property manager will take care of all the bookkeeping and make sure that you are making a profit and that money is going into the right areas.

PROS AND CONS OF PROPERTY MANAGEMENT

Now that you know what a property manager does, it is important to know the pros and cons. This will give you a broader understanding of property management so you can see both sides of the coin.

Pros

Easy and Stress-Free

Hiring a property manager means that the rental process is going to be a lot easier for you. You will not need to stress out about your tenant's maintenance of the property or any other aspect of being a landlord. You will only need to get involved if something very important requires your attention, and your property manager will contact you regarding this.

Understand the Market

Property managers will have experience in the real estate market, and that means they can make decisions with a wealth of knowledge. This might be something you do not have, so bringing this kind of professional on board could help you see better returns on your investment.

Build a Wall Between You and the Tenants

If you are the type of person who does not want to deal with the social aspects of having tenants, then a property manager is a great choice. It creates a barrier between you and your tenants, so you do not have to deal with them or have any direct contact with them.

Oversee Maintenance and Problems

Running a rental property means that maintenance needs to be taken care of and problems need to be solved. The property manager will call the tenant if there is a problem or if maintenance is needed in a certain area. The manager will also handle all maintenance schedules and ensure your property runs smoothly throughout the year.

Cons

Poor Performance

There is always a risk that your property manager will perform poorly and not meet your expectations. Therefore, it is essential to choose the right property manager, but sometimes, things go wrong, even with all the right steps being taken.

Troublesome Employees

When hiring a property manager, you are essentially relinquishing a lot of control to that person. This means they can hire staff or contractors to help with the maintenance, cleaning, and anything else on the property. There's always a risk of troublesome employees working on your property, and sometimes, this could even be the property managers themselves.

Loss of Revenues

When hiring a property manager, you have to pay them for their services. This is typically a percentage of your rent or revenue. The percentage will vary depending on the property manager or the company they work for. Often, this is somewhere between 5 and 10 percent.

Pay for Fees

On top of the percentage payment that you owe them, there may also be additional fees you need to pay. Some property management companies require a placement fee if they find a new tenant for your property. It is important to understand the contract when working with a property manager so you know what costs you might be liable for.

IDEAS TO GENERATE MORE INCOME FROM YOUR RENTAL PROPERTIES

You can make some additional income from your rental property in many ways. Some investors choose to stick to the basics and just generate revenue through the rent they charge, but you can get a little creative and expand your money-making opportunities. These ideas are not going to work for every property or for every investor.

However, you can try one or two of these options to increase the revenue you make through your rental properties.

Rent out fully furnished apartments and rooms. You can charge a bit more when you are renting out fully furnished apartments and rooms. People are more willing to spend when a living space is aesthetically decorated and taken care of.

Offer storage space. If you have additional space in your garage or spare room, you can offer it as a storage space. People are always looking for places to store their extra furniture and items.

Minimize resident turnover. If you are trying to ensure that your property makes the most profit, it is important to minimize your turnover. If you have long-term tenants, it means that you are getting a steady rental income without having to do much work. This means you must provide them with excellent service and ensure that you meet their needs.

Add services and amenities. See if you can add a service or amenity that could be beneficial to your tenants. For example, you could offer a laundry or cleaning service since this is something that people often need. You can add additional amenities like a pool, play area, or air conditioning to add greater benefits to your property.

Reinvest your profits. The money you make from your rental doesn't need to be spent immediately. Instead, you can use this money to reinvest to continue growing your profits. Even though you may not be using the money you're making immediately, you are increasing your overall net worth, and it will be valuable in the future.

Use dynamic pricing strategies. A dynamic pricing strategy means you change your prices based on what is going on in the market. If you are trying to find tenants when there is a lot of demand, then you can increase your prices since people will be willing to pay more. You can decrease your price and offer a discount to be more attractive and competitive in the quieter season.

Increase energy efficiency. Electricity and energy cost a lot of money, so get an energy professional into your property to see how you can use energy more efficiently. This can save you a lot of money in the long run, and it is also kinder to the environment.

INTERACTIVE ELEMENT: CREATING A PROPERTY MANAGEMENT PLAN

Creating a property management plan is crucial when it comes to running a rental property. Without a plan, things can get overlooked, and this will make things harder for you in the future. Follow these steps to create a robust property management plan.

Step 1: Taking Care of Your Property's Needs

Property's existing issues:

____

____

____

Trends in the local rental market:

____

____

____

Legal requirements:

____

____

____

Step 2: Setting Goals

Long-term goals:

____

____

____

Short-term goals:

____

____

____

Financial goals:

____

____

____

Tenant satisfaction goals:

____

____

____

Property-specific goals:

____

____

____

Step 3: Create Your Budget

Income:

Name	Amount

Expenses:

Name	Amount

Savings:

Name	Amount

Step 4: Make a Maintenance Schedule

Indoors:

Name	Budgeted Amount	Date

Outdoors:

Name	Budgeted Amount	Date

Plumbing:

Name	Budgeted Amount	Date

Electrical:

Name	Budgeted Amount	Date

Landscaping:

Name	Budgeted Amount	Date

HVAC:

Name	Budgeted Amount	Date

Other Upkeep:

Name	Budgeted Amount	Date

Now that you're familiar with long-term rentals, let's move on to short-term rentals and why they're profitable.

SHORT-TERM RENTALS

Active listings on Airbnb exceeded 7.7 million by the end of 2023, increasing 18 percent year-over-year with sustained double-digit supply growth across all regions. And in 2023 alone, hosts earned more than $57 billion (Airbnb, 2024). This shows how much money there is to be made through short-term rentals and platforms like Airbnb. If you have not considered short-term rentals, then this may be your sign to start thinking about it.

WHAT ARE SHORT-TERM RENTALS?

A short-term rental is also known as a vacation rental. It is a property the owner rents out to people who will only stay there for a short period. The property must be fully furnished, and all necessary amenities must be provided to the guests. With short-term rentals, we refer to the people staying in the property as guests rather than tenants because they are not staying there on a long-term basis. The guests are also not responsible for taking care of the property in the ways a tenant would. There are completely different expectations between the two, and the goal of a short-term rental business is to make sure there are consistent bookings of the property.

Short-term rental properties are a growing market. We are seeing it become more and more accessible through companies like Airbnb and VRBO. These are platforms where somebody with a property posts it as a listing, and people looking for a short-term rental can easily view and book. It is an alternative to a hotel so that guests can get a unique experience as well as competitive pricing. A host, or the owner of the property, also has a good chance to make even more money than with a long-term rental. This is because people are willing to pay more per night when they are booking a vacation or short-term stay. If you have good guest turnover, you will have a high chance of making good money through short-term rentals. As with anything, short-term rentals have pros and cons, and it's important to understand these before diving in.

PROS

Flexibility

There is a lot of flexibility in how you choose to run a short-term rental. If you only want to rent out your property on certain days, then you can do that. You can bring in guests as often or as seldom as you would like. Some people choose to rent their homes or their main property on a short-term rental basis when they are traveling. For example, if you plan a two-month European vacation, you can rent out your home to make additional money while you're not there. Another example of this flexibility would be if you have a rental property that is a bit farther away from you and you are only in the area on the weekends. You could choose to rent out your property on the weekends when you can attend to your guests, and it's most convenient for you.

Most of the short-term rental platforms and websites allow you to choose when you want to rent out your property. If there is a time when you do not want to accept guests, you can block that out on the calendar so people cannot book. This gives you complete control over when you are accepting guests and when it is going to be the most convenient for you.

Higher Cash Flow

With short-term rentals, you have the opportunity to make a lot of money. All you have to do is a bit of quick math to figure this out. A property could bring in $1,500 per month for rent on a long-term basis. Renting out a property as a vacation rental allows you to charge $1,500 for a week. That means you could potentially earn four times as much money using a short-term rental strategy.

The reason for this huge difference in pricing is that when you set a fee for a short-term rental, you are doing it on a per-night basis. But for a long-term rental, you have to set a per-month rental price that must be locked in for the duration of the lease. Something else to consider with short-term rentals is that you can change the nightly fee whenever you want. When vacation properties are in high demand, you can increase the price in order to generate more profit. You can also lower the price in the low-demand seasons to attract more people to your vacation rental. There are a lot of pricing strategies that you can use when it comes to short-term rentals that are simply not available with a long-term rental. This maximizes the amount of profit that you can make.

Fewer Tenant Legal Disputes

With a short-term rental, there is a lower likelihood of you having large legal disputes with your guests. A guest will typically stay for no longer than a week and then move on. However, with a long-term tenant, there are a lot of legal aspects to take into consideration. A prolonged tenant and landlord relationship can lead to legal action based on disagreements. These kinds of legal disputes can be costly as well as time-consuming.

It is important to note that there are tenant laws that protect short-term renters in the same way they might protect long-term rentals. Staying up-to-date with all the relevant property laws will make your life a lot easier in the long run. You will cover your back and ensure that you are meeting all the relevant legal standards.

CONS

Risk of Prolonged Vacancy

There are risks when it comes to short-term rentals. While the potential for a larger income is definitely there, there is also the risk of a prolonged vacancy. When this happens, you will not be making any money through rental income for the duration of the vacancy. There is no guarantee that you will get consistent bookings and guests. With a vacation rental, you have to understand the market. Some months are booming, and people are booking their vacations like crazy, while other months are much slower. In the slower months, you may struggle to get people to book with you, which means that you will be losing out.

With a prolonged vacancy, you will still be liable for the utilities on the property. With a long-term rental, the tenants have to pay the utilities, but this is not the case with a short-term rental. You will have to pay the mortgage and any other bills that come with the property, even if you're not making money at that moment. If there are prolonged vacancies, you will also need to make more of an effort to go and check on the property, as there is no one there to report potential issues like plumbing problems, damages, or electrical faults.

In seasons when there are not a lot of bookings, it is still important for you to maintain the general cleanliness of the property. You don't know when you will get new guests, and making a good impression is important. That means that even if nobody is in the property, you still have to make sure it is up to standard.

More Time and Property Upkeep

Since the guest turnover in a vacation rental property is high, you are required to spend more time on your rental property. This is not a passive income because you have to turn over the property and ensure it's ready for your next guest. When one guest checks out, you have to go in, clean the property, and make sure all the necessities have been replaced. Then, you will need to check in the new guests and make sure they have everything they need. You also have to be on call should your guests need something from you or have an emergency.

With short-term rentals, the goal is to give your guests the best experience possible. You will only get guests and have good ratings on the platform if you provide exceptional service. This means you will need to be there for your guests and provide them with the service they want.

You may also need to do regular maintenance and upkeep checks more often. Some guests may not be as careful as you would like them to be. Remember that when guests check into a place for a holiday, they don't want to think about anything serious. Their main goal is to relax or have fun. In that case, they might be a bit more careless with handling things, which means more maintenance is going to be required from you. Of course, they shouldn't destroy your property, but if they are a little clumsy with their luggage or decide to move around the furniture, then there will be scuffs and scratches that you may need to take care of. With long-term rentals, a lot of these minor issues need to be taken care of by the tenant, but this is not the case with short-term rentals.

Fewer Tenant Screening Options

With a short-term rental, the primary goal is to get as many people in and out quickly as possible. That is how you are going to make the most money. However, this does mean you do not have the opportunity to screen your tenants as you would in a long-term rental. At the start of your short-term rental endeavor, you may accept any potential guest who wants to book with you just so you can make some money and get some reviews on the rental platforms.

Some screening and security measures have been implemented with platforms such as Airbnb and VRBO. However, this is not a comprehensive screening process. It verifies basic information like a phone number, email address, and government ID. Then, there are reviews on the platform that you can check out. Just as a guest can rate and review you on the platform, the people who own the properties can write and review those who stay with them. It is always a good idea to look at these ratings and reviews to ensure that the person hasn't been destructive or inconsiderate. However, in many cases, the person may not have reviews, which means you won't have those to rely on when accepting their booking. There is always a chance that you will get a problematic guest who could cause damage to the property and violate the house rules you have set up.

INTERACTIVE ELEMENT: ARE SHORT-TERM RENTALS FOR YOU?

If you are considering the short-term rental option, then it is good to understand whether the pros outweigh the cons for you. The best way to do this is to note the cons and see how you can navigate them. Write down the cons you are most concerned about and then come up with one or two ideas that will mitigate the risks of those cons.

Short-term rentals are important to consider as a real estate investment strategy. They can make you a steady income and help you reach financial freedom. One way to operate short-term rentals is through Airbnb. We will be discussing Airbnb as an investment strategy in more detail in the next chapter.

THE AIRBNB OPPORTUNITY

Out of all these short-term rental platforms out there, Airbnb is definitely the most popular and has the furthest reach. Like many other short-term rental property sites, Airbnb is essentially designed like a marketplace. This marketplace connects people looking for accommodation with people renting out their property on a short-term basis. It has created a way for people to make additional money, and it helps people looking for a vacation find unique places at a cheaper price.

It is fairly easy to sign up on the platform. Once you have created an account and uploaded all the relevant information, you can post your listing. From here, people will be able to view your listing when they are looking for a vacation rental in the area. You have full control of when you want to rent out your property and have access to a calendar where you can open up or block out specific dates. You will also be able to chat with people who are interested in renting out your property.

Airbnb also allows you to advertise unique stays and experiences. If there is something extra special about your property or it can offer an uncommon experience, then you'll be able to advertise this as something separate. For example, if you have access to horse riding or boating cruises, you could advertise these on the platform, too.

I have written books on Airbnb and short-term rentals that could help you gain further insights into the topic. There are lots of details and information that need to be considered when you are working through a platform like Airbnb. Not to mention the tips, tricks, and hacks you can use to increase your revenue and ensure the process is as smooth as possible. If this interests you, I highly suggest you pick up one of my other books so you can set yourself up for success when it comes to your Airbnb or short-term rental.

Before diving into this topic, it is important to take into account the legal regulations surrounding Airbnb. You don't want to pay any unnecessary fees or penalties down the road. As an Airbnb host, it is really important that you understand the laws in your city, country, state, or territory. You will need to get this advice directly from your government or municipality and keep checking back regularly for any changes. You can also check the Airbnb help center, which should offer some guidance for your city. You should also visit your local government website to see the permits or licenses needed to start a short-term rental business. Some things to look into are business licenses, building codes, zoning rules, permits, tax laws, and landlord-tenant laws. With that being said, let's go through some of the basics when it comes to using Airbnb.

Creating an Airbnb Account

The great thing about Airbnb is that it is incredibly easy to create an account. First, you will need to log onto the Airbnb website and choose the sign-up option. You will be guided step-by-step through the process by the use of prompts and forms.

In order to have an active Airbnb account, you will need to verify your account, and this usually requires your government-issued ID. You also need to upload a photo for facial recognition. Once you have done that, you will have to wait up to twenty-four hours for Airbnb to review and verify your information. Once you have done that, you will be approved on the Airbnb site and can continue to build your profile.

Listing a Property, Including Niche Options

There are many steps to take when listing a property on the Airbnb site. It is highly important that you do this properly because it is the only way that you get to market yourself on the website. When you first start listing your property, you must go through various steps to present the most accurate information. Remember, not all guests are looking for the same type of property or vacation, so being specific about what you have to offer is really important.

The first thing you must do to list your property is select your property type. There are different options for property types on the Airbnb website. Currently, the options are an apartment, house, self-contained unit, unique space, bed-and-breakfast, or boutique hotel. Have a look at your property and the space you offer and see which category suits it. You can rent out a room or even part of your home, so you are not just limited to the traditional versions of the above categories. Once you have selected your property type, you will then continue to get a little more specific. There are many options, including niche options. Whatever options you choose, just make sure that you are being honest and truthful because you want to manage your guest's expectations.

You will further categorize based on the type of space you will rent out. There are three options that you can choose from. The first is an entire home or apartment, which is pretty self-explanatory. With this option, you rent out the entire apartment or space for your guests to use. That means that any guest renting out the space will expect to have all the amenities you would find in a regular home or apartment. For example, they will look for things like a kitchen, laundry facilities, cooking utensils, and cleaning supplies. Think about a family or large group coming to stay for a while and what they would need. The next type is a shared room, which is when your guest will be sharing a room with another guest or guests. This is more like a hostel where multiple guests can stay together. The guest would expect to have shared amenities and rooms. Finally, you can have a private room where the guest would have their own private room or space, but other areas of the space will be shared with other people.

Once you have handled the type of property, you'll need to move on to selecting your location. Make sure your location is as accurate as possible because your guests will book primarily based on location. Your guests will not get your exact address until you have approved their stay and are in contact with them, but there will be a map that will give them a very general idea of where your property is.

You will need to specify how many bedrooms and bathrooms you have available, as well as the amenities. You will also need to indicate how many guests you will allow to book at once to ensure a comfortable stay.

You will then need to start taking some photos of your property to upload to the Airbnb website. This is highly important because people seek out potential vacation rentals with their eyes. If your pictures are eye-catching and interesting, then you will probably get more potential guests interested in your space. Ensure that you are taking clear pictures in good lighting. You can even get a professional photographer to assist you with getting excellent pictures of your property. You also want to ensure the property is neat and there is no unnecessary clutter when taking the pictures. Essentially, you want to put your best foot forward when you are snapping those pics.

Another important aspect of listing your property on the Airbnb website is creating a title and adding a description. The title will give anyone scrolling through the Airbnb listings a quick idea of what your property offers. Remember to choose your words carefully and be truthful. Once you've got your title, you can move on to creating a description, which is a lot more detailed. You can have a look at other Airbnb listings to get an idea of what descriptions work best. Make sure you supply a list of the features and benefits of your property. There is a rather large word count allotted for the description, so make sure you are being as detailed as possible.

At this point, your listing is almost ready to go, so you need to think about pricing. For a beginner, the best way to go about it is to do some research on similar Airbnb listings in your area to see what other people are charging. When you first start, you will need to price your rental competitively to get people to book with you. The more reviews you have and the more people who have stayed at your property, the easier it is going to be to find more guests. Remember to be realistic with your pricing and that you can always change it as time goes on. When you are more established, you can increase your nightly rate to be fairly compensated. Remember to also take into consideration things like the type of rental you have, the time of year, and your location. All of these will play a big role in your pricing strategy. It is a good idea to continuously do research and look at other Airbnb listings so you know how to price your property competitively.

It is good to note that you can save your listing without publishing it and come back and fill in the rest of the details later. Since it is a fairly comprehensive listing, it can take quite a long time, and you don't have to do it all in one sitting. Once you fill in all this information, you will need to answer some questions, and then you can publish your listing to the public. All that's left now is to watch the bookings roll in.

Setting Competitive Prices

I've already mentioned how important a competitive pricing strategy is. You will need to set yourself up for success, and you can do that by taking the right steps toward pricing your property correctly. First, you will want to figure out how much your Airbnb costs you per night. This is the base from where you will work out how much you are going to charge as a nightly rate. You should aim to make a profit or at least break even. Your nightly cost will need to include your rent, utilities, taxes, and any other costs that factor into running your Airbnb or owning your property. Since a lot of the bills and expenses are calculated on a monthly basis, you can simply take your monthly costs and divide them by thirty in order to get your nightly costs.

Now that you know exactly how much your Airbnb is costing you, it is time to think about how much profit you want to make. The rate you set should be higher than the nightly rate you spend on your Airbnb. You also have to take into consideration other things, such as the time you are spending to manage your Airbnb. This may not be a solid monetary value, but you are adding value to the guest and, therefore, need to charge for it. Make sure you do market research and look at how much other Airbnbs are charging for a similar service to what you offer. Even if you have decided on a price for your nightly rate, you need to adjust for the current market. If you are overcharging, it means people will not choose you as their first option. You are probably going to lose out on potential bookings because of this. If you are undercharging, it means that you are leaving money on the table and not optimizing your potential income.

Airbnb also has a smart pricing tool that you can either turn on or off. This tool will automatically shift your price up and down, depending on what is happening in the market. The algorithm will look at the demand for properties similar to yours and then determine a price to set per night. You can also set a minimum nightly rate that the smart pricing tool cannot go below so that you still have some control over your nightly rates. If you do not want to price your listing manually, then this is definitely a good option.

Managing Bookings Remotely

You may not be available to be at your property whenever guests check in and book with you. Perhaps you have multiple Airbnb properties, or maybe you are just not in town when you are going to have guests staying with you. Having a strategy to handle your bookings and guests remotely can give you much more flexibility when you are an Airbnb host.

COMMUNICATE WITH YOUR GUESTS

Communication is always going to be key when you are managing any kind of rental. Airbnb tracks how quickly you respond to your guests, and this shows up on your listing profile. It is even more important to prioritize communication with your guests if you will not be there in person to welcome them or have an in-person conversation with them.

You should focus on communicating with your guests before, during, and after check-in and their stay. You also want to make sure that you give your guests all the necessary information. You can also check in with your guests periodically throughout the day, depending on how long their stay is. You definitely don't want to overcommunicate while they stay on your property, as this can get highly annoying. Instead, check in on them once or twice, and then make sure you're easily reachable should they need you. Check in with them to see how they enjoyed their stay, and always ask if they are willing to give you a good review on the platform.

Set Up Automated Messaging

Life can get busy, so it is a good idea to set up some sort of automated message in case you cannot respond at a certain time. This message can be a welcome to your guests and provide them with all the information they need. You can also set up automatic replies to guest questions, which will help your guests get the answers they need without you having to be involved.

Set Plenty of Reminders

You will have many different responsibilities when you are an Airbnb host, so make sure to set reminders on your calendar so you do not get distracted or forget. If you have a guest checking in or you need to do maintenance on the property, set this in your calendar as a priority for you to do.

Solicit Guest Reviews

Solicitation sounds like a bad word, but it is important to always ask for a review. Sometimes, guests do forget, and getting good reviews bumps you up on the platform and puts you in a better position to find more potential guests. You can ask for a review a few days after your guests have checked out, and you can even send an automated message for this to happen. Remember to be polite when asking for a review, as this will increase your chances of getting a positive one.

Offer Self-Check-In

These days, a lot of technology is available to make a short-term rental owner's life easier. You can implement a self-check-in system so your guests can check in without you having to be there. This is a lot more convenient for both of you since you do not have to coordinate check-in times based on availability. One option for a self-check-in would be a lockbox where you leave the key to the property and give the guest a code to access the box. You can also change the property's locks to digital locks that open with a code, fingerprint, or password. You can then change this code or password for each guest, which is an additional level of security.

Get Home Security

Since you are welcoming people into your property, it is essential that you have a home security system. You will not be on the property often enough to make sure that it is safe and secure. You want to ensure your home is secure and your guests are safe. Installing security cameras and other security systems can be very helpful. If you are installing security cameras, be aware that Airbnb has strict rules surrounding the location of the cameras. They can be outside, but no cameras are allowed inside the home or property.

Make House Rules Clear

With Airbnb, you set the house rules, so make sure these are clear to your guests before they check in. You can send out the house rules to them in advance, but then also have a printed version of the house rules in the home. Some Airbnb hosts choose to put the relevant rules in the specific areas of the house. For example, if it is a non-smoking area, you can put up signs around the property to ensure that your guests know the rules and restrictions.

Compose a Guest Book

A guest book is a great way to show your guests that you care and provide them with all the information they need to enjoy their stay. This guest book can include things like instructions for the property and how-to manuals for the amenities and technology. You can also include the house rules as well as tips and tricks for enjoying their stay. Some Airbnb hosts go above and beyond and include local attractions and features in the area that guests may enjoy experiencing.

Organize a Welcome Gift

Another way to personalize your guest experience is to have a welcome gift ready for them when they check in. Since you will not be there in person, this is a nice touch that you can add to make a guest feel welcome. You can add whatever you want to this welcome pack, but making sure that it's on theme and will be useful to your guests is important. For example, you can include some local treats, important toiletries they may need, and even a friendly note for them.

Handling Guest Inquiries

One thing that will make your life so much easier is if you can anticipate your guests' questions and answer them before they even ask. That way, you do not have to go back and forth with questions and answers that could have easily been resolved from the get-go. On top of that, it is best to have your answers locked and loaded so you can give your guests accurate information if you are on the phone with them or communicating with them through email or on the Airbnb app. You can even have answers to common questions drafted out so you can simply copy and paste them, which makes it a lot easier. Below are a few of the most common questions that guests ask and some tips on how to answer them correctly.

Where Is the Property Located?

While the address will be given to your guests as soon as you accept them and they pay, it is still important to understand that some guests do not read all the details and may ask this question. On top of the address, they will probably want to know how far it is from the amenities and the airport, as well as the directions from the airport to your property. You may also want to add some additional details on how to find your property, like the name of the building or any landmarks that could stand out to them.

Can We Check In or Out Early?

For the sake of convenience, some guests will ask if they can check in or out earlier or later than usual. Whether you accept earlier check-in or later check-out is up to you and is dependent on your schedule. If you have guests back to back, it might be difficult to accommodate these custom check-in and check-out times because you have to turn over the property and ensure it's clean and ready to go. If you cannot clean up and have the property ready for your next guest in a shorter amount of time, then it's best to let your guests know that you cannot accommodate a different check-in or check-out time. This is far better than letting them check into an untidy apartment or having the cleaning staff or you running up and down trying to get things ready while they are in the property. However, if you can accommodate them, your guests will appreciate it.

Does Your Property Have This Item?

Sometimes, guests will inquire about whether or not you have a certain item or amenity for them to use when they get to your property. To save time, you can have a list of all the items and amenities saved so you can easily send it to your guests or copy and paste this list into a message should they ask about a specific item. It is also a good idea to take as many pictures as possible of the important areas of your house so they can see what kinds of amenities and items are available.

What About a Discount?

You can't blame a guest for trying to get a discount so they can pay a little bit less. With that being said, you are under no obligation to give your guests a discount. However, you might consider selecting certain people to give discounts to under special circumstances. For example, if guests are staying for a longer time, you can offer a discount. You may also want to consider giving a discount to regular and loyal guests. Another good way to use a discount is to offer them at specific times of the year, like New Year celebrations, Christmas, or just when there is less demand in your area.

Can I Bring Someone Over, Such as a Family Member or a Friend?

Sometimes, a guest may want to invite other people over to the Airbnb once they have arrived. Sometimes, it is just for a visit, and others invite other people to stay with them. You should make sure that you are clear about your rules and policies surrounding the number of guests that are going to be on your property. Some guests want to have parties in the Airbnb, and this could get unruly and cause damage to your property. If you do not want parties in your Airbnb, then clearly state this in the rules. If you allow your guests to bring over other people, make sure they know the perimeters, such as how many guests can visit and when they need to leave.

Maintaining the Property

Maintenance is one of the most important things you can do for your property. When you run an Airbnb, it means there will be a lot of traffic in and out of your home. Maintenance is of the utmost importance because it shows that the house meets the standards your guests require and that you are not leaving things too long before you start making fixes and changes. Having a schedule and list can help you stay on track with your maintenance. That way, you won't accidentally forget something.

Some things need to be done weekly. You will find a list of those things below.

- Inspect all plumbing and water sources for leaks.
- Wash windows and doors and inspect for cracks or damages.
- Double-check that all the locks in the house are working correctly.
- Check furniture.
- Check that all safety systems and fire extinguishers still work.
- Check for any indication of pests.
- Do a general clean and tidy up of the house.
- Test all remote controls and electronic devices.
- Check electrical outlets and light fixtures.
- Ensure all items are packed away where they need to be.

Becoming a Superhost

The title of Superhost is coveted among Airbnb hosts. Before we get into the rest of the topic, it is important to know what a Superhost is. A Superhost is somebody who has an above-average rating due to exceptional service and the provision of amazing guest experiences. When you get to Superhost status, you will get a badge displayed on your profile so that everybody can see it on the listing page. You can also charge a good amount more because you are reliable and now have an elevated status on the platform.

There are a few criteria that you need to meet in order to become a Superhost. The first criterion is that you have a minimum of three stays, which equals up to one hundred nights stayed, or a minimum of ten trips or reservations booked with you. You will also need to ensure that you keep the standard of a 90 percent response rate to potential guests who have questions or are looking to book with you. Your cancellation rate needs to be under one percent to show that you don't just cancel on your guests whenever you feel like it. Another incredibly important criterion is that you have a review score of 4.8 or more.

Once you have met all of these criteria, then you will be considered a Superhost. This is not something that you need to apply for. Instead, this is awarded automatically once you have met all the criteria. The review process takes place once every quarter, so you have a chance to be awarded a Superhost badge every three months. If, for any reason, you no longer meet the criteria, your badge will be removed, and you will need to work your way back up to being a Superhost.

INTERACTIVE ELEMENT: PLAN YOUR FIRST AIRBNB LISTING

Having a plan to start your very first Airbnb is so important. You must plan your listing and get everything in order before jumping in. I have written two books on becoming a successful Airbnb host. These could be essential reading should you want to become an Airbnb host. Here are the titles:

How to Set Up and Run a Successful Airbnb Business: *Outearn Your Competition with Skyrocketing Rental Income and Leave Your 9 to 5 Job Even if You Are an Absolute Beginner*

How to Unleash Your Airbnb's Full Potential: *The Complete Step-by-Step Guide to Maximizing Bookings, Rental Income, Setting Up Automation and Optimizations for Your Short-Term Rental Business*

You can also get in touch with other people in the Airbnb community. More experienced people will be able to share a wealth of knowledge with you. I have created a Facebook group just for this purpose. I would encourage you to join and get an inside look at the world of Airbnb. Here are the details:

Name: Airbnb Host Community

URL: www.facebook.com/groups/airbnbhostcommunity

QR Code:

After exploring Airbnbs, it's now time to focus on long-term success and wealth-building strategies. In the next chapter, we will explore how to ensure sustainable growth and maximize your real estate investments over time.

LONG-TERM SUCCESS
AND WEALTH-BUILDING

"Real estate cannot be lost or stolen, nor can it be carried away. Purchased with common sense, paid for in full, and managed with reasonable care, it is about the safest investment in the world."

— FRANKLIN D. ROOSEVELT

PROPERTY REHAB

Property rehab is simply rehabilitating a property that may be in poor condition to make it live up to its full potential. You are essentially going to be restoring a piece of real estate to increase its functionality and appearance and raise the value of that property. There are many steps to consider when you do this, but it can be worth it if you do it right.

Property Condition Assessment

The first thing you will need to do is assess the property's current condition. This will give you a starting point so you can identify any big issues that need your attention. Ensure you do this assessment thoroughly and get professionals involved when necessary. You definitely don't want to be shocked by an enormous expense down the road.

Create a Checklist

Once you have done your assessments, you need to organize all of your information into a checklist. This will help you easily work through each thing that needs to be done for the renovation project. Doing this ensures that you understand the task at hand and keeps everything organized so you don't accidentally miss something.

Make a Budget

When it comes to real estate, everything costs money, so it is important to have a budget. Based on your checklist, try to figure out the estimated amount that you would need for each item. You also need to be prepared for emergencies and unforeseen expenses. Sometimes, you just don't know the full cost of something until you do it, so it is important to have some cushioning in your budget.

Find a Contractor

A good contractor will save you a lot of money but also a lot of time and stress. Choose a contractor with a lot of experience and a good track record. You also want to make sure the contractor you choose has experience with the type of renovations and improvements you are doing to your property.

Debris and Trash Removal

This is by no means the most glamorous part of the process, but you will need to organize the removal of any debris or trash on the property. This is not just for aesthetic purposes but for safety reasons as well. Accidents can happen if there are random items lying around.

Depending on how much trash and debris is on the property, you may need to hire a service to assist you.

Interior Renovations

The most exciting part of any kind of rehabilitation or revamp of a property is probably the decorating, but you cannot start there. You first need to take care of structural issues and any other major problems before you move on to the design aspects. These are what's going to cost you the most money, and they may also be safety concerns. Dealing with this first is in the best interests of everybody who takes up residence on this property.

Work on the Exterior

The exterior of the house is also important because you want to increase curb appeal. The outside of the property is the first thing people see, so if you can draw them in from the get-go, you have a much better chance of increasing the value and getting people interested in either purchasing your property or renting it out from you. Take care of the lawn and exterior of the home and anything they can see from the street view.

Finalize the Project

Now is the time to do a walk-through to ensure all the work has been carried out to your liking. Don't simply trust your contractors or other people to approve everything. It is important for you to be involved in the finalizing process and make sure that you check everything thoroughly.

SELLING YOUR PROPERTY

There are many reasons why you may want to sell your property. It could be due to a life event, or it could be a strategic decision. There is no right or wrong answer to the question of when to sell your property, but you need to think about it before you do it. It is a big decision, and you want to make sure that you are thinking it through and considering all the options before you go through with the sale.

Below are some reasons why you might sell your property:

- In the case of a major life event, you may no longer be able to handle the maintenance or responsibility of the property.
- Your other investments bring in more income than this one.

- Your cap rate is sitting below the risk-free rate of return.
- You no longer find joy in owning this property but find it in something else that is more important to you.
- Other options may be more lucrative for your investments, and you want to explore those.
- The tax laws have changed, and now homeowners are getting stuck with excessive taxes.
- Your property is simply too expensive for you to handle at this moment.
- You no longer want to own this property for a personal reason.

As you can see, there are many reasons why somebody might not want to own a specific piece of property any longer. If you have considered it and examined all your options, it is perfectly okay to look into selling your property.

If you have decided that selling your property is the best way forward, it is important to think about ways to maximize your profit from the sale. One of the best ways to do this is to avoid as many taxes as possible when selling your property. There are various ways in which you can do that, and one way is through something called tax harvesting. In order to do this, you will be offsetting your capital gains with losses so that you can reduce the amount you are paying in tax. For example, if you see that your property has increased in value over the years, but you have other investments that have decreased in value, you can sell the other investments at a loss so you can balance out your overall capital gains and pay less tax. You could also use a 1031 exchange to reduce the amount you are paying in tax. As mentioned, you can use this exchange to purchase a similar property to avoid capital gains taxes. You could also use Section 121 exclusion, with which you can exclude up to a maximum amount of $500,000 if you are married and filing jointly on your capital gains. You can only do this by converting an investment property into your and your spouse's primary residence. If you are a single person, then this will be cut in half, and the benefit is $250,000.

When selling your rental property, there are other things to consider to increase the amount you will get from the sale. While considering capital gains tax is important, it's not the be-all and end-all. One of the best things you can do is to hire a professional who understands real estate investing and can help you through the process. This may result in you saving so much money in the long term that it will be worth it. You should also consider completing any repairs, renovations, or upgrades you had in the works. Even some repairs or renovations make a significant difference in the selling price of your property. You also need to ensure you are marketing your property well to attract buyers with money to spend. These are key to getting the price you deserve when you are selling your current real estate.

REINVESTING PROFITS

Once you have determined that selling your property is the best for you and you have received some profit, you need to decide what you will do with that profit. It may seem tempting for you to spend as much of it as possible. However, this is not usually the best way to go. Reinvesting that profit into other investment types is a much better long-term approach. You have already worked hard to build up your current real estate investment and make a profit, and you don't want to lose it by making a few bad purchasing decisions.

There are many things that you could invest your money into. With real estate, so many options are available that it is difficult to choose just one. Diversifying your investments is one of the best things you can do for the health of your future portfolio and to ensure you make the most profit possible. If you haven't already looked into a REIT, then this is the time to do so. This is a way that you can invest your money into real estate without being an active participant in managing your property. We have already done a deep dive into this kind of investment, so if you want a recap, it is best to go back to Chapter 1 and get all the information you need.

You can also diversify your investment portfolio through different types of real estate. If you have sold a property and are looking to invest in real estate differently, there are many categories you can look into. You can look into the geographical location of the properties you invest in. If all of your real estate investments are in one area, you can expand this by purchasing in a different city or even state. It does mean you will need to do some research on the state laws when it comes to real estate, but if you are willing to do that, you could make a very secure investment in a different geographical location.

You can also look at the type of properties that you are investing in and do something a little different. For example, if all of your property investments are long-term real estate investments, you can have a look at short-term rentals as an option. Different real estate investments will help you diversify your portfolio. You may also want to try a different investment strategy, such as house flipping or holding your investments for a longer time so they increase in value. Perhaps moving to a more active or passive investment is something that could also appeal to you, depending on your goals and what you have experienced in the past.

When you reinvest the money you have made through one of your investments, you are taking advantage of compounding your profits. You are essentially accelerating the growth of your wealth over time to increase it at an exponential rate. The more money you put into your investments, the more money you could potentially get out of it. This is why it is so important to think continuously about how to invest and get more out of your investments. The goal is to take advantage of the investment market so you can maximize your profits and ensure you are seeing the best returns possible.

WHY INFLATION IS AN ALLY

Whenever the topic of inflation is brought up, it typically has a negative connotation to it. This is understandable because when the price of things increases, your general profit may decrease since you are paying more money for the upkeep of your property. However, inflation can work to your benefit. When inflation hits, it means that the general prices of things increase, which also means that rent increases and the amount people will spend on properties will also increase. Essentially, you can charge a lot more rent or sell your property for more when experiencing higher inflation. This works best if you purchased your investment property when inflation was lower and the general price of things was also lower.

You can use inflation to your advantage when it comes to your real estate investment. One way is to focus on properties that generate a steady cash flow. When your real estate investments generate high cash flow, you can make more money when interest increases. If the prices of everything are already increasing, it means that you will probably be able to charge more rent on your properties and make more money. In this case, it might also be a good idea to go for short-term leases rather than longer-term ones. If you know that inflation will be a risk soon, you may want to lock in shorter-term leases so that you can increase the rent prices should inflation occur. If you and your tenant have a long-term lease, that means that you have to accept their rental payments at a fixed rate until the lease is terminated. A shorter-term lease means you can change the agreed-upon rental price based on factors such as inflation.

Diversifying your investment portfolio is a good way to protect yourself from interest rates. Diversification is incredibly important. You are investing, which means you are spreading out your investments and effectively lowering the risk you are facing. Where one investment may have a negative outlook when it comes to inflation, another investment might give you positive benefits when faced with inflation.

A huge part of being an investor is being knowledgeable about what is going on in the economy and the general market. While you can never fully predict what will happen with the economy, monitoring economic indicators is still a good idea. This way, you can prepare for any changes in the state of the economy. This may mean that you need to make different investments, sell your investments, or invest more heavily in what you currently are investing in. There will always be trends in the market, and staying aware and up-to-date with these will allow you to make better investment decisions. You can try to follow professionals on various social media platforms, newsletters, magazines, and other types of content. This will keep you in the loop with what is happening and help you be constantly notified when things are changing so you know what to expect. It is always better to be prepared rather than to be caught off guard.

INTERACTIVE ELEMENT: REFLECTION QUESTIONS

It is always important to reflect when it comes to your investment decisions. As you move through life, your investment choices will look different based on various factors. The goals you set five years ago might not be relevant now, and you will need to shift your goals and thought patterns to move into something better for the future. As you gain more experience in real estate investing, you may realize that your investment style changes, and so do the things you need and want. Ask the reflection questions below every once in a while so you can see where you stand when it comes to your investments:

- What are your long-term and short-term goals regarding your finances and real estate investing?
- How will you use real estate to help you reach your financial and personal goals?
- In which ways do you plan to diversify your investment portfolio?
- What strategy are you going to use to reinvest your profits from your current investments into future investments so you can build long-term wealth?

With a comprehensive understanding of long-term success strategies in real estate, you're now equipped to navigate the market confidently and build substantial wealth.

INSPIRE NEW INVESTORS TO GET STARTED!

You're about to begin one of the most exciting and rewarding ventures you've ever committed to—and this is your chance to inspire others and let them in on how to break into real estate investment.

Simply by sharing your honest opinion of this book and a little about your own story, you'll inspire new readers to take the plunge—and you'll show them exactly where they can find all the information they need to make a success of it.

Thank you so much for your support. I wish you every success with your investments!

Scan the QR code to leave a review

CONCLUSION

Investing in real estate is one of the most rewarding journeys you can go on. It definitely takes a lot of work, but all the effort you will put in will be worth it. When you invest in real estate, you are also investing in your future. There is a reason so many people want to get into real estate. Now that you have reached the end of this book, you have all the tools you need to become a successful real estate investor. Just remember that all it takes is one small step at a time. You don't have to put pressure on yourself to become a multimillionaire in a matter of months. Taking a few small steps at a time is the best way to approach investing in real estate. Focus on one aspect first and then keep building on that momentum.

There are so many types of real estate out there that you can find one that suits your needs and financial goals. If you are a beginner investor and don't have a lot of funds to play with, then you can start small by investing in a real estate investment trust. This is a great place to start, so you can get a feel for investing in real estate without actually purchasing a property. From there, you can continuously build up and then take steps toward other types of real estate investments. As long as you have a plan and are taking action to stick to it, then you are on the right path. There is no one way to be a real estate investor, so it is up to you to create a strategy and a plan that is going to work for you and your finances. The power is completely in your hands, and you can tailor your investment strategy while using the principles in this book to help guide you.

You've learned the essentials of real estate investing, from financing and purchasing properties to managing short-term rentals and leveraging long-term strategies. Now, it's time to put these insights into action and start building your real estate empire!

If you have found this book helpful, I'd really appreciate it if you gave it a positive review on the platform where you purchased it. This will help to extend my reach and ensure more people are well-equipped for the fulfilling journey of investing in real estate. Don't forget to check out my other books as well!

GLOSSARY

1031 Exchange: This allows for tax to be deferred by selling a property and using that money to buy a new property without paying capital gains tax on the sale.

Amortization: An accounting method to spread loan payments over a certain time. The payments will cover the principal and interest.

ARM: Also known as adjustable-rate mortgage. With this type of loan, the interest rate adjusts or changes over time.

Amenity: This refers to an extra feature or appliance that a property has.

Appreciation: When the value of a property increases over time due to market demand, improvements, or inflation.

APR (Annual Percentage Rate): The yearly cost of a loan, including all additional fees and rates.

BRRRR: This refers to an investment strategy where you buy, rehab, rent, refinance, and repeat.

Cash Flow: The net amount being transferred in and out of an investment after income and expenses.

Cap Rate (Capitalization Rate): This is used to assess how profitable a real estate investment will be by dividing the NOI by the purchase price.

CMA: A comparative market analysis, which is a report on the market value of a property based on a comparison of similar properties in the same area.

Collateral: Pledging an asset for a loan so if you default on the loan, the lender can repossess it to get their money out.

Depreciation: The value of an asset decreases over time due to various factors.

Equity: The difference between the market value and the amount owed on the property.

Fair Market Value: The estimated price a property can be sold for on the current market.

HELOC: Also known as Home Equity Line of Credit, it allows a borrower to take out credit up to a certain limit by leveraging equity in a property they currently own.

Homeowners Association (HOA): An organization that manages the affairs and operations of a certain group of properties that are owned or rented by multiple different people.

HVAC: Heating, Ventilation, and Air Conditioning system.

Interest Rate: A percentage fee that is charged on a loan.

Leverage: To use a loan or credit to purchase a piece of real estate.

Liquidity: Signifies how quickly an asset can be sold or converted into cash.

LMI (Lenders Mortgage Insurance): Insurance that protects the lender if the borrower defaults on a loan.

LTV: This stands for loan-to-value ratio and is used to calculate the potential risk of a loan compared to the value of the property.

NOI: This stands for net operating income and indicates the income generated after subtracting the expenses.

Principal: The original amount of money borrowed, without the additional fees or interest.

REIT: Also known as a Real Estate Investment Trust. This entity pools together investment capital from multiple investors to purchase, operate, or finance properties to generate investment returns.

ROI (Return on Investment): Evaluates the profitability of an investment. This is calculated by dividing the net profit by the investment cost.

REFERENCES

"3 Highly Motivational Real Estate Success Stories - New Silver," January 25, 2024. https://newsilver.com/the-lender/real-estate-success-stories/.

"7 Pros and Cons of Owning a Short Term Rental | Short Term Rental Manager," April 20, 2018. https://shorttermrentalmanager.com/7-pros-and-cons-of-owning-a-short-term-rental/.

"10 Common Rental Property Repairs Landlords Need to Know About | Travelers Insurance," November 14, 2022. https://www.travelers.com/resources/home/landlords/10-common-rental-property-repairs-landlords-need-to-know-about.

"20 Expert Tips for Successfully Managing an Airbnb Remotely." https://awning.com/post/manage-airbnb-remotely.

"50 Questions To Ask Before Investing in Real Estate." https://www.linkedin.com/pulse/50-questions-ask-before-investing-real-estate-camaplan.

Admin. "Land Investing - How To Make Money in 9 Steps." *Best Real Estate Investment Company in Lekki, Lagos, Nigeria* (blog), May 16, 2022. https://eystone.ng/land-investing/.

Guest Author. "How and Why You Need to Diversify Your Real Estate Portfolio - Stessa." https://www.stessa.com/blog/how-and-why-you-need-to-diversify-your-real-estate-portfolio/.

Booking Ninjas. "What Is a Residential Property? Types, Features, and Benefits." https://www.bookingninjas.com/blog/what-is-a-residential-property-types-features-and-benefits.

Brown, Jerry. "27 Loan Terminologies You Must Know." Forbes Advisor, February 9, 2021. https://www.forbes.com/advisor/personal-loans/loan-terminologies/.

Cain, Sarah Li. "10 Key Questions To Ask When Buying A House." Bankrate, July 17, 2024. https://www.bankrate.com/real-estate/questions-to-ask-when-buying-a-house/.

Contributor, Guest. "8 Strategies for Real Estate Investing During Inflation." REtipster, August 3, 2023. https://retipster.com/8-strategies-for-real-estate-investing-during-inflation/.

DeAngelo, Nic. "Understanding Compounding in Real Estate." *Saint Investment* (blog), September 28, 2023. https://saintinvestment.com/blog/understanding-compounding-in-real-estate/.

Dieker, Nicole. "Why Is Good Credit So Important?" Bankrate, November 3, 2023. https://www.bankrate.com/credit-cards/advice/why-is-good-credit-so-important/.

Drake Law. "Key Legal Factors to Consider Before Investing in Real Estate." https://www.drakelaw.ca/legal-insights/key-legal-factors-to-consider-before-investing-in-real-estate.

Elphick, Dean. "Airbnb Superhost: How to Become a Superhost on Airbnb." Little Hotelier, October 10, 2022. https://www.littlehotelier.com/blog/get-more-bookings/airbnb-superhost/.

Ferran. "10 Ways To Make More Money From Rental Properties." *June Homes Blog* (blog), January 23, 2024. https://junehomes.com/blog/2024/01/23/make-more-money-from-rental-properties/.

Fettke, Kathy. "Top 60 Real Estate Definitions for Investors to Know." *RealWealth* (blog). https://realwealth.com/learn/real-estate-definitions/.

FortuneBuilders. "House Hacking: A Beginner's Guide," September 21, 2022. https://www.fortunebuilders.com/p/what-is-house-hacking/.

Griggs Homes. "What Is Property Development and How Does It Work?" https://www.griggshomes.co.uk/what-is-property-development-how-does-it-work.

Hamed, Eman. "The Complete Beginner's Guide to Investing in Long-Term Rentals." *Learn Real Estate Investing | Mashvisor Real Estate Blog* (blog), March 7, 2019. https://www.mashvisor.com/blog/beginners-guide-long-term-rentals/.

Harrington, Dennis. "The Rise of Renters by Choice." Multifamily Executive, May 18, 2022. https://www.multifamilyexecutive.com/property-management/demographics/the-rise-of-renters-by-choice_o.

"Highlights From the Profile of Home Buyers and Sellers," November 13, 2023. https://www.nar.realtor/research-and-statistics/research-reports/highlights-from-the-profile-of-home-buyers-and-sellers.

"How Much Should I Charge for Rent: Tips to Rental Rates." https://www.mysmartmove.com/blog/how-much-charge-for-rent.

https://prenohq.com/. "How to Start an Airbnb: A Beginners Guide." https://prenohq.com/blog/how-to-list-your-property-on-airbnb/.

Investopedia. "5 Negotiating Strategies When Selling Your Home." https://www.investopedia.com/articles/mortgages-real-estate/12/playing-hardball-when-selling-your-home.asp.

Investopedia. "Calculating Net Operating Income (NOI) for Real Estate." https://www.investopedia.com/terms/n/noi.asp.

Investopedia. "Capitalization Rate: Cap Rate Defined With Formula and Examples." https://www.investopedia.com/terms/c/capitalizationrate.asp.

Investopedia. "Commercial Real Estate: Definition and Types." https://www.investopedia.com/terms/c/commercialrealestate.asp.

Investopedia. "Fixed-Rate Mortgage: How It Works, Types, vs. Adjustable Rate." https://www.investopedia.com/terms/f/fixed-rate_mortgage.asp.

Investopedia. "How Airbnb Works—for Hosts, Guests, and the Company Itself." https://www.investopedia.com/articles/personal-finance/032814/pros-and-cons-using-airbnb.asp.

Investopedia. "How to Profit From Inflation." https://www.investopedia.com/articles/investing/080813/how-profit-inflation.asp.

Investopedia. "Interest-Only Mortgage: Definition, How They Work, Pros and Cons." https://www.investopedia.com/terms/i/interestonlymortgage.asp.

Investopedia. "Loan Terms: Specific Terms Defined and How to Negotiate Them." https://www.investopedia.com/loan-terms-5075341.

Investopedia. "REIT: What It Is and How To Invest." https://www.investopedia.com/terms/r/reit.asp.

Investopedia. "Rent-to-Own Homes: How the Process Works." https://www.investopedia.com/updates/rent-to-own-homes/.

Investopedia. "Residential Rental Property Definition, Tax Pros & Cons." https://www.investopedia.com/terms/r/residentialrentalproperty.asp.

Investopedia. "What Is a 1031 Exchange? Know the Rules." https://www.investopedia.com/financial-edge/0110/10-things-to-know-about-1031-exchanges.aspx.

Investopedia. "What Is Comparative Market Analysis (CMA) in Real Estate?" https://www.investopedia.com/terms/c/comparative-market-analysis.asp.

Investopedia. "What You Should Know About Real Estate Valuation." https://www.investopedia.com/articles/realestate/12/real-estate-valuation.asp.

"Key Financial Metrics for Real Estate Investors | Cg Tax, Audit & Advisory," October 24, 2023. https://www.cgteam.com/key-financial-metrics-for-real-estate-investors/.

Landon, Dena. "The Top 10 Metrics Every Real Estate Investor Should Know (and Why) - Stessa." https://www.stessa.com/blog/10-real-estate-investing-metrics/.

Lodgify. "All About Short-Term Rentals," n.d. https://www.lodgify.com/guides/business/short-term/.

Lodgify. "What Is a Vacation Rental?" n.d. https://www.lodgify.com/encyclopedia/vacation-rental/.

Mann (Silvermann), Baruch. "How Does Inflation Affect Real Estate? Here's What You Need to Know." Entrepreneur, December 2, 2022. https://www.entrepreneur.com/money-finance/how-does-inflation-affect-real-estate-heres-what-you-need/433953.

Marketing. "Giving Rehab Property a Makeover: A Real Estate Investor's Guide." Reedy & Company, December 7, 2023. https://www.reedyandcompany.com/blog/giving-rehab-property-a-makeover-a-real-estate-investors-guide/.

Martin, Allison. "Cash-Out Refinancing: What It Is, How It Works." Bankrate, September 5, 2024. https://www.bankrate.com/mortgages/cash-out-refinancing/.

McCracken, Madison. "The Importance of Thorough Tenant Screening Process." *Bay Property Management Group* (blog), April 6, 2022. https://www.baymgmtgroup.com/blog/tenant-screening/.

Memphis Investment Properties. "7 Benefits of Owning a Rental Property," November 8, 2021. https://www.memphis investmentproperties.net/7-benefits-of-owning-a-rental-property/.

NerdWallet. "How to Buy a House: 15 Steps in the Homebuying Process," March 19, 2024. https://www.nerdwallet. com/article/mortgages/home-buying-checklist-steps-to-buying-house.

NerdWallet. "How to Get Preapproved for a Mortgage," April 25, 2024. https://www.nerdwallet.com/article/mort gages/how-to-get-a-mortgage-preapproval.

New Western. "Marketing Your Investment: Step-by-Step Guide on Selling Your Investment Property Like the Pros." https://www.newwestern.com/guide/selling-a-rental-property/.

Newsroom. "Airbnb Q4-2023 and Full-Year Financial Results." Airbnb, February 13, 2024. https://news.airbnb.com/ airbnb-q4-2023-and-full-year-financial-results/.

Oak, Red. "Top 7 Reasons Why 90% of US Millionaires Invest In Real Estate & Why You Should Follow the Lead." *Red Oak Development Group* (blog), August 3, 2022. https://redoakvc.com/top-7-reasons-why-90-of-us-millionaires-invest-in-real-estate-why-you-should-follow-the-lead/.

Ostrowski, Jeff. "What Is A HELOC (Home Equity Line Of Credit)?" Bankrate, April 24, 2024. https://www.bankrate. com/home-equity/what-is-heloc/.

Passive Real Estate Investing. "From Zero to 35 Rentals in 4 Years – A Client Success Story," January 30, 2018. https:// www.passiverealestateinvesting.com/from-zero-to-35-rentals-in-4-years-a-client-success-story/.

Rajkhar. "Tax Saving by Investing in Real Estate." Reddit, 2024. https://www.reddit.com/r/realestateinvesting/com ments/1blsscr/tax_saving_by_investing_in_real_estate/.

"Real Estate Risks: What It Is and How to Avoid Them." https://www.mandanibay.com/blog/risks-of-real-estate-investment-and-how-to-avoid-them/.

Richards, Laurie. "What Is A Balloon Mortgage And Why Is It Risky?" Bankrate, July 15, 2024. https://www.bankrate. com/mortgages/what-is-a-balloon-mortgage/.

Rocket Mortgage. "Lease Option: Definition And How It Works." https://www.rocketmortgage.com/learn/lease-option.

Rocket Mortgage. "Seller Financing: How It Works, Pros And Cons And If It's A Good Idea." https://www.rocketmort gage.com/learn/seller-financing.

Rocket Mortgage. "Top 6 Tax Benefits Of Real Estate Investing." https://www.rocketmortgage.com/learn/tax-bene fits-of-real-estate-investing.

Rocket Mortgage. "Understanding The BRRRR Method Of Real Estate Investment." https://www.rocketmortgage. com/learn/brrrr.

Rodriguez, Amanda. "Understanding NOI/Cap Rate & How to Calculate Them." *Learn Real Estate Investing | Mashvisor Real Estate Blog* (blog), July 10, 2023. https://www.mashvisor.com/blog/noi-cap-rate/.

Rohde, Jeff. "What Is Due Diligence in Real Estate? A Simple Guide and Checklist." https://learn.roofstock.com/blog/ what-is-due-diligence-in-real-estate.

Samurai, Financial. "When To Sell An Investment Property: Every Indicator To Consider." *Financial Samurai* (blog), August 17, 2019. https://www.financialsamurai.com/when-to-sell-an-investment-property/.

"Self-Management vs. Property Company: Which Is Better? | BiggerPockets Blog," May 12, 2023. https://www.bigger pockets.com/blog/property-management-vs-self-management.

Sharkey, Sarah. "Putting A Down Payment On Investment Property: What To Know." Quicken Loans, October 20, 2023. https://www.quickenloans.com/learn/down-payment-on-investment-property.

Strategies for Influence. 2019. "Robert Kiyosaki - Rich Dad Poor Dad." Strategies for Influence. November 17, 2019. https://strategiesforinfluence.com/robert-kiyosaki-rich-dad-poor-dad/.

"Successfully Estimating Renovation Costs in Real Estate." https://www.dealmachine.com/blog/successfully-estimat ing-renovation-costs-in-real-estate.

Team, BnB Hosts. "How to Handle The Most Common Airbnb Guest Enquiries Like a Pro." *BnB Hosts* (blog), September 24, 2019. https://www.bnbhosts.com.au/common-airbnb-enquiries/.

"The 7 Best Short Term Rental Sites | Uplisting.Io." https://www.uplisting.io/blog/the-7-best-short-term-rental-sites-for-hosts.

The Balance. "How You Can Build (or Lose) Equity in Your Home." https://www.thebalancemoney.com/definition-of-equity-1798546.

"The Ultimate 35-Point House Rehab Checklist." https://www.theinvestorsedge.com/blog/the-ultimate-36-point-house-rehab-checklist.

"The Ultimate Airbnb Maintenance Checklist and Schedule | Minut." https://www.minut.com/blog/airbnb-mainte nance-checklist-and-schedule.

Todd, Jonny. "Viewing a House Checklist: Key Questions to Ask When Buying." Ellis & Co, July 26, 2022. https://www.ellisandco.co.uk/guides/buying/viewing-a-house-checklist-8457/.

Tom. "How to Get Your Airbnb Pricing Strategies Right: 7 Steps." *Host Tools* (blog), July 24, 2020. https://hosttools.com/blog/short-term-rental-tips/airbnb-pricing-strategies/.

Tross, Kasey. "The 6 Types of Commercial Real Estate Property." *VTS* (blog), May 8, 2023. https://www.vts.com/blog/the-6-types-of-commercial-real-estate-properties.

TRVLGUIDES [Learn How To Travel]. "How To Create An Airbnb Account [Or Change Or Delete It]." https://trvl guides.com/articles/create-airbnb-account.

Ugazu, Yassine. "Glossary of Real Estate & Vacation Rental Investing Terms." *Learn Real Estate Investing | Mashvisor Real Estate Blog* (blog), August 24, 2023. https://www.mashvisor.com/blog/real-estate-investing-terms/.

Wall Street Prep. "Net Operating Income (NOI) | Formula + Calculator." https://www.wallstreetprep.com/knowledge/noi-net-operating-income/.

"What Is a Variable Rate Mortgage and How Do They Work | L&C." https://www.landc.co.uk/mortgage-guides/vari able-rate-mortgage.

"What Is the Due Diligence Period in Real Estate? - Experian," November 4, 2022. https://www.experian.com/blogs/ask-experian/what-is-due-diligence-period-real-estate/.

"What Is Real Estate Appreciation?" https://smartasset.com/investing/real-estate-appreciation.

"What Is Underwriting In Real Estate? Full Guide." https://www.metawealth.co/post/what-is-underwriting-in-real-estate-explained.

"What's a REIT (Real Estate Investment Trust)?" https://www.reit.com/what-reit.

Wieland, David. "Council Post: Assessing Three Types Of Risk In Real Estate." Forbes. https://www.forbes.com/coun cils/forbesrealestatecouncil/2020/08/05/assessing-three-types-of-risk-in-real-estate/.

Yale, Laura Grace Tarpley, CEPF, Aly J. "Saving for a Down Payment: Strategies to Achieve Homeownership." Business Insider. https://www.businessinsider.com/personal-finance/mortgages/tips-for-saving-for-a-down-payment.

"Your Essential Guide to Navigating Real Estate & Your Credit," July 27, 2023. https://mathesonattys.com/blog/real-estate-and-your-credit/.

Yuhenyo. "Property Is Severely Under Valued by Potential Lender Bank." Reddit, 2023. https://www.reddit.com/r/AusPropertyChat/comments/180asha/property_is_severely_under_valued_by_potential/.

Zillow. "75% of Recent Home Buyers Have Regrets about Their New Home." https://www.prnewswire.com/news-releases/75-of-recent-home-buyers-have-regrets-about-their-new-home-301477283.html.

Zinn, Dori. "Flipping Houses: A How-To Guide For Beginners." Bankrate, July 8, 2024. https://www.bankrate.com/real-estate/flipping-houses/.

IMAGE REFERENCES

BP, Steve. *Calculator, Calculation, Insurance Image.* July 9, 2014. Photograph. https://pixabay.com/photos/calculator-cal culation-insurance-385506/.

Kuhar, Milivoj. *Man Climbing on Ladder Inside Room.* February 2, 2018. Image. https://unsplash.com/photos/man-climbing-on-ladder-inside-room-Te48TPzdcU8.

Li, Kostiantyn. *A House Made out of Money on a White Background.* October 20, 2021. Image. https://unsplash.com/pho tos/a-house-made-out-of-money-on-a-white-background-1sCXwVoqKAw.

Mallorca, Tierra. *White and Red Wooden House Miniature on Brown Table*. June 14, 2019. Photograph. https://unsplash.com/photos/white-and-red-wooden-house-miniature-on-brown-table-rgJ1J8SDEAY.

Tingey Injury Law Firm. *A Wooden Gavel on a White Marble Backdrop*. May 13, 2020. Photograph. https://unsplash.com/photos/brown-wooden-smoking-pipe-on-white-surface-6sl88x150Xs.

Wheeler, Blake. *Housing Development American Fork*. April 4, 2017. Photograph. https://unsplash.com/photos/aerial-photography-houses-zBHU08hdzhY.

THE ULTIMATE HOUSE FLIPPING AND BRRRR REAL ESTATE INVESTING BEGINNER'S BOOK

BUILD WEALTH THROUGH FIX-AND-FLIP AND
THE BUY, REHAB, RENT, REFINANCE, REPEAT
STRATEGY—EVEN IF YOU'RE ON A TIGHT BUDGET

INTRODUCTION

Financial freedom is the goal, right? I don't think there are many people out there who wouldn't want financial freedom in their lives, where they can say they have built up enough wealth so that finances are not a huge source of stress for them. There are many people who claim to have found the answer to financial freedom with their hacks and business ideas, but the truth is that real estate is one of the most solid investments to ensure financial freedom and wealth building.

Real estate is one of the longest-standing investments available. If you talk to members of the older generation, you will quickly discover that many of them are advocates of investing in real estate. This is because, in general, the return on investment in real estate far outperforms many other traditional investments over the long run. Even though stocks and bonds are good investments, real estate tends to perform better than those. It is one of the most stable, trustworthy, and rewarding investments available.

You might be one of the people who feel that real estate investing is either out of reach or very intimidating. If this is the case, that is okay because you are not alone. We all start somewhere. The truth is, I was definitely apprehensive when it came to real estate investing and whether it was a good option. I only started investing in real estate out of necessity because I needed somewhere to live, and I didn't have much money to pay for it. As a new immigrant family, we didn't have all the resources in the world. The only thing I could afford was an old, broken-down house, but I was willing to put in the work. After a few years of renovating, I refinanced the house, and it was worth much more than I had paid for it. The cash-out I received from refinancing was used to access the equity in my house and put a down payment on a two-bedroom apartment. I used it to start my short-term rental business, and my real estate investment journey began. I know it can be intimidating to start, but I was able to do it, and now I want to help others create the same for themselves.

Before we get ahead of ourselves, let's take some time to define what real estate investing is. Real estate is property that can include land and anything that is permanently attached to or built on it. Typically, real estate is divided into five main categories: commercial, residential, industrial, raw land, and special use land. You can invest in any one of these types, but as a first-time or beginner investor, residential tends to be the better option because it is more accessible and requires less specialized knowledge. When you invest in real estate, you are purchasing the property, land, or home. Then you can either rent or sell the property to make a profit. This is a very simple breakdown of what real estate investing is, as there are many different strategies that fall under this umbrella. The two main strategies we are going to focus on in this book are house flipping and the BRRRR (Buy, Rehab, Rent, Refinance, Repeat) method. We will be diving more into both of these in this book, but let's give you an overview of the BRRRR method. This is a strategy where you buy a property that might need a bit of work and renovate it to increase its value. Then you rent it out for additional income and eventually refinance the property to access equity to fund your next investment property. If this all sounds like another language, don't worry, we are going to cover this and house flipping to help you along your journey. The important thing to know is that both are great strategies to help build your wealth as a beginner real estate investor and see significant gains with your investments.

There are many myths surrounding real estate investing, which discourage a lot of people from even giving it a try. I want to put these myths to rest. You don't need to be wealthy to start investing, nor do you need to be a landlord, own a house, or time the market perfectly. At the end of the day, all you need to do is be willing to start and ensure that you are taking the right steps to reach your goal. While there are risks involved in investing in real estate, the truth is that any investment carries some level of risk. As the saying goes, "no risk, no reward." However, you must do your best to mitigate these risks and ensure that you are not making rushed decisions. It is important to understand that sometimes we need to take a step in the right direction for things to work out. There are numerous success stories of people who started investing in real estate and have now seen significant returns on their investments. You can be one of those success stories, too.

In this book, we will go through a three-part framework that outlines the key elements for investing in real estate through house flipping and the BRRRR method. The first part is the foundational section of the book, where we will learn about the two main strategies we will discuss. Then we will move on to part two, which focuses on taking action and making the right moves to find, fix, rent, or sell the property. The final part, part three, will dive into building smart and growing big. In this section, we will discuss how to grow your investment and ensure that you are making smart decisions to protect yourself and your investment.

My hope for you is that by the end of this book, you will have the confidence to start investing in real estate using your chosen strategy. Both house flipping and the BRRRR method are great ways to begin your real estate investment journey, but it is important to understand what they are and what your first step should be. So, without any further delay, let's dive into Chapter 1, where we will discuss these strategies.

PART ONE

LEARN THE STRATEGIES

FLIP VS. BRRRR—WHICH ONE'S RIGHT FOR YOU?

In 2024, the US real estate market saw a notable shift: While traditional home sales faced challenges, investors found opportunities in alternative strategies. Notably, 41% of residential real estate investors reported higher earnings compared to the previous year (Pisano 2024). These figures highlight the potential of informed investment choices.

UNDERSTANDING HOUSE FLIPPING AND THE BRRRR STRATEGY

You may or may not have heard of house flipping before, but I am sure that you have watched a TV show where someone buys houses and renovates them. After the renovations are completed, they sell the house and make a profit. This is the basic principle of house flipping. When someone wants to flip a house, they must conduct extensive research to find a property within a reasonable price range. Then, they will assess what needs to be done to improve the value of the home. This could involve larger projects, such as adding an extra bedroom or bathroom, or removing the entire floor and replacing it with something more modern, durable, and functional. It could also include smaller tasks like repainting, refurnishing, and adding new finishes to the existing amenities and furniture.

Unlike many other real estate investment strategies, when you flip a house, the goal is to make a profit as soon as possible. Remember that a property is a significant investment, and if you are going to put a lot of money into it, you also want to ensure that you can recoup your investment as quickly as possible. Many people who invest in house flipping aim to flip houses frequently so that they can consistently achieve a good return on their investments. If done correctly, flipping houses can be a highly effective investment strategy that yields substantial profits. In fact, in 2024, house flipping generated a median profit of $73,500 per property (Gratton 2025a). That is an impressive return on investment for a strategy that allows you to access your profits relatively quickly after making the investment.

But before you pick up your drill and paintbrush, you need to be aware of the main aspects that lead to house-flipping success. It's not as easy as simply making a property attractive and then selling it off. You will first need to consider the overall market appreciation in the neighborhood where you are going to purchase your property. The truth is that some neighborhoods are better than others when it comes to investing. If a neighborhood has a bad reputation, lacks amenities, or is unsafe or difficult to navigate, then the likelihood of making a good profit is quite slim. People will always prefer to pay a little more to live in a better area, even if the property is smaller than what they would have gotten in a less desirable area.

Another important factor to consider is how much value the improvements will add to the property. You'll need to carefully evaluate which improvements to make based on what will add the most value and, therefore, yield the most profit. Some improvements are merely nice to have; they may enhance the property's appearance or feel, but they do not significantly increase its value when you are trying to resell. Since the goal of property flipping is to maximize profit, it is important to consider which types of renovations and improvements will generate income and which ones may not be worth the investment.

Let's shift gears and discuss something that is often mistaken for house flipping but can be considered a level up from traditional house flipping. It is called the BRRRR method, which stands for Buy, Rehab, Rent, Refinance, and Repeat. The goal is to purchase distressed properties, fix them up, rent them out, and generate income from them. While this is happening, you are building equity, which you can then use toward your next property. Unlike house flipping, you retain possession of the property because you are renting it out for income rather than selling it. This way, it is not a one-time profit but rather a source of income over a longer timeframe.

In order for this method to work, an investor will need to make sure they can make enough money through their rent to cover the mortgage. If they are only able to rent out the property for less than the amount they have to pay on their monthly mortgage payments, it means that they will not be making a profit, and this investment is going to be a losing battle.

In order to almost guarantee that you will make a good profit from this method, you need to ensure that you are purchasing a property at a discounted price. The cheaper you can buy a property, the more potential you have to make a larger profit. With that said, you must conduct thorough research to ensure that the area, as well as other factors, will work in your favor. There is no point in purchasing a property that is cheap if it has absolutely nothing else going for it. We will dive deeper into the BRRRR method in Chapter 5, so stay tuned for an in-depth exploration of the method later in the book.

For now, let's discuss some of the numbers you might expect in a successful BRRRR deal (Blankenship 2023b). Let's say you have a property that you are looking to purchase, and it costs $100,000. The closing costs are $5,000, with the rehab costs being around $25,000. All in all, this means that the total cost for which you will need to secure a loan would be $130,000. The monthly rent is $1,200, which means that the annual rent taken in would be $14,400. After you have completed all of the renovations, the new value of the property is $180,000, and your new loan amount, which is 80% of the appraised value, is $144,000. This means your cash pullout would be $14,000.

The new monthly mortgage payment, with a 4% interest rate over 30 years, would be $687. Now you have $14,000 freed up, which you can use as the down payment on another property, allowing you to repeat the BRRRR method. If the monthly mortgage payment is $687 and the monthly rent you will be charging is $1,200, it means that you are making a significant profit that you can reinvest into the mortgage or use to finance another property, depending on what works best for you. This is how the BRRRR method operates in real life.

PROS AND CONS

As you can probably tell, there are some definite similarities between house flipping and the BRRRR method. While those similarities are important, it is even more crucial to note the differences when deciding which method you will use to build your property investment portfolio. Both strategies start by acquiring an undervalued property and then renovating it to increase its value. The difference lies in the exit strategy: House flipping focuses on selling the property as quickly as possible to make a profit, while the BRRRR method emphasizes renting out the property and creating equity so you can continue investing.

House Flipping

Pros

With house flipping, there are plenty of pros that make it attractive to many investors. One of the most appealing aspects is the potential for a quick profit. When a house flip is done correctly, you can achieve faster returns on your investment compared to most other real estate strategies. Once your house is on the market and sold, you will receive almost immediate profits from it. The goal of house flipping is to renovate and sell the house as soon as possible to secure these quick profits. Additionally, as a house flipper, you will be improving a property's value through upgrades and renovations, allowing you to see the value you are creating on the property as it unfolds.

You will also begin to gain a wealth of market knowledge simply by the nature of house flipping. You will be buying and selling properties quite often, which means you will develop a better understanding of the real estate market in your local area. This knowledge is invaluable as you continue your real estate investment journey. If you are investing in real estate in other ways, choosing house flipping can be a great way to diversify your current portfolio. You can expand your portfolio and increase your potential profit by engaging in something a little different and more hands-on.

Cons

One of the biggest potential downsides to house flipping is the risk of significant financial losses due to unforeseen problems or inadequate research conducted prior to purchasing the property. When it comes to any form of real estate investing, some risk is always involved; therefore, it is crucial to understand what you are getting into before you jump in. Additionally, house flipping is resource- and time-intensive, which means it requires a considerable amount of work as well as a substantial financial investment.

In addition to the money and resources needed to complete a house-flipping project, you must also consider the time commitment and the potential stress of the process. As an investor, you will need to be present every step of the way as the property undergoes renovation. This is essential to ensure that everything runs smoothly, and if any issues arise, you will need to be there to address them to achieve the desired outcome. If you have ever undertaken any building project, you know that unexpected challenges can arise, and many aspects may not go according to plan. This can be highly stressful and may require more resources, time, and money than you initially anticipated. This is why it is so important to be resilient in your thinking and quick on your feet when choosing to invest in this manner.

BRRRR Method

Pros

With this method, there are numerous advantages that make investing in this way very attractive to many investors. One of the biggest draws is simply that you have access to leverage, allowing you to withdraw a significant portion of your initial investment to invest in another property. This way, you are using your current investment to fund your next investment without actually using your own physical money. Additionally, this approach allows for more cash flow than many other investment opportunities, including the house-flipping method.

Another significant benefit is that you are enabling yourself to build equity through the natural appreciation and value of the property while renting it out. This is because you maintain ownership of the property for a longer period than you would with house flipping. There are also considerable tax benefits associated with owning a rental property, which can certainly be a positive aspect. Finally, there is the advantage of being able to expand and grow your real estate investment portfolio, allowing for a more diversified investment strategy that can lead to greater gains and provide some safety for your investments.

Cons

While refinancing a property does create leverage, there are also risks associated with refinancing. Nothing is ever guaranteed; a property appraisal might come in much lower than you expected, which means you may not receive as much money as you had anticipated. This could result in being tied up financially, leaving you without enough funds to invest in your next property right away. Additionally, you must consider that over-leveraging can pose a risk, especially if you are attempting to leverage your current investments recklessly by continuously borrowing without proper research or by trying to make quick money.

One definite negative aspect to consider if you choose the BRRRR method is the fact that you will be managing multiple properties simultaneously. The goal is to refinance and then have enough money to buy another rental property, repeating the process for as long as possible. This means you will have quite a few rental properties to manage, and rental properties are not a passive source of income. You will need to oversee those properties as well as manage your tenants, which could become a full-time job if you do not hire someone else to handle it.

Like any other real estate investment strategy, overall market volatility must be taken into consideration. Even if you have conducted all the necessary research, property values and rental rates are never set in stone. What you expect to gain from your property may not align with what you actually receive.

Finally, another potential drawback to consider is that the BRRRR method adds a level of complexity that exceeds many other property investment strategies. You will constantly be trying to balance buying, rehabbing, renting, and refinancing to keep this investment strategy moving forward. This is not as straightforward as it appears on paper, as there are many moving parts, and your different properties may be at various stages of the process. Balancing everything will require a significant amount of your time and energy, ensuring that you make the right decisions in each area. It is also important to note that the more properties you take on, the more complex the situation will become. Therefore, you will need to decide for yourself when it is a good time to stop and when you can purchase another property and continue the process.

SO, WHICH STRATEGY SUITS YOU BEST?

When it comes to investing in real estate, there are many different goals that people are trying to achieve. It is important to understand what your goals are so that you can make the right choices. Let's discuss some of the most popular investment goals and which type of real estate investment would be best suited for each.

Short-Term Cash Generation

If you are someone who needs a quick turnaround time to get your money out of your investment as soon as possible, then house flipping is a better option. With house flipping, you can expect to see returns within a few months, and it offers a very clear path toward achieving your short-term returns.

Long-Term Wealth Building

If your goal is to build wealth gradually over a longer period, then the BRRRR method of real estate investing is a better choice. You are essentially building equity over the years, even if you don't have physical cash in hand. Eventually, your properties will appreciate in value, and you will also be able to purchase many more properties through this method, thereby building your real estate investment portfolio. This approach works well for people who do not need quick cash or who have longer-term financial goals.

People with Limited Capital

If you are someone who is starting off with limited capital, you can definitely get involved in both house flipping and BRRRR. However, house flipping is a bit riskier, and in many cases, you will need a large amount of money available to purchase the property and renovate it quickly. While you can take out loans for this, you must handle your finances very well to ensure that you don't go into debt or overextend yourself.

With the BRRRR method, you can get involved with a lower amount of capital on hand. This is because you are refinancing your properties and pulling out a majority of your original investment so that you can reinvest it. Essentially, you are using the same money to continue investing without having to invest more than the original amount. Just bear in mind that whichever form of real estate investing you are trying to pursue, some capital will be needed to get started, and real estate investing is a type of investment that requires significantly more upfront than many other types of investing.

Passive vs. Active Investors

Some investors prefer to be more hands-on and active in their investments, while others favor a more passive approach. Neither is right nor wrong, but it is important to understand what you are getting into and what you can handle. In general, house flipping is a more hands-on type of investment. During the time you are renovating the property, you'll need to oversee the entire process to ensure that everything is going well. You are also responsible for managing the finances and the contractors. Additionally, you must get involved with marketing and selling the property.

Many people don't realize how much work this entails because they hope to simply give directions to the contractors and then only get involved at the end when it's time to sell. However, this is not realistic. If you do not have the time or the capacity to be hands-on with the property, then house flipping might not be the best choice for you.

The BRRRR method is hands-on at the beginning, but once everything has stabilized, it becomes a more passive form of income. Once you have your properties and have found tenants, you don't really have to do much because you become a landlord, and you only need to get involved if there is a problem. The only other time you will have to be very hands-on is when you purchase another property and need to renovate it in order to rent it out again. You are in control of how many properties you have, so if you do not have the capacity to renovate and reestablish a property, then you can simply manage the ones that you currently have, and they will still bring you an income, even if you're not doing much.

EVALUATING SUITABILITY BASED ON PERSONAL FACTORS

Every investor is different, and that means it is essential to evaluate how suitable an investment style is based on your personal factors. Many different elements come into play when considering an investment style, and asking the right questions will yield the best results. Remember that there are no right or wrong answers, but it is important to be completely honest with yourself so that you can identify which investment style will be best for you.

Time Frame Considerations

When it comes to the timeframe in which you can access your investment funds, each of these investment methods offers something different. BRRRR is more about creating long-term wealth, which means you don't always have immediate access to your funds, whereas house flipping provides much quicker returns. If you are trying to determine which option is best for you, consider asking yourself some of the following questions:

- How soon do I need to see results and financial returns from my investments?
- Am I looking for something that will provide a quick profit, or do I want to build something that will last for a long time?
- Can I commit to the hands-on renovation process for the next couple of months, or do I prefer something more steady over time?

Cash Flow vs. Lump Sum

With house flipping, you can expect to receive a lump sum of money once you sell your property for a profit. You will not receive any additional money from this investment after it has been sold. In contrast, with the BRRRR method, you can anticipate smaller returns on investment over a longer period because you will be earning rental income while renting out the property. Here are some questions you can ask yourself to determine whether you prefer long-term cash flow or a short-term lump sum:

- Do I need a one-time payout, or am I more comfortable receiving small amounts of money consistently each month?
- Would I be disciplined enough to manage my finances properly if I received a lump sum from a house flip?
- Is it better for me to have an automatic monthly income that can help supplement my day job or cover some of my regular expenses?

Tax Implications

Whenever we talk about money, one aspect that always needs to be considered is the tax implications. When you are considering house flipping, you must understand that the profits you earn will be taxed as ordinary income. However, with the BRRRR method, you benefit from aspects such as depreciation and other tax deductions. With rental properties, you receive tax deductions that arise from homeownership as well as deductions that are specific to rentals. Here are the questions to ask yourself:

- Am I fully aware of the tax implications that come with receiving a large profit from a house flip?
- Do I believe that there are benefits to tax rates, depreciation, mortgage interest, and other tax advantages associated with rentals?
- Do I fully understand property tax in my state and what the implications are for both of these investment methods?

Risk Assessment

Any kind of investment comes with a certain level of risk; however, some investments are riskier than others. Additionally, you must consider the types of risks you will incur with each method. For example, when it comes to house flipping, you need to account for the risks of market fluctuations as well as unexpected renovation surprises. Not everything is clear-cut with this type of investment, and while you might plan to sell your property for a specific amount, this may not reflect the reality of the situation when you put the house on the market. Sometimes, the housing market takes a dive, and properties are simply selling for much less than you might have predicted. The risk of unexpected renovation costs is another significant concern, and anyone who has renovated a property will tell you that there are far more surprises than you might anticipate. You only fully understand the extent of the damage or the renovation costs while you are in the thick of it.

There are also definite risks associated with renting out a property. For example, you must be aware that tenant management comes with its own challenges. You might encounter a difficult tenant who makes your life incredibly challenging or one who simply does not pay their rent on time. This has implications for your financial planning, and it can be quite difficult to evict someone, depending on the laws in your country or state. Another risk associated with the BRRRR method is refinancing risks. In some cases, the process is not as straightforward as applying for refinancing and then simply getting approved. Nothing is set in stone until you have signed all of the papers.

With all of these risks in mind, here are some questions that can help you assess which kinds you can tolerate and which ones are simply not worth it for you:

- Am I capable of handling risks such as a delayed permit, a burst pipe, or a property that cannot be sold quickly?
- Do I prefer the risks associated with tenant issues or refinancing, or the risks related to market timing and renovation?
- If things do not go according to plan, which would stress me out the most: sitting on a property that is not selling or dealing with a rental property that is vacant for an extended period?

Personality Fit

Another important aspect to consider is your personality. Each one of us is unique, and that means we all have our own personalities, which come with particular strengths, weaknesses, and preferences. Some people are more tolerant of risk, while others are more patient, and we also have individuals who might be a bit more cautious. Here are some questions that you can ask yourself to understand how your personality fits into the type of investment strategy you are considering:

- Do I like the idea of managing a property, making quick decisions, and being hands-on, or do I prefer something more stable and a slow burn when it comes to my investments?
- Does the idea of dealing with tenants and managing a property excite me or drain me?
- Do I prefer a predictable income that might take longer to establish, or am I able to handle short-term stress for a bigger short-term payoff?

In this chapter, we covered the differences between house flipping and the BRRRR method in real estate investing. It is crucial to understand both before you commit to a property investment. Regardless of which investment method you choose, one of the biggest challenges that beginners face is limited funds. In the next chapter, we will dive into practical methods to begin real estate investing without having substantial capital at your fingertips.

HOW TO GET STARTED
WITHOUT A LOT OF MONEY

According to a 2023 report by the National Association of Realtors, only 26% of home buyers paid cash for their homes, while 74% relied on financing options (2024).

FINANCING OPTIONS THAT DON'T REQUIRE HUGE SAVINGS

Financing is undoubtedly a significant consideration when it comes to real estate investing. Most people simply do not have the capital to invest in cash and will need to explore various financing options to make their real estate dreams come true. The very idea of financing a property can deter people from investing because it seems like a tedious and difficult process.

However, this is not necessarily the case, as there are financing options that offer flexibility and are more beginner-friendly.

FHA Loan

One option could be a Federal Housing Administration (FHA) loan, which is a loan insured by the government. With this type of loan, you are required to provide a lower down payment than with other, more traditional loans from a financial service provider or a bank. It is also more accessible for beginners because you might not need as high a credit score to be approved for this type of loan. These loans were designed to help people in lower-income brackets purchase property.

Even though the requirements for an FHA loan are lower than those for other types of property loans, there are still some criteria that must be met to obtain one. For example, you will need to have a credit score of at least 580 to qualify. A down payment is also required for this loan, but it can be as low as 3.5% (Segal 2025). Compared to the much higher down payment percentages required for other loans, this is significantly more accessible for people who do not have substantial finances or cash on hand. If you have a credit score lower than 580, you can still access this loan, but it will require a higher down payment. As you can see, there is a lot of flexibility with an FHA loan, making it more accessible to many people.

There are also some basic qualifications you need to meet to be considered for this type of loan. Some of these requirements include having a Social Security number, legally residing in the US, being of legal age, having a qualifying credit score, providing proof of employment, and demonstrating sufficient income to handle the loan. As with any other loan process, there are no guarantees that you will receive the loan. You will need to apply and go through the process, and once you are approved, you will have access to the funds.

One important aspect of this type of loan is the fact that the property needs to be your principal residence. This means that you cannot use this loan to finance property that you do not live in. This does put some restrictions in terms of investment potential, as you won't be able to use this loan to purchase a property to flip or to purchase a property immediately to rent out.

However, a detached or semi-detached house, townhouse, condominium, or anything similar can be FHA approved, and you can rent out a part of your residence. Typically, this method is called house hacking, where you live within a part of the property and rent out another part of it. Essentially, you are using the rent that you are getting from part of your property to pay off your entire mortgage, so you are living in the property for free.

VA Loan

This is a type of loan that is available through the US Department of Veterans Affairs. It helps active service members and their spouses become homeowners. This type of loan can be used to either purchase a property or build, improve, and repair one. It can also be used to refinance an existing mortgage. This type of loan has significant benefits over other types of loans if you are a veteran. There is no down payment required, and sometimes there is no private mortgage insurance required. Even though this is a type of loan that sounds very appealing to most people, there are only a few people who will qualify for it based on their veteran status. If you are a veteran or the spouse of a veteran, then you can consider this as an avenue for you.

Hard Money Lenders

A hard money loan works very differently from other types of loans you obtain from a bank or financial service provider. This type of loan is issued by an individual or a private company to help someone purchase a property. A hard money loan is backed by the property rather than the creditworthiness of the person taking out the loan. When you take out a traditional loan, you must prove that you will be able to pay it back with interest; however, with a hard money loan, you are putting up the property as collateral. If you are unable to repay the loan, the lenders can take the property from you and sell it to recover their money.

Since a hard money loan is backed by collateral rather than your credit score or borrowing history, it is much easier to obtain this type of loan. However, it is important to be aware that with this type of loan, you will be paying significantly more interest. The interest rate is set by the person or entity loaning you the money and can range anywhere from 10% to 18%. This can be risky if you plan to pay off the loan over a long period. If you are taking out a loan to flip a house, this could be a good option because you will be repaying the loan relatively quickly, so the interest won't have as much of an effect.

Private Lenders

A private lender is an individual or a company that offers a loan outside of a traditional mortgage loan. The entity or individual will fund the loan from their own resources. Since it is private, the person or entity loaning you the money will set the terms and conditions, which can vary greatly depending on who you are obtaining the loan from.

Even though these types of loans are privately managed, there are still some criteria that you need to meet in order to access them. Just bear in mind that this is definitely not set in stone, and you will have to talk with the lender to properly define their requirements. Typically, a down payment of around 20% or more is expected, as well as having the property professionally appraised for its value. You will also need a good credit score, which should be above 620, along with proof of income to demonstrate to the lender that you have the necessary funds to repay the loan (Martin 2025).

ALTERNATIVE ENTRY POINTS THAT DON'T REQUIRE BUYING RIGHT AWAY

In some cases, you might not want to purchase a property outright. There are some excellent options to still be able to have a property and make money from it without following the traditional methods.

House Hacking

House hacking is becoming increasingly popular for those looking to invest in real estate. We have already briefly mentioned what it is, but let's do a quick recap. House hacking is when you generate income from your home and then use that income to pay off your mortgage, allowing you to stay in the property for free. This can be done by dividing your property and living in one section while renting out the other for income. It is typically easier to house hack if you purchase a multifamily property, as it is simpler to divide it into different sections.

There are other ways to house hack without having a multifamily home; you just have to be a little more creative. For example, you could find a roommate to share your space with. You could also rent out your garage, yard space, or extra room as storage for people to keep their belongings. If you live in a densely populated area where parking is hard to come by, you could rent out a parking space. All of these options are great for house hacking, and you can even implement more than one, depending on the size and layout of your property.

Partnership

Another avenue you could explore is a real estate partnership. This is where you combine the strengths of two people to split the work and make things easier for both parties. In a partnership, there is typically a financial component as well as a time and effort component. One person might have the funds, while the other might have the expertise, time, and resources to manage the property and handle all of the real estate affairs. You can think of this as an active participant and a passive participant. These two different strengths, when combined, can lead to a lucrative investment opportunity for everyone involved.

When entering into a partnership with someone else, it is crucial to hash out all the details and draw up a contract so that everyone knows their responsibilities. Doing this at the beginning means that nobody will overstep their boundaries, which will cause much less friction down the line.

You could have a real estate limited partnership or a general partnership that falls under this category. In a real estate limited partnership, there is a general partner and a limited partner. The limited partner is the one who funds the investment, while the general partner takes care of the day-to-day operations regarding the investment. If you enter into a general partnership, it means that there is more than one person who will be a general owner and will be responsible for the day-to-day management and decisions regarding the investment. In this case, each partner will have equal rights and responsibilities in decision-making and all other matters concerning the property.

Wholesaling

Real estate wholesaling is an interesting approach to real estate investment. With this strategy, you purchase a property and then almost immediately sell it for a profit. You won't need to make any significant improvements or changes to the property; essentially, you are just acting as the middleman. For the strategy to work, you will need to be on the lookout for great deals when properties go on sale. You are looking to purchase a property that is sold below its market value so that you can make a profit when you resell it.

The turnaround time for property wholesaling should be quite quick to limit risks and enable you to receive your profit as soon as possible. This is typically done with distressed properties and individuals who are looking to sell their properties quickly. Once you find a property, you'll need to contact the seller and discuss how a wholesale real estate transaction works. You will then need to obtain a property contract, which must include the right to assign the contract to another party. You are not purchasing the property; rather, you are the person who will find someone to buy it. You will need to agree on how much the seller wants to make from the property so that you can keep the remainder as your profit.

Once all of this is in place, you will need to find a cash buyer. This is important because the seller will want the money as quickly as possible, and you will want your profit as well. Once everything is finalized, all you need to do is reassign the contract to the buyer and close the deal.

REAL EXAMPLES OF LOW-BUDGET DEALS

Jackson is someone who has a lot of experience in real estate and wants to use a hard money loan to help him make another real estate investment. As he was doing his research, he came across a distressed property that was in a really good neighborhood. He could see the potential in this property; all it needed was a little bit of love and some hard work. He knew that if he didn't make a move on this property, it was likely to be sold quite quickly, given that it was cheap and in a good area. He decided to take out a hard money loan since this was going to be the easiest and fastest option for him to obtain financing for the property.

Once he had access to the funds, he purchased the property, and it was time to get to work. He started renovating and updating the property to make it more modern and usable. Since it was an older property, it was very sturdy and well-made, so there weren't any huge structural changes that he had to make. He made sure to choose renovations that would provide a maximum return on his investment. He also ensured that he selected contractors he trusted and who were reputable in the real estate market. He didn't have the time or the money to waste on redoing something due to a botched job by an unreliable contractor.

The entire renovation process took about three months, and at this point, it was time to put the property on the market. Since the quality of work was high and the property looked great in a good area, it sold pretty quickly and at the price he was aiming for. He made a great return on investment through the profit he gained from the property. He was also able to pay off his hard money loan very quickly, so the high interest rate did not impact him significantly. This built his confidence in house flipping and real estate investing, so he continued doing it and made sure to conduct thorough research to make the process smoother and maximize his profit.

SIMPLE FIRST STEPS

Working toward your first real estate deal is an incredibly exciting process, but there are also steps you need to take to ensure that you are doing it properly. Let's take a look at these.

Check Your Credit Score

The first thing you'll need to do is check your credit score. Having a good credit score will significantly open up your options for obtaining a loan and financing your real estate investment. They say knowledge is power, so knowing your credit score is essential. This will help you determine whether you need to work on improving your score, and then you can create a plan to do this effectively over the next few months and years.

It is relatively easy to check your credit score. All you need to do is enter your information on your credit bureau's website, and it should pull up your credit information. You should actually check your credit score fairly often to ensure that there aren't any errors in your credit report and to confirm that you are moving in a positive direction.

Research Local Loan Programs

Every state has different loan programs, so it is important to understand which ones will be available to you before you even begin trying to finance a property. Simply conducting some internet research will help you discover what programs are available and what you need to do to qualify for them. If you don't qualify for a loan right now, you can create a plan to build yourself up to the point where you do qualify for one.

Make a List of Local Investor Meetups or Groups

Sharing ideas and knowledge with other investors is crucial. This is why getting together with other real estate investors is so important. You will gain insights and knowledge that you can't obtain anywhere else, plus other investors will be able to provide you with accurate advice based on their real experiences. They might also be able to assist you on your real estate journey, so making these connections is highly important.

You can look at social media or conduct an internet search to find your local investor meetups and groups. It might seem daunting to try joining one of these associations, but you'll find that people are much more helpful and friendly than you might think. Building your network is one of the most important things anyone can do in their professional life. We all need a helping hand sometimes, and having people who are in the same field as you is a great way to receive the right assistance and advice.

Talking to a Local Real Estate Agent or Mortgage Broker

When you are dealing with real estate, you will need to contact a real estate agent or a mortgage broker at some point. Doing this as early as possible is a great idea. Real estate agents possess extensive knowledge of the local real estate market, and they can help you understand the market you are trying to enter and what you need to do to be successful. They can offer guidance and tips on how to search for the right property, and they can assist you throughout the entire real estate process. A mortgage broker is an expert in the mortgage process, and they can help you understand what you need to do to qualify for a mortgage with a favorable interest rate. Building relationships with these types of professionals will aid you in your real estate investment journey and ensure that you are not scrambling to find these experts when you are ready to start investing or buying.

Investing can often seem very complicated and expensive, but there are many low-barrier ways to begin investing. Whether it's choosing nontraditional financing options or using an entry strategy like house hacking, you can definitely enter the real estate market with confidence as a beginner. Your first step does not have to be significant; it just needs to be intentional.

Hopefully, you now have the confidence to embark on your real estate journey. In the next chapter, we will shift gears so that you can learn how to find good deals and evaluate potential properties, setting yourself up for success. It is possible to start your real estate journey without a large down payment or the perfect financial situation. However, you do need to know how to identify the right property, and that will be our focus in the next chapter. The goal is to find undervalued properties, which will work for both house flipping and the BRRRR method.

TAKE ACTION AND MAKE SMART MOVES

FINDING THE RIGHT PROPERTIES

In 2024, approximately 10% of real estate transactions were off-market deals, highlighting the growing importance of alternative sourcing methods in a competitive market (Dodge 2025).

EXPLORING PROPERTY SOURCING METHODS

Having a solid plan to secure financing for your real estate investment is the first step. Now that that's out of the way, we can focus on how to find potential investment properties. Just because you can afford a property or it looks good on the outside, doesn't mean it will make a great investment. Therefore, it is important to understand what you are doing when searching for a real estate investment property.

Multiple Listing Service (MLS)

A multiple listing service is a database that a real estate agent creates based on the information they have for a particular area. This is a handy tool for real estate agents because it allows other agents to see the MLS and connect buyers to various listings. Someone looking to purchase a property can also consult an MLS to find information about properties that are on the market and then make comparisons. Typically, this kind of database is electronic and online, making it easily updated and accessible for everyone. You can contact your local real estate agent and ask for their MLS if you cannot easily find it online. You will need to partner with a real estate agent in the area to gain access to some of these databases.

There is a wealth of information available on an MLS that can help you make better decisions when searching for a potential property. The information in each database will depend on the real estate agent who set it up. However, some information you can expect to see includes sales data, the structural components of the property, the interior features, and any special attributes.

Off-Market Deals

Most properties that are up for sale can be found on a multiple listing service, but there are also other ways to find a property. These are known as off-market homes, and they might provide you with the opportunity to access a better deal through a private avenue. They are more exclusive than the properties listed on an MLS, and only a single real estate agent will handle the buying and selling of them.

The reason a real estate agent might want to keep this information to themselves is that it results in less competition in the real estate market. It is also better for flexible negotiation since buyers and sellers can speak directly with one another to come up with a deal that works best for everyone. Additionally, there won't be the added pressure of traditional real estate sales timelines or the stress of having multiple people making offers on the property at the same time.

Finding an off-market listing can be a bit more difficult. Your best bet is to contact your local real estate agent and ask them directly if they have any off-market homes currently available. Another avenue to explore is online property websites. You might need to survey quite a few properties to find what you're looking for. However, if there are filters, see if you can filter by unlisted or for-sale-by-owner options.

Another important tool when looking for off-market properties is networking and approaching homeowners directly. If you have a network, see if you can put out feelers to indicate that you are interested in purchasing an off-market property, and then simply wait to see who responds. Your network is a very powerful tool because you never know who can assist you in your real estate investment journey. Building a network is something you will continuously do as you meet more people. This will be an ongoing part of your real estate journey, so working on your networking skills is key.

APPLYING INVESTMENT RULES

There are a few very helpful investment rules that you can use when investing in real estate. The rules you will be using will also depend on the type of real estate investment you are pursuing and what you plan to do with your property.

70% Rule for Flipping

The 70% rule is a great guideline for flipping a house. Essentially, when you take on a house-flipping project, the goal is to purchase your property for as low a price as possible so that you can reap a much larger profit when you sell. If you spend too much money on buying the house and on renovations, you will struggle to achieve any reasonable profit when you sell the house. This is why it is important to know what the home's sale price will be before you start making any purchases. This is where the 70% rule comes in to help you.

With the 70% rule, you should not pay more than 70% of your property's after-repair value, subtracting the cost of the repairs and renovations you will be making to the property. The after-repair value is simply the amount that the property could possibly sell for after you have fixed it up. To use this rule, you will need to estimate how much you think the property will sell for, multiply that by 70%, and then subtract your estimated renovation costs.

From here, you will arrive at the maximum amount you can pay for a property while still achieving a good profit. Just remember that this rule is simply a guideline to help you determine how much a property is worth or how much you should be paying for it. It is not a hard and fast rule that you must abide by. Other factors may come into play that could sway your decision or change the amount you need to pay for a property.

Also, remember that this method relies on many estimations, which means there are limitations to its accuracy. This is why it is crucial to spend some time researching the market and ensuring that you understand its ups and downs. This will also provide you with an indicator of what you can expect from the market and help you make better decisions going forward.

1% Rule for Rentals

The 1% rule is a useful guideline that you can apply with the BRRRR method or any other real estate investing strategy where you plan to rent out a property. With this rule, you simply multiply the purchase price of the property, including any necessary repairs, by 1%. The resulting figure will represent the amount of monthly rent you can set as your baseline when renting out the property. Although this is not a hard and fast rule, it provides a good estimate of your potential monthly cash flow when renting out your property.

It offers a starting point, but it is advisable to consider other factors, such as the general market rate in your area. You may have acquired a property at a bargain price and are paying a very low amount for a property in a desirable location. In this case, you might be able to charge more for rent than what the 1% rule suggests. You would use the 1% rule as your baseline and then take additional factors into account to maximize your rental profit.

UTILIZING ANALYTICAL TOOLS

These days, there are numerous tools at your disposal. You can leverage these to your advantage and simplify your real estate journey.

After-Repair Value (ARV) Calculators

The formula to calculate the after-repair value is straightforward: After-Repair Value = Purchase Price + Renovation Cost. However, you do not need to do the math yourself, as there are online calculators that perform all the calculations for you. These tools are user-friendly and accurate because they also consider other factors, such as the location of your property. One of these calculators can be found here: https://tools.reikit.com/comps/.

Return on Investment (ROI) Calculators

The goal of an investment is to make you money, so knowing the return on investment (ROI) is vital. This knowledge will help you predict how much you will gain from your investment. You can use this information to decide whether this is a good investment. The ROI is expressed as a percentage; therefore, the higher the percentage, the better the investment. There are two methods that can be used to calculate ROI: the cost method and the out-of-pocket method.

The basic formula for calculating ROI is as follows:

ROI = (Investment Gain − Investment Cost) / Investment Cost

Let's discuss the cost method first. With this method, you take into consideration the total cost of the investment. This encompasses the price you paid to buy the property and the cost of any renovations or improvements made. For example, if you bought a property for $100,000, spent $20,000 fixing it up, and then sold it for $160,000, you would calculate it as follows:

(160,000 − 120,000) / 120,000 = 33%

The out-of-pocket method is based on your invested money. It factors in the use of borrowed or leveraged money, so you would typically see a higher number when calculating the ROI. Let's use similar numbers as above. The purchase price of the property is $100,000, with a down payment of $30,000. The renovations cost you $20,000, which makes your out-of-pocket expenses $50,000. You sold the property for $160,000. Now, use these numbers to calculate ROI:

(160,000 − 120,000) / 50,000 = 80%

A good ROI calculator can be found here: https://www.calculator.net/roi-calculator.html.

Deal Analysis Software

There is a lot that goes into analyzing a deal, but you do not have to do everything yourself because there are platforms that do most of it for you. The ones I recommended you check out are:

- DealCheck: https://dealcheck.io/
- DealMachine: https://www.dealmachine.com/
- PropStream: https://www.propstream.com/
- Mashvisor: https://www.mashvisor.com/

SELECTING THE RIGHT MARKET AND NEIGHBORHOOD

It is crucial to choose the right neighborhood when investing in real estate. This decision can make or break your investment, so it is essential to conduct thorough research when selecting the neighborhood. A real estate market analysis is also known as a comparative market analysis. This is where you analyze the current market values of properties and compare them to the property you are considering buying or selling. This is one of the best and easiest ways to conduct a real estate market analysis.

When performing this type of comparative market analysis, the goal is to help you decide whether or not you should invest in a specific area. This is especially helpful if you are wondering about purchasing a property in two or three different cities. You can compare and determine which option is better. This type of market analysis also helps you identify elements that could potentially hinder the success of your investment in certain areas. Additionally, you will gain insight into the demographics of the area, allowing you to fully understand the future potential of the neighborhood. All of these factors are essential for understanding your potential investment. Let's delve into more detail about the steps you will need to follow to conduct a market analysis.

Step 1: Be Informed About the Market

The first step is always to be informed about the market. You need to understand the market you are working with in order to make the best decisions regarding it. In this initial step, you should look at things from a global or broad perspective without delving deeply into the specifics or details. This broad perspective is necessary to form the foundation of your analysis and ensure that you understand the situation from a larger viewpoint.

The real estate market is always evolving and changing, so it's important to stay on top of what is happening, as well as observe the trends. Take a look at what the real estate market looks like now and how it is performing. You can gain valuable insights into what the market might look like by examining economic indicators; if the economy is doing well, it will likely be reflected in the real estate market as well.

It is also a good idea to analyze your competitors to see what they are offering or doing so that you can gain a better understanding for yourself. If they are being more aggressive with their investment strategies, try to understand why this is the case, and then see if you can apply a similar strategy to your investments. It is not advisable to simply copy someone else's investment strategy or analysis of the market, so make sure that you conduct your own research and support what you observe with your competitors using your knowledge and expertise.

Step 2: Know the Customers in the Market

Knowing your customers is vital when you are trying to understand a market or when you are investing in real estate in general. This can also be referred to as understanding the current demand in the market. Who is looking for what kind of property? How many people are searching for property? What is attracting potential customers to certain properties? These are all great questions to start asking yourself so that you can fully understand the potential customers in the market.

A good starting point is to ask yourself how many customers are currently in the real estate market and how this is changing over time. A market analysis is not something you will conduct at one static point; rather, it is something you will continuously perform to track changes to understand how things are evolving. See if you can identify whether the demand is increasing, decreasing, or remaining the same. You will also need to know who your real estate customers are and where they are located. Examine their consumption rates and behaviors. It might also be beneficial to understand what the budget of your customers is, as well as the common factors that tend to trigger a purchase.

Step 3: Study in Detail What Your Competitors Already Offer

You might not be too excited about having many competitors, but you can use your competition to your advantage. When you have direct competition, it means that you and a few others are all competing for the same customers or potential investment opportunities. This indicates that your competitors have been researching matters pertaining to you and your investments as well. Consequently, you can obtain vital information by studying their behavior and gaining a deeper understanding of it.

The first thing you will need to do is figure out who your competitors in the market are. They could be individual investors or even larger companies. Try to determine their investment strategies and whether or not they have been successful over the long term. Examine their trends as well as any public financial data you can find. All of this will help you understand your competitors more deeply, and it will also assist you in grasping the market in which they operate. If someone else has made a mistake that did not work out, you can learn from their errors rather than repeating the same ones yourself. This will help you achieve greater success in a shorter period of time, so it is definitely something you should not overlook.

Step 4: Analyze the Factors That May Influence the Market

There are many factors that could potentially influence the market that may not be directly related to actual real estate. For example, there may have been technological developments, or new laws and regulations might have been enacted. There may also be a new real estate trend that emerges, making certain properties more attractive than others.

Step 5: Collect Data to Determine If the Project Is Viable and Secure

Data collection is an underrated but very important part of real estate market research. When you collect data, you are essentially gathering information that will assist you in determining whether a project is a good investment or if it is something you need to move on from. Some of the data you will need to collect includes demographic and socioeconomic information. This is important because it will help you understand the demand for the property and what is happening in the area. For example, if there is an area experiencing a large influx of younger families, this indicates that it is an affordable area, and the demand for housing will likely increase over the next few years.

You can use various tools to help you collect and analyze the data for the property or area in which you are looking to invest. Some of the most helpful tools include property management software, such as a real estate CRM system, which helps you manage your real estate portfolio. You can also examine heat maps, which will show you where there is high demand for properties and where there is potential for growth. You might even want to conduct property surveys in the area to gain a more hands-on understanding of what is happening locally.

Evaluate a Neighborhood Before Investing

When it comes to investing in property, it can be more important to invest in a good area than to focus solely on a specific property. When you consider purchasing a property, you will likely choose an area first and then look for properties within that area to see if anything meets your needs and standards. Typically, it does not work the other way around, where you would search for a specific property and then evaluate the area to see if it suits your requirements. A specific neighborhood or area will have benefits and amenities that align with the lifestyles of certain individuals, which is why selecting the right neighborhood is so crucial for investors.

Regardless of who your target customer or tenant is, it is important to consider the amenities that are close to your potential property investment. The more amenities that are nearby, the better your chances of attracting the right kinds of tenants. It is true that different demographics will desire different amenities. For example, a young single person who is just starting out in their career might want to be closer to city life, with social meetup spots like restaurants and bars nearby, whereas families are looking for proximity to good schools, parks, and family-friendly facilities. In general, you would like the neighborhood you are investing in to have good schools, restaurants, shops, gyms, medical facilities, and recreational activities close by.

Another key indicator of a good area is its proximity to employment. Many people choose to live close to where they work, so if there are many job opportunities in an area, it will be attractive to a lot more people. This doesn't necessarily mean that it has to be in the economic hub, but being near an area with more job availability is advantageous. You should also consider factors like crime rates, as everyone would prefer to live in a place with a lower crime rate.

If you want to get a good idea of what is happening in a specific neighborhood or area, it is advisable to get in your car and drive around or walk through the neighborhood. You will see what is actually going on, apart from what you can research. If you notice a lot of rundown properties where it appears that the residents do not take pride in their homes, this is not a good sign. It is also a red flag if you see many signs indicating "for rent" or "for sale." You don't want a large number of vacant properties in an area, as this indicates that people do not want to live there and that more people are moving out than moving in. The only exception would be a neighborhood or area with a lot of new development and new builds, as this will naturally have more properties for sale or rent.

Even though it can seem like a tedious job, doing your research on the neighborhood and the properties you want to invest in is a key part of the real estate investment journey. It is going to save you a lot of time, money, and resources in the long run, and you'll be thankful that you spent a little extra effort doing the groundwork before putting down your money for an investment. The great thing is that there are many tools available that can really help you ensure you have the best chance at a successful investment, so it is a good idea to use these to your advantage. The goal is to be able to make the most informed decisions you can as you embark on your real estate investment journey.

Now that you can identify promising properties, your next step is to understand how to effectively rehabilitate a property to maximize its value and your potential returns. In the next chapter, we will dive into the renovation process so that you can understand key elements such as budgeting, planning, and executing successful property rehabilitation.

REHAB WITHOUT REGRET

In 2024, Americans spent an estimated $603 billion on home remodeling, with 46% of home buyers being less willing to compromise on the condition of the home when purchasing (National Association of Realtors 2025). This highlights the importance of well-executed renovations in the real estate market.

THE REHAB PROCESS

There is a lot that goes into the rehab process when it comes to real estate. Knowing the full extent of what is expected is fundamental to ensuring your success. Let's discuss some of the things you will need to consider as you embark on this journey.

The first thing you need to do is plan and work out your design for your property. Many people like to skip this step because it seems like a waste of time, and they believe it will take too long. If you are the type of person who just likes to dive into something, then the planning and preparation phase is probably the part you will dislike the most. However, it is one of the most important things you can do to ensure a smooth process from start to finish.

Think about building a house from scratch; you will want to make sure that the foundation is set and solid before you start with anything else. If you do not have a solid and secure foundation, as you continue building your house, there is a risk that the foundation will give way, ruining all the hard work you have put in throughout the rest of the process. Then, you will need to break down everything you have done and start from the bottom again. I'm sure this is not something you want to do, which is why it is important to recognize that planning and preparation are the foundation of everything else that comes afterward.

If you are undertaking a larger renovation, you will also need to consider the time and resources required for the demolition. You might want to remove a certain part of the property to create space for something else, or it may simply be an eyesore that you wish to eliminate. Following that, the rebuilding phase will commence, during which you will begin to see tangible progress toward making the space look the way you envision. In some cases, the rebuilding phase may not take too long; however, if you are making significant changes to the property, you should plan for it to be quite resource-intensive and time-consuming. Additionally, you will need to consider the installation of essential systems such as plumbing, HVAC, electrical, and mechanical components. All of this is crucial to ensure that your property and home function at their best and meet all safety standards.

Once you have the structure and these important elements in place, you can move on to your walls and flooring. It may be the case that you do not need to break down or build up much, so you would only need to redo the flooring or certain walls. Other tasks you might need to undertake include adding cabinets, appliances, and final touches. This is definitely the more enjoyable part of the process, as you can see your vision coming to life; however, it requires careful planning and time to get it right. Along the way, you may discover that some of your initial plans do not work out as expected, necessitating adjustments. This is a very normal part of the process, and it is something you should anticipate. Let's discuss in more depth the steps you will take as you navigate the rehabilitation process.

Step 1: Make a Plan

As mentioned above, it is crucial to start your process by making a solid plan. This is where you establish your priorities so you know exactly what you will be working on first and how you will proceed through the process. It also helps you stay on track and ensures that you do not get caught up in details that are not important.

Step 2: Set a Budget

Part of the planning process is budgeting, which is essential. It is easy to go off course and spend significantly more money than you have available. When you budget, you can allocate your funds to the most important items and ensure that you will not run out at crucial moments. When budgeting, make sure to keep about 10% to 20% of the total amount for unforeseen circumstances and expenses. As much as planning is essential, unexpected bumps in the road can arise, and it is important to have the finances to help you navigate through them.

Step 3: Hire a Contractor

Once you have set your budget, it is time to hire your contractors. If you have been through the renovation process before, you probably have one or two contractors with whom you are comfortable. If not, then it is time to start interviewing. Take your time with this, as you will be entering into a contract with this person and including them in a significant portion of the renovation process. Ensure that they have the necessary skills, certifications, and experience to help you achieve your goals. Do not choose the cheapest or most convenient option in this case.

Step 4: Talk to Your Insurance Company

You will need to ensure that you have the necessary insurance coverage, so call your insurance company before and after the renovation process is completed. Remember that when you renovate a property, it increases in value; therefore, the amount for which you were insured at the beginning of the process may not be sufficient afterward.

Step 5: Secure Permits and Order Materials

Before you start breaking ground on your renovation, it is important to ensure that you have all of the necessary permits and materials. Every county and state has different requirements regarding permits and what they allow in general. Understanding the permits you will need will help you ensure a smooth process and avoid incurring any unnecessary fines. At this stage, you should also begin securing your materials for the remainder of the building process.

Step 6: Start Demolition

Once all of this is done, you can start the demolition of the property. This is not always necessary, and it really depends on the size of your project. However, if you are undertaking significant renovations, then demolition is an important step. Even something as simple as relocating a wall requires some demolition, so keep this in mind.

Step 7: The Installs

Once the demolition is complete, you can begin rebuilding and installing the necessary and important elements. For example, you will need to finish the patching, drywall, sanding, painting, flooring, appliances, and cabinetry.

Step 8: Add the Finishing Touches

Once all that is done, it is time for you to add the finishing touches to your property. You'll want to incorporate some fixtures and hardware that will make things look appealing. This will include lighting, door handles, a backsplash, and even sealing the floor so that it looks crisp and new. You can also add other design elements, but it depends on what you are doing with the property. If you are renting out the property and choosing to do so fully furnished, then you'll need to furnish the property and ensure that it attracts the type of tenant you want. If you are planning to sell the property, then you do not need to worry about furniture or making things look pretty.

ESTIMATING COSTS AND AVOIDING SURPRISES

It can be very easy to let the cost of revamping your property skyrocket without proper planning. Expenses can quickly add up, and because you are likely to spend smaller amounts of money on many different items, it might be difficult to track. Being able to estimate your costs effectively will help you avoid any surprises down the line and ensure that you have enough money for the most important aspects of your renovation journey.

Step 1: Pick Your Projects

When you purchase a property with potential, you might have a long list of different things you want to do to increase its value. However, not all of these things will be realistic based on your timeline or budget. This is why it is so important to select the projects you want to tackle during your renovation. Since you are renovating to increase the potential profit of your property, it is best to write down a list of all the things you want to do and then prioritize them based on what would add the most value. Adding an extra bedroom or bathroom might be more beneficial than retiling the kitchen. Even though it might be nice to install new floors in the kitchen and it would increase the value, adding an extra room will be much more valuable and yield more money in the long run. It's all about planning and being smart about where you invest your money so that you can achieve the best returns while spending the least.

Step 2: Research the Costs

You will need to understand the costs associated with each of your renovation projects. There are many hidden costs that are not immediately obvious, which means that conducting thorough research will help you uncover these hidden expenses, allowing you to obtain an accurate representation of how much you will be spending. For something like retiling a floor, you will need to spend money on tiles, but that is not the only expense. You will also need cement or adhesive to adhere the tiles to the floor, as well as grout. Additionally, you might require a sealant, tools to complete the tiling job, and equipment to remove the previous flooring.

You will also need to consider the contractors or professionals you will hire to complete this job. You can consult a contractor with a specific skill set for the project you wish to undertake and ask them for an estimate of how much everything will cost, including labor. Be sure to add a little extra as a buffer in case unexpected costs arise.

Step 3: Keep a List of All Your Cost Estimates

Keeping a list will help you track all of the cost estimates you made during the planning stage. You can update this list, but it is also important to do your best to adhere to it throughout the process. This list should organize your total budget into different categories, so you know how much is allocated to each area. You can break this down into specific percentages, with the highest percentage going toward the most expensive or most important items.

Step 4: Set Your Savings Goal

Once you have estimated the costs of everything you want to do, it's time to start saving and budgeting. This is something you need to do in advance so that you have enough time to save for all the renovations you want to undertake. Depending on the type of project you are going to pursue, whether it's flipping a house or following the BRRRR framework, you might need a larger amount of money. You will be able to leverage some of the expenses through a loan so that you aren't paying the majority of the expenses out of pocket or in cash. However, it is a good idea to have some physical funds available for renovating the property. Once you know your total savings goal, you can break it down into smaller amounts to start working toward that goal.

Step 5: Collect Bids from Contractors

Now is the time to interview and collect bids from contractors. Remember what we discussed earlier: the cheapest, most convenient option might not be the best one. This is why it is so important to do your research and conduct interviews with each of your contractors. If you can obtain reviews or referrals from other people you trust who have used these contractors, that is even better, as it provides firsthand experience of how good or bad they are. You can also conduct some online research to find out if there are any online reviews, which will help you better understand your potential contractors.

Step 6: Schedule Your Renovation

Once all of this is done, your planning is almost complete, and it's time to schedule your renovation. This includes ensuring that all elements are aligned so you can start on a specific day. You will want to make sure that you have all the appropriate materials and contractors available around the same time to avoid losing precious hours due to missing materials or unavailable contractors. It helps to schedule a bit in advance to ensure that everything goes according to plan and that you have everything you need. This also gives you some time to prepare for the process ahead, which might be quite a significant task to undertake.

HIGH-ROI UPGRADES AND DIY TIPS

ROI stands for return on investment, and it refers to the amount of profit you will make after completing your investment in relation to how much money you spent. Every investor seeks to achieve a higher ROI, which means spending less money to generate more profit. Certain renovations and DIY projects yield a much higher ROI, and those are the areas you can focus on to ensure you maximize your profit. Let's discuss a few of these options, and then you can decide which ones will be best for you.

One upgrade that can bring a higher ROI is a garage door replacement. In many cases, the garage door is one of the first things people see when they enter a property. Having a modern, clean, and aesthetically pleasing garage door will significantly enhance curb appeal. Additionally, it is not very expensive, so you could potentially double your ROI with just this improvement. Continuing with the theme of curb appeal, you can replace your entry door to create a more expensive and modern look. This is something that people will notice from the outside, and they will expect something amazing on the inside as well. Plus, there is nothing better than walking through a beautifully designed doorway.

One of the most frequently used rooms in a house is the kitchen, which truly attracts potential buyers. Updating and replacing a few key elements in the kitchen can significantly increase a property's perceived value. These updates include updating countertops, replacing hardware, installing new flooring, repainting walls, and improving lighting. You can also make a few adjustments by rearranging certain amenities to enhance user-friendliness.

Everyone loves an outdoor space for enjoyment and entertaining, which is why a deck could be a great addition to your property. An outdoor deck is one of the features that truly attracts buyers to a home. The most popular types of decks are wood and composite, so you will need to choose which one best suits your needs and budget. Composite decks are more expensive, but they offer a better return on investment and are highly durable.

Another room that can significantly enhance resale value is the bathroom. There is nothing better than a modern and relaxing bathroom. When bathrooms are outdated and old-looking, they do not feel as welcoming or inviting, which can deter many potential buyers or renters from purchasing or renting a property. Adding new fixtures, tiles, lighting, and decor can greatly help modernize and improve a bathroom.

A few other aspects to consider are window replacements. This is especially relevant if the house is quite old and the windowpanes appear incredibly outdated. You can also look into replacing the floors or the roof if these elements are not up to standard or do not look as nice as they could. This depends on how much money you have to spend on renovations and should be considered last, after you have evaluated the other areas we have already discussed.

Now, remember that some tasks can definitely be done by yourself, while others require professional assistance. While it might be tempting to do everything yourself to cut costs, this can lead to bigger issues down the line. Therefore, make sure that you only undertake DIY projects that are suitable. For example, you can certainly repaint walls, replace small fixtures, change the lighting, install simple tiles, install kitchen cabinets or doors, update knobs and door handles, clean the gutters, power wash the outdoor area, and tidy up the outdoor landscape. Tasks that you should definitely hire a professional for include electrical work, plumbing, major renovations, siding, roof repairs, and structural or foundational repairs.

RECOGNIZING AND AVOIDING RED FLAGS

On this journey, there are some red flags that you should do your best to avoid in order to prevent any wasted money down the line. When looking for a potential property in which you will be investing, this is when you need to be extra alert. Certain issues can cost you significantly more money and simply won't be worth renovating, and these are the things you should avoid.

The number one item on the list is foundation problems. If a house has foundation issues, it means that you will essentially have to redo the entire house, as you will need to dismantle the existing structure before fixing the foundation. This is definitely not worth it and will require a lot of work and money. You should also look out for signs of wear and tear and an outdated design in the property. Some homes have been around for a very long time, and the general wear and tear of the structure of the property may not be what it should be. It might take considerable work and renovations to ensure that the house is modern and fully functional before you can sell or rent it out.

Another aspect to consider is safety concerns or limited functionality with certain features of the property. You want to make sure that the property is 100% safe, and you also want to ensure that it is user-friendly. If the current layout or design of the property doesn't align with how modern people live, then it's really not going to be worth it. For example, I have seen properties where the bathrooms are outside of the main building, which seems like a nightmare for anyone living in that home on a day-to-day basis.

Significant issues like water damage, pest problems, and general environmental concerns are also things you will need to avoid if you are trying to achieve a higher ROI. The goal is to spend the least amount of money while obtaining the most returns, so when these major issues arise, it will require a lot of time, energy, and resources to resolve, making it potentially not the best choice for an investment.

Spotting Unreliable Contractors

You will need a reliable contractor throughout the process, so it's important to spot any potential red flags early on to avoid engaging further with a bad contractor. There are a few things you can consider red flags when getting a quote or thinking about moving forward with a specific contractor. One thing to be wary of is if the contractor is asking for a large down payment or if the contract is very vague. It is easy to be taken advantage of in both of these cases, so it's important for you to read through the contract and ensure it is highly specific to the job and the tasks that need to be completed. Additionally, make sure that you do not have to pay an unnecessarily large down payment that is nonrefundable should the job not be done as needed.

Another red flag to consider is if the contractor has a lot of bad reviews or no reviews at all. You want a solid track record to ensure that this person will do what they say and is good at their job. If there are no reviews or no one for you to call for references, then this is definitely something you can consider a red flag, and you should move on from this potential contractor.

An estimate or bid that is extremely low is also a red flag because it could indicate that this person does not know their worth, is just starting out, or is simply trying to make a quick buck without planning to do the job properly.

You can also learn a lot from a person's communication skills. If they are not communicating effectively, missing your messages, or simply going silent for long periods, then this is not someone you want to work with on a long project. You will also need to verify your potential contractors to ensure that they have the necessary licenses; if the information does not match up, then this person is probably shady and not someone you want to work with.

Other things that can be considered red flags include asking for upfront cash payments, appearing unprofessional, or even being under the influence of alcohol or other substances. All of these behaviors are simply unprofessional, and you don't want to work with someone who will bring negative energy to your project. You want someone professional and reliable.

At the end of the day, the planning phase is likely one of the most important phases of any renovation or real estate journey. It will be extremely helpful if everything is planned properly, as this ensures that things will go much more smoothly for you moving forward. It will also help you build a proper strategy and avoid potential mishaps and mistakes because you've already planned for or anticipated them before they occur. Even though it might seem tedious, it is definitely worth it to do your research and take your time with the planning process.

Now that you have a solid understanding of the renovation process, you are ready for the next step. This will involve diving into the BRRRR strategy. In the next chapter, we will fully explore how to leverage the buy, rehab, rent, refinance, repeat method to build a scalable and profitable real estate portfolio.

THE BRRRR PROCESS

The BRRRR method is a fantastic approach to entering real estate investing due to its structured nature. Many people have found success with it, but it's important to understand the process before diving in. When you fully comprehend the process and what goes into something like this, you can make better decisions, and you can navigate this type of real estate investment much more effectively. There are numerous individuals with fantastic success stories related to this method of real estate investing, and you can be one of them.

THE BRRRR STRATEGY: A CLOSER LOOK

There are five specific steps in the BRRRR method, and each letter represents something very important. In this section, we will discuss each of these steps and explore them in greater depth so that you fully understand each one.

Buy

The first step is to buy a property. This is what the "B" stands for in BRRRR. In this initial step, you need to ensure that you are purchasing the right property to maximize your investment. This step is not only the first but also the most important. If you buy the right property, it will make all the other steps much easier and ensure that you achieve a great ROI. The goal is to purchase a property as cheaply as possible, with as few issues as possible. You should be looking for a property that is below market value. Distressed or undervalued properties can offer significant rewards after the rehabilitation process.

During this phase, you will need to conduct market research to find the right property. It will take some time, and you are unlikely to find an ideal property within the first few days. Don't get disheartened; make sure to take your time so that you don't rush into something that could cost you later on. Once you have located your ideal property, it is time to start applying for a loan to purchase it. You will also need to obtain the appropriate licensing and registration required for the potential renovations you will be undertaking.

Rehab

The second step is the rehab step. This step focuses on a lot of what we discussed in the previous chapter. It's all about renovating and rehabilitating the property so that it is ready for your potential tenant. During this step, you will also ensure that you are selecting the right contractors to work on your project.

Rent

Once your property is ready, it is time to rent it out. The goal is to secure reliable tenants who will be able to pay you your weekly or monthly rental fee so that you can make a profit. It's not only about finding the right tenant but also about setting the right rental rate to ensure a consistent cash flow. There is a lot that goes into this, but conducting some market research and evaluating how much you want to charge based on what similar properties in the area are charging is a good start. Doing this at the beginning will help you get a better idea of what you can expect once your property is up for rent.

This step also includes marketing your property to get the word out and find the right tenant. The goal should be to have as many options as possible so that you can make the best choice. Marketing could involve strategies such as online ads, newspaper ads, word-of-mouth, or even posters and billboards. It all depends on your area and what will give you the most reach.

Once the word is out and people start applying to rent your property, you will need to conduct interviews and check references to ensure that you choose the right person. You should be very wary of anyone who applies without any references. Also, make sure you perform a credit check to ensure that the person renting can afford to pay the rent.

Refinance

Once you have your tenant, it is time for the fourth step, which is refinancing. With this step, you can pull out equity from the property to use for purchasing another property and repeating the process. This step requires a lot of accounting and ensuring that your finances are in order. Throughout this process, you must manage your property well and maintain it so that your tenants are happy. You will also need to communicate effectively with your tenants and ensure that you are meeting all of the lease agreements on your end.

Repeat

The final step is to repeat, which means that you will start again with the buying process and follow the steps once more. The goal of the BRRRR method is to grow your portfolio and maximize your profit. When you repeat the strategy, it means that you will manage multiple properties simultaneously. This does require some strategy, which may mean that you need to acquire software to assist you with property management. You might also consider hiring a property manager who will take care of the day-to-day operations of your properties while you focus on building your portfolio.

RISKS BEFORE INVESTING

As with any kind of investing, there are definitely risks associated with this method. It is important to understand these risks before proceeding so that you aren't going in blind. It will also help you to develop some contingency plans should one of these risks become a reality for you.

The first and probably the biggest risk is over-leveraging. There is great potential to make a lot of money through leveraging, which is why this method is so attractive; however, over-leveraging is something you need to watch for. Over-leveraging is essentially borrowing too much money and then being unable to pay it back. You might be tempted to stretch your borrowing capacity to secure the deal you want, but when you borrow too much money, you negatively impact your cash flow, making it difficult to repay the loan.

Another point regarding over-leveraging is that if the market experiences a downturn, your property value may decline. If you have a very small buffer between the money you've leveraged and what you possess, this could lead to significant problems. It could place you in a negative equity situation, which could complicate refinancing and obtaining loans. You want to ensure that your property can stand on its own two feet, even in the event of a market downturn. It is important not to rush into the next deal quickly after renting out one of your properties. You want to ensure that the properties you currently own are secure and can operate independently before you attempt to invest further.

Another risk is underestimating the rehabilitation costs of a property. This is something we have mentioned before, and it is incredibly common. The truth is that you never truly know how much the rehabilitation will cost until you are in the thick of it. This is why it is important to do your best to estimate, but also to have a buffer amount so that if something unexpected arises, you have funds to cover it.

Along the same lines, the risk of overestimating the after-repair value is very real. This occurs when you believe that you can rent or sell your property for much more than what is actually reflected in reality. This may happen because you didn't conduct your research properly, or the market has shifted since you made your estimates. This is why it is so important to stay up-to-date with your local real estate news and to be more conservative with your estimates.

Since the BRRRR method is all about renting and finding tenants, there is a risk of getting a bad tenant who could cause more issues than benefits for you. For example, a tenant could cause property damage, lead to legal disputes, or fail to pay their rent, and all of this will be your responsibility. Another risk associated with renting is that the market may not be in your favor. It could be difficult to find a tenant, which means you will have a higher vacancy rate, and every month your property remains vacant is money lost.

Another risk involves challenges with refinancing. You may find it difficult to secure favorable refinancing terms, which means you will not be getting a good deal on your loan, and it will cost you more than you expected. Even worse, you might not be able to obtain a loan or refinance your property at all. This is why it is so important to ensure that your credit score is good and that you have established relationships with lenders so that they trust you.

KEY CONSIDERATIONS DURING REFINANCING

When refinancing your property, your aim is to secure a lower interest rate or to completely change the repayment terms of your current mortgage. This helps you save on your monthly payments, allowing you to free up more finances for other purposes. In this case, you will have more money to invest in other properties and continue growing your real estate investment portfolio.

When you refinance your mortgage, you have the opportunity to lower the interest rate you currently have, which means that over the long term, you will be paying much less for the property. You might also be able to lower the monthly premium you need to pay and obtain a shorter loan term, which all adds up to additional savings. Refinancing also allows you to change your current mortgage product to something more beneficial or better suited to you at this moment. Sometimes, we might choose an option that seems like a good idea, but as time goes on, a better option becomes available for refinancing. One of the biggest benefits of refinancing is that you can cash out some of your equity and then secure a larger loan. When you have some of your equity in cash, you can use that to reinvest in another property or area.

While there are many positive aspects to refinancing, it is also important to consider the negatives while you are trying to make this decision. There are always risks involved when it comes to investing and finances. Since refinancing is essentially like taking out a new loan, you are agreeing to new loan terms and new loan amounts, and you will likely have to pay all the closing costs again. These costs cover fees, underwriting, title deed services, and appraisal. You might expect to pay somewhere between 3% and 6% of the balance of your loan for these closing costs.

Another thing that people don't often consider is the time and research you need to do in order to select the right loan and lender. This is similar to the process you would have undertaken when you first started looking for a loan for your property investment. You likely didn't jump into the first loan or mortgage you were offered, and you would have needed to do your research to ensure you were getting the best deal. The same principle applies here, so you need to be aware that you will need to invest a lot of time and effort. It is also important to understand that your credit score might take a hit because you are taking out a new mortgage. This will likely not last very long, but be prepared for a drop in your score that could last anywhere from a few months to a couple of years. This might not be all that bad, depending on what your credit score currently is.

It is important to understand your loan-to-value (LTV) ratio so that you can know how much you owe on your current mortgage relative to the value of your property. This is an essential ratio to grasp when you are trying to refinance your property. It can significantly impact your ability to secure a favorable interest rate on your new mortgage and may also determine your eligibility for certain loans. If your LTV is on the higher side, it will be more difficult for you to obtain a loan.

Calculating this number is relatively simple; all you need to do is divide the amount you currently owe on your mortgage by the value of your property and then multiply that number by 100. You will obtain a percentage, which will represent your LTV. Depending on the type of refinancing loan you intend to pursue, you might only need a percentage of 97% or lower to qualify (Kenton, 2023). However, for certain options, such as a cash-out refinance, you will need an LTV of about 80% (Parker, 2025).

When you are going through the refinancing process, it is important to ensure that you have all your ducks in a row and that all your documentation is ready to go. You can start collecting this information as early as possible to make the process smoother when you reach the refinancing stage. You will need proof of rental income, property appraisal, and renovation receipts, to name a few of the required documents. Additionally, you can contact your preferred loan provider to inquire about any other documentation they require, ensuring that you have everything on hand to facilitate the process.

SAFELY ACCESSING EQUITY

When you are following the BRRRR method, it is important to safely access equity with as little risk to yourself as possible. We have already mentioned the cash-out refinance, which is a great way to access equity safely. With a cash-out refinance, you will use the equity in your current property to access cash, allowing you to purchase another property. This is not a second mortgage, which means it is distinct from a traditional line of credit. Essentially, you are replacing your current mortgage with a new loan that will include the balance you owe on your current property plus the equity you are borrowing to make your next investment.

All the other benefits of refinancing are still available with a cash-out refinance. For example, if there are better interest rates now than there were when you first took out your mortgage, you will benefit from lowering your overall interest rate with your new loan. This is definitely the way to go when you are following the BRRRR method, and many investors have done the same.

While leveraging can be a great tool to help you make more money through diversifying your real estate investments, there is a risk of over-leveraging. When you over-leverage, you put yourself in more debt than you can handle, or the amount of debt you have on your property exceeds its current market value. This makes it difficult to recover your funds.

The good news is that over-leveraging can be avoided. If you do your research and ensure you conduct your due diligence before purchasing a property or taking out a mortgage, you can mitigate this risk. You need to understand all the expenses that will arise from purchasing the property so that you aren't taken by surprise and require a much higher loan than expected. This means you will need to comprehend the property's expenses right from the start. Once you do that, you should also ensure that your debt-to-equity ratio is less than 70% to make sure it is manageable and that you will have good leveraging power.

It is also good practice to stick to a few investment properties rather than trying your hand at multiple investments, as these can be difficult to manage. If you are a beginner, then just stick to one or two additional properties so that you can get a feel for the BRRRR method. Once you are comfortable, you can move on to more properties. Remember that real estate investing is not a get-rich-quick scheme, which means you will likely need to take your time to ensure that you aren't losing any money.

CALCULATING CASH FLOW AND SETTING RENTS

When you are ready to start renting out your property, it is important to set the right rent so that you are not selling yourself short or making less money than you possibly could. At the end of the day, you want to maximize your profits so you can increase your cash flow. This begins with researching how much others are charging for rent for comparable properties. Look for a property that is very similar to yours and located in the same area, and see what others are charging. This will give you a good indication of how much people are willing to spend in that area for your type of property. You can easily conduct this research by visiting property websites like Zillow and even Craigslist. Remember that you will likely be able to charge more money after you have made your improvements and renovations, so you can also hire a home appraiser to help you determine the value of the property and how much you can charge in rent if you are finding it difficult to locate comparable properties.

Another factor to consider is the laws in your area, as many regions have limits on landlords regarding how much they can charge for rent. This means that the amount you charge for rent may not be entirely up to you. Rent control laws are a very real consideration depending on the city, state, or country in which you live. You'll need to ensure that you understand these laws so that you're not violating them and becoming liable for repercussions.

You will also need to check for seasonality, which means that certain seasons or times of the year will have more demand for rental properties than others. A simple example would be if you are situated in a college town; it is more likely that you will find a renter during the school term, as that is when students will flock to the town and need a place to stay. During peak times, you'll be able to charge more for rent than when demand is much lower.

A common rule that you can use when determining how much you can charge for rent is the 1% rule. It is a simple calculation where you multiply the property's value by 1%. The number you obtain will be an estimate of what you can expect to charge for rent. However, this is a very rough estimate, so it is important to take into consideration other factors such as demand, location, and market conditions. This will provide you with a starting point, and then you can conduct further research to refine the amount you will be charging for rent.

EFFECTIVE PROPERTY MANAGEMENT

When it comes to managing your property, the first thing you need to do is ensure that you find the right tenant. Finding good and reliable tenants will make things much easier for you down the road. It means that you will have someone living in your property whom you can trust, making your income more reliable and ensuring that your property is well taken care of. This is why it is so important to take your time when looking for tenants and not rush the process just to fill the vacancy.

The first step is to advertise your rental property to get the word out that you have a vacancy. This is not as simple as quickly putting up an ad on a property website and hoping for the best. You want to put your best foot forward to attract high-quality potential tenants. Firstly, you need to understand who your target market is. Look at your property and consider who your ideal tenant would be. For example, if you have a studio apartment in the middle of a big city, your tenant will likely be a couple or a single person with a career who wants to be close to the city center. You can then tailor your advertising to this specific tenant. Highlight aspects that they would find important and what they are looking for in a place to stay. If your property is a larger home with a garden and is close to good schools, your target market might be a family with small children. In this case, you should emphasize safety, amenities, children's activities, space, and other factors that parents of young children would consider important. This is what your target audience is looking for, so when they search for something, you want to be at the top of the search results.

Putting your best foot forward in advertising your property also involves taking high-quality photos. One of the biggest mistakes I see people making is that the photos they take of their properties are so poor that they deter potential applicants. Ensure that you take photos when the lighting is good, and it is also a good idea to clean up the space to make it look appealing. You might want to hire a professional to help you take stunning pictures. Once you have your photos, you will also want to create a detailed listing that highlights all the positive aspects of your property to attract your target tenant.

You don't only have to advertise on property websites because social media is also a great tool. Additionally, people you know could spread the word, and it is more likely that you will find a good-quality tenant through word-of-mouth and your network than by sifting through thousands of applications from random individuals. Speaking of your network, it is always a good idea to broaden it by speaking to local real estate agents and attending real estate investment events. This way, you can build connections with people who could possibly help you find the right tenant for your property.

Once you have a few applicants, it is time to start the tenant screening process. This is where you conduct background checks and delve deeper into who your potential tenants are so that you can make the right choice. The screening process begins with the rental application. You'll need to have your potential tenant fill out an application and provide all of their basic information to get started. This information will include their name, contact information, employer, and rental history. Your potential tenant might also want to provide additional information to help you make your decision. To ensure that you are not overwhelmed with thousands of applications from individuals who would not qualify, you can set some applicant requirements in your advertisement to immediately disqualify those you would not consider. These minimum requirements could include a certain income level or credit score.

Now that you have all of your applicants' basic information, you can run some checks to ensure that you have good candidates. These checks will include credit history, rental history, and an overall background check. This is important because you want to get a clear idea of how financially responsible your potential tenant is, as well as their rental history, so that you can spot any red flags early on. You can also run a criminal history check if you wish. However, it is important to note that you cannot discriminate against someone based on their criminal history unless the crime is related to their past or present tenancy.

Once you have completed all of your screenings and background checks, you can review what you have learned about your potential tenants and then narrow down the applicants. Once you have a good number of quality applicants, you can conduct interviews to see if you get along with your prospective tenants or if there are any red flags that you might notice when speaking with them. It is a good idea to plan what you are going to ask them in advance so that you can accurately compare your potential tenants and ensure that you are asking the most important questions. If there is anything concerning that arose in your background checks, you can also ask them to elaborate, as there may be a valid reason for it, which could provide you with peace of mind.

There is a lot that goes into building a solid foundation for the BRRRR method. It is important to do this groundwork to ensure that whatever steps you take beyond this will have the best chance of leading you to success. In the next chapter, we will take some time to explore how incorporating short-term rentals can further enhance your rental income and investment returns.

"Every person who invests in well-selected real estate in a growing section of a prosperous community adopts the surest and safest method of becoming independent, for real estate is the basis of wealth."

— Theodore Roosevelt

Everyone wants financial freedom, but the majority of people have no idea how to achieve it. To them, it will always be a dream—unless, that is, they see just how possible it is. I told you at the beginning of our journey together that I was unsure about real estate investing at first. To begin with, it was just about making sure my family had somewhere to live. It was only when I refinanced that house and used the equity to acquire another property that I realized what I could do with real estate investing.

Real estate is one of the most solid investments you can make, and the return you can get from it is, in most cases, far higher than it is for other forms of investment. I had to prove this to myself before I believed it, but now my goal is to help other people see just how possible it is. I talk to so many people who tell me that they're not wealthy enough to invest in property or that they don't even own their own house so they couldn't possibly consider it. They assume that these things are barriers, which means they don't even look into it.

I want to show people that there are fewer barriers to real estate investing than most people realize. I'm sure you've heard the expression, "Give a man a fish, and you feed him for a day. Teach a man to fish, and you feed him for a lifetime." That's how I view sharing what I know about real estate investment: I want to teach as many people as I can to build their wealth over their lifetime—and you can help me, simply by leaving a short review online.

By leaving a review of this book on Amazon, you'll help new readers to find it and understand that they, too, have the power to make money from real estate.

Anyone who's even slightly curious about whether they could make real estate investing work for them is looking for guidance—and your review will help them to find it. Together, we can help more people to make sure that financial freedom has a chance of becoming a reality instead of remaining a dream. I don't know about you, but that's a world I want to live in.

Scan the QR code to leave a review

Thank you so much for your support. Now, let's get back to business!

USING AIRBNB TO SUPERCHARGE RENTAL INCOME

The global short-term rental market is estimated to be worth $135 billion, reflecting a 9.7% increase from 2019 to 2023 (Achen 2025). This growth highlights the lucrative opportunities available to property owners who effectively leverage platforms like Airbnb. I have personally found success with Airbnb, which has far exceeded my expectations. Once I decided to truly get involved and create a plan, I was able to see significant financial gains through the Airbnb platform, and it is the reason I am so passionate about real estate.

WHEN AIRBNB IS A STRATEGIC CHOICE

When it comes to renting out your property, you don't have to do it solely on a long-term basis. A long-term strategy is great for many people, but you can definitely earn a substantial amount of money through Airbnb and short-term rentals. If you have never considered Airbnb as an option, let this be your sign to at least think about it.

Whether your Airbnb will be successful depends on several factors. Properties located in tourist-heavy areas or near major stadiums and events will have the highest chance of generating a steady income. Since Airbnb is a short-term rental strategy, the goal is to achieve higher occupancy rates, which means more people booking with you over time.

The type of property you have may not matter, as there are many different ways to rent out a property on Airbnb. It offers very flexible options, so you are likely to find one that is best suited to you. Firstly, you could rent out an entire standalone house. This means your guests will have access to the rooms, facilities, amenities, and anything else on the property. This arrangement is quite desirable, as guests enjoy having all the space to themselves, and it provides them with additional privacy.

You could also rent out an apartment or a condo in a larger building or complex. In this case, you would be renting out whatever is in that apartment, such as the rooms, living area, bathrooms, and kitchen. There will also be some shared areas and amenities, such as the laundry room, swimming pools, outdoor amenities, and entrances. Another option is to rent out a private room on Airbnb. This works if you have a space in your home that is not currently being used. Your guests will have their own private room, but they will need to share spaces like the living area, dining area, kitchen, and possibly the bathroom.

The final option is the shared room option, where one bedroom is shared by multiple guests. Think of a dormitory where several people sleep in one room using separate beds or bunk beds. There will also be shared rooms and amenities, such as the bathroom and kitchen. This will be a very affordable option for most guests, but it's not universally appealing, so only those who are on a budget would be attracted to something like this.

As you can see, there are many different options when it comes to renting out an Airbnb. Something good to know is that there are quite a few amenities that stand out from the crowd and make a property even more attractive on the Airbnb platform. Remember, people are booking with Airbnb because they're looking for a short-term rental, either for a vacation, business trip, or some other personal reason. In most cases, they are looking for a comfortable place to stay, and if they are on vacation, they will want some special amenities. A pool or hot tub is a great draw, and people will be willing to pay more for this. Staying with the water theme, if you have a property near the waterfront or with beach access, this is also a great draw. Everybody loves a view of the water, plus there are so many things to do, including water sports or even just relaxing on the beach. Water is not the only thing that attracts people; they also love outdoor and mountain views, so any of those options would be really good locations for an Airbnb.

If you have interesting architecture, a luxury bathroom, or unique amenities, such as a theater room, then these features will also attract more people. In the case of individuals wanting to book an Airbnb for business reasons, having an office space will be key and a significant attraction. What will attract your potential guests depends on their needs and your location. If you're situated in a city center or an economic hub, you are likely to attract more people who are coming to the city for work trips, and catering to them will be important. However, if you have a property that is more on the outskirts, where there are plenty of views, activities, and water attractions, you are likely to attract more people who are there for a vacation.

On Airbnb, you can also advertise experiences, not just property rentals. You can curate specific experiences in your area that potential guests would be excited to participate in, such as rides, city tours, sightseeing tours, and fun activities. You can add these experiences to your Airbnb booking package to make it even more attractive for people looking for a fun holiday experience. You can provide guests with tips and tricks for the area, as well as guide them to restaurants or provide maps of the area where they can go hiking, biking, swimming, or skiing. You might also be able to provide them with locations for museums and historical sites so they can explore while they're in the area. Remember that with Airbnb, you are essentially creating an experience rather than just renting out a place for people to stay. The more effort you put into creating a wonderful experience for your potential guests, the better your chances are of receiving positive reviews and more bookings.

Airbnb is a short-term rental platform, which means that when you engage with it, you'll be involved in short-term rentals. Short-term rentals require significantly more hands-on work and effort because you need to ensure that your guests are well taken care of, and you must prepare the property for the next guests after your current ones check out. There is indeed a lot that goes into managing an Airbnb, which is why I have written two books on this specific topic.

You can find both of my books on Amazon by using this link: https://www.amazon.com/stores/author/B0BH5891HS/

These books have already helped many people build the Airbnb business of their dreams, so I'm confident they will be useful to you if this is something you are considering as well.

Additionally, I have a Facebook community group specifically for Airbnb and short-term rental owners. This is a great place for people to connect and receive helpful tips and tricks along their Airbnb journey. Feel free to join this group to gain valuable insights and connect with others who are on the same journey as you.

Name: Airbnb Host Community
URL: https://www.facebook.com/groups/airbnbhostcommunity
QR Code:

You can choose to have either a short-term or a long-term rental. Both options have their pros and cons, so it is better to understand these before you choose a strategy. Let's discuss them in more detail.

Short-Term Rentals

For most of this book, we have been discussing long-term rentals or at least considering them as an option. Now we are going to switch gears and talk about the pros and cons of short-term rentals so that you fully understand this method.

Pros

A significant advantage of short-term rentals is that they offer a lot of flexibility. You can decide when you want to rent your property out and when you want to keep it vacant or live in it yourself. For example, if you own a beach cottage that you want to use for family vacations a few weeks a year, you can rent that property out through short-term rentals during the times you are not going to be there. This way, your property does not remain vacant and unused for the majority of the year, but you still have the option to enjoy a vacation home when you want it. This flexibility also allows you to be much more hands-on with your property, enabling you to check and inspect it whenever you need to. This means you can conduct more frequent maintenance checks compared to if someone were living on your property on a long-term basis and would prefer not to be disturbed as often.

Short-term rentals also provide the opportunity to earn significantly more money than long-term rentals. Consider this: When you book a vacation, you pay per night. If you multiply the per-night rate at an average vacation rental by 30 days, this amount would be much greater than what someone would pay for monthly rent at the same property. If your property has a good booking rate, with people staying fairly often, you will definitely be making more money than if you were renting it out on a long-term basis.

Another major benefit is that you are far less likely to encounter legal disputes with a short-term rental than with a long-term one. Tenant rights and laws can lead to lengthy legal disputes, whereas in a short-term rental situation, the guest is only staying for a few days. They are unlikely to have the time to engage in any significant arguments or disagreements that could lead to legal action.

Cons

There are some downsides to short-term rentals that are important to be aware of. One of the biggest risks is the possibility of long vacancies for the property. You can never truly predict the market, and there is a chance that your property will not receive as many bookings as you would like. Additionally, you must take into consideration the seasonal market and the type of property you have. If you own a beach vacation home, it is likely that during the winter, there will be few people interested in booking with you. In this case, you might experience a season where you do not have any guests for months on end. There is also significant competition for short-term rentals, and if you have found a good area for an Airbnb, it is likely that other Airbnbs are in the vicinity.

Since different people are coming in and out of your property all the time, you must consider the fact that this could result in increased wear and tear on the amenities and the general structure of the property. It is also important to recognize that people might be a bit more careless while on vacation, so the chances of scuffs, scratches, and other minor damages could increase. You also need to remember that while you may have a certain standard for how you like to take care of things or live in a house, this standard may not be the same for other people. Spills, stains, and damage are all common and may require you to perform regular maintenance and refurbishment more often.

Another downside is the risk of neighbor complaints due to unruly or loud guests. Even if your guests are well-behaved, there may be inconveniences that you inadvertently cause your neighbors, such as parking congestion or a buildup of dirt and trash. Since your guests will be staying on a short-term basis, they may not be familiar with the norms of the neighborhood, which could lead to behaviors that irritate your neighbors.

With a short-term rental or an Airbnb, you do need a high level of involvement since there is a high turnover rate of guests. You'll have to ensure that the house is cleaned and restocked before your next guest checks in. On top of that, you might also need to be available should there be an issue that a guest needs help with. Remember that you are essentially providing a service to your guests, so being on call is simply part of the job. You want to make sure your guests have the best experience, and this means that you need to assist them when they need it. If not, they might leave a negative review, which could heavily impact your future bookings.

Another thing to consider is that maintenance is much more urgent with a short-term rental because you want to ensure your guests have the best quality stay and that their satisfaction level is high. If there are non-urgent or smaller maintenance tasks, you might be able to schedule them for a later date with a long-term rental, but this is not the case with a short-term rental. Additionally, you can't perform maintenance when your guests are on the property, as this will not go well for your ratings or your overall guest experience. This means that you might need to conduct maintenance by not taking any bookings for a certain period or by scheduling it outside of business hours, which might result in you paying higher fees for your contractors.

Long-Term Rentals

Let's have a look at some of the pros and cons of long-term rentals.

Pros

The huge benefit of a long-term rental is that the income stream is much more predictable. You and your tenant will agree on a rental amount that will be paid to you regularly, and you can expect this amount on a specific payday. This allows you to know how much money is coming in and to budget accordingly. This arrangement is a commitment between you and your tenant, and you can rely on this consistent payment.

Long-term tenants also tend to take better care of the property since they view it as a long-term stay and as their home. This creates a sense of ownership, and they feel responsible for the space. They are also likely to report any maintenance issues quickly so that they can be resolved before escalating into something bigger.

With a long-term rental, there is a lower likelihood of long vacancy periods, and the turnover rate is significantly smaller. This results in much less work for you because you don't have to market the property and find new tenants constantly. Additionally, your tenants will need to give you notice before they pack up and leave, which gives you some time to find new tenants.

Cons

There are a few downsides to long-term rentals that are important to consider. Firstly, there isn't much flexibility when it comes to your property. You won't be able to use your property for personal purposes until the lease agreement has ended. Your tenants have exclusive use of the property, and you have very little control over what occurs. Additionally, you need to respect your tenants' privacy, so you can't always check up on or inspect the property.

You also need to be well-versed in the legal landscape and tenant rights surrounding long-term rentals. If you have problematic tenants, they could use this to their advantage, which could disadvantage you and pose significant challenges. It can be very difficult to evict a tenant, even if they are not paying rent or taking care of the property. There are strict rules and guidelines that you must follow to address these situations, and it could take months or even years to achieve the desired outcome.

Another downside is that you may have to deal with problematic tenants, which can be incredibly time-consuming. Unlike short-term rentals, you don't get to restart with a new group of people after a few days. The issues that arise with long-term rentals stem from the fact that tenant and landlord relationships are much more complex, time-consuming, and resource-intensive. You may need to engage in extensive communication, problem-solving efforts, and negotiations. You might also need to involve other professionals, such as lawyers and property experts, to help resolve the issues. All of this can be incredibly time-consuming and expensive.

Airbnb and short-term rentals, in general, are great strategies for renting out your property to many people. There are some factors you need to consider to ensure that this is something you can handle. It might require significantly more time and effort on your part because you have to manage the property and ensure your guests are happy at all times. However, the positives and benefits are definitely worth it if you have the time and capacity to do this. You can potentially earn much more money with a short-term rental, plus you get the opportunity to meet a variety of interesting people from all around the world. It is crucial to assess your properties and the current market to determine if Airbnb is a suitable avenue for increasing your rental income. You could use Airbnb for one or two of your properties in your real estate portfolio while keeping the others as long-term rentals, allowing you to have a variety of income streams. Ultimately, it is up to you and the strategy you wish to pursue.

In understanding how Airbnb can boost your rental income, it's essential to establish a solid legal and financial foundation. This is important regardless of the rental strategy you use with the BRRRR method. In the next chapter, we will discuss the business structures, financial planning, and legal considerations necessary for long-term success in real estate investing.

PART THREE

BUILD SMART AND GROW BIG

LET'S TALK LEGAL, FINANCIAL, AND BUSINESS MATTERS

According to the IRS, all rental income must be reported on your tax return, and in general, the associated expenses can be deducted from your rental income (Internal Revenue Service n.d.). This is why it is important to know the ins and outs of legal and financial matters.

CHOOSING THE RIGHT OWNERSHIP STRUCTURE

Choosing the right ownership structure is crucial when you are investing in real estate. Your two main options are individual ownership or LLC ownership, which stands for limited liability company. With individual ownership, it is incredibly simple and involves owning the property in your name. There is less paperwork and administration required for this option. With an LLC, you separate your personal assets from your property or real estate investment. This means that should there be a lawsuit or claim against your property, your personal finances and wealth will be protected. It means that your investment is owned by a separate entity; even though you own that entity, you are not personally liable. If there is a claim or a lawsuit regarding your property, it will go through the LLC rather than your name. Basically, just as if an individual sues a company, the CEO of the company is not personally responsible for paying that claim out of his or her own pocket. It is covered by business expenses, and the business takes care of it separately from any personal assets.

Another thing to consider is the tax implications that come with both methods. When you own a property individually, you will need to file taxes on your rental income as part of your personal tax return. If your properties are under an LLC, there is a completely different way to file your taxes. The income you generate from your properties is not taxed at a corporate level, so you will need to file Form 1065 and then report the income on your individual tax return.

When it comes to how easy it is to use either of these methods, there are definitely advantages and disadvantages to both. For example, if you have the property under individual ownership, you can easily access funds from your bank or financial service provider without the additional work of setting up an LLC. However, with an LLC, there are additional protections against creditors, plus you can establish a board of directors for better decision-making as your business grows. When you own a property in your personal capacity, there is no protection against personal liability, so you will have to take full responsibility if there is legal action, and your personal assets might be at risk of being repossessed if there are any financial issues.

UNDERSTANDING PERMITS, INSURANCE, AND CONTRACTS

When purchasing a property to renovate or improve, it is important to understand all of the permits and contracts that you will need in order to do so legally and safely. Undertaking these improvements without proper research can put you at risk of engaging in illegal activities, making you liable for fines or even jail time. It is also important to remember that most states and municipalities have different regulations, so you'll need to research your specific area to find out what permit contracts or legal frameworks are in place to ensure compliance. Although the permit process can vary from place to place, some basics are important to understand, regardless of where you live.

Not every small home improvement will require a permit, but larger projects that involve electrical, mechanical, and structural changes will likely need one. Any of these changes must comply with local codes, and you will need a basic plan in place before applying for a permit. Examples of projects that might require a permit include fencing, new windows, plumbing, electrical work, siding, water heaters, and renovations that exceed a certain total cost. Smaller tasks, such as painting, installing new walls, minor electrical work, new countertops, or adding fixtures and faucets, typically do not require a permit.

In addition to obtaining the necessary permits, you should also consider getting insurance to cover your property and renovations. At the end of the day, many things could go wrong, and you don't want to be out of pocket for any unexpected events. Having insurance will protect you and your property, ensuring that you have the funds available to handle emergencies. Unfortunately, there are many instances where an unexpected emergency occurs, and the property owner does not have enough money to address it. In such cases, the property owner may need to sell the property to mitigate their losses, or the property may remain in disrepair for years until the owner can save enough money to continue with the renovations. This results in wasted time and lost revenue, which is definitely something you want to avoid.

There are many different types of insurance available, and if you obtain general home insurance, it might be covered under that umbrella. Looking for some sort of umbrella policy might be your best option because it means that you only have to pay one insurance bill rather than multiple different insurance premiums. It is always a good idea to compare insurance premiums in terms of their cost and the benefits you will receive from them. You also want to ensure that the claims process is straightforward, so look for insurance providers that have good reviews and real-life examples of people being able to access their claims quickly.

As mentioned earlier, many things could go wrong when you own a property. The type of insurance you will obtain depends on the type of property you have as well as your location. In certain areas, there are greater risks for specific issues than in others. For example, some areas have a higher chance of flooding or fires, and in such cases, you want to ensure that your insurance policy covers these and other natural disasters. Other aspects you want your insurance policy to cover include liability, loss of income, and rent guarantee insurance. You should also consider obtaining insurance for workers' compensation and builders' risk insurance, especially if you are undertaking a larger project with many workers on-site. If something were to happen to the workers, you might be liable for their medical expenses, so having this insurance means that it will not come out of your pocket.

You also need to have the right contracts when you are involved in property investment or purchasing a property. There are many different types of contracts available, but there are five that you should consider, which are the most common in this context. The first is a purchase agreement, where the buyer and the seller agree to transfer ownership of a specific property. All the details regarding the sale and transfer of the property will be included in this contract.

The next common type of contract is an assignment contract. This is specifically for wholesaling, as it facilitates the property sale between the current homeowner and a separate buyer who is not the wholesaler.

Another contract is a lease agreement, which is a contract between the tenant and the landlord. This contract outlines the expectations of both parties, as well as the rent that the tenant needs to pay to the landlord.

Power of attorney is another important contract, necessary when the owner of a property grants permission for their attorney or another individual to act as their proxy in the transaction.

The final common contract is a subject-to contract. With this contract, the person buying the property will take over the seller's existing mortgage payment without needing to go through the entire process of obtaining their own mortgage, undergoing a credit check, or making a down payment.

TAXES AND RECORD-KEEPING

Whenever you are earning income, regardless of how or where it is coming from, you need to keep the taxes in mind. You must ensure that you are paying your taxes correctly; otherwise, you could face hefty fees and possible jail time if you are purposely avoiding paying taxes or evading the tax authorities. Unfortunately, taxes are a normal part of society, and we all have to comply, so making sure that we know what we are liable for will benefit us in the long term.

Rental income needs to be reported and taxed, so if you are using the BRRRR method, this is something you need to consider. This type of income is reported by you on Schedule E (Form 1040), though you might receive a Form 1099-MISC from your property manager if they collected rent on your behalf and are required to report it (Internal Revenue Service 2024). If you are filling out your taxes online, the program will automatically prompt you to complete the appropriate forms, such as Schedule E. It is typically a good idea to get someone with experience to assist you with your tax return, especially if you are not familiar with the process. This will help you avoid any mishaps and allow you to save money on your taxes.

Many categories are tax-deductible when you are working with real estate. This is a great benefit, and it's important to know what these deductions are so that you can effectively lower your taxable income and the amount of taxes you will be paying. Some expenses that can be deducted include mortgage interest, property tax, operating expenses, depreciation, and repairs.

It is very important that you keep thorough records of your income, expenses, and any financial transactions related to your property. This will help you with your tax filing process and allow you to analyze your finances. It is recommended that you keep a record for at least three years. You may choose to keep your financial and tax records for longer, just in case, but this is definitely the minimum. When you maintain a record of all your income and expenses, it will make tax preparation much easier because you will have everything on hand. If the IRS requests certain proof or documentation, you can quickly provide it, which will reduce the amount of time you spend going back and forth. It also makes the process significantly less stressful.

In general, you must have documentary evidence, including items such as checks, bills, receipts, and emails that can support your expenses. A good rule of thumb is that if you have spent any money on or for your property, you should keep the evidence of this safely. You can retain hard copies, but you can also scan or take pictures of the hard copies and save them digitally, making it easier to keep track of what you have. Additionally, you can keep a record of any travel expenses related to rental property repairs. You may want to consult a tax professional to find out if there are any other tax deductions you could qualify for. Although hiring a tax professional does incur a cost, they are usually worth it because they can make your life much easier and save you money in the long run by helping you reduce your tax liability.

SETTING UP BUSINESS ACCOUNTS AND SYSTEMS

It is not necessarily mandatory, but it is a good idea to set up separate bank accounts for your property business and your personal account. While it might seem like a tedious process to establish these different accounts, it will definitely be worth it in the long run, as it simplifies your finances and makes tax season much easier for you.

There are numerous benefits to having a separate account for your business or property investments. One is that it prevents the co-mingling of funds. It is easy to let your business and personal funds become mixed, making it difficult to determine which goes where, especially if everything is in one account. When everything is combined, it can be very challenging to track your expenses and report them for financial and tax purposes. Having a clear separation between your accounts simplifies everything, allowing you to prevent overspending in certain areas. It also helps protect your personal assets and funds.

When you have a separate account, your general accounting for your rental property will be much easier because you can easily track your income and expenses. If you need to review your spending, you can be confident that the expenses in your property account are solely for your property and nothing else. This will reduce the overall preparation time when you are preparing for taxes and financial accounting in general.

As your portfolio grows and you acquire more properties, having a separate bank account makes managing your finances significantly easier. You can also establish a separate bank account for each of your properties, allowing you to track how well each one is performing. This will also be beneficial when you apply for financing from lenders, should you wish to refinance a property or purchase another one.

As your portfolio grows, you might want to start hiring people to assist you with certain areas of your business. This could include property management, accounting, or general administrative duties. These individuals will then become part of an employee payroll, and it will be much simpler if there is a separate account from which you pay these employees. You will also be able to pay your vendors from this account, ensuring that you do not overspend in that area. You will know exactly how much money is in your account, how much you have to spend, and what you need to budget for.

In addition to having these separate accounts, you can also utilize accounting software to help automate and streamline financial management. These days, we really do not have to do all the tedious work ourselves; we can use software and apps to assist. This makes everything much easier and provides us with additional insights that might be more difficult to obtain if we were doing everything on our own. Some good options include QuickBooks, AppFolio, Stessa, and Buildium.

BUILDING YOUR REAL ESTATE TEAM

As your real estate portfolio grows, you can't do everything on your own. It becomes incredibly important to bring people onto your team to help you focus on the things that really matter. Additionally, it is always a good idea to seek advice and assistance in various areas of property management and investing. There are many different roles you fill as a real estate investor, and outsourcing some of this workload will greatly assist you in balancing your tasks.

You might not be able to hire people for every single step of the process at the beginning, but you can always start somewhere and build your team as you progress. One of the first individuals or groups you can bring on board is a driver. This is not someone who will drive you around, but rather someone who will help you find properties that meet your investment criteria. This approach provides you with more options, increasing your chances of finding the right property.

The great thing about this role is that you don't necessarily have to hire a professional to fulfill it. When you first start out, consider reaching out to friends and family members who could be your initial drivers. All you need to do is inform them that you are looking for a specific property that meets your ideal criteria. If they are on the lookout for such properties, they can funnel any leads they find to you, allowing you to decide whether to pursue those options. As you continue your real estate investing journey, you will be able to recruit more drivers who will help you maintain a pipeline of potential property investments.

The next person you can bring on board is called a lead manager. This individual will take the leads provided by the drivers and call around to find the most qualified leads. They will gather more information about the properties that have come their way to identify which ones will be the best fit for you and your goals. It is important for this person to have good interpersonal skills, as they will be interacting with many people while discovering more about the properties.

You might also need an acquisitions manager, who is responsible for closing deals and acquiring the properties. They will receive information from the lead manager and then analyze the properties to determine how much you can offer. They need to possess excellent negotiation skills as well as a solid understanding of the real estate market. This knowledge will help them make better deals and understand what is realistic. The next step involves someone called a disposition manager, who handles the sale of the property after you have flipped and revamped it. They will work to sell your property to a list of qualified buyers to ensure that the sale goes through quickly. If you are not looking to sell the property, then you do not specifically need this person.

Another key member of your team would be a marketing manager or a marketing lead. Since you are on the hunt for new properties and also trying to sell your current properties, marketing will be crucial. Marketing can require a lot of time and effort, especially if you have multiple properties. They will assist by designing your marketing initiatives and working on strategies and plans to help promote your properties. They will also play a key role in attending networking events and conferences to meet more people who could potentially bring in additional leads.

On top of what we have just discussed, there are some other really important members of your team that you will need to get on board. This will include a lender who will provide you with funds while you are in the property market and looking to purchase properties. While you can apply for loans and go through banks and other avenues, having a lender or someone you know you can work with easily will greatly improve the process. Mutual trust will allow things to go more smoothly. If you have a designated person you know you can approach when you need a loan or some extra money, it will be beneficial.

You will also need a real estate agent to assist you with buying and selling properties, as well as a contractor who will help with building and renovating your property. Another important person will be an accountant who will handle the financial and tax aspects.

Some honorable mentions in terms of people you might want on your team include property managers who will manage the day-to-day operations of your property if you cannot do it yourself. They will handle the tenants and the individuals who work on the property daily, so you do not have to be on-site all the time. You might also want to consider getting an appraiser, inspector, or real estate attorney on board. Finally, consider hiring an insurance agent you can trust to help you obtain the best insurance products.

A lot goes into being an investor in real estate, and it's important to have all the finer details sorted out as soon as possible. You'll need to establish an appropriate ownership structure, understand the legal requirements, and maintain accurate financial records to ensure that your business is running at its optimum capacity. You might also want to bring on more people to assist you in areas where you may not be fully competent or where you simply need help. Once you have all of these in place, it will form a foundation for the next step, which is considering how you want to exit your investments effectively. This is exactly what we will be discussing in the next chapter.

EXIT STRATEGIES AND LONG-TERM PLANNING

Current data from CBRE and NCREIF indicates that over 68% of real estate investors in Q1 2025 revised their exit strategy within 18 months of acquisition (The Luxury Playbook 2025). This highlights the importance of having an exit strategy and adapting it to ensure that it remains effective in the current market and your specific situation. The real estate market is constantly changing, which means we sometimes need to be flexible with our plans regarding the properties we purchase. You might have acquired a property for a specific reason, such as renting it out, but upon further inspection and additional research, you may discover that this is not a renter's market. Consequently, you might need to sell your property or consider another strategy to profit from your investment.

TO SELL OR REFINANCE

When you are involved in real estate investment, you have a choice between mortgage refinancing and selling the property. Both options come with their own pros and cons, so it is important to understand your goals and what you hope to achieve. You also need to assess the housing market to determine which option will suit you better. While refinancing may have been your original plan, you might come to realize that selling could offer more benefits. It is always best to keep an open mind when investing in real estate, as circumstances can change, and you want to be flexible enough to achieve the best results.

Mortgage Refinancing Pros and Cons

When you refinance your property, you are essentially replacing your current mortgage with a new one. The monthly payment you make will now be applied to the new mortgage. There are many different refinancing options available, each with varying rates and terms. If you are using the BRRRR method, you will need to refinance your properties at some point. There are definite benefits to refinancing, including a lower interest rate, debt consolidation, and the opportunity to make home improvements.

When you refinance, you also have to take into consideration a few negatives or drawbacks that come with it. For example, you need a good credit score in order to secure a favorable rate on your refinance. If not, you will find it very difficult to obtain a new loan, which might even end up costing you more money. If you take a cash-out refinance, this can lower the equity in your home, which can be a significant disadvantage, especially if overall housing market prices decrease. Finally, another major downside to consider is that refinancing extends your debt timeline, meaning that you will need to pay back money for a longer period than you might have initially anticipated.

Selling Pros and Cons

Selling your home is another option you can explore. There are many reasons you might choose to sell your property, even if you are currently trying to implement the BRRRR method. This could be because you realize that the home is not generating the amount of money you expected, or perhaps you have too many properties in your portfolio, making it difficult for you to manage them.

One of the biggest benefits of selling your house is that you gain access to immediate funds as soon as the sale goes through. You receive a lump sum, and then you can do what you wish with that money. It also allows you to reduce your overall debt because you can sell your house, pay off your debts, and then take the profit from the sale. If you have owned your property for a significant amount of time or have improved it to the point where it has increased in value, you can sell your house for a much larger profit margin.

The downsides of selling your house include market-dependent value. This means that, because the housing market is always fluctuating, if you choose to sell your house when the market is low, you will receive a lower price than what you deserve or desire. Another factor to consider is that you will need to have your home reappraised if you want to sell, and this comes with additional costs. Selling also means dealing with uncertain timelines. Sometimes houses sell in a matter of days, while in other cases, it can take months or even years to sell. If you're looking to make quick money from selling your property, this may not be possible depending on the current market demand.

There are many reasons people choose to sell rather than rent, even if they are following the BRRRR method. Life can be unpredictable, and it's important to adjust your goals or priorities accordingly. For example, if you have financial goals and have determined that refinancing will not help you achieve them, then selling might be the better option. Perhaps your rental property is not generating much income, making it less worthwhile to keep. In cases where you co-own property with someone else and there is a death, divorce, separation, or a general partnership dispute, it might be better to sell so that everyone can recoup their investment rather than attempting to maintain a joint rental. Another reason people consider selling is if there is a significant issue with the property that will require too much time and resources to resolve. As you can see, there are many reasons to sell your property, and it all depends on your current situation and your goals.

UTILIZING 1031 EXCHANGES AND UNDERSTANDING TAX IMPLICATIONS

A 1031 exchange is a process that allows an investor to defer capital gains tax when selling an investment property. This is permitted because the proceeds are reinvested into another property that is very similar to the one being sold. Essentially, it is a swap from one property to another. While this may sound like an excellent idea since you do not have to pay the capital gains tax immediately, the truth is that it can be very difficult to find a similar property to the one you currently own. You also need to ensure that the new property is located in an area you like and meets all your other requirements, even if it is similar and qualifies.

There are some timing rules that come into play with the 1031 exchange. The first is the 45-day rule, which indicates that once the property has been sold, the intermediary entity will receive the money. As the seller, you will not be able to accept the cash immediately; otherwise, it will jeopardize the 1031 treatment. Within the 45 days, you must designate the property you are replacing your current one with in writing. You can designate up to three properties, as long as you intend to close on one of them. In some cases, you may designate more than three.

The other rule is the 180-day rule, which requires you to close on your new property within 180 days after selling your previous property. You can also purchase a replacement property before selling the one you currently own and still qualify for this exchange, but the same 45- and 180-day time windows will apply.

If you engage in a 1031 exchange, you will need to report this to the IRS. You must submit Form 8824 along with your tax return for the year in which the exchange occurred. In this form, you will need to provide descriptions of both properties, the dates they were transferred, and your relationship with the person or people with whom you exchanged properties. You will also need to indicate the value of each property.

One important tax implication to be aware of is depreciation recapture. This occurs when the IRS collects tax on the depreciation you claimed after selling your assets for more than their book value. Within this category, there are two types of properties you might need to calculate: 1245 property and 1250 property.

Using Section 1245 property includes the depreciation of the property when calculating the profit from its sale. Let's say you bought a property for $100,000, and each year you claim $10,000 as depreciation deductions, which means you are lowering your taxable income by $10,000 every year. After five years, you would have claimed $50,000, making your adjusted cost basis $50,000. This is because you subtracted the amount you have deducted over the five years from the original cost. Let's say that in this scenario, the housing market is really bad, and when you sell your property, you sell it for only $70,000. This might seem like a loss because you originally spent $100,000 on the property when you first bought it, but the IRS calculates things differently. Instead of comparing it to the original sale price, they adjust the value of the property based on the deductions. So, if the new value is $50,000 and you sold it for $70,000, it means that you have made a $20,000 profit. That $20,000 is subject to depreciation recapture, which means that you will be paying your regular income tax rate on that amount.

The next topic we will cover is Section 1250 gains. With this, the real estate investor benefits from a favorable depreciation recapture, as business equipment is taxed separately at a regular income rate, while real estate depreciation recapture is capped at 25%. To qualify for this, you will need to use straight-line depreciation. This means you will need to claim equal deductions every year over the lifespan of your property. When it comes time to sell your property and you sell it for more than the original price, the final sale price will be divided into two parts. The profit you make up to the amount of depreciation you've already claimed in previous years is subject to a maximum recapture rate of 25%. The profit that exceeds the original purchase price will be taxed at a lower long-term capital gains rate, which is around 15% for most people.

Speaking of capital gains, it is important to understand what they are and how they impact your taxes. Capital gains tax is simply the tax imposed on the profit after you have sold your property or any other asset. You have made gains from your investment, and those gains need to be taxed as profit since they qualify as income. Using the 1031 exchange is a good way to lower your capital gains tax, but there are also other strategies, including converting your second home into your main residence or investing in Opportunity Zones, which are designated areas that offer tax benefits for real estate investors. It is always a good idea to consult with an accountant or tax practitioner to help you minimize the amount you will pay in capital gains tax so that you can save as much money as possible.

BUILDING A SUSTAINABLE REAL ESTATE PORTFOLIO AND SCALING UP

As you continue on this real estate journey, you will want to ensure that you are building a sustainable real estate portfolio—something that lasts for a long time and continues to generate income. A strong portfolio will help establish a solid financial foundation for you, even in the face of changes in the housing market.

When building your real estate investment portfolio, it is important to have a long-term perspective so that you can set your objectives and goals correctly. Doing this will help streamline your choices as you begin to build your portfolio. You must know where you are going before you start taking steps to get there. Consider factors such as how much time you can dedicate to your real estate investment portfolio and the amount of work or effort you are willing to invest.

Once you know what you want to achieve from your real estate investing, it's time to choose a starting point. For first-time investors, it is crucial not to try to do too much at once. Even if you have the finances to invest in multiple properties, it is best to start small so that you can acclimate to real estate investing and understand its implications for your lifestyle. Starting small also allows you to gain a good understanding of real estate before committing to something larger. You might consider options like house hacking, as it is easier to qualify for a loan in this scenario and can help you pay off the main property in which you reside.

The next step is to consider how you will grow your portfolio. While it may seem appealing to expand your portfolio annually by continuously adding properties, exponential growth is far more advantageous. It demonstrates a greater increase over time. Linear growth involves investing in rental properties of the same or similar value every few years; while this approach will yield growth, it may take some time before you see anything substantial. However, if you create a portfolio that grows exponentially, you can use your rental income to leverage and accumulate more equity, allowing you to purchase additional properties that generate more income. This is the beauty of the BRRRR method. It enables you to leverage your investments and increase your income over time. Consequently, you will be able to acquire more properties in a shorter period, resulting in significantly higher profits.

If you want to have an edge in the real estate game, it is essential that you fully understand your local real estate market. This is especially important while you are still growing your real estate portfolio. If you are considering purchasing properties that are very far away from you, the truth is that you don't always know what's happening in your rental home or what is going on in the neighborhood. This poses challenges when you are trying to make decisions about your real estate investments, and there may be things that you are missing. If you keep your real estate investments in areas that you know well and can easily travel to, it will be much easier for you to keep track of things and ensure that you are getting the most out of your real estate investment. It is also easier to monitor your local market because you are there, and it will interest you since it impacts you personally, not just in your investment space.

As your real estate investment portfolio starts to grow, it is crucial to understand that diversification is key. When you diversify your real estate investments, you essentially protect yourself while maximizing your returns. A non-diversified portfolio is one in which you are only investing in one type of real estate or property. For example, you might only invest in apartments that are close to the city center. When you diversify, you spread your investment across different types of properties and locations. This is important because if something were to happen with one type of investment or property, it would not impact your entire portfolio as severely, since you have many different types within your portfolio. In the example where you own three apartments in the city center, if something were to happen to the city and it no longer becomes a popular place to live, you would essentially lose your revenue from all three of your investments. However, if you invest in a multifamily home in the suburbs, one apartment in the city, and an Airbnb vacation rental, even if something happens to the apartment in the city, the other two investments in your portfolio will still be generating income, so you will remain secure.

A good rule of thumb for diversification is the 60/20/20 rule. This is where you have 100% of your portfolio divided into three smaller categories. You can split it up however you like, but traditionally, 60% of your portfolio is allocated to multifamily residential properties, 20% goes to vacation rentals, and the last 20% is for private equity real estate funds. With this kind of diversification, you get the best of all worlds in real estate investing. You invest in long-term and short-term real estate, as well as funds, all of which have different levels of profit generation and security. You don't have to stick to these ratios, and it's best to find something that works best for you, but this is definitely a great starting point as you try to diversify your investment portfolio.

COMMON MISTAKES TO AVOID

There are many mistakes that you could make or be making when investing in real estate. Understanding these common mistakes early can help you avoid them as you move through this journey. If you know to expect something that could cause a problem down the line, you will recognize it quickly, and you might not have to deal with it at all. Let's talk about some of the most common mistakes when it comes to real estate investing.

Underestimating Costs

Underestimating the total cost of a house flip or rental is a very common mistake. It is easy to miscalculate the overall costs of renovating a house if you have not done it before. There are many things you might not think about until you reach the point where you need them. This is why it is important to conduct thorough research. You can also obtain quotes and appraisals to ensure you know what the costs will be. Then, you'll need to create a detailed budget and do your best to stick to it throughout the process.

Not Doing Enough Research

Research is a crucial step when you are going to invest a significant amount of your money in something. If you don't conduct your research properly, it could lead to bigger issues down the road. For example, if you don't research the city or area you are buying in and that area is in decline, you could end up unable to sell or rent out your property for as much as you would like when the time comes. Remember to conduct market research as well as research on contractors, materials, and anything else you might think is necessary.

Choosing the Wrong Location

When it comes to property, location will always be one of the most important factors to consider. People typically want to move to a specific area and then look for their dream house; it's not the other way around. Finding an area that is safe, clean, and easily accessible is crucial. You also want to ensure that the neighborhood has increasing or stable property values, as this improves your chances of getting the amount you want when you sell your property. If you can find an up-and-coming neighborhood or area, it will be a great benefit to you because it means you can buy at a lower rate and have a greater chance of making a profit.

Over-Improving the Property

Yes, there is such a thing as over-improving your property. This means that you are making more improvements than are necessary to achieve a good profit. Certain improvements will yield a good return on investment, while others, although nice, are not as worthwhile. When you are making an investment, every step you take needs to be aligned with your end goal. You want to maximize your profit while minimizing your expenses. This is not about cutting corners; rather, it is about being smart with your money to ensure that you are making worthwhile changes.

Rushing the Process (Timeline)

We all want to get things done as quickly as possible, but when it comes to real estate, it is not advisable to rush the process. This is especially true when renovating your property. Rushed work can lead to mistakes and problems that will cost you significantly to fix down the line. Quality will always be more important than speed. While you do not want things to be delayed unnecessarily, taking your time with each step is crucial to ensure that you are doing everything thoroughly.

Not Having an Exit Strategy

It is essential to have an exit strategy because you do not want to hold on to a property longer than necessary or end up selling it for a much lower price than you intended. Lost profit can lead to larger financial problems, especially if you have a strict budget or specific financial goals to achieve. Before purchasing a house to flip, make sure you have considered an exit strategy. This could involve selling the property if you are unable to find the right tenant, or if you have flipped the property and cannot find buyers, you might consider renting it out for some income. This way, you have a backup plan in case things do not work out as you had planned.

Not Enough Patience

A true professional is someone who takes their time to wait for the right property and the right buyer. It can be very tempting to rush through things, but this is not a good long-term strategy. Just because a house is cheap and the current owners appear desperate to sell does not mean that it will be a good buy for you. Remember to practice patience and take a breather between big decisions so that you know you aren't rushing into things.

It is crucial to understand your investment strategies and to reevaluate them from time to time to ensure they remain relevant in the current environment and real estate market. Consider implementing a few of the methods and suggestions we have discussed in this chapter to help you grow your investment business sustainably. Long-term planning is essential, and the next step is to put all of your knowledge into action. In the next chapter, we will discuss executing your first real estate investment deal to set your future up for success.

YOUR FIRST DEAL

My first deal wasn't anything flashy or massive. We were new immigrants, so we did not have a lot of disposable income to purchase the best properties in desirable areas. We bought an old, rundown house in the countryside because it was all we could afford. My wife and I had a newborn baby, and I had started a new job, so there was a lot we were still trying to figure out. The house needed a lot of work, but we were ready to roll up our sleeves and do most of the renovations ourselves. This included tasks such as installing new floors, building a new kitchen and laundry room, painting, replacing the doors, and landscaping the garden.

My little family lived in this house for two years before we decided to get the property revalued. I originally bought the house for $282,000 and paid a 20% deposit. The rest was financed through a mortgage. Once the property was revalued, it was worth $345,000, which meant we had gained quite a bit of equity in just two years. From there, I decided to refinance and was able to borrow up to 80% of the new value. This meant I could borrow $276,000. The refinance replaced the original mortgage and gave us about $50,000 in cash-out equity. This amount was perfect for a deposit on a two-bedroom apartment, and we still had some money left over, so we decided to refinish the apartment and run it as a short-term rental. This marked the true start of my real estate investing journey and how I got into Airbnb.

If I'm being honest, those first couple of years didn't truly feel like I was making a real estate investment. I was just trying to make the best of my situation by improving the home where I lived. This hard work really paid off and became a catalyst for my real estate investment journey. My family and I took the first step and started small. We learned as we went along and chose to reinvest whatever we earned. These small steps made a huge difference in the long run. I gained momentum, and I used this to keep going. Eventually, my property portfolio grew one deal at a time. I know that if I hadn't taken that first step with my very first house and then purchased that apartment, I would never be where I am today. One smart move in the right direction is all it takes to change the entire game.

STAYING MOTIVATED WHEN DEALS GO WRONG

Even with the best-laid plans, a deal can still go wrong, or the market might not work in your favor. Even people who have been in the real estate game for decades can go through seasons when things are just not working out for them. You will likely face challenges for many reasons; some of them will be within your control, while others won't be. Regardless, it is essential to keep yourself motivated during hard times.

The first thing you need to do is control the things that you can. When things are not working out the way you wanted them to, it is important to understand what you can change and what you can't. If you have made a mistake or miscalculation, this is something you can fix going forward, and you don't have to deal with this bad patch for too much longer. For example, take a look at all of your listings and see if you are overpricing them for the market. Remember that the market changes all the time, and just because something has historically worked does not mean it will continue to do so forever. You might need to adjust your pricing strategy to attract more people to your properties.

It is also a good idea to examine your listings and see if there are any issues that are making them hard to sell. This might relate to how your listings are marketed or to the properties themselves. Perhaps there is something that is dissuading people from renting or buying from you. Put yourself in the shoes of a potential renter or buyer and view things from their perspective. You can even ask a friend, family member, or a completely impartial third party to review your listings and see if anything stands out as a red flag. If you identify any issues, you can make the necessary changes to make your listings more attractive.

Let's say you have checked your properties and have done all the work to ensure that your listings and properties are as attractive as possible. However, you are still not receiving the interest you had hoped for. In this case, it could simply be a rough patch, and it's something you just have to ride out until the market picks up and you can gain momentum once again. If you've been in the real estate game long enough, you will quickly notice that there will be a few times when you encounter these rough patches, and all you need to do is stay motivated until the wave is over. Things will definitely pick up again and return to normal, or even improve beyond normal.

While you're waiting for things to return to an optimal level for your investments, you can work on your mindset. The first step toward cultivating a more positive mindset is to figure out your "why." You've probably heard something along these lines before, but it's such a key part of anything you are trying to achieve. The goal is to uncover the deep reasoning behind your decision to embark on this journey in the first place. Sometimes, it can be easy to forget why we are doing something when we are in the thick of a problem. Reflecting on the beginning, when you first started, will help reawaken some of that passion and fire. Perhaps you wanted to start real estate investing to become financially free or independent. Maybe you want to create a better life for your family and children. Or perhaps you want to have enough money to retire early. Whatever your reasoning or your "why," write it down and keep it with you so that you have something to refer back to each day or when things get difficult.

The next thing you need to do is avoid any negativity from people who are either not in the field or who are simply glass-half-empty types. Whenever you are trying to achieve something great, there will always be individuals who have their own biases and negativity that they want to share with you. Such negativity can easily derail you and make you think the situation is far worse than it actually is. If there are negative people around you, it is an indication that you should not share your strategies or struggles with them. Of course, it is important to have people with whom you can bounce around ideas, but if someone is merely negative and not helping you find solutions, then that person is not the right ally for you. You don't have to cut them off completely, but you should distance yourself from them regarding your real estate investments and that aspect of your life. It is important to find someone who is positive and uplifting in that space to help you stay motivated and keep moving forward.

It might also be worthwhile to examine your current goals and see if they are realistic for where you are right now. If you are feeling like a failure, it could be that your goals do not align with the reality of your situation, making you feel worse than you should. By reevaluating your goals and making them a bit more realistic, you will feel as though you are making progress and actually reaching them, rather than feeling that you keep falling short.

Remember that anyone who has achieved greatness in any sphere of life has faced challenges. Challenges are completely normal, and they can provide a great learning experience if you allow them to. You may be in a difficult situation right now, but you will push through and emerge stronger on the other side if you keep going and maintain a positive outlook. You can look at other people's success stories to see how they have overcome struggles and what they did to build themselves up when times were tough. As you read about others' real estate investment journeys, you will quickly notice that everyone encounters some sort of bump in the road or challenge. Mindset is everything when it comes to reaching your goals and finding success.

THE 90-DAY ACTION PLAN

Having a 90-day plan will provide you with structure, allowing you to clearly work toward your first deal. This plan will serve as a guideline to help you take action. It can be all too easy to read something in a book and, once you reach the final page, fail to apply the information you have learned. A solid plan will help you move forward and allow you to see results. You can modify this action plan as you see fit, but make sure to create a plan for yourself and stick to it. You will find that you learn much more about real estate and investing simply by being active in the field.

Month 1

In the first month, the focus will be on research and analysis. This is what we discussed in the first part of this book. Feel free to revisit that section for a refresher on how to take action during the research and analysis phase. In this phase, you will do your best to thoroughly research the different types of investing and decide which one you want to pursue. Consider writing a pros and cons list tailored to your situation to help you determine which real estate investment strategy aligns with your goals and lifestyle.

You can further deepen your understanding of what you have already learned in this book by researching online and exploring the opinions of others. If you have joined my Airbnb Facebook group, you can ask for advice there or simply read what others have to say and see how you can apply it to your own plan or strategy. Additionally, you can attend real estate investing seminars or networking events to enhance your knowledge and skills, as well as to meet others in the same field.

It is also a good idea to create a simple matrix that includes several factors. You will use this matrix to compare each investment style, helping you understand which one is best suited for you. You can include as many factors as you like, but the four recommended factors are the pros of the strategy, the cons of the strategy, the minimum investment required, and the time commitment involved. Once you have completed this matrix, you can start comparing and identifying which option best suits your needs.

	Pros	Cons	Minimum Investment Needed	Time Required
Strategy 1				
Strategy 2				
Strategy 3				
Strategy 4				

Month 2

In month two, it is time for you to choose your tools. It is important that you select the right ones because, as they say, a builder is only as good as his tools. Choosing the right tools to work with will make your life much easier and more efficient. They will need to align with your overall goals and strategy.

Since there are so many tools available, it is essential for you to conduct some comparisons to help you make a decision. You can also create a matrix to compare different factors and then decide from there. Again, you can include as many factors as you deem fit, but the following are recommended: features, upfront investment, recurring investment, learning curve, and potential ROI.

	Features	Upfront Investment	Recurring Investment	Learning Curve	Potential ROI
Tool 1					
Tool 2					
Tool 3					
Tool 4					

Once you have completed the tools matrix, you will need to choose which ones you want to pursue. You do not need to have a large variety; rather, pick a few that will truly make the biggest impact on your real estate investment journey. You can always add more to your list as your portfolio grows or as you need them. Many tools require you to pay some kind of subscription, so you don't want to commit to too many while you are still in the beginning stages. Reach out to people who have a similar investment style and see if they have any recommendations, and ask how they use them. Also, remember to give yourself some time to learn how to use these tools effectively and navigate any of the platforms you will be using. Some have a steeper learning curve than others, so don't forget to allow yourself that time to learn before you need to use them.

Month 3

In the third month, you will be making your very first deal. This is where the rubber meets the road, and you will do your best to make your first investment. You have all the information from your research and your tools, so now it is time for you to get moving and try to close a deal. With the BRRRR method, the goal is to find a property to purchase so that you can renovate it and then rent it out. At this stage, you need to be on the hunt for the right property. This might mean getting on the phone and making calls or scouring the internet to see what your options are. You might even need to jump in your car and drive around your neighborhood to see what is actually happening in the area and if any potential properties catch your eye.

Commit to doing something each day toward meeting your goal. This way, you maintain momentum and ensure that you don't lose what you have built up. Make notes about what you are doing and how it is turning out for you. For example, if you are pursuing the right property, start writing down exactly what is being said and how you are being received by others.

Making these notes is crucial at the beginning because it will help you identify patterns that may or may not be working, allowing you to change your approach or lean into a positive aspect.

You may not close your very first deal within the 90-day or three-month period, and that is completely okay. The goal of having this plan in place is to provide you with something to work toward and to help you build the habit of taking action. Once you reach the end of your 90 days, reevaluate your plan and assess how far you have come. You may have closed a deal, or you may not have; if you have, that's fantastic! If you did not manage to close a deal or find the right property, it doesn't mean you have to go all the way back to the drawing board. You can simply review your journal as well as the matrix you used while researching and discovering. This will provide in-depth information to help you make better decisions in the future and possibly create a more effective strategy.

Real estate investing is an exciting journey, and now that you have reached this point, you have a clear action plan. Congratulations! This is where things start to happen, and you get to see your knowledge transform into action. At this point, you are equipped to begin your real estate investing journey, and you are at one of the most exciting moments in your life. Real estate changed my life, and I'm sure it will do the same for you.

SHARE THE OPPORTUNITY!

Your journey is just beginning, but you still have a chance to help others out on theirs. If you take just a few minutes to leave a short review, you'll help them find it and launch their adventure with real estate investments.

Simply by sharing your honest opinion of this book and a little about your own experience, you'll inspire new readers to try it out for themselves—and you'll show them exactly where they can find all the information they need to get started.

Thank you so much for your support. I wish you every success in your ventures.

Scan the QR code to leave a review

CONCLUSION

When I first started out as a young real estate investor, I don't think I fully understood how much it was going to change my life. I had seen other people invest in real estate, and it was something that definitely piqued my interest. However, I did not know where to start. It took me a long time to find my footing, and eventually, I began to gain traction. The more I engaged in it, the more I developed a passion for real estate investing. Then the BRRRR method came along, and I knew that this was something I needed to get involved in.

This is probably where you are in your journey. It's the exciting beginning phase, where there is so much opportunity and possibility in front of you. It is time for you to harness this feeling and the knowledge you have already gained from this book and take steps forward to build a better future for yourself and your family. Regardless of what your goals are, investing in real estate is a powerful tool to help you achieve them. Keeping the end goal in mind is what will keep you motivated as you progress through your real estate investment journey.

Remember that, regardless of what you do, the most important thing is to build a solid foundation. Learning, researching, and absorbing as much knowledge as you can is a crucial step. This will help you create a solid plan as you move forward with your investments. It will also enable you to recognize any red flags or potential problems because you have this knowledge tucked away in your memory bank. Even though it might not be the most exciting part of the process, it is crucial, and you shouldn't skip it. One challenge I like to set for myself is to read one article or watch one video about real estate investing every day. This way, I keep the information fresh in my mind, and it helps me reorient my brain back to what is truly important. On top of that, it helps me gain more knowledge about the market, even though I'm only spending a short amount of time each day on this knowledge-seeking. Try it out and see if it works for you.

As much as building up your knowledge bank is important, it is also essential for you to take action. If all you do is learn, read, and research, then you will never reach the point where you actually move forward and purchase your first investment property. It can be scary because it is such a significant financial commitment, but it is something you need to do if you want to become a successful real estate investor. Trust your instincts and the knowledge you have, and you will do great. Remember to surround yourself with people who are more experienced in this area and seek their advice whenever you need it. This will help you continue to grow and avoid common mistakes that many other investors might have made. It is never a bad idea to expand your circle and network, so make sure you are doing your best to build a strong team.

There are many moving parts when it comes to real estate investing and the BRRRR method. It can seem overwhelming to juggle everything, but once you take one small step and continue taking other small steps afterward, you will see that it is not that difficult. You will start to build momentum, and once you have your first property rented out and leverage that to acquire your second property, you will gain a good understanding of this method and how to use it going forward. You are about to embark on an exciting journey, and I know you will do well. It all begins with a single deliberate step and embracing the process. Remember to stay committed to your goals and let each experience propel you toward financial freedom and lasting success. I sincerely wish you nothing but success and happiness as you start investing in real estate and making your dreams come true.

GLOSSARY

1031 Exchange: This allows for tax to be deferred by selling a property and using that money to buy a new property without paying capital gains tax on the sale.

Appraisal: An estimate of the value of a property provided by a professional.

Appreciation: The increase in the value of a property or another investment over time.

ARV: After-Repair Value, the estimated value of a particular property once renovations are completed.

BRRRR: A real estate investment strategy that stands for Buy, Rehab, Rent, Refinance, and Repeat.

Cash Flow: The income generated from rent after subtracting expenses.

Cash-Out Refinance: A type of refinancing where you take out a new mortgage for more than what you currently owe and pocket the extra cash to use as needed.

Closing Costs: Fees that are due at the end of the property purchase process.

Contractor: A person who is hired to perform repairs and renovations on a property.

Credit Score: A three-digit number that shows how well someone manages debt. Lenders use it to evaluate loan eligibility and determine borrowing terms.

Debt-to-Equity Ratio: A way to measure financial risk by comparing how much debt is owed on a property to how much equity (ownership value) the owner has.

Deed: A document that allows a property to be transferred from one owner to another.

Due Diligence: A period just before finalizing the sale of a property during which an investigation takes place.

Equity: The difference between the market value and the amount owed on the property.

Exit Strategy: The plan for making a profit from a real estate investment without retaining ownership.

Flipping: Buying a property, fixing it up, and selling it again in a short time with the goal of making a profit.

Individual Ownership: When one person owns a property outright, with complete control and full responsibility for it.

Interest Rate: A percentage fee that is charged on a loan.

Leverage: To use a loan or credit to purchase a piece of real estate.

LLC (Limited Liability Company): A business structure that lets you own real estate while protecting your personal assets from potential risks or lawsuits.

LTV: This stands for loan-to-value ratio and is used to calculate the potential risk of a loan compared to the value of the property.

MLS (Multiple Listing Service): A shared database where real estate agents list properties for sale, making it easier for buyers and sellers to connect.

Opportunity Zones: Designated areas that offer tax benefits for real estate investors.

Property Manager: A person who is hired to manage a rental property, including tenants, maintenance, and the general day-to-day operations of the property.

Real Estate Agent: A professional with the necessary licenses to assist with buying and selling properties.

Refinance: A method of recovering your capital on a property by replacing your current loan with another one that potentially offers better terms and interest rates.

ROI: Return on Investment, a percentage or ratio that indicates how profitable an investment is or will be.

REFERENCES

Achen, P. 2025. "2024 Vacation Rental Stats Roundup." Rent Responsibly, March 3. https://www.rentresponsibly.org/2024-vacation-rental-stats-roundup/.

Airbnb. n.d. "Success Stories." Accessed July 3, 2025. https://www.airbnb.co.za/resources/hosting-homes/t/success-stories-27?locale=en&_set_bev_on_new_domain=1750448390_EAZjk5MmEyMmJiMT.

Akins, H. 2024. "Spring Cleaning: What Rental Property Documents to Keep, What to Toss, and When." REI Hub, August 26. https://www.reihub.net/resources/rental-property-document-retention/.

All Property Management. 2024. "Landlord's Guide to Rental Property Accounting." December 12. https://www.allpropertymanagement.com/blog/post/landlord-rental-property-accounting/.

Allred, C. 2025. "How to Choose the Right Real Estate Broker." *Investopedia*, April 29. https://www.investopedia.com/updates/real-estate-broker/.

AmeriMac Appraisal Management. 2024. "Can Your Neighborhood Affect Your Property Appraisal? Key Factors to Consider." August 13. https://www.amerimacmanagement.com/about/blog/can-your-neighborhood-affect-your-property-appraisal-key-factors-to-consider/.

Araj, V. 2024. "House Hacking Incorporates a Variety of Ways You Can Use Your House to Pay Living Expenses. Learn What House Hacking Is and How You Can Make It Work for You." Rocket Mortgage, April 3. https://www.rocketmortgage.com/learn/house-hacking.

ArchEyes Team. 2023. "Home Renovations You Shouldn't DIY: A Guide to Professional Help." ArchEyes, September 24. https://archeyes.com/home-renovations-you-shouldnt-diy-a-guide-to-professional-help/.

Ashton, D. 2024. "What Is the BRRRR Method (and How Does It Work)?" University of the Built Environment, September 9. https://www.ube.ac.uk/whats-happening/articles/what-is-the-brrrr-method/.

Birk, C. 2025. "Complete Guide to the VA Home Loan." Veterans United Home Loans, August 1. https://www.veteransunited.com/va-loans/.

Bitton, D. 2023. "How to Find Tenants: Everything You Need to Know." DoorLoop Hubs, April 3. https://www.doorloop.com/hub/find-tenants.

Blankenship, M. 2023a. "7 BRRRR Method Risks You Should Know Before Investing." Call Porter, October 6. https://callporter.com/blog/brrrr-method-risks/.

Blankenship, M. 2023b. "The BRRRR Method vs. Flix & Flip: What's The Difference?" Call Porter, October 19. https://callporter.com/blog/the-brrrr-method-vs-flix-flip/.

Blankenship, M. 2024a. "5 Common Types of Real Estate Investing Contracts." Call Porter, March 1. https://callporter.com/blog/real-estate-investing-contracts/.

Blankenship, M. 2024b. "7 Real Estate Investing Calculators You Can Use for Free." Call Porter, December 31. https://callporter.com/blog/real-estate-investing-calculators/.

Boldyreff, K. 2020. "House Hacking 101: What It Is and How It Works." Northpointe.com, May 28. https://www.northpointe.com/learn/homes-real-estate/house-hacking-101-what-it-is-and-how-it-works/.

Brock, M. 2024. "What Is a Real Estate Portfolio and How Do You Build a Collection of Real Estate Investments?" Rocket Mortgage, March 27. https://www.rocketmortgage.com/learn/real-estate-portfolio.

Cartier, B. 2024. "Rental Property Accounting & Bookkeeping 101: Landlord's Guide." *Stessa*, December 23. https://www.stessa.com/blog/rental-property-accounting-101/.

Casago. 2024. "What Makes a Good Airbnb Property? A Guide to Amenities, Fees & More." Casago, September 1. https://casago.com/blog/airbnb-property-guide/.

Cepf, L. G. T., and M. Grace. 2025. "Finding the Right Real Estate Agent: Everything You Need to Know." Business Insider, April 11. https://www.businessinsider.com/personal-finance/mortgages/how-to-find-real-estate-agent.

Chen, J. 2024. "Multiple Listing Service (MLS): Definition, Benefits, and Fees." *Investopedia*, July 9. https://www. investopedia.com/terms/m/multiple-listing-service-mls.asp.

Collins, D. 2023. "What Is Wholesale Real Estate? This Guide Will Help You Understand the Basics, How the Selling Process Works, and Best Practices." December 21. https://www.rocketmortgage.com/learn/wholesale-real-estate.

Conde, A. 2023. "What Is a Real Estate Partnership?" SmartAsset, October 20. https://smartasset.com/investing/real-estate-partnership.

Crace, M. 2024. "Hard Money Loans, Unlike Traditional Loans, Are Based on the Collateral That Secures the Loan." Rocket Mortgage, February 22. https://www.rocketmortgage.com/learn/hard-money-loans/.

Dar, S. 2025. "Why Landlords Need a Separate Bank Account for Rental Property." Baselane, May 28. https://www. baselane.com/resources/separate-bank-account-for-rental-property/.

Davis, M. 2025a. "How to Find Your Return on Investment (ROI) in Real Estate." *Investopedia*, June 1. https://www. investopedia.com/articles/basics/11/calculate-roi-real-estate-investments.asp.

Davis, M. 2025b. "Real Estate Agent vs. Mortgage Broker: What's the Difference?" *Investopedia*, March 14. https:// www.investopedia.com/articles/financialcareers/10/real-estate-agent-mortgage-broker.asp.

Dehan, A. 2025. "Hard Money Lending: Guide to Hard Money Loans." *Bankrate*, February 28. https://www.bankrate. com/mortgages/hard-money-lenders/.

Dixon, A. 2025. "Determining How Much You Should Charge for Rent." Smart Asset, January 30. Accessed July 12. https://smartasset.com/mortgage/how-much-you-should-charge-for-rent.

Dodge, A. 2025. "What Does Off-Market Mean in Real Estate?" FastExpert, April 25. https://www.fastexpert.com/ blog/what-does-off-market-mean/.

DoorLoop. n.d. "The 2023 BRRRR Method Ultimate Guide for Real Estate Investors." Accessed July 8. https://www. doorloop.com/hubs/brrrr.

Dossey, J. 2023a. "4 Best Strategies to BRRRR Deals with No Money." Call Porter, October 12. https://callporter.com/ blog/brrrr-method-with-no-money/.

Dossey, J. 2023b. "Investing in Real Estate: 7 Steps to Your First Deal." Call Porter, May 11. https://callporter.com/ blog/guide-to-investing-in-real-estate/.

Drake Law. 2025. "Key Legal Factors to Consider Before Investing in Real Estate." June 16. https://www.drakelaw.ca/ legal-insights/key-legal-factors-to-consider-before-investing-in-real-estate.

Duncan, A. 2024. "Staying Motivated in a Tough Market." Agent Monday, December 23. https://www.agentmonday. com/how-to-stay-motivated-in-a-tough-market/.

Evans, K. 2024. "Understanding Off-Market Listings: A Strategic Tool for Real Estate Agents." *Luxury Presence*, August 13. https://www.luxurypresence.com/blogs/off-market-listings/.

Fairless, J. 2022. "Real Estate Horror Stories from Five Active Investors." Best Ever Commercial Real Estate, June 9. https://www.bestevercre.com/blog/real-estate-horror-stories-five-active-investors.

Fraraccio, M. 2025. "Buying an Existing Business? How to Finance Your Purchase." CO—by US Chamber of Commerce, January 31. https://www.uschamber.com/co/run/business-financing/financing-buying-an-existing-business.

Freitas, T. 2025. "What Is an FHA Loan?" *Bankrate*, May 9. https://www.bankrate.com/mortgages/what-is-an-fha-loan/.

Gibson, J. 2025. "Factors to Consider Before You Refinance Your Mortgage." *Investopedia*, March 24. https://www. investopedia.com/mortgage/refinance/9-things-to-know-before-you-refinance-mortgage/.

The Ginther Group. 2024. "Setting Real Estate Goals: Buying, Selling, or Investing." December 23. https://theginther group.com/tips/buying-selling-investing-goals/.

Goade, C. 2023. "Is a Stack of Cash Better than Slow but Steady Returns? A Look at Flipping and the BRRRR Method." BiggerPockets, November 5. https://www.biggerpockets.com/blog/flip-vs-brrrr-real-estate.

Goff, K. 2023. "What Is the 70% Rule in House Flipping?" *Bankrate*, February 21. https://www.bankrate.com/real-estate/70-percent-rule-house-flipping/.

Grace, M., and A. J. Yale. 2025. "Understanding the Loan-to-Value Ratio (LTV) and What It Means for Mortgage

Borrowers." Business Insider, March 28. https://www.businessinsider.com/personal-finance/mortgages/loan-to-value-ratio-mortgage-refinancing.

Graham, K. 2024. "An FHA Loan Is a Government-Backed Loan That Allows You to Buy a Home with Less Strict Financial Requirements." Rocket Mortgage, November 20. https://www.rocketmortgage.com/learn/fha-loans.

Gratton, P. 2025a. "Flipping Houses: How It Works, Where to Start, and 5 Mistakes to Avoid." *Investopedia*, February 6. https://www.investopedia.com/articles/mortgages-real-estate/08/house-flip.asp.

Gratton, P. 2025b. "What Is Depreciation Recapture?" *Investopedia*, February 25. https://www.investopedia.com/terms/d/depreciationrecapture.asp

Harris, V. 2019. "How to Get Started in Real Estate Investing: Your 90 Day Plan." Mashvisor Real Estate, January 17. https://www.mashvisor.com/blog/get-started-real-estate-investing-90-day-plan/.

Hayes, A. 2024. "Loan-to-Value (LTV) Ratio: What It Is, How to Calculate, Example." *Investopedia*, September 26. https://www.investopedia.com/terms/l/loantovalue.asp.

Heath, K. 2024. "Lender or Realtor: Who Should You Talk to First Before Buying a House? FastExpert, March 13. https://www.fastexpert.com/blog/lender-or-realtor-who-to-talk-first-before-buying-house/.

Hendricks, M. 2023. "How Private Money Lending Works." SmartAsset, March 19. https://smartasset.com/personal-loans/how-private-money-lending-works.

Henson, T. 2024. "Flipping vs. Renting—Which Real Estate Strategy Is Best for Long-term Gains." Beach Front Property Management Inc., December 18. https://bfpminc.com/flipping-vs-renting-which-real-estate-strategy-is-best-for-long-term-gains/.

Hrovat, J. 2024. "Maximizing Short-Term Rental with the BRRRR Method." UpRev, October 15. https://www.uprev.co/post/maximizing-short-term-rental-brrrr-method.

Huff, J. 2023. "BRRRR vs. Flipping: A Comparison of Real Estate Investment Strategies." Jacobs & Co. Real Estate, November 8. https://www.jacobsandco.com/blog/brrrr-vs-flipping-a-comparison-of-real-estate-investment-strategies/.

Hughes, E. 2025. "Completing My First BRRRR Property." Rental Income Advisors, April 28. https://www.rentalincomeadvisors.com/blog/my-first-brrrr-property.

Internal Revenue Service. n.d. "Tips on Rental Real Estate Income, Deductions and Recordkeeping." Accessed July 14. https://www.irs.gov/businesses/small-businesses-self-employed/tips-on-rental-real-estate-income-deductions-and-recordkeeping.

Internal Revenue Service. 2024. "Publication 527: Residential Rental Property." https://www.irs.gov/publications/p527.

The Investopedia Team. 2023. "4 Tips for Joining an Investment Club." *Investopedia*, September 16. https://www.investopedia.com/articles/01/062001.asp.

Jamal, A. 2021. "How to Diversify Your Real Estate Portfolio." *Forbes*, August 3. https://www.forbes.com/sites/forbesbooksauthors/2021/08/03/how-to-diversify-your-real-estate-portfolio/.

Johnson, M. 2023. "6 Renovation Projects That Pay Off for ROI, According to an Expert." *Architectural Digest*, September 25. https://www.architecturaldigest.com/story/renovation-projects-and-their-roi-according-to-an-expert.

Jones, R. n.d. "Setting Effective Property Investment Goals: How to Achieve Success in 2025." Property Investments UK. https://www.propertyinvestmentsuk.co.uk/5-steps-property-success-goal-setting/.

J. P. Morgan Chase. 2023. "How to Use the BRRRR Method in Real Estate." March 31. https://www.chase.com/personal/mortgage/education/buying-a-home/brrrr-method.

Kagan, J. 2021. "VA Loan: Definition, Eligibility Requirements, Types & Terms." *Investopedia*, November 27. https://www.investopedia.com/terms/v/valoan.asp.

Karani, A. 2020. "How to Evaluate a Neighborhood Before Investing." Mashvisor Real Estate, December 27. https://www.mashvisor.com/blog/evaluate-a-neighborhood-investing/.

Knaack, E. 2024. "Building a Successful REI Team & Keeping Them Accountable." *Deal Machine* (blog), May 16. https://www.dealmachine.com/blog/how-to-build-a-team.

Kopp, C. M. 2020. "1% Rule in Real Estate: What It Is, How It Works, Examples." *Investopedia*, November 11. https://www.investopedia.com/terms/o/one-percent-rule.asp.

Langager, C. 2025. "Reducing or Avoiding Capital Gains Tax on Home Sales." *Investopedia*, February 23. https://www.investopedia.com/ask/answers/06/capitalgainhomesale.asp.

Lecko, D. 2021. "What Is ARV in Real Estate & How to Calculate." *Deal Machine* (blog), December 23. https://www.dealmachine.com/blog/what-is-arv-in-real-estate.

Lombardo, T. 2024. "Maximizing Returns: The Power of Evaluating Neighborhoods for Residential Real Estate Investment Success." Carolina Venture REI, February 5. https://carolinaventurerei.com/evaluating-neighborhoods-for-residential-real-estate-investment-success/.

Lubin, D. 2023. "3 Types of Loans to Maximize the BRRRR Method." Kiavi Funding, Inc., December 15. https://www.kiavi.com/blog/three-types-of-loans-to-maximize-the-brrrr-method.

Lubin, D. 2024. "How to Calculate a Profitable BRRRR Property." Kiavi Funding, Inc., March 25. https://www.kiavi.com/blog/how-to-calculate-a-profitable-brrrr-property.

The Luxury Playbook. 2025. "10 Best Real Estate Investment Exit Strategies (+ Examples)." April 17. https://theluxuryplaybook.com/real-estate-investment-exit-strategies/.

Maldonado, J. D. 2022. "What's the Story of Your First Deal?" BiggerPockets, June 22. https://www.biggerpockets.com/forums/48/topics/1046282-whats-the-story-of-your-first-deal.

Martin, E. J. 2025. "What Is a Private Mortgage Lender?" *Bankrate*, March 10. https://www.bankrate.com/mortgages/what-is-a-private-mortgage-lender/.

Moeen, A. 2024. "ARV Calculator—After Repair Value." Omni Calculator, April 23. https://www.omnicalculator.com/finance/arv

Moore, A. 2024. "Case Study: A Real Estate Success Story with Hard Money Funding." Lending Bee, May 13. https://lendingbeeinc.com/blog/case-study-a-real-estate-success-story-with-hard-money-funding.

myRealPage. 2025. "Why Reinvesting in Your Real Estate Business Is Essential and How to Do It." myRealPage, May 5. https://myrealpage.com/real-estate-marketing/reinvesting-real-estate-business-essential/.

National Association of Realtors. 2024. "Highlights from the Profile of Home Buyers and Sellers." November 4. https://www.nar.realtor/research-and-statistics/research-reports/highlights-from-the-profile-of-home-buyers-and-sellers.

National Association of Realtors. 2025. "Remodeling Impact." April 9. https://www.nar.realtor/research-and-statistics/research-reports/remodeling-impact.

Nesbit, J. 2025. "What Is the 70% Rule in House Flipping and Does It Show How Much to Pay for a Distressed Property?" Rocket Mortgage, February 19. https://www.rocketmortgage.com/learn/what-is-70-rule-in-house-flipping.

Nichols, B. 2023. "Mastering BRRRR: The Power of Refinancing in Real Estate." *Deal Machine* (blog), December 3. https://www.dealmachine.com/blog/mastering-brrrr-refinancing-in-real-estate-investing.

Nicola, G. 2025. "Flipping vs. BRRR: Which Real Estate Investment Strategy Is Right for You?" Tallbox, March 28. https://www.tallboxdesign.com/flipping-vs-brrrr-which-strategy-is-for-you/.

Nock Deighton. n.d. "ROI (Return on Investment) Calculator." Accessed June 29. https://www.nockdeighton.co.uk/investment-calculator.

Nowacki, L. 2024a. "Breaking Down the 1% Rule in Real Estate: What You Should Know Before Investing." Rocket Mortgage, February 27. https://www.rocketmortgage.com/learn/1-rule-real-estate.

Nowacki, L. 2024b. "Understand the BRRRR Method of Real Estate Investments." Rocket Mortgage, May 16. https://www.rocketmortgage.com/learn/brrrr.

Olson, L. n.d. "10 Types of Insurance for Real Estate Investors to Consider." Obie Insurance. Accessed July 2. https://www.obieinsurance.com/blog/insurance-for-real-estate-investors.

Pallardy, C. 2025. "How to Find and Buy Off-Market Homes." *Investopedia*, March 17. https://www.investopedia.com/articles/personal-finance/121415/how-find-and-buy-offmarket-homes.asp.

Paquette, A. 2019. "Success Story of the Week: Will FHA work for you?" *Athena Paquette* (blog), August 8. https://athenapaquette.com/success-story-of-the-week-will-fha-work-for-you/.

Parker, T. 2025. "Home Improvements That Require Permits." *Investopedia*, April 17. https://www.investopedia.com/financial-edge/1012/home-improvements-that-require-permits.aspx.

Peterson, L. 2025. "How many hours per week does it take to manage a successful Airbnb?" L'abode Accommodation, April 21. https://labodeaccommodation.com.au/time-spent-on-an-airbnb/.

Pisano, N. 2024. "Residential Real Estate Investing in 2024: More Rent Money, More Rental Problems." Clever, July 22. https://listwithclever.com/research/residential-real-estate-investing-2024/.

Plati, A. 2024. "How to Conduct a Real Estate Market Study: The Perfect Guide." October 21. https://www.netquest.com/en/blog/how-to-conduct-real-estate-market-study-perfect-guide.

Ramsey Solutions. 2025. "How to Create a Home Renovation Budget." March 27. https://www.ramseysolutions.com/real-estate/home-renovation-budget?srsltid=AfmBOorAz3wQZNv1mvhEhlIaFeKSAP-z-S5H9BlBA5AMzkdS0Ifp YAbS.

Reiff, N. 2025. "Do-It-Yourself Projects to Boost Home Value." *Investopedia*, March 18. https://www.investopedia.com/articles/mortgages-real-estate/08/diy-home-projects.asp.

Rodriguez, C. 2024. "To Flip or to BRRRR?" BiggerPockets, March 9. https://www.biggerpockets.com/forums/48/topics/1127968-to-flip-or-to-brrrr.

Rogers, E. 2025. "What You Need to Know About Building Wealth with the BRRRR Method in St. George." Red Rock Real Estate, February 3. https://www.relocatetosunnystgeorge.com/blog/what-you-need-to-know-about-building-wealth-with-the-brrrr-method-in-st-george.

Rosenberg, E. 2025. "Ultimate Guide to BRRRR Method For Real Estate Investment." Baselane, May 14. https://www.baselane.com/resources/brrrr-method-for-real-estate/.

Segal, T. 2024. "Hard Money Loan: Definition, Uses, and Pros & Cons." *Investopedia*, May 7. https://www.investopedia.com/terms/h/hard_money_loan.asp.

Segal, T. 2025. "Federal Housing Administration (FHA) Loan: Requirements, Limits, How to Qualify." *Investopedia*, March 27. https://www.investopedia.com/terms/f/fhaloan.asp.

Shehaj, E. 2022. "The Ultimate 60-Day Action Plan for the Paralyzed Newbie Longing for a First Deal." BiggerPockets, July 29. https://www.biggerpockets.com/blog/60-day-newbie-action-plan.

Shour, E. 2025. "Should You Hire a Property Manager? The Pros & Cons." Stessa, April 15. https://www.stessa.com/blog/should-you-hire-property-manager/.

Shugrue, D. 2023. "How to Plan Your Home Renovation Costs." *Budget Dumpster* (blog), December 4. https://www.budgetdumpster.com/blog/budget-home-renovation.

Sprenkle, B. 2024. "The Dilemma on Whether to Refinance or Sell." American Apartment Owners Association, June 4. https://american-apartment-owners-association.org/property-management/the-dilemma-on-whether-to-refinance-or-sell/?srsltid=AfmBOorvn4BfX0OGOJGafoPelEyfNera-1-FN3rAlWXGI5QpqvG5EAxY.

Stammers, R. 2021. "Should You Buy and Hold Real Estate or Flip Properties?" *Investopedia*, January 27. https://www.investopedia.com/articles/mortgages-real-estate/08/flipping-flip-properties.asp

Stohler, N. 2024. "How to Find Off-Market Properties: 13 Winning Methods." Azibo, June 28. https://www.azibo.com/blog/how-to-find-off-market-properties.

Subel, M. 2024. "Home Remodeling Steps: A Checklist to Help Plan and Organize Your Renovation." Dave Fox, August 29. https://www.davefox.com/resource-center/whole-home-remodeling-steps-checklist.

Talbot, A. 2025. "What Is 'House Hacking' and How Is It Helping Millennials and Gen Z Buy Houses?" Webster First Federal Credit Union, January 22. https://www.websterfirst.com/blog/what-is-house-hacking-definition/.

Travelers. 2023. "10 Common Rental Property Repairs Landlords Need to Know About." February 28. https://www.travelers.com/resources/home/landlords/10-common-rental-property-repairs-landlords-need-to-know-about.

Turner, B. 2020. "The BRRRR Origin Story: How I Discovered This Amazing—No Money—Real Estate Strategy." BiggerPockets, July 11. https://www.biggerpockets.com/blog/brrrr-origin-story.

Vazquez, J. 2024. "The Difference Between Rehabbing a Flip, Short-Term Rental, Corporate Rental, Long-Term Rental, and BRRRR Strategy." Graystone Investment Group, August 30. https://graystoneig.com/articles/the-difference-between-rehabbing-a-flip-short-term-rental-corporate-rental-long-term-rental-and-brrrr-strategy.

Villegas, F. 2024. "Real Estate Market Analysis: What It Is & How to Do It." QuestionPro, April 10. https://www.questionpro.com/blog/real-estate-market-analysis/.

Wall Street Prep. 2024. "After-Repair Value (ARV)." February 20. https://www.wallstreetprep.com/knowledge/after-repair-value-arv/.

Webber, M. R. 2024. "The Top Renovations That Increase Home Value in 2024." *Bankrate*, May 13. https://www.bankrate.com/homeownership/home-renovations-that-return-the-most-at-resale/.

Welty, S. 2025. "Short-Term Rental vs. Long-Term Rental: 12 Things to Know." Good Life Property Management, May 19. https://www.goodlifemgmt.com/blog/short-term-rental-vs-long-term-rental/.

White, J. 2025. "What's a Good Return on Investment (ROI)?" SmartAsset, May 28. https://smartasset.com/investing/whats-a-good-return-on-investment-roi.

White, M., and A. Conde. 2024. "How to Start Wholesaling Real Estate in 7 Steps." Smart Asset, July 29. https://smartasset.com/mortgage/how-to-get-started-wholesaling-real-estate.

Williams, T. 2022. "Look for these 12 red flags to avoid hiring bad contractors." Architectural Digest, March 14. https://www.architecturaldigest.com/story/bad-contractors-red-flags-warning-signs.

Wood, R. W. 2024. "What Is a 1031 Exchange? Know the Rules." *Investopedia*, December 16. https://www.investopedia.com/financial-edge/0110/10-things-to-know-about-1031-exchanges.aspx.

Woodman, C. 2023. "How to Scale Your Real Estate Portfolio." New Silver, May 24. https://newsilver.com/the-lender/how-to-scale-your-real-estate-portfolio/.

Woodman, C. 2025. "Over Leveraged Real Estate—What Is It and How to Avoid It." New Silver, March 24. https://newsilver.com/the-lender/over-leveraged-real-estate/.

Woodward, E. 2024. "The BRRRR Method: What It Means and What It Stands For." *Bankrate*, February 23. https://www.bankrate.com/real-estate/brrrr-method-in-real-estate/.

Young Entrepreneur Council. 2023. "How Real Estate Investors Can Find Off-Market Properties." *Forbes*, February 14. https://www.forbes.com/councils/theyec/2023/02/14/how-real-estate-investors-can-find-off-market-properties/.

Zinn, D. 2024. "How to Flip a House: A Beginner's Guide." *Bankrate*, July 8. https://www.bankrate.com/real-estate/flipping-houses/.

IMAGE REFERENCES

Anke, Peggy. 2018. *Airbnb*. Image. Pixabay. May 19. https://pixabay.com/photos/airbnb-air-bnb-apartment-3399753/.

Cytonn Photography. 2018. *Two People Shaking Hands*. Image. Unsplash. March 23. https://unsplash.com/photos/two-people-shaking-hands-n95VMLxqM2I.

Danilyuk, Pavel. 2021. *Couple Holding Blueprint of a House*. Image. Pexels. May 18. https://www.pexels.com/photo/couple-holding-blueprint-of-a-house-7937668/

Kindel Media. 2021. *People Holding a Key*. Image. Pexels. April 16. https://www.pexels.com/photo/people-holding-a-key-7579192/.

Lehner, Stefan. 2021. *A Room That Has Some Tools in It*. Image. Unsplash. October 18. https://unsplash.com/photos/a-room-that-has-some-tools-in-it-biRt6RXejuk.

McBee, David. 2018. *High Angle Shot of Suburban Neighborhood*. Image. Pexels. October 28. https://www.pexels.com/photo/high-angle-shot-of-suburban-neighborhood-1546168/.

Mils, Alexander. 2019. *Fan of 100 U. S. Dollar Banknotes*. Image. Unsplash. March 27. https://unsplash.com/photos/fan-of-100-us-dollar-banknotes-lCPhGxs7pww.

RDNE Stock Project. 2021. *Person Wearing Silver Ring Holding Red Pen on White Printer Paper*. Image. Pexels. May 25. https://www.pexels.com/photo/person-wearing-silver-ring-holding-red-pen-on-white-printer-paper-8052843/

Thirdman. 2021. *Shallow Focus Photo of a Realtor Posting a Sold Sticker*. Image. Pexels. June 24. https://www.pexels.com/photo/shallow-focus-photo-of-a-realtor-posting-a-sold-sticker-8470803/.

ABOUT THE AUTHOR

Frank Eberstadt is an accommodation manager and bestselling author of books on Airbnb and real estate investing.

His books address property management and business growth in short-term rentals, guiding readers to seek and capitalize on opportunities in the market while nurturing successful businesses along the way.

Frank is the accommodation manager for an investment group operating hotels and motels in Australia. He has established his own successful Airbnb business, and has grown his portfolio to six properties. Frank began his first Airbnb business from the ground up and knows how hard it can be to break into property listings and attract guests. Using his extensive experience in the accommodation industry, his aim is to lay out a clear, step-by-step path that even complete newbies can follow to success.

Frank's interest in vacation property stems from his many years traveling as a solo backpacker, something he now does with his family. These two very different traveling experiences have fed into his awareness of what makes a successful vacation rental, and have been key to his success as an Airbnb business owner.

Frank still loves to travel, and enjoys surfing, but more than anything, he loves to spend quality time with his family, no matter where their adventures take them.